LEE EDWARDS and **ARLYN DIAMOND** are colleagues in the Department of English at the University of Massachusetts at Amherst. Ms. Edwards has also co-edited a non-fiction collection entitled *Woman: An Issue* and is planning a book on Virginia Woolf as a political writer. Ms. Diamond is a medievalist who has written on Middle English romances and about the feminist Germaine Greer. Their interest in exploring the role of women in literature led to the editing of *American Voices, American Women* and they are currently at work on a collection of feminist criticism.

AMERICAN VOICES, AMERICAN WOMEN

EDITED WITH AN INTRODUCTION BY
**LEE R. EDWARDS AND
ARLYN DIAMOND**

 BARD BOOKS / PUBLISHED BY AVON

AVON BOOKS
A division of
The Hearst Corporation
959 Eighth Avenue
New York, New York 10019

First Bard Printing, November, 1973.
Second Printing

BARD TRADEMARK REG. U.S. PAT. OFF. AND
FOREIGN COUNTRIES, REGISTERED TRADEMARK—
MARCA REGISTRADA, HECHO EN CHICAGO, U.S.A.

Printed in the U.S.A.

For Tillie Olsen, who leads the way

CONTENTS

INTRODUCTION   11

Harriet Prescott Spofford
THE AMBER GODS   21

Elizabeth Stuart Phelps
THE STORY OF AVIS   65

Mary Wilkins Freeman
A NEW ENGLAND NUN   151

THE REVOLT OF "MOTHER"   165

ONE GOOD TIME   181

OLD WOMAN MAGOUN   199

Kate O'Flaherty Chopin
LILACS   221

THE GODMOTHER   233

Mary Hunter Austin
A WOMAN OF GENIUS   257

Dorothy Canfield Fisher
A DROP IN THE BUCKET   341

Susan Keating Glaspell
A JURY OF HER PEERS   359

Jessie Redmon Fauset
PLUM BUN "HOME"   385

PLUM BUN "MARKET"   397

PLUM BUN "PLUM BUN"   423

INTRODUCTION

This anthology began with our suspicion that there were significant American women writers about whom we had never heard, and, more importantly, that these women had something to say to us. This suspicion gained further encouragement from the women's movement and the series of discoveries and rediscoveries about women's past that the movement has inspired. The American literary tradition has always been subject to change and we are attempting here to broaden it. Just as Afro-Americans had to insist that their experience and literature were an integral part of American culture and then brought to light the documents which legitimized their insistence, so too must women.

We finished reading for this collection with a drastically changed sense of what we mean by the tradition of American literature and the habit of mind, male and female, which produced it. It was disappointing to find that critics who could perceive the greatness of works like *Walden* and *Moby Dick* did not also consider other works potentially as revealing of America's psyche. Why not study works by women whose heroines loved the wilderness as much as Natty Bumppo did, or who themselves longed for the freedom to wander or create? Did these critics ever think to look? Why should we be left with a picture of a literature obsessed with escape from women whose view of the world was bounded by the parlor and the kitchen? Or for that matter, why should we accept the idea that the parlor and the kitchen are unimportant places, respectable, and boring?

As every woman knows and most men now recognize, the maps of our culture have been drawn by men whose vision was focused on their own experience of the world and who confused one landscape with an entire terrain. For the most part the followers of those maps—students, teachers, scholars, critics, editors, publishers—were themselves male. Developments were circular: definition encourages publication; certain authors are kept in print; out of print works become unavailable, and are unable to exert a countervailing pressure.

At our beginnings, the Puritan leaders defined themselves as something new in the history of the world, and since then Americans have continued to see themselves as different—not inheritors of European tradition but fugitives from it. If post eighteenth-century British fiction was social, domestic, concerned with the relationship between manners and morals, and produced frequently by women acknowledged to be great writers, much of what we traditionally see as American literature is profoundly and self-consciously masculine, anti-social, undomestic, concerned with neither social manners nor social morality, and is, as Hawthorne says, "romantic." The romancer denies the prophet's statement that there is nothing new under the sun, endorses the individual out of harmony with social norms and emphasizes not simply the possibility of extraordinary experience but its almost religious nature.

From its beginning, then, America and its literature combined romantic conventions with Puritan consciousness. Flying the City of Destruction, the Puritans brought with them not only a contempt for the petty social concerns of Vanity Fair, but also a concept of the proper relations between men and women based on adherence to the most conservative Biblical doctrines. The Christian wife had to atone for the sin of Eve by her submission and self-effacement. Woman's very existence was a temptation, even if only a temptation to forget ultimate judgment in the comfort of home. If such is the case, then men must be homeless and women abandoned. Hester is the occasion for Dimmesdale's sin in *The Scarlet Letter;* Thoreau knows that a man can live in the woods only if he lives alone; Ahab would renounce his search for Moby Dick if he thought too much about his young wife on shore. Even such seemingly non-Puritan writers as Faulkner, Hemingway, and Mailer are still terrified by the spectre of Eve with an apple in her hand.

Puritanism, moreover, is connected with not only what is romantic but also what is epic in American literature. The myth of the *Mayflower* and that of the frontier meet in a common distrust of woman and what she represents. For the Puritans, woman was evil—menacing and destroying men and goodness. Her only salvation was to be a bloodless saint, an object for veneration rather than an individual consciousness. For the frontier hero and his creator it is civilization which is corrupt. Since, however, civilization is seen as the realm of females and "feminized" men, a distrust of civilization is equivalent to a distrust of women. The basic assumption behind such a notion is that femininity and wilderness are, as we have been told, implacably opposed. The perception that what strangles men may strangle women too is alien to those writers and critics responsible for the accepted version of the myth of the frontier.

The fascination with Wilderness, Apocalypse, and Escape as defining themes has obscured two realities: First, that women writers and/or characters were just as American as their male counterparts and therefore shared their longings; and second, that there is more to American literature and the American experience than Armageddon and the Santa Fe trail. The selections represented in this collection document these neglected realities. They force us to acknowledge not only these authors' literary and real lives but also the importance of their visions, permitting us to define the American experience in a more varied way.

* * * * *

Despite striking differences in style, tone, and overt subject, the writers reprinted here relate to one another in their common sense of conflict. The identities of their female protagonists are formed, of necessity, out of a developing awareness of the difficulties in reconciling their private selves with public expectations of them as women. As a result, these fictions are psychological rather than cosmological in focus. Often isolated in their unhappiness, the women portrayed here are convinced that they are abnormal to sense a tension between social duty and psychological integrity. Male protagonists in American fiction frequently share this sense of isolation, but there is a long historical and literary tradition to justify their alienation. For women, no such tradition was available, and each author and heroine had to recreate her own struggle without the guidance of positive alternative modes of being. The situation persists, but women may now know that the struggle need never have been a solitary one.

In Elizabeth Stuart Phelps's *The Story of Avis* (1877)

and Mary Austin's *A Woman of Genius* (1912), the central figure is torn between her sense of her own large talents and ambitions on the one hand and the demands of love and domesticity on the other. In one of the earlier novel's several turning points, Philip Ostrander, the young professor who has successfully wooed Avis, is pressing for a more immediate wedding than she desires. Unlike Philip, Avis is happy to be merely engaged and mistrusts the condition of marriage. Ostrander appeals to her to recognize that situated as he is—lacking a wife to make a home for him and care for his creature comforts, and to entertain his colleagues—he is unable to "command his best conditions." Moved by his plea, Avis consents to marry immediately, and Phelps's comment on the consequences of this assent is notable for its pointedness, as well as its restraint:

> Long years after, these words came back to Avis Dobell's memory, like the carven stone into which time has wrought meanings that the sculptor's mind or hand was impotent to grasp.

At the book's conclusion Phelps can free Avis only by destroying Philip. But Avis' freedom, as the author well knows, has come too late: " 'It is of no use,' said Avis wearily, 'my pictures come back upon my hands . . . My style is gone . . . I work as if I had a rheumatic hand . . . But the stiffness runs deeper than the fingers' . . ." Beyond the limits of this plot, moreover, Phelps uses her final pages to speculate on the new turnings that new lives might produce:

> We have been told that it takes three generations to make a gentleman: we may believe that it will take as much, or more, to make a WOMAN. A being . . . physically educated by mothers of her own fibre and by physicians of her own sex—such a woman alone is fitted to acquire the drilled brain, the calmed imagination, and sustained aim, which constitutes intellectual command . . . such a creature only is competent to the terrible task of adjusting the sacred individuality of her life to her supreme capacity of love and the supreme burdens and perils which it imposes upon her.

A man in whom the sources of feelings are as deep as they are delicate . . . whose affection becomes a burning ambition not to be outvied by hers, whose daily soul is large enough to guard her, even though it were at the cost of sharing it, from the tyranny of small corrosive care which gnaws and gangrenes hers —such a man alone can either comprehend or apprehend the love of such a woman.

The actress heroine of *A Woman of Genius,* Olivia, is fiercer in her devotion to her gift and less determinedly moral than Avis. Phelps and Austin in their works, like Charlotte Brontë in *Jane Eyre,* reveal that the price of conventional marriage is the destruction of one of the partners. Male writers, too, have realized this truth. They, however, attempt either to deny it by assuming that women survive in marriage because they are incapable of being alive in the way that men live or by denouncing the women rather than the pattern for producing this situation.

Near the end of *A Woman of Genius,* Olivia and her friend (soon, we suspect, to be her husband), Jerry, discuss Olivia's autobiography. Their conversation, like Phelps's musings at the end of *Avis,* underlines the need for new forms to produce healthy, non-destructive relationships between men and women:

"Where is the justice in making us so that we can't do without loving and then not be happy in it?"

"I don't believe it is the loving that is wrong; it is the other things that are tied up with it and taken for granted must go with loving, that we can get on with."

"Marriage, you mean?"

"Not exactly . . . living in one place and by a particular pattern . . . thinking that *because* you are married you have to leave off this and take up that which you wouldn't think of doing for any other reason."

"You mean . . . I know," he nodded; "my wife was always wanting me to do this and that, on the ground that it was what married people ought, and I couldn't see where it led or why it was important. But what if it should turn out that the others are wrong and we are right about it?"

"Oh, I think we are *all* wrong. People like us are

after the truth of life, and marriage is the one thing
that society won't take the trouble to learn the truth
about."

For Harriet Prescott Spofford and Kate Chopin the central conflict is not between talent and the bourgeois marriage of romantic lovers, but between the accepted image
of the chaste marble figure of the good woman and the
realities of women's emotional lives. Spofford's "The
Amber Gods" is an extended monologue by the heroine,
Giorgione Willoughby, expressing an intense sensuality
which is both compelling and terrifying in its self-absorp-
tion. The sequel Spofford wrote to this story is absolutely
conventional in its defeat of such egoism by the self-
effacing love of Giorgione's proper Victorian sister. Although Spofford finally kills Giorgione she cannot overcome the force of her creation, who says of herself: "I
am used to admiration . . . it is my food; without it I
should die of inanition; but do you suppose I care any
more for those who give it to me than a Chinese idol does
for whoever swings incense before it? Are you devoted to
your butcher and your milkman?" If Galatea could speak
her mind, might she not make the same admission?

In her fiction Spofford keeps returning, fascinated and
appalled, to the figure of an imaginative and sexual
woman who refuses to deny herself, and in a world which
demands only beauty, charm and passivity of women, uses
her energy to force the world to satisfy her desires. Chopin
does not feel the need to depict her female characters as
monsters merely because they are aware of their own
needs and powers. Instead, she chooses in "Lilacs" as well
as in her increasingly well-known novel, *The Awakening*,
to celebrate female sensuality at the same time as she
shows the price for it exacted from women by external
society and internalized social values. In "The Godmother" she shows that it is just such self-denying and absolute
love for another—thought of as women's great gift—
which is monstrous. Obsessed with protecting her godson,
Tante Elodie condones his murderous actions and thereby
destroys him.

The remaining authors—Mary Wilkins Freeman, Dorothy Canfield Fisher, Susan Glaspell, and Jessie Redmon
Fauset—are concerned with more apparently conventional people, who do not consciously feel the need for

values and lives other than the traditional ones. For them, too, nonetheless, the ordinary and accepted is potentially —and sometimes actually—crippling.

Freeman's and Fisher's New England village women and Glaspell's prairie matrons, bound by poverty and limited experience, fight heroic battles on tiny battlefields. Even the most barren lives, we learn from these heroines, can reveal an unsuspected strength of will and capacity for imaginative action. The results may be comic, as in Freeman's "One Good Time," in which the heroine breaks out to sow one wild oat, or "The Revolt of Mother," in which the title figure, after years of unrelenting housewifery, demonstrates that her meekness was only self-imposed. Or, they may be horrifying, as in Glaspell's "A Jury of Her Peers" and Freeman's "Old Woman Magoun," where murder becomes the inevitable response to masculine brutality and the inability of women to cope with isolation and legitimate fear. Finally, they may be tragic, as in Fisher's "A Drop in the Bucket," whose complacent heroine is a loving parody of Freeman's village spinster. Content with her position as a lady and happy with the order that "The New England Nun" chooses over the chaos and dependence of married life, Cousin Tryphema is forced to see the ugliness of existence beyond her village.

The nobility of her response to suffering is echoed in all the stories. The protagonists' acquiescence in what is expected of them is finally the result of conscious choice, producing a curious kind of integrity which ultimately breaks the barriers of convention. Thus, the wives in Glaspell's story choose to conceal from their husbands their knowledge that the spiritual death imposed on a lonely farm wife by her husband justifies her actual murder of him. This concealment is part of the guilt they must bear, as women, for failing to reach out to her in time. "Mother," in the story of her revolt, is willing to live in a barn, if she can satisfy her sense of justice in no other way. The village minister's inability to deal with what he perceives as her eccentricity is the visible sign of how conventional mores fail when faced with such women.

Jessie Redmon Fauset ends her novels with happy marriages, but only after the heroine has shown herself to be practically independent of matrimony, thus in a limited way fulfilling Phelps's and Austin's dreams. Angela Murray, *Plum Bun*'s central figure, is born in Philadelphia. She is bourgeois, talented, and black. Like the masculine hero of the *bildungsroman*, she has to leave the safety of her home and test herself in hostile surroundings, in this case a white world some of whose values she has assumed. Fauset finally creates a situation in which Angela can accept her blackness without thereby accepting the imposition of any limits on her potentialities.

The variety and richness of these works suggest that women's experience is not limited to a mindless preoccupation with cradles and cooking and clothes, and that an understanding of previously neglected writing by American women can deepen our understanding of the entire human experience. More and more, students of American literature are coming to see its fiction as centered on love and death. They are right, but their depositions state only half the case. The women American men were rushing to the sea and to the woods to escape were not wistfully expecting the return of their husbands and sons so they could tidy them up and send them out to work. They too had fantasies of escaping, if necessary over the dead bodies of the men who thought their women really preferred tatting and waiting. A cry for help echoes in all these works, for reconsideration of the nature of feminine identity, for re-evaluation of the relationship between men and women, and for redefinition of the content and meaning of the American experience.

Harriet Prescott Spofford (1835–1921)

Although some of her most romantic work seems to deny such a background, Harriet Prescott was born and raised in New England. Her father was a merchant who went West to make a fortune, and returned an invalid. The family was often hard-pressed financially, and before she was twenty, she began publishing, in Boston, story-papers to earn much-needed money. From childhood she had been involved with literature, reading widely and writing. Thomas Wentworth Higginson recognized and sponsored her talents when she was still in school. She first came to wide public notice in 1858, when *The Atlantic Monthly* accepted "In the Cellar," first checking to make sure the story was not the work of a more likely author than a sheltered New England girl.

She published copiously for more than fifty years: novels, poetry, short stories, books on household management, articles, essays, and reviews. Her husband, Richard Spofford, a lawyer whom she married in 1865, encouraged her writing. Except for the death of their only child, they seem to have led a happy life. She had many friends, especially among other women authors, and during the 1860's and 1870's enjoyed a respectable literary reputation. Her popularity waned at the end of the century, to be revived in the 1900's with the publication of a series of New England stories, some of which were collected in *The Elder's People* (1920). She alternated between the realistic mode and lush romanticism, the latter perhaps best represented by her first volume of short stories, *The Amber Gods* (1863). The title story is reprinted here. Her works, at their best, show a remarkable ability for rich description, particularly of colors and textures; imaginative characterization; and the convincing creation of worlds she knew only through reading.

[References: There is a full-length critical biography: Halbeisen, Elizabeth K. *Harriet Prescott Spofford.* Philadelphia: Univ. of Pennsylvania, 1935; useful also is Rose Terry Cooke's chapter on Spofford in, *Our Famous Women.* Hartford: Worthington, 1884.]

THE AMBER GODS

FLOWER O' THE PEACH

We've some splendid old point-lace in our family, yellow
and fragrant, loose-meshed. It isn't every one has point
at all; and of those who have, it isn't every one can
afford to wear it. I can. Why? O, because it's in character.
Besides, I admire point any way,—it's so becoming. And
then, you see, this amber! Now what is in finer unison, this
old point-lace, all tags and tangle and fibrous and be-
wildering, and this amber, to which Heaven knows how
many centuries, maybe, with all their changes, brought
perpetual particles of increase? I like yellow things, you
see.

To begin at the beginning. My name, you're aware, is
Giorgione Willoughby. Queer name for a girl! Yes; but
before Papa sowed his wild-oats, he was one afternoon in
Fiesole, looking over Florence nestled below, when some
whim took him to go into a church there, a quiet place,
full of twilight and one great picture, nobody within but a
girl and her little slave,—the one watching her mistress,
the other saying dreadfully devout prayers on an amber
rosary, and of course she didn't see him, or didn't appear
to. After he got there, he wondered what on earth he
came for, it was so dark and poky, and he began to feel
uncomfortable,—when all of a sudden a great ray of sunset dashed through the window, and drowned the place
in the splendor of the illumined painting. Papa adores
rich colors; and he might have been satiated here, except
that such things make you want more. It was a Venus;—
no, though, it couldn't have been a Venus in a church,
could it? Well, then, a Magdalen, I guess, or a Madonna,
or something. I fancy the man painted for himself, and
christened for others. So, when I was born, some years
afterward, Papa, gratefully remembering this dazzling little
vignette of his youth, was absurd enough to christen *me*

First published in *The Atlantic Monthly*, 5 (Jan. and Feb., 1860),
7-18 and 170-185.

Giorgione. That's how I came by my identity; but the folks all call me Yone,—a baby name.

I'm a blonde, you know,—none of your silver-washed things. I wouldn't give a *fico* for a girl with flaxen hair; she might as well be a wax doll, and have her eyes moved by a wire; besides, they've no souls. I imagine they were remnants at *our* creation, and somehow scrambled together, and managed to get up a little life among themselves; but it's good for nothing, and everybody sees through the pretence. They're glass chips, and brittle shavings, slender pinkish scrids,—no name for them; but just you say blonde, soft and slow and rolling,—it brings up a brilliant, golden vitality, all manner of white and torrid magnificences, and you see me! I've watched little bugs— gold rose-chafers—lie steeping in the sun, till every atom of them must have been searched with the warm radiance, and have felt that, when they reached that point, I was just like them, golden all through,—not dyed, but created. Sunbeams like to follow me, I think. Now, when I stand in one before this glass, infiltrated with the rich tinge, don't I look like the spirit of it just stepped out for inspection? I seem to myself like the complete incarnation of light, full, bounteous, overflowing, and I wonder at and adore anything so beautiful; and the reflection grows finer and deeper while I gaze, till I dare not do so any longer. So, without more words, I'm a golden blonde. You see me now: not too tall,—five feet four; not slight, or I couldn't have such perfect roundings, such flexible moulding. Here's nothing of the spiny Diana and Pallas, but Clytie or Isis speaks in such delicious curves. It doesn't look like flesh and blood, does it? Can you possibly imagine it will ever change? Oh!

Now see the face,—not small, either; lips with no particular outline, but melting, and seeming as if they would stain yours, should you touch them. No matter about the rest, except the eyes. Do you meet such eyes often? You wouldn't open yours so, if you did. Note their color now, before the ray goes. Yellow hazel? Not a bit of it! Some folks say topaz, but they're fools. Nor sherry. There's a dark sardine base, but over it real seas of light, clear light; there isn't any positive color; and once when I was angry, I caught a glimpse of them in a mirror, and they were quite white, perfectly colorless, only luminous. I looked like a fiend, and, you may be sure, recovered my temper directly,—easiest thing in the world, when you've motive enough. You see the pupil is small, and that gives more expansion and force to the iris; but sometimes in an evening, when I'm too gay, and a true damask settles in the cheek, the pupil grows larger and crowds out the light, and under these thick brown lashes, these yellow-hazel eyes of yours, they are dusky and purple and deep with flashes, like pansies lit by fire-flies, and then common folks call them black. Be sure, I've never got such eyes for nothing, any more than this hair. That is Lucrezia Borgian, spun gold, and ought to take the world in its toils. I always wear these thick, riotous curls round my temples and face; but the great braids behind—O, I'll uncoil them, before my toilet is over.

Probably you felt all this before, but didn't know the secret of it. Now, the traits being brought out, you perceive nothing wanting; the thing is perfect, and you've a reason for it. Of course, with such an organization, I'm not nervous. Nervous! I should as soon fancy a dish of cream nervous. I am too rich for anything of the kind, permeated utterly with a rare golden calm. Girls always suggest little similitudes to me: there's that brunette beauty,—don't you taste mulled wine when you see her? and thinking of yourself, did you ever feel green tea? and find me in a crust of wild honey, the expressed essence of woods and flowers, with its sweet satiety?—no, that's too cloying. I'm a deal more like Mendelssohn's music,—what I know of it, for I can't distinguish tunes,—you wouldn't suspect it,—but full harmonies delight me as they do a wild beast; and so I'm like a certain adagio in B flat, that papa likes.

There, now! you're perfectly shocked to hear me go on so about myself; but you oughtn't to be. It isn't lawful for any one else, because praise is intrusion; but if the rose please to open her heart to the moth, what then? You know, too, I didn't make myself; it's no virtue to be so fair. Louise couldn't speak so of herself: first place, because it wouldn't be true; next place, she couldn't, if it were; and lastly, she made her beauty by growing a soul in her eyes, I suppose,—what you call good. I'm not good, of course; I wouldn't give a fig to be good. So it's not vanity. It's on a far grander scale; a splendid selfishness,—authorized, too; and Papa and Mamma brought me up to worship beauty,—and there's the fifth commandment, you know.

Dear me! you think I'm never coming to the point. Well, here's this rosary;—hand me the perfume-case first, please. Don't you love heavy fragrances, faint with sweetness, ravishing juices of odor, heliotropes, violets, water-lilies,—powerful attars and extracts that snatch your soul off your lips? Couldn't you live on rich scents, if they tried to starve you? I could, or die on them: I don't know which would be best. There! there's the amber rosary! You needn't speak; look at it!

Bah! is that all you've got to say? Why, observe the thing; turn it over; hold it up to the window; count the beads,—long, oval, like some seaweed bulbs, each an amulet. See the tint; it's very old; like clots of sunshine, —aren't they? Now bring it near; see the carving, here corrugated, there faceted, now sculptured into hideous, tiny, heathen gods. You didn't notice that before! How difficult it must have been, when amber is so friable! Here's one with a chessboard on his back, and all his kings and queens and pawns slung round him. Here's another with a torch, a flaming torch, its fire pouring out inverted. They are grotesque enough;—but this, this is matchless: such a miniature woman, one hand grasping the round rock behind, while she looks down into some gulf, perhaps, beneath, and will let herself fall. O, you should see *her* with a magnifying-glass! You want to think of calm, satisfying death, a mere exhalation, a voluntary slipping into another element? There it is for you. They are all gods and goddesses. They are all here but one; I've lost one, the knot of all, the love of the thing. Well! wasn't it queer for a Catholic girl to have at prayer? Don't you wonder where she got it? Ah! but don't you wonder where I got it? I'll tell you.

Papa came in, one day, and with great mystery commenced unrolling, and unrolling, and throwing tissue papers on the floor, and scraps of colored wool; and Lu and I ran to him,—Lu stooping on her knees to look up, I bending over his hands to look down. It was so mysterious! I began to suspect it was diamonds for me, but knew I never could wear them, and was dreadfully afraid that I was going to be tempted, when slowly, bead by bead, came out this amber necklace. Lu fairly screamed; as for me, I just drew breath after breath, without a word. Of course they were for me;—I reached my hands for them.

"Oh, wait!" said Papa. "Yone or Lu?"

"Now how absurd, Papa!" I exclaimed. "Such things for Lu!"

"Why not?" asked Lu,—rather faintly, for she knew I always carried my point.

"The idea of you in amber, Lu! It's too foreign; no sympathy between you!"

"Stop, stop!" said Papa. "You sha'n't crowd little Lu out of them. What do you want them for, Lu?"

"To wear," quavered Lu,—"like the balls the Roman ladies carried for coolness."

"Well, then, you ought to have them. What do you want them for, Yone?"

"Oh, if Lu's going to have them, I *don't* want them."

"But give a reason, child."

"Why, to wear, too,—to look at,—to have and to hold, for better, for worse,—to say my prayers on," for a bright idea struck me,—"to say my prayers on, like the Florence rosary." I knew that would finish the thing.

"Like the Florence rosary?" said Papa, in a sleepy voice. "Why, this *is* the Florence rosary."

Of course, when we knew that, we were both more crazy to obtain it.

"Oh, sir," just fluttered Lu, "where did you get it?"

"I got it; the question is, Who's to have it?"

"I must and will, potential and imperative," I exclaimed, quite on fire. "The nonsense of the thing! Girls with lucid eyes, like shadowy shallows in quick brooks, can wear crystallizations. As for me, I can wear only concretions and growths; emeralds and all their cousins would be shockingly inharmonious on me; but you know, Lu, how I use Indian spices, and scarlet and white berries, and flowers, and little hearts and notions of beautiful copal that Rose carved for you,—and I can wear sandal-wood and ebony and pearls, and now this amber. But you, Lu, you can wear every kind of precious stone, and you may have Aunt Willoughby's rubies that she promised me; they are all in tone with you; but I must have this."

"I don't think you're right," said Louise, rather soberly. "You strip yourself of great advantages. But about the rubies, I don't want anything so flaming, so you may keep them; and I don't care at all about this. I think, sir, on the whole, they belong to Yone for her name."

"So they do," said Papa. "But not to be bought off! That's my little Lu!"

And somehow Lu, who had been holding the rosary, was sitting on papa's knee, as he half knelt on the floor, and the rosary was in my hand. And then he produced a little kid box, and there lay, inside, a star with a thread of gold for the forehead, circlets for wrist and throat, two drops, and a ring. O such beauties! You've never seen them.

"The other one shall have these. Aren't you sorry, Yone?" he said.

"Oh no indeed! I'd much rather have mine, though these are splendid. What are they?"

"Aqua-marina," sighed Lu, in an agony of admiration.

"Dear, dear! how did you know?"

Lu blushed, I saw,—but I was too much absorbed with the jewels to remark it.

"Oh, they are just like that ring on your hand! You don't want two rings alike," I said. "Where did you get that ring, Lu?"

But Lu had no senses for anything beyond the casket.

If you know aqua-marina, you know something that's before every other stone in the world. Why, it is as clear as light, white, limpid, dawn light; sparkles slightly and seldom; looks like pure drops of water, sea-water, scooped up and falling down again; just a thought of its parent beryl-green hovers round the edges; and it grows more lucent and sweet to the centre, and there you lose yourself in some dream of vast seas, a glory of unimagined oceans; and you say that it was crystallized to any slow flute-like tune, each speck of it floating into file with a musical grace, and carrying its sound with it. There! it's very fanciful, but I'm always feeling the tune in aqua-marina, and trying to find it,—but I shouldn't know it was a tune, if I did, I suppose. How magnificent it would be, if every atom of creation sprang up and said its one word of abracadabra, the secret of its existence, and fell silent again. O dear! you'd die, you know; but what a pow-wow! Then, too, in aqua-marina proper, the setting is kept out of sight, and you have the unalloyed stone with its sea-rims and its clearness and steady sweetness. It wasn't the thing for Louise to wear; it belongs rather to highly nervous, excitable persons; and Lu is as calm as I, only so different! There is something more pure and simple about it than about anything else; others may flash and twinkle, but this just glows with an unvarying power, is planetary and strong. It wears the moods of the sea, too: once in a while a warm amethystine mist suffuses it like a blush; sometimes a white morning fog breathes over it: you long to get into the heart of it. That's the charm of gems, after all! You feel that they are fashioned through dissimilar processes from yourself,—that there's a mystery about them, mastering which would be like mastering a new life, like having the freedom of other stars. I give them more personality than I would a great white spirit. I like amber that way, because I know how it was made, drinking the primeval weather, resinously beading each grain of its rare wood, and dripping with a splash to filter through and around the fallen cones below. In some former state I must have been a fly embalmed in amber.

"O Lu!" I said, "this amber's just the thing for me, such a great noon creature! And as for you, you shall wear mamma's Mechlin and that aqua-marina; and you'll look like a mer-queen just issuing from the wine-dark deeps and glittering with shining water-spheres."

I never let Lu wear the point at all; she'd be ridiculous in it,—so flimsy and open and unreserved; that's for me; Mechlin, with its whiter, closer, chaster web, suits her to a T.

I must tell you, first, how this rosary came about. You know we've a million of ancestors, and one of them, my great-grandfather, was a sea-captain, and actually did bring home cargoes of slaves! But once he fetched to his wife a little islander, an Asian imp, six years old, and wilder than the wind. She spoke no word of English, and was full of short shouts and screeches, like a thing of the woods. My great-grandmother couldn't do a bit with her; she turned the house topsy-turvy, cut the noses out of the old portraits, and chewed the jewels out of the settings, killed the little home animals, spoiled the dinners, pranced in the garden with Madam Willoughby's farthingale, and royal stiff brocades rustling yards behind,—this atom of a shrimp,—or balanced herself with her heels in the air over the curb of the well, scraped up the dead leaves under one corner of the house and fired them,—a favorite occupation,—and if you left her stirring a mess in the kitchen, you met her, perhaps, perched in the china-closet and mumbling all manner of demoniacal prayers, twisting and writhing and screaming over a string of amber gods that she had brought with her and always wore. When winter came and the first snow, she was furious, perfectly mad. One might as well have had a ball of fire in the house, or chain-lightning; every nice old custom had been invaded, the ancient quiet broken into a Bedlam of outlandish sounds, and as Captain Willoughby was returning, his wife packed the sprite off with him,—to cut, rip, and tear in New Holland, if she liked, but not in New England,—and rejoiced herself that she would find that little brown skin cuddled up in her best down beds and among her lavendered sheets no more. She had learned but two words all that time,—Willoughby, and the name of the town.

You may conjecture what heavenly peace came in when the Asian went out, but there is no one to tell what havoc was wrought on board ship; in fact, if there could have been such a thing as a witch, I should believe that imp sunk them, for a stray Levantine brig picked her— still agile as a monkey—from a wreck off the Cape de Verdes and carried her into Leghorn, where she took— will you mind, if I say?—leg-bail, and escaped from durance. What happened on her wanderings I'm sure is of no consequence, till one night she turned up outside a Fiesolan villa, scorched with malaria fevers and shaken to pieces with tertian and quartan and all the rest of the agues. So, after having shaken almost to death, she decided upon getting well; all the effervescence was gone; she chose to remain with her beads in that family, a mysterious tame servant, faithful, jealous, indefatigable. But she never grew; at ninety she was of the height of a yard-stick,—and nothing could have been finer than to have a dwarf in those old palaces, you know.

In my great-grandmother's home, however, the tradition of the Asian sprite with her string of amber gods was handed down like a legend, and, no one knowing what had been, they framed many a wild picture of the Thing enchanting all her spirits from their beads about her, and calling and singing and whistling up the winds with them till storm rolled round the ship, and fierce fog and foam and drowning fell upon her capturers. But they all believed, that, snatched from the wreck into islands of Eastern archipelagoes, the vindictive child and her quieted gods might yet be found. Of course my father knew this, and when that night in the church he saw the girl saying such devout prayers on an amber rosary, with a demure black slave so tiny and so old behind her, it flashed back on him, and he would have spoken, if, just then, the ray had not revealed the great painting, so that he forgot all about it, and when at last he turned, they were gone. But my father had come back to America, had sat down quietly in his elder brother's house, among the hills where I am to live, and was thought to be a sedate young man and a good match, till a freak took him that he must go back and find that girl in Italy. How to do it, with no clew but an amber rosary? But do it he did,—stationing himself against a pillar in that identical church and watching the worshippers, and not having long to wait before in she came, with little Asian behind. Papa isn't in the least romantic; he is one of those great fertilizing temperaments, golden hair and beard, and *hazel* eyes, if you will. He's a splendid old fellow! It's absurd to delight in one's father,—so bread-and-buttery,—but I can't help it. He's far stronger than I; none of the little weak Italian traits that streak me, like water in thick, sirupy wine. No,—he isn't in the least romantic, but he says he was fated to this step, and could no more have resisted than his heart could have refused to beat. When he spoke to the devotee, little Asian made sundry belligerent demonstrations; but he confronted her with the two words she had learned here, Willoughby and the town's name. The dwarf became livid, seemed always after haunted by a dreadful fear of him, pursued him with a rancorous hate, but could not hinder his marriage.—The Willoughbys are a cruel race.—Her only revenge was to take away the amber beads, which had long before been blessed by the Pope for her young mistress, refusing herself to accompany my mother, and declaring that neither should her charms ever cross the water,—that all their blessing would be changed to banning, and that bane would burn the bearer, should the salt-sea spray again dash round them. But when, in process of Nature, the Asian died,—having become classic through her longevity, taking length of days for length of stature, —then the rosary belonged to mamma's sister, who by and by sent it, with a parcel of other things, to papa for me. So I should have had it at all events, you see;—Papa is such a tease! The other things were mamma's wedding-veil, that point there, which once was her mother's, and some pearls.

I was born upon the sea, in a calm, far out of sight of land, under sweltering suns; so, you know, I'm a cosmopolite, and have a right to all my fantasies. Not that they are fantasies, at all; on the contrary, they are parts of my nature, and I couldn't be what I am without them, or have one and not have all. Some girls go picking and scraping odds and ends of ideas together, and by the time they are thirty get quite a bundle of whims and crotchets on their backs; but they are all at sixes and sevens, uneven and knotty like fagots, and won't lie compactly, don't belong to them, and anybody might surprise them out of them. But for me, you see, mine are harmonious; in my veins; I was born with them. Not that I was always what I am now. Oh, bless your heart! plums and nectarines and luscious things that ripen and develop all their rare juices, were green once, and so was I. Awkward, tumble-about, near-sighted, till I was twenty, a real raw-head-and-bloody-bones to all society; then Mamma, who was never well in our diving-bell atmosphere, was ordered to the West Indies, and Papa said it was what I needed, and I went, too,—and oh, how sea-sick! Were you ever? You forget all about who you are, and have a vague notion of being Universal Disease. I have heard of a kind of myopy that is biliousness, and when I reached the islands my sight was as clear as my skin; all that tropical luxuriance snatched me to itself at once, recognized me for kith and kin; and Mamma died, and I lived. We had accidents between wind and water, enough to have made me considerate for others, Lu said; but I don't see that I'm any less careful not to have my bones spilt in the flood than ever I was. Slang? No,—poetry. But if your nature had such a wild, free tendency as mine, and then were boxed up with proprieties and civilities from year's end to year's end, maybe you, too, would escape now and then in a bit of slang.

We always had a little boy to play with, Lu and I, or rather Lu,—because, though he never took any dislike to me, he was absurdly indifferent, while he followed Lu about with a painful devotion. I didn't care, didn't know; and as I grew up and grew awkwarder, I was the plague of their little lives. If Lu had been my sister instead of

my orphan cousin, as Mamma was perpetually holding up
to me, I should have bothered them twenty times more;
but when I got larger and began to be really distasteful
to his fine artistic perception, Mamma had the sense to
keep me out of his way; and he was busy at his lessons,
and didn't come so much. But Lu just fitted him then,
from the time he daubed little adoring blotches of her face
on every barn-door and paling, till when his scrap-book
was full of her in all fancies and conceits, and he was old
enough to go away and study Art. Then he came home
occasionally, and always saw us; but I generally contrived,
on such occasions, to do some frightful thing that shocked
every nerve he had, and he avoided me instinctively, as he
would an electric torpedo; but—do you believe?—I never
had any idea of such a fact till, when sailing from the
South, so changed, I remembered things, and felt intuitive-
ly how it must have been. Shortly after I went away, he
visited Europe. I had been at home a year, and now we
heard he had returned; so for two years he hadn't seen me.
He had written a great deal to Lu,—brotherly letters they
were,—he is so peculiar,—determining not to give her the
least intimation of what he felt, if he did feel anything, till
he was able to say all. And now he had earned for himself
a certain fame, a promise of greater; his works sold; and
if he pleased, he could marry. I merely presume this might
have been his thought; he never told me. A certain fame!
But that's nothing to what he will have. How can he paint
gray, faint, half-alive things now? He must abound in
color,—be rich, exhaustless: wild sea-sketches,—sunrise,
—sunset,—mountain mists rolling in turbid crimson
masses, breaking in a milky spray of vapor round lofty
peaks, and letting out lonely glimpses of a melancholy
moon,—South American splendors,—pomps of fruit and
blossom,—all this affluence of his future life must flash
from his pencils now. Not that he will paint again directly.
Do you suppose it possible that I should be given him
merely for a phase of wealth and light and color, and then
taken,—taken, in some dreadful way, to teach him the
necessary and inevitable result of such extravagant luxuriance? It makes me shiver.

It was that very noon when Papa brought in the amber,
that he came for the first time since his return from
Europe. He hadn't met Lu before. I ran, because I was
in my morning wrapper. Don't you see it there, that

cream-colored, undyed silk, with the dear palms and ferns swimming all over it? And half my hair was just flung into a little black net that Lu had made me; we both had run down as we were when we heard Papa. I scampered; but *he* saw only Lu, and grasped her hands. Then, of course, I stopped on the baluster to look. They didn't say anything, only seemed to be reading up for the two years in each other's eyes; but Lu dropped her kid box, and as he stooped to pick it up, he held it, and then took out the ring, looked at her and smiled, and put it on his finger. The one she had always worn was no more a mystery. He has such little hands! they don't seem made for anything but slender crayons and water-colors, as if oils would weigh them down with the pigment; but there is a nervy strength about them that could almost bend an ash.

Papa's breezy voice blew through the room next minute, welcoming him; and then he told Lu to put up her jewels, and order luncheon, at which, of course, the other wanted to see the jewels nearer; and I couldn't stand that, but slipped down and walked right in, lifting my amber, and saying, "Oh, but this is what you must look at!"

He turned, somewhat slowly, with such a lovely indifference, and let his eyes idly drop on me. He didn't look at the amber at all; he didn't look at me; I seemed to fill his gaze without any action from him, for he stood quiet and passive; my voice, too, seemed to wrap him in a dream,—only an instant though; then I had reached him.

"You've not forgotten Yone," said Papa, "who went persimmon and came apricot?"

"I've not forgotten Yone," answered he, as if half asleep. "But who is this?"

"Who is this?" echoed Papa. "Why, this is my great West Indian magnolia, my Cleopatra in light colors, my—"

"Hush, you silly man!"

"This is she," putting his hands on my shoulders,—"Miss Giorgione Willoughby."

By this time he had found his manners.

"Miss Giorgione Willoughby," he said, with a cool bow, "I never knew you."

"Very well, sir," I retorted. "Now you and my father have settled the question, know my amber!" and lifting it again, it got caught in that curl.

I have good right to love my hair. What was there to

do, when it snarled in deeper every minute, but for him to help me? and then, at the friction of our hands, the beads gave out slightly their pungent smell that breathes all through the Arabian Nights, you know; and the perfumed curls were brushing softly over his fingers, and I a little vexed and flushed as the blind blew back and let in the sunshine and a roistering wind;—why, it was all a pretty scene, to be felt then and remembered afterward. Lu, I believe, saw at that instant how it would be, and moved away to do as Papa had asked; but no thought of it came to me.

"Well, if you can't clear the tangle," I said, "you can see the beads."

But while with delight he examined their curious fretting, he yet saw me.

I am used to admiration now, certainly; it is my food; without it I should die of inanition; but do you suppose I care any more for those who give it to me than a Chinese idol does for whoever swings incense before it? Are you devoted to your butcher and milkman? We desire only the unpossessed or unattainable, "something afar from the sphere of our sorrow." But, though unconsciously, I may have been piqued by this manner of his. It was new; not a word, not a glance; I believed it was carelessness, and resolved—merely for the sake of conquering, I fancied, too—to change all that. By and by the beads dropped out of the curl, as if they had been possessed of mischief and had held there of themselves. He caught them.

"Here, Circe," he said.

That was the time I was so angry; for, at the second, he meant all it comprehended. He saw, I suppose, for he added at once,—

"Or what was the name of the Witch of Atlas,

> 'The magic circle of whose voice and eyes
> All savage natures did imparadise'?"

I wonder what made me think him mocking me. Frequently since then he has called me by that word.

"I don't know much about geography," I said. "Besides, these didn't come from there. Little Asian—the imp of my name, you remember—owned them."

"Ah?" with the utmost apathy; and turning to my father, "I saw the painting that enslaved you, sir," he said.

"Yes, yes," said Papa, gleefully. "And then why didn't you make me a copy?"

"Why?" Here he glanced round the room, as if he weren't thinking at all of the matter in hand. "The coloring is more than one can describe, though faded. But I don't think you would like it so much now. Moreover, sir, I cannot make copies."

I stepped towards them, quite forgetful of my pride. "Can't?" I exclaimed. "Oh, how splendid! Because then no other man comes between you and Nature; your ideal hangs before you, and special glimpses open and shut on you, glimpses which copyists never obtain."

"I don't think you are right," he said, coldly, his hands loosely crossed behind him, leaning on the corner of the mantel, and looking unconcernedly out of the window.

Wasn't it provoking? I remembered myself,—and remembered, too, that I never had made a real exertion to procure anything, and it wasn't worth while to begin then; besides not being my forte,—things must come to me. Just then Lu re-entered, and one of the servants brought a tray, and we had lunch. Then our visitor rose to go.

"No, no," said Papa. "Stay the day out with the girls. It's May-day, and there are to be fireworks on the other bank to-night."

"Fireworks for May-day?"

"Yes, to be sure. Wait and see."

"It would be so pleasant!" pleaded Lu.

"And a band, I forgot to mention. I have an engagement myself, so you'll excuse me; but the girls will do the honors, and I shall meet you at dinner."

So it was arranged. Papa went out. I curled up on a lounge,—for Lu wouldn't have liked to be left, if I had liked to leave her,—and soon, when he sat down by her quite across the room, I half shut my eyes and pretended to sleep. He began to turn over her work-basket, taking up her thimble, snipping at the thread with her scissors: I see now he wasn't thinking about it, and was trying to recover what he considered a proper state of feeling, but I fancied he was very gentle and tender, though I couldn't hear what they said, and I never took the trouble to listen in my life. In about five minutes I was tired of this playing 'possum, and took my observations.

What is your idea of a Louise? Mine is,—dark eyes, dark hair, decided features, pale, brown pale, with a mole on the left cheek,—and that's Louise. Nothing striking, but pure and clear, and growing always better.

For him,—he's not one of those cliff-like men against whom you are blown as a feather. I don't fancy that kind; I can stand of myself, rule myself. He isn't small, though; no, he's tall enough, but all his frame is delicate, held to earth by nothing but the cords of a strong will,—very little body, very much soul. He, too, is pale, and has dark eyes, with violet darks in them. You don't call him beautiful in the least, but you don't know him. I call him beauty itself, and I know him thoroughly. A stranger might have thought, when I spoke of those copals Rose carved, that Rose was some girl. But though he has a feminine sensibility, like Correggio or Schubert, nobody could call him womanish. *"Les races se féminisent."* Don't you remember Matthew Roydon's Astrophill?

> "A sweet, attractive kind of grace,
>   A full assurance given by looks,
> Continual comfort in a face."

I always think of that flame in an alabaster vase, when I see him; "one sweet grace fed still with one sweet mind"; a countenance of another sphere: that's Vaughan Rose. It provokes me that I can't paint him myself, without other folk's words; but you see there's no natural image of him in me, and so I can't throw it strongly on any canvas. As for his manners, you've seen them;—now tell me, was there ever anything so winning when he pleases, and always a most gracious courtesy in his air, even when saying an insufferably uncivil thing? He has an art, a science, of putting the unpleasant out of his sight, ignoring or looking over it, which sometimes gives him an absent way; and that is because he so delights in beauty; he seems to have woven a mist over his face then, and to be shut in on his own inner loveliness; and many a woman thinks he is perfectly devoted, when, very like, he is swinging over some lonely Spanish sierra beneath the stars, or buried in noonday Brazilian forests, half stifled with the fancied breath of every gorgeous blossom of the zone. Till this time, it had been the perfection of form rather than tint that had enthralled him; he had come home with severe ideas, too severe; he needed me, you see.

But while looking at him and Lu, on that day, I didn't

perceive half of this, only felt annoyed at their behavior, and let them feel that I was noticing them. There's nothing worse than that; it's a very upasbreath; it puts on the brakes; and of course a chill and a restraint overcame them till Mr. Dudley was announced.

"Dear! dear!" I exclaimed, getting upon my feet. "What ever shall we do, Lu? I'm not dressed for him." And while I stood, Mr. Dudley came in.

Mr. Dudley didn't seem to mind whether I was dressed in cobweb or sheet-iron; for he directed his looks and conversation so much to Lu, that Rose came and sat on a stool before me and began to talk.

"Miss Willoughby—"

"Yone, please."

"But you are not Yone."

"Well, just as you choose. You were going to say—?"

"Merely to ask how you liked the Islands."

"Oh, well enough."

"No more?" he said. "They wouldn't have broken your spell so, if that had been all. Do you know, I actually believe in enchantments now?"

I was indignant, but amused in spite of myself.

"Well," he continued, "why don't you say it? How impertinent am I? You won't? Why don't you laugh, then?"

"Dear me!" I replied. "You are so much on the 'subtle-souled-psychologist' line, that there's no need of my speaking at all."

"I can carry on all the dialogue? Then let *me* say how you liked the Islands."

"I shall do no such thing. I liked the West Indies because there is life there; because the air is a firmament of balm, and you grow in it like a flower in the sun; because the fierce heat and panting winds wake and kindle all latent color and fertilize every germ of delight that might sleep here forever. That's why I liked them; and you knew it just as well before as now."

"Yes; but I wanted to see if you knew it. So you think there is life there in that dead Atlantis."

"Life of the elements, rain, hail, fire, and snow."

"Snow thrice bolted by the northern blast, I fancy, by which time it becomes rather misty. Exaggerated snow."

"Everything there is an exaggeration. Coming here from England is like stepping out of a fog into an almost exhausted receiver; but you've no idea what light is, till

you've been in those inland hills. You think a blue sky
the perfection of bliss? When you see a white sky, a dome
of colorless crystal, with purple swells of mountain heaving
round you, and a wilderness in golden greens royally languid below, while stretches of a scarlet blaze, enough to
ruin a weak constitution, flaunt from the rank vines that
lace every thicket,—and the whole world, and you with it,
seems breaking to blossom,—why, then you know what
light is and can do. The very wind there by day is bright,
now faint, now stinging, and makes a low wiry music
through the loose sprays as if they were tense harp strings.
Nothing startles; all is like a grand composition utterly
wrought out. What a blessing it is that the blacks have
been imported there,—their swarthiness is in such consonance!"

"No; the native race was in better consonance. You are
so enthusiastic, it is pity you ever came away."

"Not at all. I didn't know anything about it till I came
back."

"But a mere animal or vegetable life is not much. What
was ever done in the tropics?"

"Almost all the world's history,—wasn't it?"

"No, indeed; only the first, most trifling, and barbarian
movements."

"At all events, you are full of blessedness in those cli-
mates, and that is the end and aim of all action; and if
Nature will do it for you, there is no need of your inter-
ference. It is much better to be than to do;—one is strife,
the other is possession."

"You mean being as the complete attainment? There
is only one Being, then. All the rest of us are—"

"O dear me! that sounds like metaphysics! Don't!"

"So you see, you are not full of blessedness there."

"You ought to have been born in Abelard's time,—
you've such a disputatious spirit. That's I don't know how
many times you have contradicted me to-day."

"Pardon."

"I wonder if you are so easy with all women."

"I don't know many."

"I shall watch to see if you contradict Lu this way."

"I don't need. How absorbed she is! Mr. Dudley is
interesting?"

"I don't know. No. But then, Lu is a good girl, and he's
her minister,—a Delphic oracle. She thinks the sun and

moon set somewhere round Mr. Dudley. Oh! I mean to show him my amber!"

And I tossed it into Lu's lap, saying,—

"Show it to Mr. Dudley, Lu,—and ask him if it isn't divine!"

Of course, he was shocked, and wouldn't go into ecstasies at all; tripped on the adjective.

"There are gods enough in it to be divine," said Rose, taking it from Lu's hand and bringing it back to me. "All those very Gnostic deities who assisted at Creation. You are not afraid that the imprisoned things work their spells upon you? The oracle declares it suits your cousin best," he added, in a lower tone.

"All the oaf knows!" I responded. "I wish you'd admire it, Mr. Dudley. Mr. Rose don't like amber,—handles it like nettles."

"No," said Rose, "I don't like amber."

"He prefers aqua-marina," I continued. "Lu, produce yours!" For she had not heard him.

"Yes," said Mr. Dudley, spacing his syllables and rubbing his finger over his lip while he gazed, "every one must prefer aqua-marina."

"Nonsense! It's no better than glass. I'd as soon wear a set of window-panes. There's no expression in it. It isn't alive, like real gems."

Mr. Dudley stared. Rose laughed.

"What a vindication of amber!" he said.

He was standing now, leaning against the mantel, just as she was before lunch. Lu looked at him and smiled.

"Yone is exultant, because we both wanted the beads," she said. "I like amber as much as she."

"Nothing near so much, Lu!"

"Why didn't you have them, then?" asked Rose, quickly.

"Oh, they belonged to Yone; and uncle gave me these, which I like better. Amber is warm, and smells of the earth; but this is cool and dewy, and—"

"Smells of heaven?" asked I, significantly.

Mr. Dudley began to fidget, for he saw no chance of finishing his exposition.

"As I was saying, Miss Louisa," he began, in a different key.

I took my beads and wound them round my wrist. "You haven't as much eye for color as a poppy-bee," I exclaimed, in a corresponding key, and looking up at Rose.

"Unjust. I was thinking then how entirely they suited you."

"Thank you. Vastly complimentary from one who 'don't like amber'!"

"Nevertheless, you think so."

"Yes and no. Why don't you like it?"

"You mustn't ask me for my reasons. It is not merely disagreeable, but hateful."

"And you've been beside me like a Christian all this time, and I had it!"

"The perfume is acrid; I associate it with the lower jaw of St. Basil the Great, styled a present of immense value, you remember,—being hard, heavy, shining like gold, the teeth yet in it, and with a smell more delightful than amber,"—making a mock shudder at the word.

"Oh, it is prejudice, then."

"Not in the least. It is antipathy. Besides, the thing is unnatural; there is no existent cause for it. A bit that turns up on certain sands,—here at home, for aught I know, as often as anywhere."

"Which means Nazareth. We must teach you, sir, that there are some things at home as rare as those abroad."

"I am taught," he said, very low, and without looking up.

"Just tell me what is amber?"

"Fossil gum."

"Can you say those words and not like it? Don't it bring to you a magnificent picture of the pristine world,—great seas and other skies,—a world of accentuated crises, that sloughed off age after age, and rose fresher from each plunge? Don't you see, or long to see, that mysterious magic tree out of whose pores oozed this fine solidified sunshine? What leaf did it have? what blossom? what great wind shivered its branches? Was it a giant on a lonely coast, or thick low growth blistered in ravines and dells? That's the witchery of amber,—that it *has* no cause,— that all the world grew to produce it, maybe,—died and gave no other sign,—that its tree, which must have been beautiful, dropped all its fruits,—and how bursting with juice must they have been—"

"Unfortunately, coniferous."

"Be quiet. Stripped itself of all its lush luxuriance, and left for a vestige only this little fester of its gashes."

"No, again," he once more interrupted. "I have seen remnants of the wood and bark in a museum."

"Or has it hidden and compressed all its secret here?" I continued, obliviously. "What if in some piece of amber an accidental seed were sealed; we found, and planted, and brought back the lost aeons? What a glorious world that must have been where even the gum was so precious!"

"In a picture, yes. Necessary for this. But, my dear Miss Willoughby, you convince me that the Amber Witch founded your family," he said, having listened with an amused face. "Loveliest amber that ever the sorrowing sea-birds have wept," he hummed. "There! isn't that kind of stuff enough to make a man detest it?"

"Yes."

"And you are quite as bad in another way."

"Oh!"

"Just because, when we hold it in our hands, we hold also that furious epoch where rioted all monsters and poisons,—where death fecundated and life destroyed,— where superabundance demanded such existences, no souls, but fiercest animal fire;—just for that I hate it."

"Why, then, is it fitted for me?"

He laughed again, but replied: "The hues harmonize; the substances; you both are accidents; it suits your beauty."

So, then, it seemed I had beauty, after all.

"You mean that it harmonizes with me, because I am a symbol of its period. If there had been women, then, they would have been like me,—a great creature without a soul, a—"

"Pray, don't finish the sentence. I can imagine that there is something rich and voluptuous and sating about amber, its color, and its lustre, and its scent; but for others, not for me. Yes, you have beauty, after all," turning suddenly, and withering me with his eye,—"beauty, after all, as you didn't *say* just now. Why don't you put some of it into—. Mr. Willoughby is in the garden. I must go before he comes in, or he'll make me stay. There are some to whom you can't say, No."

He stopped a minute, and now, without looking,—indeed, he looked everywhere but at me, while we talked,— made a bow as if just seating me from a waltz, and, with his eyes and his smile on Louise all the way down the room, went out. Did you ever know such insolence?

Papa made Mr. Dudley stay and dine, and of course we were almost bored to death, when in came Rose again, stealing behind Lu's chair, and showering her in the twilight with a rain of May-flowers.

"Now you'll have to gather them again," he said.

"Oh, how exquisite! how delicious! how I thank you!" she exclaimed, without disturbing one, however.

"You won't touch them again? Then I must," he added.

"No, no, Mr. Rose!" I cried. "I'll pick them up, and take toll."

"Don't touch them!" said Lu. "They're so sweet!"

"Yes," he murmured lower, "they share with you. I always said so, you remember."

"O yes! and every May-day but the last you have brought them to me."

"Have you the trailing-arbutus there?" asked Mr. Dudley.

"No," returned Rose.

"I thought I detected strawberries," submitted the other, —"a pleasant odor which recalls childhood to memory."

For some noses all sweet scents are lumped in one big strawberry; clovers, or hyacinths, or every laden air indifferently, they still sniff—strawberries. Commonplace!

"It's a sign of high birth to track strawberry-beds where no fruit is, Mr. Dudley," said I.

"Very true, Miss Willoughby. I was born pretty high up in the Green Mountains."

"And so keep your memory green?"

"Strawberries in June," said Rose, good-naturedly. "But fruit out of season is trouble out of reason, the Dream-Book says. It's May now, and these are its blossoms."

"Everybody makes such a fuss about ground-laurel!" said I. "I don't see why, I'm sure. They're never perfect. The leaf is hideous,—a stupid duenna! You get great green leaves, and the flowers all white; you get deep rosy flowers, and the leaves are all brown and bitten. They're neither one thing nor another. They're just like heliotropes,—no bloom at all, only scent. I've torn up myriads, to the ten stamens in their feathered case, to find where that smell comes from,—that is perfectly delicious,—and I never could. They are a cheat."

"Have you finished your tirade?" asked Rose, indifferently.

"I don't believe you mean so," murmured Lu. "They have a color of their own, almost human. infantine; and when you mass them, the tone is more soft and mellow than a flute. Everybody loves May-flowers."

"Just about. I despise flutes. I like bassoons."

"They are prophets of apple-blossoms."

"Which brings them at once into the culinary."

"They are not very showy," said Mr. Dudley; "but when we remember the Fathers——"

"There's nothing like them," said Rose, gently, as he knelt by Lu, slowly putting them into order; "nothing but pure, clear things; they're the fruit of snow-flakes, the firstlings of the year. When one thinks how sweetly they come from their warm coverts and look into this cold, breezy sky so unshrinkingly, and from what a soil they gather such a wealth of simple beauty, one feels ashamed."

"Climax worthy of the useless things!" said I.

"The moment in which first we are thoroughly ashamed, Miss Willoughby, is the sovereign one of our life. Useless things? They are worth king and bishop. Every year, weariness and depression melt away when atop of the seasons' crucible boil these little bubbles. Isn't everybody better for lavishing love? And no one merely likes these, whoever cares at all, loves entirely. We always take and give resemblances or sympathies from any close connection, and so these are in their way a type of their lovers. What virtue is in them to distil the shadow of the great pines, that wave layer after layer with a grave rhythm over them, into this delicate tint, I wonder. They have so decided an individuality,—different there from hot-house belles;—fashion strips us of our characteristics——"

"You needn't turn to me for illustration of exotics," said I.

He threw me a cluster, half-hidden in its green towers, and went on, laying one by one and bringing out little effects.

"The sweetest modesty clings to them, which Alphonse Karr denies to the violet, so that they are almost out of place in a drawing-room; one ought to give them there the shelter of their large, kind leaves."

"Hemlock's the only wear," said Louise.

"Or last year's scarlet blackberry triads. Vines together," he suggested.

"But sometimes they forget their nun-like habit," she added, "put on a frolicsome mood, and clamber out and rush all the deep ruts of the carriage-road in Follymill Woods, you remember."

"Penance next year," said I.

"No, no; you are not to bring your old world into my new," objected Rose; "they're fair little Puritans, who do no penance. Perhaps they ran out so to greet the winter-worn mariners of Plymouth, and have been pursued by the love of their descendants ever since, they getting charier. Just remember how they grow. Why, you'd never suspect a flower there, till, happening to turn up a leaf, you're in the midst of harvest. You may tramp acres in vain, and within a stone's throw they've been awaiting you. There's something very charming, too, about them in this,—that when the buds are set, and at last a single blossom starts the trail, you plucking at one end of the vine, your heart's delight may touch the other a hundred miles away. Spring's telegraph. So they bind our coast with this network of flower and root."

"By no means," I asserted. "They grow in spots."

"Pshaw! I won't believe it. They're everywhere just the same, only underground preparing their little witnesses, whom they send out where most needed. You don't suppose they find much joy in the fellowship of brown pine pins and sad gray mosses, do you? Some folks say they don't grow away from the shore; but I've found them, I'm sorry to say, up in New Hampshire."

"Why sorry?" asked Lu.

"Oh, I like it best that they need our sea. They're eminently choice for this hour, too, when you scarcely gather their tint,—that tint, as if moonlight should wish to become a flower,—but their fragrance is an atmosphere all about you. How genuinely spicy it is! It's the very quintessence of those regions all whose sweetness exudes in sun-saturated balsams,—the very breath of pine woods and salt sea winds. How could it live away from the sea?"

"Why, sir," said Mr. Dudley, "you speak as if it were a creature!"

"A hard woody stem, a green robust leaf, a delicate odorous flower, Mr. Dudley, what is it all but an expression of New England character?"

"Doxology!" said I.

"Now, Miss Louise, as you have made me atone for my freedom, the task being done, let me present them in form."

"I'm sure she needn't praise them," said I.

She didn't.

"I declared people make a great fuss over them," I continued. "And you prove it. You put me in mind of a sound to be heard where one gets them,—a strange sound, like low, distant thunder, and it's nothing but the drum of a little partridge! a great song out of nothing.—Bless me! what's that?"

"Oh, the fireworks!" said Lu. And we all thronged to the windows.

"It's very good of your uncle to have them," said Rose. "What a crowd from the town! Think of the pyrotechnics among comets and aerolites some fellows may have! It's quite right, too, to make our festivals with light; it's the highest and last of all things; we never can carry our imaginations beyond light—"

"Our imaginations ought to carry us," said Lu.

"Come," I said, "you can play what pranks you please with the little May; but light is my province, my absorption; let it alone."

It grew quite dark, interrupted now and then by the glare of rockets; but at last a stream of central fire went out in a slow rain of countless violets, reflected with pale blue flashes in the river below, and then the gloom was unbroken. I saw them, in that long dim gleam, standing together at a window. Louise, her figure almost swaying as if to some inaudible music, but her face turned to him with such a steady quiet. Ah me! what a tremulous joy, what passion, and what search, lit those eyes! But you know that passion means suffering, and, tracing it in the original through its roots, you come to pathos, and still farther, to lamentation, I've heard. But he was not looking down at her, only out and away, paler than ever in the blue light, sad and resolved. I ordered candles.

"Sing to me, Louise," said Rose, at length. "It is two years since I heard you."

"Sing 'What's a' the steer, kimmer,'" I said. But instead, she gave the little ballad, "And bring my love again, for he lies among the Moors."

Rose went and leaned over the piano-forte while she sang, bending, and commanding her eyes. He seemed to wish to put himself where he was before he ever left her, to awaken everything lovely in her, to bring her before him as utterly developed as she might be,—not only to afford her, but to force upon her, every chance to master him. He seemed to wish to love, I thought.

"Thank you," he said, as she ceased. "Did you choose it purposely, Louise?"

Lu sang very nicely, and, though I dare say she would rather not then, when Mr. Dudley asked for the "Vale of Avoca," and the "Margin of Zürich's Fair Waters," she gave them just as kindly. Altogether, quite a damp programme. Then Papa came in, bright and blithe, whirled me round in a *pas de deux*, and we all very gay and hilarious slipped into the second of May.

Dear me! how time goes! I must hurry.—After that, *I* didn't see so much of Rose; but he met Lu everywhere, came in when I was out, and, if I returned, he went, perfectly regardless of my existence, it seemed. They rode, too, all round the country; and she sat for him, though he never filled out the sketch. For weeks he was devoted; but I fancied, when I saw them, that there lingered in his manner the same thing as on the first evening while she sang to him. Lu was so gay and sweet and happy that I hardly knew her; she was always very gentle, but such a decided body,—that's the Willoughby, her mother. Yet during these weeks Rose had not spoken, not formally; delicate and friendly kindness was all Lu could have found, had she sought. One night, I remember, he came in and wanted us to go out and row with him on the river. Lu wouldn't go without me.

"Will you come?" said he, coolly, as if I were merely necessary as a thwart or thole-pin might have been, turning and letting his eyes fall on me an instant, then snatching them off with a sparkle and flush, and such a lordly carelessness of manner otherwise.

"Certainly not," I replied.

So they remained, and Lu began to open a bundle of Border Ballads, which he had brought her. The very first one was "Whistle an' I'll come to you, my lad." I laughed. She glanced up quickly, then held it in her hands a moment, repeated the name, and asked if he liked it.

"Oh, yes," he said. "There couldn't be a Scotch song without that rhythm better than melody, which, after all, is Beethoven's secret."

"Perhaps," said Louise. "But I shall not sing this."

"Oh, do!" he said, turning with surprise. "You don't know what an aerial, whistling little thing it is!"

"No."

"Why, Louise! There is nobody could sing it but you."

"Of good discourse, an excellent musician, and her hair shall be of what color it please God," quoted I, and in came Mr. Dudley, as he usually did when not wanted; though I've no reason to find fault with him, notwithstanding his blank treatment of me. He never took any notice because he was in love with Lu. Rose never took any notice of me, either. But with a difference!

Lu was singularly condescending to Mr. Dudley that evening; and Rose, sitting aside, looked so very much disturbed—whether pleasantly or otherwise didn't occur to me—that I couldn't help enjoying his discomfiture, and watching him through it.

Now, though I told you I wasn't nervous, I never should know I had this luxurious calm, if there were nothing to measure it by; and once in a great while a perfect whirlpool seizes me,—my blood is all in turmoil—I bubble with silent laughter, or cry with all my heart. I had been in such a strange state a good while and now, as I surveyed Rose, it gradually grew fiercer, till I actually sprang to my feet, and exclaimed, "There! it is insupportable! I've been in the magnetic storm long enough! it is time something took it from me!" and ran out-doors.

Rose sauntered after, by and by, as if unwillingly drawn by a lodestone, and found the heavens wrapped in a rosy flame of Northern Lights. He looked as though he belonged to them, so pale and elf-like was his face then, like one bewitched.

"Papa's fireworks fade before mine," I said. "Now we can live in the woods, as Lu has been wishing; for a dry southerly wind follows this, with a blue smoke filming all the distant fields. Won't it be delicious?"

"Or rain," he replied; "I think it will rain to-morrow, —warm, full rains." And he seemed as if such a chance would dissolve him entirely.

As for me, those shifting, silent sheets of splendor abstracted all that was alien, and left me in my normal state.

"There they come!" I said, as Lu and Mr. Dudley, and some others who had entered in my absence,—gnats dancing in the beam,—stepped down towards us. "How charming for us all to sit out here!"

"How annoying, you mean," he replied, simply for contradiction.

"It hasn't been warm enough before," I added.

"And Louise may take cold now," he said, as if wishing to exhibit his care for her. "Whom is she speaking with? Blarsaye? And who comes after?"

"Parti. A delightful person,—been abroad, too. You and he can have a crack about Louvres and Vaticans now, and leave Lu and Mr. Dudley to me."

Rose suddenly inspected me and then Parti, as if he preferred the crack to be with cudgels; but in a second the little blaze vanished, and he only stripped a weigelia branch of every blossom.

I wonder what made Lu behave so that night; she scarcely spoke to Rose, appeared entirely unconcerned while he hovered round her like an officious sprite, was all grace to the others and sweetness to Mr. Dudley. And Rose, oblivious of snubs, paraded his devotion, seemed determined to show his love for Lu,—as if any one cared a straw—and took the pains to be positively rude to me. He was possessed of an odd restlessness; a little defiance bristled his movements, an air of contrariety; and whenever he became quiet, he seemed again like one enchanted and folded up in a dream, to break whose spell he was about to abandon efforts. He told me Life had destroyed my enchantment;—I wonder what will destroy his.—Lu refused to sit in the gardenchair he offered,—just suffered the wreath of pink bells he gave her to hang in her hand, and by and by fall,—and when the north grew ruddier and swept the zenith with lances of light, and when it faded, and a dim cloud hazed all the stars, preserved the same equanimity, kept on the *evil* tenor of her way, and bade every one an impartial farewell at separating. She is preciously well-bred.

We hadn't remained in the garden all that time, though, —but, strolling through the gate and over the field, had reached a small grove that fringes the gully worn by Wild Fall and crossed by the railway. As we emerged from that, talking gayly, and our voices almost drowned by the dash of the little waterfall and the echo from the opposite rock,

I sprang across the curving track, thinking them behind, and at the same instant a thunderous roar burst all about, a torrent of hot air whizzed and eddied over me, I fell dizzied and stunned, and the night express-train shot by like a burning arrow. Of course I was dreadfully hurt by my fall and fright,—I feel the shock now,—the blow, the stroke,—but they all stood on the little mound, from which I had sprung like so many petrifactions: Rose, just as he had caught Louise back on firmer ground when she was about to follow me, his arm wound swiftly round her waist, yet his head thrust forward eagerly, his pale face and glowing eyes bent, not on her, but me. Still he never stirred, and poor Mr. Dudley first came to my assistance. We all drew breath at our escape, and, a little slowly, on my account, turned homeward.

"You are not bruised, Miss Willoughby?" asked Blarsaye, wakened.

"Dear Yone!" Lu said, leaving Mr. Dudley's arm, "you're so very pale! It's not pain, is it?"

"I am not conscious of any. Why should I be injured, any more than you?"

"Do you know," said Rose, *sotto voce*, turning and bending merely his head to me, "I thought I heard you scream, and that you were dead."

"And what then?"

"Nothing, but that you were lying dead and torn, and I should see you," he said,—and said as if he liked to say it, experiencing a kind of savage delight at his ability to say it.

"A pity to have disappointed you!" I answered.

"I saw it coming before you leaped," he added, as a malignant finality, and drawing nearer. "You were both on the brink. I called, but probably neither you nor Lu heard me. So I snatched her back."

Now I had been next him then.

"Jove's balance," I said, taking Parti's arm.

He turned instantly to Lu, and kept by her during the remainder of the walk, Mr. Dudley being at the other side. I was puzzled a little by Lu, as I have been a good many times since; I thought she liked Rose so much. Papa met us in the field, and there the affair must be detailed to him, and then he would have us celebrate our safety in Champagne.

"Goodby, Louise," said Rose, beside her at the gate,

and offering his hand, somewhat later. "I'm going away to-morrow, if it's fine."

"Going?" with involuntary surprise.

"To camp out in Maine."

"Oh,—I hope you will enjoy it."

"Would you stay long, Louise?"

"If the sketching-grounds are good."

"When I come back, you'll sing my songs? Shake hands."

She just laid a cold touch on his.

"Louise, are you offended with me?"

She looked up with so much simplicity. "Offended, Rose, with you?"

"Not offended, but frozen," I could have said. Lu is like that little sensitive-plant, shrinking into herself with stiff unconsciousness at a certain touch. But I don't think he noticed the sad tone in her voice, as she said good night; I didn't, till, the others being gone, I saw her turn after his disappearing figure, with a look that would have been despairing, but for its supplication.

The only think Lu ever said to me about this was,—

"Don't you think Rose a little altered, Yone, since he came home?"

"Altered?"

"I have noticed it ever since you showed him your beads, that day."

"Oh! it's the amber," I said. "They are amulets, and have bound him in a thrall. You must wear them, and dissolve the charm. He's in a dream."

"What is it to be in a dream?" she asked.

"To lose thought of past or future."

She repeated my words,—"Yes, he's in a dream," she said musingly.

Rose didn't come near us for a fortnight; but he had not camped at all, as he said. It was the first stone thrown into Lu's life, and I never saw any one keep the ripples under so; but her suspicions were aroused. Finally, he came in again, all as before, and I thought things might have been different, if in that fortnight Mr. Dudley had not been so assiduous; and now, to the latter's happiness, there were several ragged children and infirm old women in whom, Lu having taken them in charge, he chose to be especially interested. Lu always was housekeeper, both because it had fallen to her while mamma and I were away, and because she had an administrative faculty equal to General Jackson's; and Rose, who had frequently gone about with her, inspecting jellies and cordials and adding up her accounts, now unexpectedly found Mr. Dudley so near his former place that he disdained to resume it himself;—not entirely, because the man of course couldn't be as familiar as an old playmate; but just enough to put Rose aside. He never would compete with any one; and Lu did not know how to repulse the other.

If the amulets had ravished Rose from himself, they did it at a distance, for I had not worn them since that day.—You needn't look. Thales imagined amber had a spirit; and Pliny says it is a counter-charm for sorceries. There are a great many mysterious things in the world. Aren't there any hidden relations between us and certain substances? Will you tell me something impossible?—But he came and went about Louise, and she sung his songs and all was going finely again, when we gave our midsummer party.

Everybody was there, of course, and we had enrapturing music. Louise wore—no matter—something of twilight purple, and begged for the amber, since it was too much for my toilette,—a double Indian muslin, whose snowy sheen scintillated with festoons of gorgeous green beetles' wings flaming like fiery emeralds. A family dress, my dear, and worn by my aunt before me,—only that individual must have been frightened out of her wits by it. A cruel, savage dress, very like, but ineffably gorgeous. So I wore her aqua-marina, though the other would have been better; and when I sailed in, with all the airy folds in a hoarfrost mistiness fluttering round me and the glitter of Lu's jewels,—

"Why!" said Rose, "you look like the moon in a halo."

But Lu disliked a hostess out-dressing her guests.

It was dull enough till quite late, and then I stepped out with Mr. Parti, and walked up and down a garden path. Others were outside as well, and the last time I passed a little arbor I caught a yellow gleam of amber. Lu, of course. Who was with her? A gentleman, bending low to catch her words, holding her hand in an irresistible pressure. Not Rose, for he was flitting in beyond. Mr. Dudley. And I saw then that Lu's kindness was too great to allow her to repel him angrily; her gentle con-

science let her wound no one. Had Rose seen the panto-
mime? Without doubt. He had been seeking her, and he
found her, he thought, in Mr. Dudley's arms. After a
while we went in, and, finding all smooth enough, I slipped
through the balcony-window and hung over the balus-
trade, glad to be alone a moment. The wind, blowing
in, carried the gay sounds away from me, even the music
came richly muffled through the heavy curtains, and I
wished to breathe balm and calm. The moon, round and
full, was just rising, making the gloom below more sweet.
A full moon is poison to some; they shut it out at every
crevice, and do not suffer a ray to cross them; it has a
chemical or magnetic effect; it sickens them. But I am
never more free and royal than when the subtle celerity
of its magic combinations, whatever they are, is at work.
Never had I known the mere job of being, so intimately
as to-night. The river slept soft and mystic below the
woods, the sky was full of light, the air ripe with summer.
Out of the yellow honeysuckles that climbed around,
clouds of delicious fragrance stole and swathed me; long
wafts of faint harmony gently thrilled me. Dewy and
dark and uncertain was all beyond. I, possessed with a
joyousness so deep through its contented languor as to
counterfeit serenity, forgot all my wealth of nature, my
pomp of beauty, abandoned myself to the hour.

A strain of melacholy dance-music pierced the air and
fell. I half turned my head, and my eyes met Rose. He
had been there before me, perhaps. His face white and
shining in the light, shining with a strange sweet smile
of relief, of satisfaction, of delight, his lips quivering with
unspoken words, his eyes dusky with depth after depth of
passion. How long did my eyes swim on his? I cannot
tell. He never stirred; still leaned there against the pillar,
still looked down on me like a marble god. The sudden
tears dazzled my gaze, fell down my hot check, and still
I knelt fascinated by that smile. In that moment I felt that
he was more beautiful than the night, than the music,
than I. Then I knew that all this time, all summer, all past
summers, all my life long, I had loved him.

Some one was waiting to make his adieux; I heard my
father seeking me; I parted the curtains and went in. One
after one those tedious people left, the lights grew dim,
and still he stayed without. I ran to the window, and,
lifting the curtain, I bent forward, crying,—

"Mr. Rose! do you spend the night on the balcony?"

Then he moved, stepped down, murmured something to my father, bowed loftily to Louise, passed me without a sign, and went out. In a moment, Lu's voice, a quick sharp exclamation, touched him; he turned, came back. She, wondering at him, had stood toying with the amber, and at last crushing the miracle of the whole, a bell-wort wrought most delicately with all the dusty pollen grained upon its anthers, crushing it between her fingers, breaking the thread, and scattering the beads upon the carpet. He stooped with her to gather them again, he took from her hand and restored to her afterward the shattered fragments of the bell-wort, he helped her disentangle the aromatic string from her falling braids,—for I kept apart, —he breathed the penetrating incense of each separate amulet, and I saw that from that hour, when every atom of his sensation was tense and vibrating, she would be associated with the loathed amber in his undefined consciousness, would be surrounded with an atmosphere of its perfume, that Lu was truly sealed from him in it, sealed into herself. Then again, saying no word, he went out.

Louise stood like one lost,—took aimlessly a few steps, —retraced them,—approached a table,—touched something,—left it.

"I am so sorry about your beads!" she said, apologetically,—when she looked up and saw me astonished,—putting the broken pieces into my hand.

"Goodness! Is that what you are fluttering about so for?"

"They can't be mended," she continued, "but I will thread them again."

"I don't care about them, I'm sick of amber," I answered consolingly. "You may have them, if you will."

"No. I must pay too great a price for them," she replied.

"Nonsense! when they break again, I'll pay you back," I said, without in the least knowing what she meant. "I didn't suppose you were too proud for a 'thank you'!"

She came and put both her arms round my neck, laid her cheek beside mine a minute, kissed me, and went upstairs. Lu always rather worshipped me.

Dressing my hair that night, Carmine, my maid, begged for the remnants of the bell-wort to "make a scent-bag with, Miss."

Next day, no Rose; it rained. But at night he came and took possession of the room, with a strange airy gayety never seen in him before. It was so chilly, that I had heaped the wood-boughs, used in the yesterday's decorations, on the hearth, and lighted a fragrant crackling flame that danced up wildly at my touch,—for I have the faculty of fire. I sat at one side, Lu at the other, Papa was holding a skein of silk for her to wind, the amber beads were twinkling in the firelight,—and when she slipped them slowly on the thread, bead after bead warmed through and through by the real blaze, they crowded the room afresh with their pungent spiciness. Papa had called Rose to take his place at the other end of the silk, and had gone out; and when Lu finished, she fastened the ends, cut the thread, Rose likening her to Atropos, and put them back into her basket. Still playing with the scissors, following down the lines of her hand, a little snap was heard.

"Oh!" said Louise. "I have broken my ring!"

"Can't it be repaired?" I asked.

"No," she returned briefly, but pleasantly, and threw the pieces into the fire.

"The hand must not be ringless," said Rose; and slipping off the ring of hers that he wore, he dropped it on the amber, then got up and threw an armful of fresh boughs upon the blaze.

So that was all done. Then Rose was gayer than before. He is one of those people to whom you must allow moods, —when their sun shines, dance,—and when their vapors rise, sit in the shadow. Every variation of the atmosphere affects him, though by no means uniformly; and so sensitive is he, that, when connected with you by any intimate *rapport*, even if but momentary, he almost divines your thoughts. He is full of perpetual surprises. I am sure he was a nightingale before he was Rose. An iridescence like sea-foam sparkled in him that evening, he laughed as lightly as the little tinkling massbells at every moment, and seemed to diffuse a rosy glow wherever he went in the room. Yet gayety was not his peculiar specialty, and at length he sat before the fire, and, taking Lu's scissors, commenced cutting bits of paper in profiles. Somehow they all looked strangely like and unlike Mr. Dudley. I pointed one out to Lu, and if he had needed confirmation, her changing color gave it. He only glanced at her askance, and then broke into the merriest description of his life in Rome, of which he declared he had not spoken to us yet, talking fast and laughing as gleefully as a child, and illustrating people and localities with scissors and paper as he went on, a couple of careless snips putting a whole scene before us.

The floor was well strewn with such chips,—fountains, statues, baths, and all the persons of his little drama,—when papa came in. He held an open letter, and, sitting down, read it over again. Rose fell into silence, clipping the scissors daintily in and out the white sheet through twinkling intricacies. As the design dropped out, I caught it,—a long wreath of honeysuckle-blossoms. Ah, I knew where the honeysuckles grew! Lu was humming a little tune. Rose joined, and hummed the last bars, then bade us good-night.

"Yone," said Papa, "your Aunt Willoughby is very ill,—will not recover. She is my elder brother's widow; you are her heir. You must go and stay with her."

Now it was very likely that just at this time I was going away to nurse Aunt Willoughby! Moreover, illness is my very antipodes,—its nearness is invasion,—we are utterly antipathetic,—it disgusts and repels me. What sympathy can there be between my florid health, my rank redundant life, and any wasting disease of death? What more hostile than focal concentration and obscure decomposition? You see, we cannot breathe the same atmosphere. I banish the thought of such a thing from my feeling, from my memory. So I said,—

"It's impossible. I'm not going an inch to Aunt Willoughby's. Why, Papa, it's more than a hundred miles, and in this weather!"

"Oh, the wind has changed."

"Then it will be too warm for such a journey."

"A new idea, Yone! Too warm for the mountains?"

"Yes, Papa. I'm not going a step."

"Why, Yone, you astonish me! Your sick aunt!"

"That's the very thing. If she were well, I might,—perhaps. Sick! What can I do for her? I never go into a sick-room. I hate it. I don't know how to do a thing there. Don't say another word, Papa. I can't go."

"It is out of the question to let it pass so, my dear. Here you are nursing all the invalids in town, yet—"

"Indeed, I'm not, Papa. I don't know and don't care whether they're dead or alive."

"Well, then, it's Lu."

"Oh, yes, she's hospital agent for half the country."

"Then it is time that you also got a little experience."

"Don't, Papa! I don't want it. I never saw anybody die, and I never mean to."

"Can't I do as well, Uncle?" asked Lu.

"You, darling? Yes; but it isn't your duty."

"I thought, perhaps," she said, "you would rather Yone went."

"So I would."

"Dear Papa, don't vex me! Ask anything else!"

"It is so unpleasant to Yone," Lu murmured, "that maybe I had better go. And if you've no objections, sir, I'll take the early train to-morrow."

Wasn't she an angel?

Lu was away a month. Rose came in, expressing his surprise. I said, "Othello's occupation's gone?"

"And left him room for pleasure now," he retorted.

"Which means seclusion from the world, in the society of lakes and chromes."

"Miss Willoughby," said he, turning and looking directly past me, "may I paint you?"

"Me? Oh, you can't."

"No; but may I try?"

"I cannot go to you."

"I will come to you."

"Do you suppose it will be like me?"

"Not at all, of course. It is to be, then?"

"Oh, I've no more right than any other piece of Nature to refuse an artist a study in color."

He faced about, half pouting, as if he would go out, then returned and fixed the time.

So he painted. He generally put me into a broad beam that slanted from the top of the veiled window, and day after day he worked. Ah, what glorious days they were! how gay! how full of life! I almost feared to let him image me on canvas, do you know? I had a fancy it would lay my soul so bare to his inspection. What secrets might be searched, what depths fathomed, at such times, if men knew! I feared lest he should see me as I am, in those great masses of warm light lying before him, as I feared he saw when he said amber harmonized with me,—all things being not polarized, not organized, without centre, so to speak. But it escaped him, and he wrought on. Did he succeed? Bless you! he might as well have painted the sun; and who could do that? No; but shades and combinations that he had hardly touched or known, before, he had to lavish now; he learned more than some years might have taught him; he, who worshipped beauty, saw how thoroughly I possessed it; he has told me that through me he learned the sacredness of color. "Since he loves beauty so, why does he not love me?" I asked myself; and perhaps the feverish hope and suspense only lit up that beauty and fed it with fresh fires. Ah, the July days! Did you ever wander over barren, parched stubble-fields, and suddenly front a knot of red Turk's-cap lilies, flaring as if they had drawn all the heat and brilliance from the land into their tissues? Such were they. And if I were to grow old and gray, they would light down all my life, and I could be willing to lead a dull, grave age, looking back and remembering them, warming myself forever in their constant youth. If I had nothing to hope, they would become my whole existence. Think, then, what it will be to have all days like those!

He never satisfied himself, as he might have done, had he known me better,—and he never *shall* know me!—and used to look at me for the secret of his failure, till I laughed; then the look grew wistful, grew enamored. By and by we left the pictures. We went into the woods, warm dry woods; we stayed there from morning till night. In the burning noons, we hung suspended between two heavens, in our boat on glassy forest-pools, where now and then a shoal of white lilies rose and crowded out the under-sky. Sunsets burst like bubbles over us. When the hidden thrushes were breaking one's heart with music, and the sweet fern sent up a tropical fragrance beneath our crushing steps, we came home to rooms full of guests and my father's genial warmth. What a month it was!

One day Papa went up into New Hampshire; Aunt Willoughby was dead; and one day Lu came home.

She was very pale and thin. Her eyes were hollow and purple.

"There is some mistake, Lu," I said. "It is you who are dead, instead of Aunt Willoughby."

"Do I look so wretched?" she asked, glancing at the mirror.

"Dreadful! Is it all watching and grief?"

"Watching and grief," said Lu.

How melancholy her smile was! She would have crazed me in a little while, if I had minded her.

"Did you care so much for fretful, crabbed Aunt Willoughby?"

"She was very kind to me," Lu replied.

There was an odd air with her that day. She didn't go at once and get off her travelling-dress, but trifled about in a kind of expectancy, a little fever going and coming in her cheeks, and turning at any noise.

Will you believe it?—though I knew Lu had refused to marry him,—who met her at the half-way junction, saw about her luggage, and drove home with her, but Mr. Dudley, and was with us, a half-hour afterward, when Rose came in? Lu didn't turn at his step, but the little fever in her face prevented his seeing her as I had done. He shook hands with her and asked after her health, and shook hands with Mr. Dudley (who hadn't been near us during her absence), and seemed to wish she should feel that he recognized without pain a connection between herself and that personage. But when he came back to me, I was perplexed again at that bewitched look in his face, —as if Lu's presence made him feel that he was in a dream, I the enchantress of that dream. It did not last long, though. And soon she saw Mr. Dudley out, and went up-stairs.

When Lu came down to the table, she had my beads in her hand again.

"I went into your room and got them, dear Yone," she said, "because I have found something to replace the broken bell-wort," and she showed us a little amber bee, black and golden. "Not so lovely as the bell-wort," she resumed, "and I must pierce it for the thread; but it will fill the number. Was I not fortunate to find it?"

But when at a flame she heated a long slender needle to pierce it, the little winged wonder shivered between her fingers, and under the hot steel filled the room with the honeyed smell of its dusted substance.

"Never mind," said I again. "It's a shame, though,— it was so much prettier than the bell-wort! We might have known it was too brittle. It's just as well, Lu."

The room smelt like a chancel at vespers. Rose sauntered to the window, and so down the garden, and then
home.

"Yes. It cannot be helped," she said, with a smile. "But
I really counted upon seeing it on the string. I'm not lucky
at amber. You know little Asian said it would bring bane
to the bearer."

"Dear! dear! I had quite forgotten!" I exclaimed. "O
Lu, keep it, or give it away, or something! I don't want it
any longer."

"You're very vehement," she said, laughing now. "I am
not afraid of your gods. Shall I wear them?"

So the rest of the summer Lu twined them round her
throat,—amulets of sorcery, orbs of separation; but one
night she brought them back to me. That was last night.
There they lie.

The next day, in the high golden noon, Rose came. I
was on the lounge in the alcove parlor, my hair half
streaming out of Lu's net; but he didn't mind. The light
was toned and mellow, the air soft and cool. He came
and sat on the opposite side, so that he faced the wall
table with its dish of white, stiflingly sweet lilies, while I
looked down the drawing-room. He had brought a book,
and by and by opened at the part commencing, "Do not
die, Phene." He read it through,—all that perfect, perfect
scene. From the moment when he said,

> "I overlean
> This length of hair and lustrous front—they turn
> Like an entire flower upward,"—

his voice low, sustained, clear,—till he reached the line

> "Look at the woman here with the new soul,"—

till he turned the leaf and murmured,

> "Shall to produce out of unshaped stuff
> Be art,—and, further, to evoke a soul
> From form, be nothing? This new soul is mine!"—

till then, he never glanced up. Now, with a proud grace,
he raised his head,—not to look at me, but across me,
at the lilies, to satiate himself with their odorous snowi-

ness. When he again pronounced words, his voice was husky and vibrant; but what music dwelt in it and seemed to prolong rather than break the silver silence, as he echoed,

"Some unsuspected isle in the far seas"!

How many read, to descend to a prosaic life! how few to meet one as rich and full beside them! The tone grew ever lower; he looked up slowly, fastening his glance on mine.

"And you are ever by me while I gaze,—
Are in my arms as now—as now—as now!"

he said. He swayed forward with those wild questioning eyes,—his breath blew over my cheek; I was drawn,—I bent; the full passion of his soul broke to being, wrapped me with a blinding light, a glowing kiss on lingering lips, a clasp strong and tender as heaven. All my hair fell down like a shining cloud and veiled us, the great rolling folds in wave after wave of crisp splendor. I drew back from that long, silent kiss, I gathered up each gold thread of the straying tresses, blushing, defiant. He also, he drew back. But I knew all then. I had no need to wait longer: I had achieved. Rose loved me. Rose had loved me from that first day.—You scarcely hear what I say, I talk so low and fast? Well, no matter, dear, you wouldn't care.—For a moment that gaze continued, then the lids fell, the face grew utterly white. He rose, flung the book, crushed and torn, upon the floor, went out, speaking no word to me, nor greeting Louise in the next room. Could he have seen her? No. I, only, had that. For, as I drew from his arm, a meteoric crimson, shooting across the pale face bent over work there, flashed upon me, and then a few great tears, like sudden thunder-drops, falling slowly and wetting the heavy fingers. The long mirror opposite her reflected the interior of the alcove parlor. No,—he could not have seen, he must have felt her.

I wonder whether I should have cared, if I had never met him any more,—happy in this new consciousness. But in the afternoon he returned, bright and eager.

"Are you so very busy, dear Yone," he said, without noticing Lu, "that you cannot drive with me to-day?"

Busy! In five minutes I whirled down the avenue beside him. I had not been Yone to him before. How quiet we were! he driving on, bent forward, seeing out and away; I leaning back, my eyes closed, and, whenever a remembrance of that instant at noon thrilled me, a stinging blush staining my cheek. I, who had believed myself incapable of love, till that night on the balcony, felt its floods welling from my spirit,—who had believed myself so completely cold, was warm to my heart's core. Again that breath fanned me, those lips touched mine, lightly, quickly.

"Yone, my Yone!" he said. "Is it true? No dream within dream? Do you love me?"

Wistful, longing, tender eyes.

"Do I love you? I would die for you!"

Ah, me! If the July days were such, how perfect were the August and September nights! their young moon's lingering twilight, their full broad bays of silver, their interlunar season! The winds were warm about us, the whole earth seemed the wealthier for our love. We almost lived upon the river, he and I alone,—floating seaward, swimming slowly up with late tides, reaching home drenched with dew, parting in passionate silence. Once he said to me,—

"Is it because it is so much larger, more strange and beautiful, than any other love could be, that I feel guilty, Yone,—feel as if I sinned in loving you so, my great white flower?"

I ought to tell you how splendid Papa was, never seemed to consider that Rose had only his art, said I had enough from Aunt Willoughby for both, we should live up there among the mountains, and set off at once to make arrangements. Lu has a wonderful tact, too,—seeing at once where her path lay. She is always so well oriented! How full of peace and bliss these two months have been! Last night Lu came in here. She brought back my amber gods, saying she had not intended to keep them, and yet loitering.

"Yone," she said at last, "I want you to tell me if you love him."

Now, as if that were any affair of hers! I looked what I thought.

"Don't be angry," she pleaded. "You and I have been sisters, have we not? and always shall be. I love you very much, dear,—more than you may believe; I only want to know if you will make him happy."

"That's according," said I, with a yawn.

She still stood before me. Her eyes said, "I have a right—I have a right to know."

"You want me to say how much I love Vaughan Rose?" I asked, finally. "Well, listen, Lu,—so much, that, when he forgets me,—and he will, Lu, one day,—I shall die."

"Prevent his forgetting you, Yone!" she returned. "Make your soul white and clear, like his."

"No! no!" I answered. "He loves me as I am. I will never change."

Then somehow tears began to come. I didn't want to cry. I had to crowd them back behind my fingers and my lids.

"Oh, Lu!" I said, "I cannot think what it would be to live and he not a part of me! not for either of us to be in the world without the other!"

Then Lu's tears fell with mine, as she drew her fingers over my hair. She said she was happy, too; and to-day has been down and gathered every one, so that, when you see her, her white array will be wreathed with purple heart's-ease. But I didn't tell Lu quite the truth, you must know. I don't think I should die, except to my former self, if Rose ceased to love me. I should change. Oh, I should hate him! Hate is as intense as love.

Bless me! What time can it be? There are Papa and Rose walking in the garden. I turned out my maid to find chance for all this talk; I must ring for her. There, there's my hair! silken coil after coil, full of broken lights, rippling below the knees, fine and fragrant. Who could have such hair but I? I am the last of the Willoughbys, a decayed race, and from such strong decay what blossom less gorgeous should spring?

October now. All the world swings at the top of its beauty; and those hills where we shall live, what robes of color fold them! Tawny filemot gilding the valleys, each seam and rut a scroll or arabesque, and all the year pouring out her heart's blood to flush the maples, the great empurpled granites warm with the sunshine they have drunk all summer! So I am to be married to-day, at noon I like it best so; it is my hour. There is my veil, that regal Venice point. Fling it round you. No, you would look like a ghost in one,—Lu like a corpse. Dear me! That's the second time I've rung for Carmine. I dare say the hussy is trying on my gown. You think it strange I don't delay? Why, child, why tempt Providence? Once mine, always mine. He might wake up. No, no, I couldn't have meant that! It is not possible that I have merely led him into a region of richer dyes, lapped him in this vision of color, kindled his heart to such a flame, that it may light him towards further effort. Can you believe that he will slip from me and return to one in better harmony with him? Is any one? Will he ever find himself with that love lost, this love exhausted, only his art left him? Never! *I* am his crown. See me! how singularly, gloriously beautiful! For him only! all for him! I love him! I cannot, I will not lose him! I defy all! My heart's proud pulse assures me! I defy Fate! Hush——One,—two,—twelve o'clock. Carmine!

Elizabeth Stuart Phelps (1844–1911)

Born and raised in Massachusetts, Elizabeth Stuart Phelps came from a family of intellectuals and ministers. Her father was a professor of Sacred Rhetoric and Homiletics at the Andover Seminary, and her mother was a best-selling author of moral fictions. After her mother's death in 1852, Phelps, who had been baptized Mary Gray, adopted her mother's name.

She began writing when she was quite young; her first story was accepted by *The Youth's Companion* when she was thirteen; and her first adult story was accepted by *Harper's* when she was twenty. A prolific writer, she produced a canon whose titles would cover pages and which includes short stories, novels, essays, poetry, children's fiction, as well as temperance, religious, and anti-vivisectionist tracts. Her more significant books include: *The Gates Ajar* (1868), *Hedged In* (1870), *The Silent Partner* (1871), *The Story of Avis* (1877, excerpted here), *An Old Maid's Paradise* (1879), *Doctor Zay* (1882), *Burglars in Paradise* (1886), and *A Singular Life* (1895). Her principle themes emerged early in her career and persisted throughout her life. They include: the condition of the poor—particularly New England mill workers and fishermen; the consolation of religion; temperance; and, especially, what she called "the woman cause."

Determined from an early age to be independent, she never concealed the fact that both her writing and the money she earned by it were extremely important to her. Thus, her marriage in 1888, to Herbert Dickinson Ward, the son of an old friend and seventeen years her junior, was somewhat surprising. Ward had literary ambitions which Phelps tried to further. The two collaborated on the writing of several Biblical romances, but they—like the marriage—were not successes. In later years, Phelps's health, never very good, continued to deteriorate, and she died an invalid.

[References: Bennett, Mary Angela. *Elizabeth Stuart Phelps*. Philadelphia: University of Pennsylvania, 1939.

Smith, Helen Sootin. "Introduction." *The Gates Ajar*. Cambridge, Mass.:John Harvard Library, 1964. Stansell, Christine. "Elizabeth Stuart Phelps:A Study in Female Rebellion." *Massachusetts Review*, 13(1972), 239-256.]

THE STORY OF AVIS

CHAPTER XII

It should be remembered that the p'îng is a 'calling' or 'exclaiming' tone; the shàng is a 'questioning' tone; the kú is a 'despairing' tone; and the hiá-p'îng, an 'assenting' tone; the jă-shūng is an 'abrupt' stop.''—
CHINESE GRAMMAR.

It was in the heart of the happy winter that Ostrander, sitting one day by the study-fire with Avis, after a long walk over the frozen beach, said quietly, as if resuming a broken conversation,—

"But, Avis, is this to last forever?"

"This?" She turned to catch his meaning, dull with happiness. "It is pleasant enough to last forever, I think," she said, throwing herself back in her deep chair. She sat drowned in her furs and partially loosened cape: her check had the vivid flush that a winter-night paints upon young faces, and the fine excitement which accompanies it, hovered in her eyes.

"But our own home would be like this always," persisted he, with the vague and blessed fatuity of a lover's imagination, which, while it may perceive the trail of the serpent over Adam's Eden, or Tom Smith's, or yours, or mine, hears in its own only the rustle of the leaf upon the tree of life.

Avis, who had now lost her brilliant color, and sat quite dull and still, said,—

"I wish a man and woman could be always engaged! What are you laughing at, Philip?"

"Should you really like it to be so—for you and me?" asked Ostrander, with a smile that was grave enough.

"Certainly," said Avis promptly. "Of course I should. I am perfectly happy as we are. I think most women would be."

"But I," suggested Ostrander, "am not happy. I am tired

From *The Story of Avis*. Boston: James R. Osgood and Co., 1877.

of a homeless life; I have lived one so long!" He had never so distinctly urged his own need upon her before. Avis listened attentively. Her precious freedom—wild rebel that it was! petted, perhaps, and over-indulged—took on to her mind for the first time, faintly, the aspect of a selfish delight. To be sure, Philip had no home, like herself, no consonance of household repose and love let into his life. She had not thought sufficiently of that.

"I do not wish to press any claim or want of mine unduly," he went on gently; "but there *is* my work. I have my future to make; I don't want it to be one that my wife shall be ashamed of. Situated as I am, I cannot command my best conditions. With his home and his wife, a man must develop himself, if he ever can. With you, Avis, with *you*," he paused, much agitated, "there are no bounds but those of my own nature that will prevent my life from becoming at least a worthy if not a noble deed."

Long years after, these words came back to Avis Dobell's memory, like the carven stone into which time has wrought meanings that the sculptor's mind or hand was impotent to grasp.

"Come, now," he continued more lightly, "an honest word for an honest word, Avis! Do you suppose, if I let you go on just as you like, you would ever make a definite step towards our wedding-day?"

"No," said the woman, after a long puase. *"Never!"* She threw back her wrappings with a suffocated look, and paced for a few minutes back and forth before the brilliant fire, a silhouette in her falling feather and dark winterdress. Ostrander watched her with compressed lip and guarded eye. He was prepared for a long and serious contest, in which he had fully made up his mind not to be worsted. By gradations as fine as the shades in a woman's fancy—too fine for any man but a determined lover to be patient with—he expected her to taunt, torment, allure, baffle, but yield to him now. He had not understood (what man ever understood a complex woman?) the immortal element of surprise in her nature. He sat dumb with delight under the look and the motion with which she presently turned to him. As beautiful is the pliability of a torrent meeting its first unconquerable resistance: it surrenders as mightily as it defied.

"You are perfectly right," she said with a grave, sweet dignity; "and I have been very foolish. If you leave me to myself, I shall never make any change in any thing. If I am ever to become your wife, let it be all over with as soon as possible."

They were married in three weeks.

If ever the Christian character deepened under discipline, Aunt Chloe's should have been that character at the end of this memorable time. We are all of us a little incredulous of our neighbor's affliction; but among the radical trials of life, who could fail to rank the rearing of a motherless child to a marriage in which neither the trousseau nor the upholstery commanded the proper respect of the bride? Unless, as someone has told us, deficiency of charity be deficiency of imagination, we must feel sorry for Aunt Chloe.

Avis positively refused, at the outset, to investigate the deeps beyond the lowest deeps that underlay the nature of unbleached cotton; asked why, if a woman had money enough to buy blankets, she must sit an hour discussing the wadding of a comforter; and failed utterly to see why the marriage-certificate would not be valid without the intervention of Miss Snipper and the milk-toast. There was a compromise upon these fatal questions. Aunt Chloe retained the privilege of seeing to it that Avis entered upon the holy estate of matrimony as a lady ought, with a dozen of everything, upon sole condition that Avis herself should not be consulted. Instead, therefore, of a heavy-eyed, exhausted woman, whose every nerve was stitched into her clothes, Avis came to her wedding-day brilliant with health, and calm as the sky.

This little fact was the more memorable because it left her to her instincts, and no one knew quite how those led her to dispose of these three weeks. She was much in the open air, pacing the shore and the snowy fields; or she worked intently in the studio; or she sat alone with unshared, inscrutable moods. Ostrander would have said that he scarcely saw her in all that time. She received him quietly, but with a withdrawal which he dared not disturb. It was evident that she preferred her solitude to himself. He left her to her fancy, not altogether, perhaps, without some comprehension of it. A man does not live a celibate till thirty-one without becoming fully as conscious of the perils as of the pleasures of a wedded future. Ostrander would not have thought it possible, however, that he could put his broad shoulders beneath this sweet yoke with so slight a protest. His feeling that he accepted a sacrifice radically so much deeper than any he could ever make, overswept the superficial shrinking from change, which perhaps all but the youngest lovers feel in more or less degree upon the immediate eve of marriage. He felt impressed by his dim conception of the strong individual struggle in the nature of this woman whom he loved. His whole soul concentred itself, with a unity not habitual to him in all things, upon the effort to adjudge himself worthy of the acquiescence of her life with his. He tried to tell her so the day before their marriage. But she gave him one look which stopped the breath of his soul, for joy; and he tried no more just then.

It was the simplest of weddings. Mr. and Mrs. John Rose were there, and Barbara; but her brother was out of town on business. Barbara looked at Ostrander, and remembered the tea-rose. Ostrander looked at Barbara, and forgot it. Poor Chatty Hogarth was got over with her wheeled chair; and Frederick Maynard came to see what he was known to have pronounced "the burial of the most promising artist in New England"; and at Avis's request the family servants came in; and her father (who, as is so usual with the collegiate instructors of America, had begun life in the pulpit) married them; while Aunt Chloe, with a mind at peace with God and man upon the subject of the wedding-cake, which no New-York caterer had been allowed to handle for *her* niece, protected her silver-gray silk from her honest, sparse tears, and made it clearly understood among the guests, that Mrs. Ostrander's health had not permitted her attending her son's marriage, and that the young people would visit her in New Hampshire upon their brief little wedding-tour.

They had a relenting February day, in which the prophecy of the near spring was audible, as the whisper of one dear to us across a darkened room. The windows were flung open in the house, and the well-worn path to the studio was without frost, yielding timidly to the touch of the foot that loved it.

Avis slipped away somehow, and was missing after the wedding: her husband went in search of her. He found her, as he had expected, in the studio. The disarray of packing put a chill desolation into the room. The pictures were boxed or gone; the easels folded against the wall;

only the sphinx was left. There had been no fire in the
building that week. Avis, in the middle of the cold little
neglected place, stood shivering in her wedding-dress.

He held his arms out, smiling, but with an emotion which
he found it difficult not to call sad even at that moment.
He was so sorry to startle, to grieve, or distress her, by the
inevitable presence of his feeling. There seemed to him just
then something inexorable, like a Pagan Fate, in the nature of a mighty love. They two, standing there in the
yielding winter sunshine, seemed like children swept and
lost within it.

"Tell me," he said, seeking to dissipate the almost oppressive solemnity which the moment had assumed for
him, and coming up behind her where she stood before
the still incomplete but now strongly-indicated and im-
pressive picture, "what would you do if you had to choose
now between us,—the sphinx and me?"

"A man cannot understand, perhaps," said Avis, after a
long silence, "or he would never ask a woman such a
bitter question."

"Oh! we will have no bitter questions *to-day*," he murmured, taking a step back to look at her. There seemed
to him something strangely select and severe in her un-
ornamented dress. Only an artist could make such a bride.
Her silk drapery hung about her like the marble folds upon a statue.

"Can you understand," continued Avis, ignoring or unconscious of his look, "that I might—perhaps—choose
to stay with the sphinx to-day—and not mind it much?"

"I think I can," he said, hesitating. "No, I will not mind.
I can't be jealous even of the sphinx just now."

"And then," she added, turning sharply, so that she
stood with her face averted from him, "another day,"—

"Oh! and what the other day?"

Avis did not answer. Impetuous words bounded to her
lips; but they were checked by an instinct that she herself
did not comprehend. Her nature recoiled on itself in the
discovery that she had begun to tell him that she could
think of no price too costly by which to purchase her way
back to him.

She stood in her white dress with burning cheeks. She
wondered if, when a woman had been for half a lifetime
a happy wife, she could let her husband understand how

much she loved him. Her love seemed to her an eternal secret. Her soul spoke to his in whispers. It were unwomanly, unwifely, to lavish herself.

After a silent moment, she glided to him like a goddess, and for the first time of her own unguided, or it might be unguarded will, his wife lifted her lips to his.

They passed out together into the pliant air; and Aunt Chloe came calling about the carriage and the people; and the sky, when they looked up to it through the garden trees, lifted itself, and widened, like a joy whose nature knows no end. They passed on through the golden weather, in the solemn separateness from all our little common cares and pleasures, which to have known is to have lived, and to have missed is to hope for life beyond.

CHAPTER XIII

"In the opinion of the world marriage ends all, as it does in a comedy. The truth is precisely the reverse. It begins all."—MME. DE SWETCHINE.

"Who hath most, he yearneth most,
　Sure as seldom heretofore,
　Somewhere of the gracious more.
Deepest joy the least shall boast,
　Asking with new-opened eyes
　The remainder." . . .—JEAN INGELOW.

The reluctance with which we turn from any intense feeling, whether of pain or pleasure, to a lower level of emotion, is a psychological study for which the curriculum of Harmouth University unquestionably finds a proper place in the lecture-room, where all well-classified feelings go, but strictly in view of which, it does not regulate the academical year. Granting that the corporation agreed to honor him by the offer of a chair, Harmouth would have summoned Adam out of Eden, had the Lord chosen to create him in term-time.

It lacked still some weeks to the spring vacation, and Ostrander's bridal tour was necessarily compressed almost between two sabbath sunsets. They did not get up into New Hampshire, after all. He found himself suffering somewhat from the capricious weather; and it would be really worth more to his mother, he said, to see them in July.

The two young people came dreamily to their own home. The afternoon that they were to come, Coy and Aunt Chloe held confidential counsel in the expectant house, a passable place, which had been selected in the perplexed patience with which we adjust ourselves to all depressed ideals. Avis in the town was like a bird that has flown through a window by mistake. The sea could be heard, but not seen, from her chamber-window. The noise from the street interrupted the library. It was not quite clear where the studio was to be, unless in the attic. But there were elms in the yard, and crocuses in the garden, and the house stood at three minutes' walk from the college green. This, in view of the New-England winters, and the delicate health of the young professor, was decisive.

"I can arrange about the studio somehow," Avis had said.

"Certainly," said Ostrander, "*that* must be managed." He meant to manage it, of course. There should be no trouble about the studio. And Aunt Chloe said approvingly,—

"You do quite right, Avis, my dear, to consult Mr. Ostrander's interest first."

Avis vaguely resented this, she could not have told why. She had no principles but the instinctive code of daily love, about deifying her husband's interests, and had found women singularly weak upon this point. But it was quite reasonable that Philip should be near the college: she thought she had done no more than good manners required.

"Poor Avis," said Aunt Chloe plaintively, as she and Coy put the last touches to the small dining-room, where tea was spread for the travellers, "*would have* pink doyleys. Of course, the first cooked huckleberry will ruin them. And I told her they never could be used with English breakfast-tea, and they fade in washing beyond all belief."

"Yes, they fade like a sunrise," said Mrs. Rose demurely; "but Avis is precisely one of those women of whom you *can* say that she never will be married again. And salt sets them. Is this the china she painted? How like Avis! At first you don't understand it, then it bewitches you. See, every piece has a feather on it,—a different feather! She has wrought some fancy about her own name into this tea-table, I'll venture. Oh, I see! No, I don't; I don't see. I suppose we're not expected to see. That rose-curlew on the creamer is like—a singing-leaf, I think."

"Perhaps so," moaned Aunt Chloe. "But have you seen the vegetable-dishes? Not a handle that a servant could get hold of if her thumbs were all fingers. And that rep in the parlor, poor child, *may* last her through the summer. And when I told her how easy it was to slip down newspapers—and I'm sure you can get them up again while the door-bell rings, and a housekeeper can't begin by counting a little trouble like that—but if I'd proposed plated spoons it couldn't have been worse. Not that I've said much about it to her father; for he is so overworked, and it never does to worry a literary man: they weaken down under it like a baby under the whooping-cough. But when I come into this house, and think of those two, I am—I am very much troubled," said Aunt Chloe, stiffening suddenly at the discovery that one slow tear had rolled into the Japanese tea-pot. "Now, while she was painting all this china, she might have learned to set whitebread, at least with milk; and the yeast I could have looked after. Mr. Ostrander may dine off painted feathers a while; but he's too literary to like it long. No men are so fussy about what they eat as those who think their brains the biggest part of them, though my brother is very patient, and easy to pacify. And poor Avis knows no more what is before her than if she were keeping house with little stones and broken crockery in a huckleberry-pasture on a Saturday afternoon."

"There's a baker," said Coy soothingly, "and Mr. Ostrander is very much in love with her." But in her heart she shared Aunt Chloe's anxieties more acutely than she found it worth while to allow. Coy had a delicate loyalty about expressing them. She did not talk much about Avis, even with John himself: she wished to spare Avis the sting which pricks the brightest hours fate yields to some of us, —the knowledge, that, behind the shield we hold before our dazzling happiness, a prudential committee of our friends sits indorsing—whether in our temper, health, income, complexion, or the nature of things—a grudge against our delirium. Coy reverenced the severe old canon which bids us rejoice in the joy of the soul we love.

Mr. and Mrs. Ostrander came with the laggard March sunset. Avis moved about the house radiant and unwearied as a Hebe: even the dust of travel seemed to glitter on her. Coy and her husband, the professor and Aunt Chloe, remained, at her wish, to dedicate the pleasant tea-table. Certainly there was never a pleasanter. And the bread was Aunt Chloe's. Avis presided dreamily. The room was alive with color. She felt rather than perceived the rose-tint of the linen, the bronze prism on the peacock's plume which encircled the cup that she lifted to her lips, the Pompeiian red upon the walls, the mellowed meaning of the Japanese coloring upon the lamp-screen, the flutter of the bright ribbon at her own throat, the luminous presence of her husband's face. She lifted her eyes to him timidly for the first time across their own table. Life put a finger on its lips like a child with a secret to tell. Love was a mystery that went deepening before her. She stood with one foot on an untrod path that broadened to the sun. She shrank from the advance, nay, even from the existence, of unexplored joy. She was afraid to be so happy.

He found her, when, at an early hour, their friends had left them to themselves in the silent house, in a daydream in the middle of the parlor, just where she had bidden her father good-night. He came and stood beside her; but he, too, found it difficult to speak. He was silenced with joy: to find words for it was a task sacred and slow, like selecting an earthly lily for an angel to carry into heaven. He did not try, it seemed, and for that she liked him better; for he said only presently,—

"Are you too tired to go over the house to-night, Avis? Will it not be pleasant to see how it all looks at first? And in the morning I must get to college early."

She felt grateful to him for the easy commonplace words as they wandered up and down, hand in hand, through "that new world which is the old." She wondered how women ever became used to their husbands, and spoke of them indifferently, as Mr. Smith or Mr. Jones.

This home—their home—lifted its walls gravely about her like a temple; and this man whose wife she was, ministered therein a high priest, before whom her soul trod softly. She had never perceived before how solemn a thing it is to found a human home. Most of those experiences which make the whole world kin must become personal to become interesting. The truism was now the discovery.

Avis had contrived, it was impossible to say how,—for never did a bride take possession of a house, knowing so little what was in it,—to stamp her individuality with a delicate but distinct definition upon her home.

"It is like going from flower to flower," said Ostrander, as they strolled from room to room.

On certain points Avis had been stringent. Whatever the vague necessities in the matter of tin-ware, Aunt Chloe should not put a scarlet cricket or a purple tidy in the same room with a maroon curtain. His library was a harmony in green and gray. The little room upon whose windows the buds of the elm-tree tapped was a melody in blue. In her own room Avis had gathered the shades of the rose. The little house was a study in color. To the young man, coming out of the cold spaces of so many homeless years, it seemed, that night, like a new and glowing science, which it would take him as long to command as to possess the mysterious nature of his wife. Both awed him. He watched her with held breath as she moved, gentle with the new domestic touch and stir, that sat so strangely on her. She breathed color, he thought, as other women breathed pale air.

Avis left him presently to look over some matters for his morning class, and herself strolled about the house alone. It was one of the small surprises of life to her to find herself stroking the curtains, and patting the pillows, like other women whom she had seen in other new houses; to see that her hand lingered upon her own door-knobs even, with a caress. The thrill of possession, the passion of home, had awaked itself in a sleeping side of her nature. In her own room there was a very fine East India hammock, woven of a lithe pearl-white cord, much favored for this purpose by people of ease in tropical countries. Avis put it there, because, against the color of the walls and drapery, it had a peculiarly delicate and negligent effect, grateful to her in the confined house. Above it, against a deeply-stained panel, stood her own Melian Venus.

She flung herself into the hammock, and yielded to its light motion idly. As idly she thought of her future, of her work, of the sphinx in the cold, closed studio. Not to-morrow, perhaps, but some day, she should convert her delight into deeds.

It seemed to her a necessity simple as the rhythm of a poem, or the syntax of a sentence, that the world should be somehow made nobler or purer by her happiness. By and by she should know how to spell it out.

Her husband called her presently from the foot of the stairs, and she stole down to him with a beautiful timidity. She did not tell him what she had been thinking: she felt as if he understood. This is what it is to be happy, to believe that our thought is shared before it can be spared.

She had exchanged her travelling-dress, while she was upstairs, for a loose wrapper, over which she had thrown a shawl—a crepe shawl—that he had never seen. He put his hand upon it, and said,—

"You do not often wear this color, Avis. What do you call it?"

"It is carmine."

"It looks like a live thing."

"It is one of the colors made from the cochineal," said Avis. "I have always fancied that they throb with the life that has been yielded to make them. Do you like it, Philip?"

"Like it? How should I know? You are in it." She blushed gently: she was glad he thought the carmine suited her; she loved it too well to wear it at haphazard. One of those subtle fancies which the happiest woman does not expect to share with the man she loves, came to her just then. She would not wear this color except for him. Her soul seemed filled with fine reserves, winding corridors of fancy, closed rooms of thought, deep recesses of feeling, which she curtained from him by a lofty instinct.

The nature of the wife withdrew itself with a deeper than maidenly reticence. She feared lest her great love should put into his hands the key to a fair palace in which she would that he should be forever an expectant guest.

"What are you thinking, Avis?" he asked her suddenly. A certain contraction of her forehead which he did not know, and the familiar throbbing of the temple, arrested him.

"I was thinking," she began, and hesitated.

"Are not your thoughts to be mine, love?"

He drew her to him slowly. In the rich color of her loose drapery she had the poised, reluctant look of the fine Jacques rose.

"I was only wondering," she said. "I was thinking that there are women in the world whose husbands have ceased to love them. I can think of nothing else like that."

"You could never, under any conditions, be one of those women," murmured the young husband rapturously.

"I?" said Avis, looking for the moment perplexed. "I was not thinking of myself. I was sorry for the poor women. But I would rather be such a woman than such a man. I begin to be sorry and glad about many things, in many strange ways, new ways of which I never thought. Philip, two people who love one another might almost make the world over, it seems to me. Joy is so strong—we are so strong. God will ask a great deal of us."

"If he asks he shall receive," said the young man solemnly. He was impressed with her reverent mood: he assimilated it so perfectly, that he could have thought it was an impulse of his own which she rather had perceived and reflected. He asked her for a Bible, and himself suggested that they have prayers. With an agitated voice he sought God's blessing upon their home and upon their love.

They talked no more of lesser things after this. Avis moved about hushed and happy; she stirred, putting his books and papers in order upon the table. He watched her with eyes beaten faint by love.

"You must not tire yourself to work, dear love," she said. She had never called him so before.

Shivering like a cremona upon which a discord had been struck, Avis started, when at the newly-painted door of the new little gleaming room, there fell a sudden knock. It was the new "girl." Ostrander had forgotten that there was anybody in the house but themselves. Avis looked at her in gentle perplexity. It seemed to her a remarkable breach of good manners, that the woman should have come at all; and when she said,—

"An' what is it yez would lave me to get for your breakfast?" Mrs. Ostrander could have dismissed her on the spot.

Philip Ostrander now plunged into his life's work with the supreme vigor of joy. His ambition took on the colors of his emotion, and fired feverishly. He assumed the drudgeries of his position with the fervor of a far more conscientious temperament; and its excitements took on the character of a thrill. His really brilliant but phosphoric nature strengthened into honest flame. He was at that time in his life a marked and splendid illustration of the cohesive power of a great love. His own wife failed sometimes to fathom the almost pathetic movement with which, in those days, he would turn to her, when he came home from the lecture-room over-wearied, holding out his still thin hands, and ask her to strike a few chords for him upon the piano, saying, as he did so,—

"Harmony, harmony! Avis, I am spent for a touch of harmony."

And when her eyes only asked him what he meant, when she had satisfied him as she could, with her repressed, rich touch, he would answer that the boys had tried him, that something had jarred, that there was a discord in him.

"And you," he said,—"you quell it all." And then he spoke no more; but to himself he said, bowing his forehead on her yielding hair, "Who am I, that I should win her?"

He was then, at least, as that man should be who has gained the allegiance of a strong wife,—an awed and humble man.

Then his professional work began to partake of the gravity of his happiness. Professor Dobell brought to his daughter from the green-room of the university a report of her husband's present popularity and prospective power in the college, which excited her like fine wine. For a little while that seemed to her, added to all the other elements of deep emotion in her new life, as much excitement as she could sanely bear. Her own work she deferred resuming from day to day, but neither from that syncope of the will, nor fever of feeling, which threatens the integral purpose of a woman first intoxicated by the deification of herself, that grows from ministry to the man she loves. She reasoned herself through her honeymoon and its succeeding weeks with a steady eye. The studio was not in order; and she chose not to put into her picture—this one picture, at least—any element less permanent than repose. She decorated the dados in her hall contentedly: the sphinx could wait.

A tender sense of justice, possibly, mingled itself with this course. She had not treated Philip so well before their marriage, that she need accentuate her haste to pursue her personal aims and wishes now. Each lingering sign of physical weakness in him smote her with a rich revenge. She watched the lessening pallor of his temples with a hidden remorse of which she dared not trust herself to speak. Sometimes she stole up, and kissed the still prominent and beating vein across his forehead, darting like a vanished thought then from his outstretched arms, and silent afterwards for a long time. One day, sitting beside him in the full light, she lifted his hand, which was whiter than her own, in both her sensitive, healthful palms, and brought her lips to it with her slow and delicate, deepening touch. Then, when he restrained her, she sat crimson. She could not have said whether she was more afraid of, or more savage with, herself. She had never thought before that she could care to kiss her husband's hand.

But in these days she felt herself wasted with unsatisfied sorrow for all that she had cost him.

For him, he sat blessed and blind with love. He remembered when his daring fancy had first asked itself, "What will her tenderness be?" Her lightest endearment, he thought, meant more than the abnegation of other women's souls.

A little thing chanced at this time which gave Avis a deep pleasure, and which threw a certain glamour, even in her husband's own eyes, over his brightening popularity in the college.

During the two years of travel and study which had preceded Ostrander's connections with Harmouth, it had befallen him, one Leipsic vacation, to find himself so exhausted with the term's work, that his German physician ordered an immediate sea-voyage. Ostrander, never loath to yield himself to a new sensation, readily threw aside the laboratory life marked out for that summer, and joined a fellow-student on one of those aimless expeditions so alluring to a young, unanchored fancy, shipping on a trader, which, for aught they cared, might have been booked for the Chinese Seas or the River Styx. It chanced that they were driven by gales out of their expected course, which skirted the South Seas, and found themselves in the Paumotu Archipelago, somewhere in the track taken first by the Wilkes Expedition, and thereby opened since to navigators and missionaries. They anchored for some cause, one day, off an island to the north-east of Tahiti,—a small coral island uninhabited by man. Ostrander and his friend rowed out, overcome by an emotion which they were still young enough to try and express to one another, and beached their boat upon this maiden shore. But Ostrander, after the first thrill had spent itself, wandered away into the heart of the place, finding himself as unable to share the impression it produced upon him as he would have been to share the heart of a woman with another man. He plunged on from beckoning thicket to beckoning thicket, reeling like an intoxicated creature. When he came to himself, he was in a wild place alone. It was on the bank of a small stream, fair but fearful to him. The virgin repose of the trees, the startled look of the strange flowers, the retreat of unseen and unknown creatures rustling through the undergrowth at his approach, solemnized the nature of his delight.

Suddenly, as he sat reverent there, a bird—the island was peopled with rare birds—settled slowly over his head, and alighted on a cactus near him. It was a large creature, snow-white, and dropped like an angel from the burning sky.

A tide of feeling half terror, half joy, overswept the young man, sitting there with upturned face, gone white to the lips' edge.

Perhaps there was not a young scientist in the world but would have risked years of his life to be in Ostrander's place at that moment.

The name and nature of that bird were unknown to science; and the young man knew it. It seemed to him as if Nature laughed in his face. She held out this one sequestered, shining thought of hers, this white fancy that she had hidden from the world, and nodded, crying, "Catch it if you can! Classify my unwon mood in your bald human lore. Marry my choicest tenderness to your dull future if you will. See, I have waited for you. I have kept my treasure back from the eye and hand of other men. Yours it shall be, yours only, yours, yours!"

As for the bird, it stirred circling on the scarlet cactus. Ostrander grasped his gun, dropping to his hands and knees. The bounding of his heart delayed his shaking aim.

He sought to calm himself. His future lay balanced upon that long, shining, shuddering barrel. To capture that bird was fame: so at least the situation presented itself to the young man. When we are young, nothing seems quite so likely to happen as glory. He grew pale, with faint finger on the trigger. The bird stood perfectly still.

One day in the class-room it occurred to Ostrander to tell this story. When he had reached this point he paused, shaken by the retrospect of one of that most muscular emotions that his life had known.

"Gentlemen," he said, "the bird stood still. It turned its head and looked at me: its eyes shone with a singularly soft, pleased light. I lowered the gun. How could I fire? I crept towards it. It was a beautiful creature. It did not move: I thought it was gratified at the sight of me. It acted as if it had never seen a man before: I do not suppose it ever had. I crawled along; I stretched out my hand: and yet it did not fly. I touched it—I stroked it. With this hand I stroked that magnificent, unknown creature. It did not shrink. I took out my knife, opened it, laid it down. The bird looked at me confidingly. I put the blade to its throat; but it would not stir. It trusted me. Gentlemen, I came away—I could not kill the bird."

For a moment after the young professor told this story, his repressed feeling extended itself, like the shade of a powerful cloud, upon the class; and then the boys broke into a passion of cheers that out-rang till the old college walls trembled like a being surprised by something in its own nature that it had never perceived before. Ostrander had become the demi-god of the term.

He came home to his wife, that afternoon, much moved by this little experience. He called her several times, and, receiving no answer, sought and found her in their own room. She was in the hammock under the Venus. The weather was warm, and she was lightly covered with a white muslin *negligée*. The instinct of the English tongue has done no better yet than to level the artistic possibilities of this garment to the word "wrapper." As she lifted her head at his knock in her poised way, and, slipping from the hammock, stood to receive him, holding the long white folds of her dress, he looked at the Venus behind her, and said,—

"How like you are to one another! And I have known you so long, and never thought of it till this moment. Turn your head—so. There. Yes.—What were you doing love, when I came in?"

"I was at work."

"At work?"

"Thinking where I had better put—what I shall do about the studio?" said Avis.

"Oh the studio!—yes. We must attend to that to-morrow, immediately," said Ostrander lightly. He was thinking about the bird and the boys. He began at once to tell her about it. Her face flushed with a divine light. Nothing could have happened to *her* which would have so kindled her tender eyes. If the sphinx, standing with her patient face to the wall in the closed studio, had herself put on the wings of immortality that summer afternoon, would the woman have turned her proud head to see her fly?

They sat down side by side, like children, in the hammock. Avis touched the floor with the tip of her slender long foot; she lifted her arms timidly, and wound his hair about her finger; they looked in one another's eyes through a sweet distance, like Cupid and Psyche through the dark.

Philip Ostrander that day saw his future as the people saw the face of Moses, shining so as it must be veiled. They had been four months married, and his wife was as sacred a marvel to him as on the day when he first touched her reluctant hand. Not one charm of the bud was missing from the glory of the flower.

Deeps beyond the lowest deeps in her nature were yet unwon. His manhood gathered itself to be worthy of their mastery. He felt himself to have taken a supreme lien upon an exhaustless joy.

CHAPTER XIV

"The primal duties shine aloft, like stars."—THE EXCURSION.

"It's the drain, mem, as is playin' the fool on me, bad luck to it!"

Mrs. Ostrander's third "girl"—the third that is in point of continuity, not in cotemporaneity—met her at the front-door with these portentous words. Mrs. Ostrander, radiant from an hour in her old studio in her father's orchard, came in, shutting out the August morning, and repeated with a perplexity which would have had a touch of the superb in it, if it had not been something at once too pitiful and too ludicrous,—

"The kitchen-drain, mem, as has refused entirely to take the clane tea-leaves from the sink, but casts them back upon me hands, the vagabond!"

"I did not know there had to be—drains in sinks," said Mrs. Ostrander with an expression of recoil, "I never examined one. Could not ours be fixed to work without? What must we do about it, Julia?"

"Yez must have a man to it, mem," said she of Erin, with a sweet superior smile.

"Very well," said Mrs. Ostrander with a sigh of relief. "We will send for a carpenter at once. Mr. Ostrander shall attend to it. You can go now, Julia. Is there any thing more you wished to say?"

"It's the charmy-tartar I am lackin' for me cake, mem; and the butter is out against dinner: but that is all, mem, barrin' the limon for the pies, and the jelly-strainer, as they slipped me mind when the grocer come, being up to do the beds, mem, at the time; and the hole in the pantry-windy that lets the rain upon the flooer-barrel, as yerself complained of the mould in the biscuit. That's all I think of at the minute, savin' Mr. Ostrander's company."

"Mr. Ostrander's company?" blankly from Mrs. Ostrander.

"It's meself as well-nigh forgot it till this blissid minute, on account of ironin'-day and the breakfast so late, ye'll own yerself, mem," penitently from Julia. "But it's himself as left word wid me while yez was gone, as there would be four gentlemen to dinner."

"Have we—I suppose we have dinner enough in the house for four gentlemen?" asked Avis a little nervously. She liked Philip to feel that his friends were welcome; and she had thought, with a certain scorn, of families that were injured by the appearance of a guest on ironing-day. She was sure that a narrow hospitality must indicate either a narrow heart or a dull head. Any family in a university Faculty must, of course, be expected to receive largely and irregularly. Avis was quite used to this. But she had never been able to understand why Aunt Chloe found it a necessary condition of this state of things to make the puddings herself. The political economy of any intelligent home implied a strict division of labor, upon which she was perfectly resolved not to infringe. A harmonious home, like a star in its orbit, should move of itself. The service of such a home should be a kind of blind intelligence, like a natural law, set in motion, to be sure, by a designer, but competent to its own final cause. Besides, as Philip had said, she had not married him to be his housekeeper.

"It's the pound and half of steak for the two of you we has," observed Julia peacefully. "An' the butcher had gone before Mr. Ostrander let on a word about the gintlemin; and college gintlemin, mem, eats mostly awful."

It was not much, perhaps, to set herself now to conquer this little occasion; not much to descend from the sphinx to the drain-pipe at one fell swoop; not much to watch the potatoes while Julia went to market, to answer the door-bell while the jelly was straining, to dress for dinner after her guests were in the parlor, to resolve to engage a table-girl tomorrow because Julia tripped with the gravy, to sit wondering how the ironing was to get done while her husband talked of Greek sculpture, to bring creation out of chaos, law out of disorder, and a clear head out of wasted nerves. Life is composed of such little strains; and the artistic temperament is only more sensitive to, but can never hope to escape them. It was not much; but let us not forget that it is under the fiction of such atoms, that women far simpler, and so, for that yoke, far stronger, than Avis, have yielded their lives as a burden too heavy to be borne.

That one day wore itself to an end at last, of course,

like others of its kin. It was what Avis had already learned to call a day well wasted. She was so exhausted, what with the heat of the weather and the jar of the household machinery, that she scarcely noticed her husband, when, after their guests had gone, he came in to the cool darkness of the parlor, and threw himself in the chair beside her to say easily,—

"Tired, Avis?"

Everybody knows moments when to be asked if one is tired seems in itself a kind of insult, and to be asked in that tone, an unendurable thing. But it was not in Avis's poised and tender temper to drizzle out her little irritations as if they were matters of consequence. And her husband's greater physical delicacy had already taught the six-months' wife the silence of her own. She replied, after a moment's pause, that she should soon rest.

"I am sorry to have you concerned so much in this domestic flurry," began Ostrander. Avis turned her head with a slight contraction of the brow. To have left the colors without the drying-oil upon her easel, and surrendered her whole summer's day to the task of making one harmonious fact of the week's ironing and four round, red, hungry alumni, and then to have her moderate, but at least gracious and orderly success called a "flurry," was one of those little dullnesses of the masculine fancy which she was loath to admit in Philip,—Philip, whose fine perception, and what might be called almost a tact of the imagination, had always from the first been so winning to her.

"It must not be," proceeded her husband with some deepening sincerity in his affectionate tones. "We must have better-trained service for you."

"We must, I think,—I have been thinking it over to-day,—have more service," replied Avis. "It seemed as if Julia ought to take care of two people. And there are your college-debts to be got off, whatever happens; but I cannot think it right to get along so any longer."

"Certainly not," said Ostrander promptly: "you must have what relief you need, my dear. Do not burden yourself to worry over those debts. At most, as I have told you, three thousand would cover the whole, and a part of that is already cleared."

Avis did not answer. This point of the debts was rather a sensitive one between them. Philip thought he had explained it all to her before their marriage. Avis thought he had not made it quite clear. Of course she dimly understood that he had incurred pecuniary liabilities for his education, like other young men in America, whose belongings and beginnings were unendowed. But her way would have been to have straightened all that before incurring the risks and obligations of a home. Still, with Philip's good salary, and her own little income that fell to her from her mother,—and surely when she herself was well at work—there need be no trouble about it. And, of course, if Philip thought he explained it to her, he must have done so. It was she who had been dull. She argued this slight point with herself sometimes with an earnestness which she could not justify to herself, without a glance at some far, crouching motive set deep like a sunken danger in her thought, at which it did not seem worth while to look scrutinizingly. Any thought of her husband which was not open as the mid-day to her heart and his, was beneath the respect of attention. Her most distinct annoyance in this, and other little points which might occur to her, was, perhaps, the first baffling consciousness of a woman, that there may be laws of perspective in her husband's nature with which courtship had not made her clearly acquainted.

"It will all come right," said Ostrander in a comfortable tone, turning to go. "And now I must get to college, or I shall be late." He looked back across the long parlor; the closed blinds and dark drapery cast a moveless green shadow upon Avis's face, that made her look pale and ill. Ostrander came back. He had not reached the point of conjugal culture at which a man can go happily away, leaving a shade upon his wife's face. He came back, and said, more tenderly than a husband who has been six months' married may be expected to speak upon an especially busy day,—

"What is it, love?"

"Nothing worth getting late to recitation for, Philip."

"You tire yourself going so far and so often to your father's. We must build you a studio at home, I think."

"I do not get to father's so *often* as to tire myself," said Avis with a slight emphasis, but with a brightening brow. "But indeed, Philip, I begin to be a little impatient for my regular and sustained work. We have changed girls so much—and with all the Commencement company—something has continually happened to embarrass my plans so far. But do not look troubled, my darling. It is not all worth one such look as that."

She leaned to him lovingly; she was comforted by his tenderness; she blamed herself for adding one least anxiety of her own to his crowded cares. When he said that all this must be changed, and that she at least should not be exhausted below the level of her work, if they had to close the house, and board, her heart lightened at his thoughtfulness. Her little difficulties fused like rain-drops into a golden mist. She was sure that she saw her way through them, and beyond them, to that "energy of days" which nature had made imperative to her. When her husband called after lecture, and asked if he might go to the studio with her, and see what she was doing, her heart lifted as it did when they two stood there beneath the apple-boughs, learning love and surrender of the falling blossoms, now so long ago. She looked her future in the face with aspiration larger, because deeper than her maiden days had known. With love as with God, all things are possible.

Avis had that day retouched the sphinx. She turned the easel, and she and her husband stood before it silently. Against a deep sky, palpitant with the purple soul of Egypt, the riddle of the ages rose with a certain majesty which Ostrander may be excused for thinking few hands could have wrought upon it.

Avis had commanded with consummate skill the tint and the trouble of heat in the tropical air. It was mid-morning with the sphinx. The lessening shadow fell westward from her brow. The desert was unmarked by foot of man or beast; the sky uncut by wing of bird. The child of their union looked across them to the east.

"Staring straight on with calm eternal eyes." The sand had drifted to her solemn breast. The lion's feet of her no eye can see, the eagle's wings of her are bound by the hands of unrelenting years; only her mighty face remains to answer what the ages have demanded, and shall forever ask of her.

Upon this face Avis had spent something of her best strength. The crude Nubian features she had rechiselled, the multilated outline she had restored; the soul of it she had created.

She did not need the authority of Herodotus to tell her

that the face of the sphinx, in ages gone, was full of beauty. The artist would have said, "Who dared to doubt it?"

Yet she was glad to have wise men convinced that this giant ideal was once young and beautiful, like any other woman. If there were a touch of purely feminine feeling in this, it was of a sort too lofty to excite the kind of smile which we bestow upon most of the consciousness of sex which expresses itself in women.

A poet of our own time has articulated the speech of one phase of womanhood to one type of manhood thus,—

> "I turn from you my cheeks and eyes,
>   My hair which you shall see no more.
> Alas for love that never dies!
>   Alas for joy that went before!
> Only my lips still turn to you,
> Only my lips that cry, Repent."

With something of the undertow of these words Avis was at this time struggling in the making of her picture. Grave as the desert, tender as the sky, strong as the silence, the parted lips of the mysterious creature seemed to speak a perfect word. Yet in its deep eyes flitted an expectant look that did not satisfy her; meanings were in them which she had not mastered; questionings troubled them, to which her imagination had found no controlling reply.

"It is a great picture," said her husband heartily, after long and silent study. She flushed joyously. Just then she would rather hear these words from him than from the whole round world besides.

"I am not satisfied yet," she said. "The eyes baffle me, Philip."

"They ought to baffle you; they ought to forever: else you would have failed," he answered. "Let that picture go now. It isn't right to waste it on one blessed, unworthy sort of fellow like me. Let as much of the world as has been created fit to understand you, have the sphinx at once."

"I cannot be understood till I have understood myself," said his wife in a low voice. "The picture must wait— now—a while."

"You should know best; but I hope you'll not mistake

about it," he replied, yielding himself to the influence of the picture, with only a superficial attention to her words. "That, I have noticed, is the peril of thoroughly trained women. Once really fit to do a great thing, their native conscientiousness and timidity become, I sometimes think, a heavier brake upon their success than the more ignorant, and therefore more abandoned enthusiasm. Why, in reason, should the sphinx wait any longer?"

"Not in reason perhaps, only in feeling; and an artist can never be brusque with a feeling. The picture must wait, Philip—a little longer."

The depth of her tone arrested his scrutiny; and the eyes which she lifted, turning from the solemn sphinx to him, held themselves like annunciation lilies in a breaking mist.

It was not long after this that Professor Ostrander received imperative telegraphic summons to his old home in New Hampshire. His mother lay very ill. A succession of those little distractions incident to young people who have just yielded themselves to the monopolizing claim of their own home, together with the brief trip to the scientific convention which Ostrander had taken at the outset of the vacation, had delayed their longer and more laborious journey up to this time. Avis, upon the reception of the message, said at once that she should go with him. They set out that night, oppressed by a differing weight of feeling, of which neither cared to speak.

They found themselves in the face of a calm, inevitable death, which seemed rather an awe to the son, and an anguish to the daughter.

Avis trod the dreary oil-cloth of the narrow stairs to the sick-room with an acute sense, such as she had never known before, of what it meant to live and die in these dumb country homes. Poor, narrow, solitary home! Poor, plain, old mother, watching so long for the son who had not come. She forced herself to remember with some distinctness how imperative her husband's reasons had been for not coming before. She dismissed the neighbors and old friends who were in attendance, and herself, having sent Philip to rest within sound of her voice, watched out the night—for the first time in her life—alone with a dying face.

She found it a reticent, fine face, on whose gray solemnity sat a strange likeness to the youth and beauty of the son. Towards morning, when Mrs. Ostrander, stirring, spoke, she bent, and kissed her passionately.

"Thank you, dear," said the old lady with a painless, pleasant smile.

"I have lived without a mother," cried Avis, headlong with regret and grief. "I am so glad I am not too late! Now you kiss me, I know what it is like."

"Thank you, dear," came the answer once again quietly. "Is Philip here?"

"Oh, yes! Shall I speak to him?"

"No, do not disturb him," said his mother in the pathetic, uncomplaining tone which solitude gives to gracious age. "I would not break the poor boy's nap. And I like to see you. You are my daughter, my son Philip's wife. You made the portrait for me of my son. It was kind in Philip to send me his portrait, because I do not see him very often. You have a gentle hand, my dear. You are a good daughter."

"I am a heart-broken daughter!" cried Avis. "Why did you not send for us? We did not think—did not know— Philip did not understand how feeble a summer you have had. I can see how it has been. You did not tell us!"

"I have had—rather—a feeble summer—yes," said the sinking woman with some effort of speech; "but I have needed nothing. My son has been always a good son. I knew he would come when he could. I did not want to trouble him. I have never lacked for any thing. Did you have a pretty wedding, my dear?" Her mind seemed to slip and wander a little with this; for she spoke of Philip's father, dead now these twenty years; and then she called to him, bidding him find the wedding-slippers in the bureau-drawer, that she had saved for her son's wife; then reiterating that Philip had been a good son, and she had wanted nothing, turned to Avis once again, to say apologetically,—

"They had got so yellow, my dear, and I had not seen your foot. Philip thought they would not fit, when he was here, and I showed them to him. I'm glad you had a pretty wedding. Philip thought it was too cold for me to go. He was always careful to think when I would take cold. He was quite right. But I'm glad to know it was a pretty wedding. Raise me up, my dear, and let me look at you again."

Avis lifted her with her strong young arms easily against

the pillows, and the two turned to one another. "In the chill before the dawning" something seemed to stir from eye to eye between them, and to crawl cold about the heart of the wife, like a thought created to be of the creeping things forever, to which rectitude of gait and outrightness of speech, were forbidden.

Had Phillip—Philip, whose tenderness was like the creation of a new passion in the world—somehow, somewhere, in some indefined sense, *neglected* his mother,—his old mother, sick and alone? It was not a question for a wife to ask: it was not one for a mother to answer. Like spirits, the two women met each other's eyes, and neither spoke.

Waitstill Ostrander (such was her poetic, Puritan name) died that night. Her son was with her, tender and sorrowful, to the last. But a little before the stroke of midnight she turned her face, and said,—

"He was a good boy—he was always a good son to me. I never lacked for any thing. Your father will be pleased, Philip—that you had—a pretty wedding. Now I want—my daughter, Avis." And in Avis's arms and on Avis's heart she drew her last uncomplaining breath.

Philip and Avis were together after the funeral, drearily busied with all the little matters about the house which required the woman's and the daughter's touch before they left. Avis was standing reverently before an open bureau in their mother's room. She had just lifted from their old-fashioned swathings and scents of linen and lavender those sacred yellow satin shoes which had never ventured to the pretty wedding. Their first smooth, suave touch upon her palm gave her something almost like an electric shock. To conceal the intensity of her momentary feeling, of which she could not just then speak to her husband, she laid them down, and began to talk of other things.

"Philip," she said, "there was a woman,—a young woman in gray, I think,—who cried so bitterly at the funeral, that she attracted my attention. Do you remember? She went up and kissed poor Mother on the forehead. She had dark eyes; and I am sure the shawl was gray. Do you know who it was?"

"It might have been Jane Gray, or Susan Wanamaker, possibly: I hardly know. Both have dark eyes, and both were neighbors of Mother's," said Ostrander thoughtfully. "Susan Wanamaker was always very fond of her," he added with an increasing interest. "I think you must have heard me speak of Susan?"

"No, I do not remember that you have."

"I did not have a suitable chance to speak to her," proceeded Ostrander: "I ought to have done so. It was an old friend. All the neighbors seem to have been very kind to Mother." Thus he chatted on, to divert her, of indifferent things. Avis said nothing just then; but presently she asked,—

"Of course you added your own urgent invitation, Philip, to mine, that Mother should have come to our wedding?"

"Why, of course," said Ostrander. "But certainly she could not have come. The weather was far too cold, and I really don't know what we could have done with her exactly. But I was so absorbed then, my darling, that I am afraid I don't remember about it all as clearly as I ought."

In truth he did not; and it was this very fact, perhaps, that Avis brooded over with the most definite discontent. She had half feared, standing there with the poor little old wedding-shoe in her hand, that he would turn to her, flashing across it, and ask her if she thought him capable of a slight to his mother. That he had not even perceived that the circumstances were suggestive of neglect was in itself peculiarly painful to her. His nature had slipped so lightly away from an experience under which her own was writhing, that she felt at a loss to understand him.

She folded the white slipper with tender fingers, to take it home. Perhaps Philip could not be expected to know what a sacredness it would have added to her marriage-day to have worn it. Perhaps no man could. Perhaps this was one of the differences, one of the things that it meant to be a man, not to understand such matters. Gently she tried to think so. But she stood looking across the slope of the near church-yard to the locked, oppressive hills, with a dull pain for which she wished she could have found the tears. When her husband came up, and laid his hand upon her shoulder, stooping to see what she saw, she pointed to the mountains, and said,—

"How lean they look! How parched! And she lived— shut in here—seventy years."

"Don't grieve so!" said Ostrander tenderly. "Poor Mother

would never have been happy away from them. She always told me so when I asked her."

He kissed her, and went downstairs to see about boxing the portrait for the morning's express.

CHAPTER XV

"Only the eye of God can see the universe geometrically: man, in his infirmity, sees only foreshortenings. Perspective is, so to say, the ideal of visible things. . . . As man advances towards his horizon, his horizon retreats from him, and the lines that seem to unite in the remote distance, remain eternally separate in their eternal conveyance."

The point at which love ceases to be *per se* an occupation, is seldom more distinctly defined than the line which divides the fire of the sunset from the calm of the upper sky. Avis's love for her work was as imperious as her love for her husband, and as loyally stubborn to distraction. Said one of the greatest women of this age, "Success is impossible, unless the passion for art overcomes all desultory passions." Avis found herself, by dimly shaded gradations, approaching a condition of serious unrest. She was like a creature in whom two gods warred. Her nature bent, but could not break, under the divine conflict. Yet at this time she looked across it with firm, clear eyes. All would come right. These little household obstacles, experience would disperse. They loved each other,—what could she fear?

The winter passed dreamily. When her husband came home on the bitter nights, her eyes turned to him full of a trust as unreflective and as much in the nature of things, it then seemed, as the trust of the lily in the summer wind. He liked best to find her in the dark, opaque reds of their little parlor, and in the mood of the open fire. She sat with her books or her sketching, or in the shadow at the soft piano. The usual little feminine bustle of sewing he missed without regret. Women fretted him with their eternal nervous stitch, stitching, and fathomless researches into the nature of tatting and crochet. He rather admired his wife for sharing so fully his objection to them. Avis was that rare woman who had never embroidered a tidy in her life.

"It is as much of an exhaustion of the nervous centres to my wife to sew as it would be to me," he used to say at this time, "and as much, if not more, of a nervous waste. She shall not do it."

It did not occur to him—how should it?—that Avis's exemption from this burden was a matter requiring any forethought or management; and he expressed surprise on learning, by accident one day, that the price of two portraits which she had painted—her only finished work—that winter, had gone to cover the seamstress's bills. Avis did not chatter about such things. She had a fine power of selection in her conversation (has not someone well said that conversation is always but a selection?) which he admired.

Certain moods befell her that winter, from which he stood afar off. Sometimes, when the wild weather deterred her from the brisk walks which her sturdy, out-of-door habits had made a necessity to her, he found her pacing the house, up and down, from attic to cellar, in a fitful, and what, in a woman of less self-control, would have been a fretful way. He spoke to her, and received courteous but uncommunicative answers. Her eyes had become two beating rebels, for whom his tenderest thought could find no amnesty. Usually, at such times, she retreated to the studio (which was now established, in a manner, in the attic), and worked fiercely till the early winter dark dropped down. Then he would come up and call her, unless he were too busy. If he came, he found her gentle and calm. She leaned upon his arm as they went downstairs.

Avis left the unfinished sketch or painting patiently. She said, "By and by. After a while. I must wait a little." She was still able to allure herself with the melody of this refrain, to which so many hundreds of women's lips have shaped themselves trembling; while the ears of a departing hope or a struggling purpose were bent to hear. Life had become a succession of expectancies. In each experience she waited for her foothold upon another, before finding her poise. There is more than a fanciful symbolism in the law which regulates the drawing of the human form. We must be able to take a straight line from the head to the feet, or our picture topples over.

Women understand—only women altogether—what a dreary will-o'-the-wisp is this old, common, I had almost said commonplace, experience, "When the fall sewing is done," "When the baby can walk," "When house-cleaning is over," "When the company has gone," "When we have got through with the whooping-cough," "When I am a little stronger," then I will write the poem, or learn the language, or study the great charity, or master the symphony; then I will act, dare, dream, become. Merciful is the fate that hides from any soul the prophecy of its still-born aspirations.

The winter was over. In the elm-tree outside of Avis's chamber-window a robin was building a nest, with an eye that withdrew itself like a happy secret. Avis watched the bird with a blind sympathy. She held out her hand, and the little creature ate from it after a decorous hesitation. She felt a lowly kinship with the brooding, patient thing.

In May her baby was born,—a son. Avis was a little sorry for this, but she did not like to say so: it seemed a rude disloyalty to the poor little fellow. But when his father asked her if she were not content, she said,—

"If I had a daughter, I should fall down and worship her."

It was a delicate, ailing baby, and seemed at first a mere little ganglion of quivering nerves. It cried a great deal.

"I don't see what the child has to cry for!" said Avis, looking a little offended.

The baby's grandfather was there the day that she said this. He put on his spectacles at the precise angle and with the peculiar rub which he reserved for a pet philosophical problem, and with a lordly reverence took the child's fingers—poor little sprawling antennae—upon his own.

"What Aristotle and Leibnitz and Kant," he said loftily, "would have yielded their lives to know, you ask, Avis, over-lightly. Philosophy will be no longer a fragment, but a system, when it has commanded the psychological process by which one infant is led to weep."

Aristotle might have had a chance to find out, Avis thought, if he could have had the pleasure of studying her child for the first three weeks of its life. But the professor watched the child gravely. He had a deep respect for a being who could baffle Aristotle.

"That baby has cried ever since it was born!" Avis wailed one night, exhausted with sleeplessness. "I wish somebody would take it out of my sight and hearing for a while."

"Why, Avis," said her husband, "don't you care—don't you feel any maternal affection for the little thing?"

"No," cried every quivering nerve in the honest young mother; "not a bit!"

Perhaps, indeed, she was lacking in what is called the maternal passion as distant from the maternal devotion. She was perfectly conscious of being obliged to learn to love her baby like anybody else; and really she did not find the qualities which that unfortunate young gentleman developed during the early part of his existence, those which she was wont to consider lovable in more mature characters. She felt half ashamed of herself for being the mother of so cross a baby. She had supposed that children were gifted by their Creator with some measure of respect for the feeling of others. This child seemed to be as deficient in it as a young batrachian. It mortified her, like an evidence of ill-breeding. Avis had never lived in the house with a baby; neither had Ostrander. Their vague ideas of the main characteristics of infancy were drawn as, I think I may safely say, those of most young men and women are at the time of marriage, chiefly from novels and romances, in which parentage is represented as a blindly deifying privilege, which it were an irreverence to associate with teething, the midnight colic, or an insufficient income.

Avis herself had not escaped the influence of these golden, if a little hazy pictures. While she knew, or supposed that she felt, many things not expected of her, and failed to feel others which it was proper to feel under the conditions of maternity, yet she cherished in her own way her own ideals. But of these she did not talk, even to her husband. These it was only for her child and herself to understand. Over these, as over her wedded fancy, Nature drew a veil like those casement screens, which to the beholder are dense and opaque, but to the eye behind them glitter with a fair transparency through which all the world is seen divinely new. And then motherhood was a fact which had never entered (as in the case of most women) upon her plans or visions of life. It was to be learned like any other unexpected lesson.

But the spring was budding; and in the robins' nest at the window the fledglings chirped; and the tender air stole in on tiptoe; and her strength waxed with the leaping weather; and God made people to love their children: so it must all be well. The kind of dumb terror with which she had lain listening to the child's cry gave place to a calm exultance. Now, in a fortnight, in a week, in days, to-morrow, she could be at work.

To be sure the baby was a fact; but he was matched by another,—the nurse: from so fair an equation it was not too much to expect a clear solution.

She came out into the sunshine with bounding heart. The soul of the spring was in her. Her most overpowering consciousness was one of deep religious fervor. She thanked God that her life's purpose, for which she believed He had created her, would be more opulently fulfilled by this experience. The baby would teach her new words to tell the world,—His sad, wrong world that the birth of a little child had saved. She felt a deepening respect for the baby. She kissed her fervently. It seemed singularly obtuse in him to double up his seriously inartistic fist, and put her eye out with blind and smarting tears.

"I hope you like him, Avis," said Coy a little doubtfully, one day in June. He was so pre-eminently uninteresting compared with her baby, that she really felt some uncertainty on the nature of Avis's feelings; and then Avis said so little!

"Certainly," said Avis, looking up rather wearily from the week's wash which she was sorting,—a snowdrift fatally deepened by all these little garments whose name and nature were still a mystery to her, and, if the truth must be told, produced more a sense of irritation than of poetry on her fancy, since she did not see that her love for her son required that she should know whether the scallop on his flannel petticoat was ironed the wrong way,—"certainly I like him; but I don't understand why, when he is put on the bed, he doesn't go to sleep. It is very inconvenient,—crying so, when it is proper for him to take a nap. Why," said Avis, lifting her grave eyes, *I find him a great deal of trouble!*"

Coy, who thought it quite in the order of things that her baby should be three months the older, since naturally Avis couldn't get on (she never had) in any real *thing* that had got to be *done* without her advisory council,—Coy gasped, and felt it useless to remonstrate that morning, even about the little shirts which poor Avis was understood to have trusted the nurse to sew.

We hear and think much of the marked days of life, the signal-stations of gloom or gladness, the wedding, the birth, the burial, the day that lent its ear like a priest to love's first confession. One may dare assert that among these

> "Days which quiver to their roots
> Whene'er you stir the dust of such a day,"

there strikes in the lives of most of us one deeper than they all,—that day when we heard the first bitter word from lips which would once have breathed their last to win our kisses. Do you not remember how the sun struck out the figure in the carpet? The refrain of the bird that flew singing past the window? What the pattern of the sofa-cushion was on which you sat gazing? How the Parian Venus tumbled from the bracket, when, going out, he slammed the door? How she swept away to the piano, and the little polka that she played with bent head to hide the tears? You turned that carpet, you covered the cushion long ago, for economy's sake, you thought. Ah, me! It must have been for economy, too, that the broken Venus was never mended, but lies hidden in your bureau-drawer; and let me hear you play that little polka if you dare!

Avis's baby selected one July night, when the thermometer stood at ninety degrees in the heart of the little town, to cry, with a perseverance worthy of so noble a cause, from nine o'clock in the stifling night till three in the exhausted dawn, doubtless for reasons which were metaphysically satisfactory to himself. Philip Ostrander, not finding in them any distinct bearings upon the natural sciences, was, as might be expected, less of an enthusiast in the matter. He took his pillow, and vacated the scene of action. He had some time since reached the stage at which a man first perceives the full value and final cause of the "spare room,"—an institution not created, as we have crudely supposed, for a chance guest, but for the relief of the father whose morning duties clearly require a full night's rest. It certainly was plain enough that Mr. Ostrander could not conduct the morning recitation if he had been kept awake all night; and his weak lung forbade his carrying the baby, Avis said.

The poor girl wore that terrible July out as best she might, in the deepening reserve which motherhood only of all forms of human solitude knows.

On this particular morning she came down late and wan. The fierce, free fire of her superb eyes had given way to the *burnt-in* look of anxious patience, which marks a young mother out from all other young creatures in the world. Her husband sat with a disturbed face at a disorderly table.

"Avis," he began, without looking up to see how she was, "the cracked wheat is soggy again."

Avis for a moment made no reply: she could not for sheer surprise. The husband's tone, breaking in upon her exhaustion of mind and body, gave her something of the little shock that we feel on finding our paper give out in the middle of an absorbing sentence. When she spoke, she said gently, but with some dignity,—

"I am sorry, Philip: I will speak about it."

"And the cream," proceeded Philip, "is sour. The steak was cold; and the coffee will give me a bilious headache before night. I really don't see why we can't have things more comfortable."

"We certainly must, if they are so very uncomfortable," replied his wife with rather a pale smile, striving, she could hardly have told why, to turn the discussion into a jest. "But you remember you didn't marry me to be your housekeeper, Philip!"

Philip Ostrander pushed his chair back without a smile, folded his napkin with the peculiar masculine emphasis which says, I can hold my tongue, for I am a gentleman; but it is doggedly hard work! Then turning, with averted face murmured through his closed teeth,—

"Yes, I remember. I don't know what we were either of us thinking of!"

With this he took his hat and strode away to college, in the sacred summer light, to conduct the morning prayers of a thousand perceptive and receptive boys.

Avis sat for a little while at the uninviting breakfast-table; she tasted the cold coffee, and sent Julia away with her sympathetic if a little bitter tea: she felt too weak to eat. She looked out into the elm-branch, and saw the empty nest which the May robin had left, and dimly thought what an unpleasant look it had, and dimly thought she would get Julia to pull it down. It seemed quite necessary not to think of anything except the nest. Her eyes burned feverishly. She threw herself upon the lounge, and lay with both hands pressed upon them, still as the coins that press the lids of the dead. Presently she rang the bell sharply, and in a strung, strained voice bade that the nurse be ordered to bring the child.

He came, poor little fellow! looking as wan as his mother, but as innocent of having made himself an unpleasant fact in the family life as a tuberose is of yielding too strong a sweetness. Avis caught him with something not unlike the passionate love which Arria may have felt for the dagger, and hid her broken face upon the baby's neck, as if she would have hidden it there forever from all the world.

When Ostrander came home, he sought his wife all over the house. She was not to be found. The cook said she took her hat and went out an hour since; and the nurse explained, that in throwing back the nursery blinds to give the important message which the cook had forgotten to deliver to the grocer's boy, she had thought it likely it was Mrs. Ostrander as she saw just beyond the top of the cart, turning Elm Street to the beach.

Ostrander pursued her impatiently in the blazing sun. He perceived the flutter of her dress far down against the light-house; and, when he had overtaken her, he found her creeping along in the shadow formed by that great gorge so memorable to them both. She did not see him or hear him, and so crawled along in an aimless, dreary fashion which it gave him a nameless terror to see.

Her figure looked so broken, so beaten, and weak, that it for the first time occurred to him that the effect of a little conjugal quarrel upon a nature like that of his wife's was not altogether a calculable one. His own words once spoken in that spot came back to him as he made his penitent way along the purple gorge, looking from torn side to torn side.

"It was a perfect primeval marriage. The heart of the rock was simply broken."

Had Avis wrought herself into that frenzy of wounded feeling in which weaker women have courted death, as a man with lacerated spinal nerves courts the *moxa?* He overtook her without her hearing his light step, and, manlike, trusting to the sensation to interpret the emotion, barricaded her with both arms, and folded her to his shamed and sorry heart. But Avis glided from his touch like a spirit. Her bent figure heightened grandly, and her unwon maiden eyes seemed to look again from a great height down upon him, where she had swept and stood upon the jutting cliff.

Ostrander at that moment felt that to have been permitted to gain the allegiance of the heart we love, is but the most tentative and introductory step towards the durability of a happiness whose existence depends upon our being found worthy to retain what we have won; and in feeling this he felt deeper than he could reason into the joy and pain and peril which weld two individual human souls into the awful fusion which we call marriage.

But he said only,—

"Avis, I was a brute!"

"No," she said bitterly, "you were only a man." Then repenting, with swift nobility she came to him,—

"Now it is I who am wrong. Forgive me, Philip!"

"*You?*"

He gathered her tenderly. She did not repel him: she was worn out with the strain of the night and the glare of the long walk. She did not cry; but she lay in his arms with a dry, sobbing sigh which alarmed him. He caressed her passionately. He sought her pardon in the soul of every sweet sign love had taught him in its first dizzy hours. She submitted quietly, but with an unresponsiveness which afterwards he remembered with disquiet perplexity.

The scar which an unkind word leaves upon a large love, may be invisible, like that of a great sin upon the tissues of the repentant soul; but for one as for the other, this life has no healing.

Avis did not choose to talk about cracked wheat. There were other things in the world to say. And it was impossible to express, without giving them both useless pain, her inherent, ineradicable, and sickening recoil from the details of household care. And Philip, distraught with his deepening responsibilities at the college, naturally ceased to inquire so often how matters went in the studio. Avis faced her circumstances with such patience as she could command. A weaker woman lets conditions override her, be the lash a divine frenzy or a chronic neuralgia. Avis sadly turned the tense muscle of her strong nature now to secure a gracious home. The thong which has stung the aspirations of all women, since Eve, for love of knowledge, ate and sinned, goaded her on. She said to herself, "It will be a matter, at most, of a few months. When I have mastered this one little house, life waits; and art is long." She made haste to be wise in wisdom that her soul loathed, to clear the space about her for the leisure that her patient purpose craved. But sometimes, sitting burdened with the child upon her arms, she looked out and off upon the summer sky with a strangling desolation like that of the forgotten diver, who sees the clouds flit, from the bottom of the sea.

CHAPTER XVII

"Men think that it is ungrateful to the Creator to say that it is the design of Providence to keep us in a state of constant pain; but . . . were our joys permanent we should never leave the state in which we are; we should never undertake aught new. That life we may call happy which is furnished with all the means by which pain can be overcome: we have, in face, no other conception of human happiness."— KANT.

"The worst of it is the babies," said Aunt Chloe, giving a severe twist to her flower-pots, that would have estranged the devotion of anything else than the verbenas. But verbenas are not sensitive: one knows about how far one can go with them. "I don't see but the worst of it always *is* the babies, in this world," she proceeded, and prayed next minute to be forgiven for so unevangelical a sentiment. Aunt Chloe was so stubborn to the advance of civilization, that she still held that the Lord never sent more mouths than he could fill. She would have thought it very unwomanly to confess to Avis her conscious lack of enthusiasm at the birth of this second child. She blamed herself, that in her honest heart poor Avis's experience of motherhood gave her so much more anxiety than pleasure, and attributed it all to the fact that Mr. Ostrander would use homoeopathic remedies for the croup. And now—

"Who is going to prepare Avis for this?" asked Aunt Chloe, turning her back on the verbenas without ceremony, and standing on tiptoe laboriously to remove a bit of lint from her brother's coat-collar while she spoke: it was not necessary that they should meet each other's eyes. When a literary man is in any kind of trouble, he does not want his women-folks to know too much about it: that, Aunt Chloe thought might be easily understood, even in a business family. When the professor said shortly,—

"I suppose I must tell her myself," going out, and letting the wind take the door behind him, she said, "Poor Hegel!" and wondered if the arbutelon overheard her. And then she went to start a lemon-cream for his dinner. She remembered that she gave him lemon-cream the day the president vetoed that plan about the post-graduate courses; and what a comfort it seemed to be to her brother! And then perhaps poor Avis would taste of it; and there really was no hurry about the child's shirts. Aunt Chloe, like the rest of the world, had expended all the poetry of her allegiance upon the first baby. It did not seem so necessary to crochet the edges of things for this one, poor little lassie; and she had put fully five cents a yard less into the flannels.

Mrs. Ostrander's little girl was four weeks old, four weeks that very day, as the professor—Heaven knows how!—chanced to remember on the way to his daughter's house. He was rather proud of himself for thinking of it, and made the most of the little matter. He was nervous over what he had to say. He thought he had never seen Avis looking so poorly. He took the child from her, for she held it rather listlessly across her arm upon the rose-red lounge: he lifted the little maiden upon his knee well-nigh as tenderly as if she had been a leaf from the "Rhetoric" or "Poetic" in the original autograph. When the boy ran in, he gave him a cough-lozenge, and said,—

"And how is Van Dyck, to-day?" with a sense of unusual originality of expression. In his heart the professor was rather glad that day, that the boy had not taken a family name. Avis had never been heard to express a wish to name her son for his father. She did not try to explain either to herself or to another why this was. We do not always remember that a woman seeks and finds two perfectly distinct beings in one and the same man. For herself, she can afford to love a human creature; for the father of her child she demands a God. That very weakness in his nature upon which she will abnegate herself, which perhaps she will lower the tone of her own soul to idealize into a perversion of strength, she will defy like a lioness in its transmission to her son. But Avis did not talk —even to her own husband—much about her children. There were throes of the soul in her strong motherhood, which it was no more possible to share than to share a physical pang.

When the professor had repeated, "And how is Van?" and asked the four-weeks' baby (in the anxious tone of a man who expects a reply) if she were sitting quite comfortably, he found that he had exhausted his nursery vocabulary; and when he had said helplessly,—

"Are you quite well to-day, my dear?" and when Avis replied that she was gaining slowly every day, his mind proved to be perfectly barren of any further phrases logically consequent upon the premise formed by the morsel of humanity upon his knee. He began therefore, at once, but with a certain hesitation to which Avis's transparent face became magnetically alive,—

"I came for a special purpose to-day, Avis: I want to have a little talk with you about—your husband."

"Van," said his mother immediately, "run into the nursery." She spoke to her two-years' baby in a tone which assumes both intelligence and obedience in the listener. "Mary Ann, take the child—take both the babies, and do not bring them back till they are sent for.—Now, father, what is it? What has Philip done?"

She raised herself upon the pillow with a sharp motion. The deep circles about her eyes seemed to widen, like the circles in the sea into which a blazing jewel is sinking.

"He has not done anything," said the professor nervously; "and that is exactly the trouble."

"Do you mean," asked Avis in a rapid, business-like tone, "that my husband is not giving satisfaction in the university?"

"Somebody must tell you," pleaded the poor professor. "I thought you would rather—perhaps—it would be I."

"Walk the floor, Father," said Avis, after a moment's silence: "you will feel a great deal more comfortable. Don't mind me."

The professor, with a sigh of relief, thrust back his chair, and trode heavily to and fro: the floor of the room shook beneath its faded roses.

"Now," said Avis, after a slightly longer pause than before,—"now tell me all about it. I am quite ready to hear. Stop! To begin with, does Philip know this?"

"N-n—I do not know. Probably not. There has been no direct expression of dissatisfaction made to him as yet. How sensitive he is to the indirect command of the situation, it is not possible to say. There is a committee of the Board in town to-day: that is why I have annoyed you with it. Probably the matter will be taken up at once in some form. I thought you would prefer, and he, that you should be forewarned."

"Thank you, sir!" said Avis in a low voice.

"The trouble is"—began the professor, and stopped.

"The trouble is?" prompted Avis gently.

"That your husband does not attend to his business," said her father desperately. "The department is running behind. It ought to be one of the most brilliant in the college. Under Professor Cobin's day it acquired a prestige, which, of course, makes it difficult for a younger man, *any* younger man. I thought Mr. Ostrander was equal to these difficulties. He is not: that is about all."

"Still I don't understand," urged Avis. "Is not Philip enough of a man for the position? Did you overestimate his ability to start with? In plain words, has not he the brains for it?"

"He has the brains for anything!" exclaimed the professor irritably, "that he chooses to apply himself to. It is not his ability that has been overrated."

"What, then?" insisted Avis. "Does my husband *shirk?*"

She brought the ugly word out with a keen emphasis with which it was not possible to parley. "Certainly," she added with a momentary flash, "he is not an idle man: he works hard. Philip is rather overworked than underworked. I think he is always busy. I do not in the least understand where all this activity has gone to, if it has not gone into the department."

"It is not easy to say where it has gone," replied her father nervously. "I doubt if he knows himself. It is not quite fair to call a man a shirk, perhaps, while he is occupied in so many—but the trouble is, they are not the right directions. He bends himself to too many things. Now it is electricity; now it is magnetism; then it is a process for utilizing coal-gas. Just now it is a new method for blowing up caterpillars—blowing up fiddlesticks! His business is in his class-room. He ought not to see one inch beyond the faces of those boys this five years. He ought to absorb that morning recitation as the old Hebrew prophets swallowed the scroll on which the word of God was written. Every fossil ought to be a poem to him. He shouldn't be able to *say Old Red Sandstone without a thrill!* He should have conquered his lecture-room by this time. There is a soul in science: he should have handled her body reverently for her soul's sake. He should have overwhelmed that class with his inspirations, as the deluges have overmastered the mountains. When every man in it worth educating could get an enthusiasm out of a chip of granite; when a man he'd marked down on examination would huzza for him in the street; when the college papers were afraid to lampoon him,—then he might have taken to his magazine-writing, and his whatnot, and the more welcome. *When the college could afford to be proud of him* was the time to let the world know that such a man as Philip Ostrander was in it. Well"—the professor brought himself up short before his daughter's sofa with burning eyes—"I am tiring you, Avis. It is a great pity: it is all a pity."

"Then Philip has done—none of this?" proceeded Avis authoritatively. "He has been impatient, volatile—he has"— She paused.

"He has shirked the drudgery of the class-room," said her father in a lower and calmer tone. "He got weary of it. He has dissipated himself in unconsequent ways. He has no more business to be giving popular lectures on physiology, or writing poetry for the newspapers, than I have to set up a milliner's shop on the college green. It is too bad, too bad. But, my dear, I'm tiring you."

"The trouble," began Avis, hesitating.

"The trouble with your husband, my child," said the professor with something of gathering enthusiasm in his manner, as though he propounded a well-involved meta-physical problem to a rather superior class,—"the trouble is an extraordinary lack of intellectual constancy. It—it really is nothing worse, my dear," he added soothingly. "It does not prevent him from possessing all those do-mestic virtues which have doubtless endeared him to you; and I must say," tremulously—"to myself as well. I have been very much drawn to the young man, as to—a—son. After we have adjusted ourselves to this—blow, my dear, something else will open for him. I see no reason for in-dulging in any undue—regrets. As for yourself"—

"Should Philip resign at once?" demanded Avis in the metallic tone which resolutely suppressed feeling gives to a tender voice.

"It may be—I cannot tell till after the meeting of the Board. It is impossible to say what will be done, or when, about a successor. But it will not be expected that his resignation shall take effect before the end of the year.

That will give us six months to look about us in," added the professor rather miserably.

He came and stood beside his daughter, looking compassionately at her. He did not seek to offer her a consolation which her nature would inevitably reject. Her lip did not tremble. She had the half-recoiling but wholly patient look of one who was adjusting herself to a familiar experience in a slightly altered form. She put up her hand, and said only,—

"Thank you, Father!"

And he said,—

"There, there, my dear!"

And then the little boy ran in, with Mary Ann and the baby behind him.

Avis gathered both the children in her arms with a quick and passionate motion. Her heart said, "Oh! what have we done to bring them into this world? What have we done? What can we do?" But her lips said nothing at all.

"The little folks interfere with the studio just now," said the professor awkwardly, coming back when he was across the threshold of the room. He was sick at heart to say some tender word. "If her mother had lived," he thought, "this might somehow have been spared." Whenever Avis was in any trouble, he always said, "If her mother had lived"— The great professor was as unconscious of any logical flaw in this sweet inconsequence, as the lover is of the laws regulating the circulation of the blood in the lip he kisses.

"Yes, Papa," said Avis, falling back into the pretty girlish fashion of speech that she had scarcely outgrown before her marriage.

"But as soon as you are about again—and—the little girl begins to grow, we shall have some more pictures I hope, my dear?"

"Yes, Papa," patiently. But she said nothing more. It did not seem to help anything to talk about it. And then the baby began to cry—her little daughter—her woman-child. Avis looked at her, and said, "You too, *you too!*" It seemed to her just then more than she could bear, to know that she had given life to another woman.

When her husband came to her with the news, a day or two after, she had so far adjusted her mind to it, that she was able to receive its announcement from himself in the only way which—long after—she could have recalled without regret.

He came in looking very pale. She had heard him coughing in the hall: the day was damp. He threw himself heavily upon the lounge, and said,—

"Has your father told you what has happened?"

"Yes, Philip."

"How long since?"

"On Tuesday."

"Some way or other," said Ostrander irritably, "I have offended Cobin. He has been more or less cavalier in his treatment of me this long while. When it's time for a man to die, he never can understand why other men are alive. He opposed me about the museum; he complained of my Star Course Lectures; I haven't raised a point in Faculty meeting this year, that he hasn't voted down. I attribute this disaster entirely to the cause which has ruined so many a young man,—the jealousy of his senior colleague."

Avis made no reply. She could not speak just then. It did not seem a sane expense of words, which, at best, must be hard to choose. She let him dribble on petulantly for a few minutes. Her boy at her knee was vociferously claiming it an evidence of extraordinary maternal depravity, that his little sister was not allowed rubber-boots with which to go to walk with him. The child's voice and his father's chimed together oddly. She stood apart from them,—these two intensely wrought male personalities, with whose clamorous selfism it was impossible to reason. It struck her unpleasantly at that moment that Van might be like his father, if he lived to grow up. She pushed the boy a little away from her, then drew him penitently back.

"What in Heaven's name is going to become of us," Philip was saying, "is more than I can see. The mere mortification of it is enough to kill a stronger man than I am."

"Never mind, dear," said Avis, exactly as she spoke to the child. She came up, and bent over the lounge, passing her strong hand across his forehead and hair, with the magnificent, maternal motions which her fingers had learned more slowly than those of most women, but more passionately. When he said,—

"My head aches horribly!" she stooped and kissed him, and said,—

"My poor boy!"

It was impossible for her to render anything more reasonable than tenderness to a humiliated man.

"It is hard for you, coming just now," said Ostrander, rather as an afterthought. "I wish the children were not both babies. It's a confoundedly tough thing for a man with a young family to be turned adrift in this way. I should have thought," irritably, "that your father's influence might have prevented it. But it seems he couldn't or didn't exercise it. I shall write my resignation to-morrow, and get it off my mind. Ought you to stand so long, Avis?"

"It does not hurt me"; but she sank wearily down upon the edge of the lounge. Philip did not move to make room for her, but lay with his brows knotted with pain, and his restless eyes flitting about the room. She slipped down upon her knees, and so knelt, crouched and cramped, till the life of her sensitive hand had spent itself upon him.

"The pain is gone, thank you," he said at last politely. Avis rose at once, and took a chair. In these days, if she caressed her husband, it was with a sufficient and distinct reason: the time had tripped by when he expected her to sit within reach of his hand, within vibration of his breath, within the maze of all that sweet young folly which is wiser than the lore of the ages to those who love. It was so with all married people, she supposed.

"Whatever," began Philip, "is to turn up next"—

"Whatever we do next, I hope we shall be able to persevere in it," suggested Avis gently. She was not a woman of reproaches. Philip Ostrander's wife never "nagged" him. He shrugged his shoulders now, and said,—

"Perhaps it is all for the best. I was worn out with that eternal class-room," rather sullenly. Then he complained of the draught, and said that he had taken cold, and asked what on earth the baby was crying about now.

Avis's heart brooded over him, seeing him so irritable and weak, as if he had been a wounded thing. She drew a little nearer, and began to plan and purpose for him, as she would for an excited boy who had got into a scrape. She brought the whole machinery of her superb imagination to bear upon their future. She presented it to him in the colors of courage and the ardors of hope. She spoke with a cheer and assurance that rang hollow to her own forebodings. Ostrander warmed at this tremulous fire. He talked of his command of the languages, of his medical education. He thanked Heaven that he had never been a man of one idea; and now, whatever versatility it had pleased Providence to endow him with would serve them through this emergency till another position offered. Avis listened, and said,—

"Yes, Philip." She sat with her face turned from him.

"Of course it will be impossible to meet the first annoyance of this by living along here," said Ostrander in a tone that admitted of no reply. "I must get abroad for a month or so at the end of the year; but I think we can manage that. And, as soon as I return, I shall take to lecturing. It is impossible that we should get into a very tight place. I am not sure that the freedom of such a life will not be better for my health. Whenever I get strong enough to go under the harness of all this drudgery again, some other college will be ready for me. At least, a good American can always go West. We won't give up the ship for one blunder, Avis."

He put out his hand to her affectionately; he thanked her for her courage and consideration; he was afraid he had overwearied her in her state of health. His spirits and his tenderness rose together. And Avis to herself said, with a leap of her strong heart, "No, we will give up nothing, not for many blunders." She gathered him under the wing of her great love with a kind of fierce maternal protection; her husband,—the man who had won her lost freedom from her; life of her life, and soul of her soul; hers in his weakness as once in his glittering strength; hers in the fault and folly as in the beauty and the brilliance of his nature; still hers, for still he loved her: nothing could snatch that from her,—her one sure fact, abiding calm above the gusty weather of her life. Philip loved her: let the rest go. Why should she fret?

"It will all come right," she said, letting her hand drop reticently into his. "There are two of us, Philip, to try again."

She was glad to see him catch the glow of her strong spirit so quickly. She smiled when he got up nervously, and walked the room, calculating the expenses of the European trip. It pleased her better, she said to herself, than if he had stayed where he was, and stopped to fondle her. And she never told him, when, her strained nerves being too receptive, she caught the headaches which she had cured.

She threw herself down wearily, and watched him. She thought she could never have noticed before that uncertain curve in his delicate lips; perhaps that little something in the shape of his hand, which had always troubled her—was it a deficiency in the organ of tenderness? either the cause or the effect, as Lavater would have put it, of some weakness in the nature? Ah, well! Poor Philip! Her heart assumed a new burden, as if a third child had been born unto her. Was it possible that her soul had ever gone upon its knees before the nature of this man? So gentle had been the stages by which her great passion had grown into a mournful compassion, her divine ideal become this unheroic human reality, the king of her heart become the dependent on its care,—so quietly this had come about, that, in the first distinct recognition of it all, she felt no shock; only a stern, sad strain upon the muscle of her nature. There was, indeed, a certain manhood in her—it is latent in every woman, and assumes various forms. Avis possessed it only in a differing degree, not in differing kind, from most other women,—an instinct of strength, or an impulse of protection, which lent its shoulders spontaneously to the increasing individuality of her burden.

She spoke to her husband out of a deepening self-restraint, down whose solitary corridors she did not suffer herself to look too closely. She bowed to the great and awful law of married story, by which, so surely as life and love shall one day wear themselves to death and calm, we may know that it shall befall the stronger to wear the yoke of the weaker soul.

But late that night, when the wind was high about the house, and the firelight, dying, flung wild shapes upon the walls, Avis got up, and went into the little room where her children were, to think it all over alone with them. She could not sleep. The shadow of their disordered future, of her own dishonored aspiration, of bedraggled ideals, of clambering fears, sat heavily upon her. Her thought flickered confusedly, now upon her own unfitness for the cares of motherhood, now upon the lapse of time before they should have Van's school-bills to pay. Then as the child stirred, coughing slightly, she must sit mourning about it, and wondering what else he had inherited from his father besides his delicate lungs. Then her imagination flew like a bird into a clouded sunrise, across the future of her little daughter. She turned from one little face to the other; she gathered them under her knotted arms half savagely, as if she would shut them in from the chance of this awful gift called life, which she had imposed upon them. It seemed to her a kind of mortal sin that she should have bestowed upon her children a father whom she might not bid them kneel to worship. She felt a sense of personal guilt for every pain or peril that was in store for these two poor little confiding creatures—her children, their children—to be reared in a sick and poor and struggling, and perhaps (Heaven only knew) an inharmonious home.

"Nothing can make this right," she said, and fell upon her knees beside them, constrained by that mute prayer without ceasing, through which all lofty motherhood draws the breath of its strong life.

CHAPTER XVIII

"The effects of weakness are inconceivable, and I maintain that they are far vaster than those of the most violent passions."—CARDINAL DE RETZ

"Ce temps où le bonheur brille et soudain s'efface,
Comme un sourire interrompu!"—VICTOR HUGO.

It is said that Greenland, five or six centuries ago, was temperate. Parts of Siberia were once mild. Sulphur past the point of fusion, at a higher degree of temperature, consolidates again.

Perhaps most married people reach a point where, for the time being, they consider their union with each other to be the greatest mistake of their lives. Fortunate are they who pass this period, as the younger and more irritable passion may, within a year or two after the wedding-day. It is the slowly growing divergence, as it is the slowly gathering attraction, which is to be feared. That tether galls most terribly from which the satin surface is longest in wearing down.

Avis and Philip Ostrander had been married three years and a half.

She was thinking of this one night rather sadly, more leisurely indeed than she might often think of any thing in that careworn summer. Beneath the pressure of their increasing anxieties and the more clamorous strain of the nursery, her elastic strength had at length surrendered. For the first time in her life, she had been dangerously ill.

Stung with the immediate needs of their position, in the heart of July she had put the new-born baby off her knee, and gone up into the hot attic studio to finish a portrait. Then came the old and commonplace story: any woman knows it. Why the children must needs select that precise time to have the whooping-cough? why the cook must get married the week before Commencement? why Philip must just then and there have an attack of pleurisy? why the New-York relatives, unheard of for years, should come swarming in on class-day? why she herself should come down with diphtheria the evening that Philip's resignation was accepted?—such questions eternity alone can be long enough to answer to the satisfaction of some of us. A fig for the mysteries of fate, free-will, foreknowledge absolute, the origin of species or pre-Adamic man! when in teeth of it all, flat comes the professor with rheumatism, and Aunt Chloe even cannot be spared to High Street.

It was very kind in Barbara Allen to make the offer. Really, there was no one else to be had. And Barbara was always kind: she certainly had a genius for the sick-room, as Philip and Avis agreed. Avis accepted the attention gratefully, dropped her household in Barbara's hands as glady as the escaping soul may drop the dying body, and proceeded immediately to be as ill as she knew how. Her sickness was characteristically intense, and culminated rapidly. Stirring one day, out of the famine of exhaustion which renders that disease, when fatal, a peculiar prolongation of the agony of dissolution, she caught an expression upon her husband's face which absolutely aroused her.

"Philip," she said, "am I going to die?"

"Oh, God knows!" he had cried, before he could be silenced. Avis had not thought of it before. She lay a few moments perfectly quiet. She did not,—like that great creature to whom late happiness brought an early death, to whose genius love was superadded, only that both might mercifully sleep before the conflict of ages should befall which has set these two at odds in women,—she did not cry out,—

"God will not separate us, we have been so happy!"

No, not that.

Afterwards she remembered that she did not think about her husband at all. In one supreme moment the whole future of two motherless children passed before her. One of those clairvoyant flashes which sometimes seem to make motherhood a form of prophecy, flared out across these unconscious lives for whose creation she was responsible. Oddly enough the thing presented itself to her in isolated pictures, as if she had been turning the leaves of an illustrated book. She saw Van—a large boy in jackets that did not fit—coming home with his rubber-boots wet: nobody told him to change them, so he had the lung-fever; and the nursing was poor, so he got the cough.

As distinctly, she saw him skulking in from college one night (a moonlit night); he swore as he came up the steps; there was something wrong, but he did not tell his father. Van would never confide in his father. Then she saw her little daughter. Avis was sure that she knew what her daughter was like, before the child was a week old, —a reticent, solitary little girl, hating her patchwork, always down by the sea; as full of dreams as a dark night, and as impenetrable,—her daughter, brought up by another woman. There probably would be a step-mother. Rather a pretty woman, Avis thought she would be (Philip' taste was fastidious), well-bred and a little dressy, a member of a Harmouth reading-club, but without a career; probably her bread would always rise; and she would turn the studio into an excellent lumber-room, with everything done up in camphor, and carefully shaken twice a year on account of the moths.

"Doctor," she repeated, "is it death that is the matter with me?" The baby, as her mother spoke, began to cry from the adjoining room; not crossly, as the boy used to, but with a low, confiding wail. Avis could never be impatient with her little girl's cry. Van, too, came trotting up vociferously, demanding, behind the sick-room door, to be let in and ask Mamma why he couldn't get the kitty through the ice-cream freezer. His voice, as his father hushed him, died away rebelliously. A singular upheaval of the moral nature seemed to Avis to take place in herself; something stronger, because more vital than the revolt of the will or the physical recoil against death. Her children assumed the form of awful claims upon her conscience; they presented a code to her, absolute, imperious, integral with the law of God.

"It is wicked" she said aloud, "it is wicked for the mother of two little children—babies—to die. Doctor, you should have told me I was in danger of committing such a mistake. I will not do it. Do you understand? I will not die! Call in my husband. Tell him to kneel down there and pray. God understands about this. It is my duty to live."

Magnificently she set herself moment by moment to conquer death. She counted the dropping of the medicine which she could not swallow, the passing of her pulse, the beating of her heart, the ticking of the watch. She cast the whole force of her nature upon that die. Her will rang iron to the crisis. She repeated at intervals,—

"It is my duty to live."

She continued the struggle for three days, growing weaker. On the fourth she swallowed brandy; on the next her medicine; beef-juice on the next. Every physician knows such cases. "The soul makes her own body," said the great physician Stahl.

Avis recovered rapidly.

Perhaps the inevitable reactions of convalescence told more heavily upon Ostrander than upon most people. His mercurial sensitiveness to discomforts rose as the excitement of danger ebbed. The annoyances of sickness acted upon him like cologne upon a blooded dog. (If any reader fail to understand the force of this simile, let him put the experiment in practice.) Ostrander had never been able to remain within hearing of the children's cough. Once when the boy was ill, long ago, worn with watching, Avis had asked him to take the baby a while. He said, "Oh, certainly!" and paced the floor with Master Van, who was black in the face with vocal disapprobation of the arrangement, for half an hour. Then Avis heard Philip say through his clinched teeth,—

I'll get a nurse for this child to-morrow, if it costs twelve dollars a week.

She never asked him to take the babies again.

On this particular night, when it occurred to Avis to lie thinking just how long they had been married, he had come up after tea and said,—

"Nicely to-night, Avis?" And she had said,—

"Thank you, Philip!" And he had asked,—

"If we leave the doors open, will it not rest you to hear a little music before I go out?" And she had repeated,—

"Thank you, Philip!" And then he had said,—

"Pellet makes a mistake using so much camphor in your case," and had kissed her forehead, and gone away.

She tore the bandage off her throat when he had gone. Philip was always fastidious about scents; no wonder this kept him out of the sick-room so much. She felt a little solitary, listening to Barbara's fine execution downstairs, as the twilight came on. But she was glad and grateful to have Philip amused. Barbara was playing the "Adelaide," then the operas, "Trovatore," "Lucia," "Faust." Every thing she touched to-night had the sway of familiarity:

every thing was full of arias, of—it was not easy to say what. Barbara was not a woman of strong emotions. She possessed, however, abundant sensitiveness to strong effects.

Avis thought how long it was since her husband had asked *her* to play to him. She remembered the day when he said beneath his breath,—

"What a touch!"

But now Barbara had begun to sing. She sang,—

"Oh! dinna ye mind, young man, she said,
   When the red wine ye were spillin',
How ye made the cup gae round and round,
   An slighted Barbara Allen?"

Barbara was still playing, when, pliant to the quiet temper of returning strength, Avis fell asleep. When she waked, it was late, and the house was still.

The door was open into the hall. Philip, in coming up, must have forgotten it. He usually came in, but, now that she was so much better, sometimes merely looked in, on his way to the little blue room which he occupied. Avis rose to shut the door: as she did so, she glanced at her watch. It was two o'clock.

The gas in the hall was still lighted; and they could not afford to waste gas in these days. Thinking it a pity to wake the nurse, and feeling her strength rather rising than falling with the exertion, Avis flung over her wrapper a shawl,—the carmine one,—folding it about her face and head, and crept along, hand over hand upon the balusters, clinging with care. Her bare feet made no sound upon the carpeted stairs: not a board creaked beneath her tread she noticed, as she crawled down.

Halfway down the stairs, she was surprised to hear the sound of a voice, low and irregularly articulate; no— voices—two. The sound came from the parlor; and then she saw that the parlor-door, too, was open, and that the room was still lighted like the hall.

She was for the moment slightly startled. There was usually a little tramp and burglar panic in Harmouth in the early autumn nights, and usually with some reason. Then she remembered that Philip had said something of an appointment with an Englishman, with a notion about making telegraphy subservient to audible speech. But she crept on to make quite sure and safe, staggering a little, holding by the wall, and so into the doorway.

It was not the Englishman.

CHAPTER XIX

PRO: "How long remained the fickle true to thee?"
EPI: Her vision still is true: 'tis ever near me."

GOETHE'S PANDORA.

Barbara Allen sat on the piano-stool, leaning backward, one elbow upon the music-rack, and the poise of her pleasant figure resting upon the bruised white keys.

The sheets of music lay scattered about; one or two had fallen to the floor: they lay with disordered leaves. A hand surprised by some momentary disturbance would have dropped them so. Barbara's touch was habitually self-possessed; that of few women more so. Barbara's head was bent. Her bronze curls fell against her cheek, sweeping clean that fine profile from the comb to the curve of the neck. There were traces of agitation upon her face.

Philip Ostrander sat beside her. He had drawn his chair, so that its edge and the edge of the piano-stool collided. The hardly-acquired housekeeper's impulse in Avis noticed this, even at that moment, and she thought how the varnish was getting rubbed.

One of Ostrander's arms was stretched out, his hand resting upon the bass keys. It could not be strictly said that it encircled Barbara's waist; but there was no back to the piano-stool, and Barbara was tired. In his other hand he held, alas! he held her own. There were dimples in Barbara's fingers; she had cool, clear-cut, conscious nails. She had put her hand in Ostrander's, so that the profile of the thumb and first finger was presented to view; a constitutional amendment on nature, which a hand not altogether of the smallest may surely find legitimate. Nature had as yet suffered no such surprise in Barbara as to enable her to forget this; but then Barbara had never allowed a man to hold her hand before.

Ostrander's eyes were fastened upon Barbara's face. They wore the look which a woman accustomed to the admiration of men would feel, whether through the lid of her eye or her coffin. You think you can watch a woman as you will, sir, because she happens to be at the other end of the room? transfigured in conversation with the hostess? netted in the labyrinth of a crocheted shawl-strap? up to the ears of her soul in the poem or the sonata? promising the next polka to your rival? or adoring the Tintoretto, with her cool, round shoulders to you? Do you fancy that you can lift an eyelash that she will not know it, any more than you can pass a comment on the weather that she will not hear?

Barbara's lashes swept her flushed cheek; but she would have seen Ostrander's look through her back-hair.

Ostrander's face wore a peculiar illumination when he admired anything,—a statue, a picture, or a woman. The corners of his mouth quivered a little, and his lips parted in a smile beside whose silent homage a spoken word would have seemed a definite rudeness. There was a re-fined, cool light in his eye, too, which Barbara exceedingly admired. She had never seen a man look just like that. His whole bearing was that of one swayed by a delicate in-toxication, in which all that was noblest, calmest, and most permanent in himself, deferred to the object which had excited it.

It was this book which his wife—years past, now, there in the garden-studio, when the apple-blossoms fell about them—used to surprise, looking up suddenly from her painting; and then sit lifting her beautiful head gravely beneath it. It was this look which his wife surprised now.

Philip Ostrander was called a man of great discretion in his relations to women. It is doubtful if his most way-ward fancy had ever betrayed him into a positive social imprudence before.—What, then, would he have done with Barbara's hand?

When Avis saw him lift it, prisoned there like a bird against his leaning shoulder, she stirred, and would have uttered his name. Her lips made no sound; but her trailing dress rustled upon the floor. Barbara started. Philip turned slowly around.

His wife in the doorway, haggard from her mortal sick-ness, stood colossal. She was paler, perhaps, than need be, in that red drapery. She gathered it, for it had fallen almost to her knee, in one hand. The other was thrust into the empty air. She had never reminded him of her great Venus as she did at that moment. In the blind ac-tion of her arm and figure was something of the same shrinking as of a creature from whom a shield had been torn away. The real or fancied similarity in her features, too, was emphasized by the way she held her head.

By degrees her pallor deepened dreadfully. Her features seemed to grow thin and sheer like a marble medallion of a spirit.

Philip Ostrander looked from her to Barbara's curls; and his eyes dropped like a falling star.

Barbara drew away her hand swiftly. He would not have had her do this: it was an implication which, he began angrily to say to himself, the circumstances did not call for. He roused himself at this, and said in his easy way,—

"Why, Avis!"

But Barbara said nothing.

Avis also said nothing—nothing at all. She advanced a step or two into the room, and in silence pointed to the little Egyptian clock upon the mantelpiece, whose bronze sphinx told the hour,—seven minutes past two o'clock. With the other hand she pointed to the door.

Barbara arose at once. She said she had no idea it was so late; she muttered something about being very sorry, and that she was afraid Avis would take cold. Barbara had never got into such a strait before. She was frightened.

Avis did not stir when Barbara left the room, but stood, still pointing with a grand sweep of her arm to the open door. Perhaps never in her youth and joy and color had she possessed more beauty than at that moment. It is undeniable, explain it as you will, that Ostrander's most conscious emotion just then was one of overpowering admiration for his wife. He felt a kind of terrible taunting pride in her. He did not believe there was another such woman in the world. He could have flung himself at her feet, if he had dared.

His eyes, as hers transfixed them, seemed suddenly to reel; then came on their dead, dense look. He appeared to watch her from a vast distance like a being from another sphere; as a dumb animal watches a human face; or the victim of some pitiable mania regards the sane.

"Don't be offended over a little thing, Avis," he began, collecting himself, stumbling into the weakest thing he could have said.

He wished hotly that she would have burst into reproaches, accusations, into a passion of repulse or rebuke.

The woman who does this puts herself at radical disadvantage with most men. Perhaps, mingled with the unworthy consciousness of this little psychological fact, a nobler impulse stirred in Ostrander's heart. Perhaps he knew that he deserved the worst she could have given, and it might have been a certain relief to him just then, to get what he deserved.

But Avis answered him not a word. Her lip curled slightly,—his wife's lip,—curled above him as she stood looking down. A single articulate syllable would have broken the exquisite edge of her scorn; but she did not utter it. He felt under her silence as men may under crucifixion, which does not permit the victim even to writhe.

"You are making a mountain out of a mole-hill," he said irritably, rising with his fugitive look, determined to put an end to this dumb and dangerous scene; "and it is a terrible imprudence for you to be here in the cold. You will have a relapse tomorrow. Let me help you up the stairs."

Advancing, he put out both hands, and would have touched, supporting her. But Avis, with a slight, imperious gesture, waved him away.

"Very well," he said, "have it as you will." He stood to watch her from the bottom of the stairs, anxious for her, till he should see her safely up. She had swept by him with a certain strength, but tottered on the first stair. He sprang and caught her; held her for one moment so impetuously, that his trained ear detected the irregular, sluggish beating of her heart,—a paralytic beat. It alarmed him, and he said hurriedly,—

"You are not fit to get up by yourself. Don't be so hard on a man, Avis!"

But she disengaged herself, and crawled up alone. He followed at a little distance to catch her, if she fell. Thus they reached the landing; and she went on into the faded rose-red room, and shut the door. The wind was rising as she went in. She crawled weakly into bed, and lay with her hands crossed, listening to it. It blew all night fitfully, like the resolve of some great live, lawless nature; but it rose perceptibly from hour to hour. Towards morning it lulled.

In the morning Aunt Chloe came over, and Barbara sent up word, that, if she could be spared, perhaps she had better go home. Avis replied that she should like to see her. Barbara came awkwardly enough. She had been crying, and her front-hair was out of crimp. Avis looked at her with gaunt, insomniac eyes: it was evident that she had not slept, but she was quite at ease. She thanked Barbara for all her kindness, and bade her a grave good-by.

Barbara looked sullen for a minute; then a quiver ran through the bronze curls. She began to sob.

"Pray don't," said Avis wearily. "I am not quite strong enough—to—see people cry. But I understand your feeling. It is so dangerous for a woman to commit an indecorum! Society does not excuse her as it does a man. Will you ask Aunt Chloe to bring the children up?"

Avis spoke gently. A certain terror fell upon her at finding in her own heart no sting sharper than that of a sad scorn. She had rather hoped that she might find herself a little jealous of Barbara. She hung over her love for her husband as we hang over a precious, diseased life, of which we have not the courage to despair. She fanned it wildly. Better fire than frost! Better the seething than the freezing death! But all her soul was numb. She looked calmly at Barbara's curls and fresh maiden colors and attitudes. She could not be jealous of so slight a thing. With a sickening dismay she perceived that Philip—he too—began to seem to her small and far, like a figure seen in the valley of an incoherent dream. She felt as if she had suddenly stepped into a world of pygmies, and had a liliputian code to learn before she could take up the duties of citizenship therein.

Barbara stopped crying. She stole downstairs with dry, startled eyes. *An indecorum? Society? Excuse?* Barbara repeated the words confusedly. Two weeks ago she would have regarded the supposition that any human lip would ever tell her she had been indecorous, with a pleasant unconcern, like that with which she regarded the habits of the cavemen, or the subject of unconscious cerebration. Barabara thought she ought to see Philip Ostrander at once, and ask him if he thought any harm was done. But he was in the study, and the door was locked. When he came out, he asked where she was, and his little boy told him she had gone.

Now, Barbara forgot to take her sun-umbrella. It was the middle of the afternoon before Ostrander saw it— a pretty purple silk toy—hanging by the clutch of a little ivory hand upon the hat-tree. Ostrander saw it, and thought he had better carry it over to her: he must walk somewhere. Under the circumstances it would be more fitting that Barbara should not come for it; it would be pleasanter, indeed, for Avis, he said to himself: and Avis had expressed no wish to see him to-day. He put on his hat and strolled out, carrying the parasol. A delicate perfume hung about it, something that he had never known any woman but Barbara to use: he remembered that he fancied it when she was taking care of that gunshot wound. Barbara had certainly been very kind to them both. It was not right that his wife's over-scrupulousness should react unpleasantly upon her. The least that a sense of honor demanded of him now was to see to it that Barbara should not in any manner suffer from his folly. If he did not guard her, nobody would. No man with a spark of chivalry in him would allow the woman whom he had so unfortunately drawn into a trifling imprudence, to meet the consequences of it unwarned or unshared. . Then, too, he would not be misunderstood himself in the affair, if he could help it. If he had said anything that sounded indiscreet,—and he could not remember that he really had,—it would be better to explain to Barbara precisely what he did mean: there should be no mistake in the thing anywhere. There was no need that any man with a sound head should get into that fog-bank of relations in which men and women were always going astray for simple lack of a clear understanding each of what the other wanted. He thought the sooner he had a talk with Barbara the better.

He went to her brother's house, and she presented herself at once: her eyelids were still delicately discolored, like rain-beaten flowers, with tears. Ostrander did not go in, but stood in the hall, hesitating. He said,—

"Here is your parasol." And Barbara thanked him; and then there was an awkward pause.

"I want to see you—a few moments," said Ostrander gravely.

"There is company in the parlor," replied Barbara, with downcast eyes.

"It is pleasant on the beach this afternoon," urged Ostrander impulsively. It did not seem quite possible now to go home without seeing Barbara alone.

Barbara said, "Just as you like." She got her hat, and

they went out in silence together into the hot summer afternoon.

When they reached the beach, he said, "It will be cooler on the water." Nothing but commonplaces occurred to him.

He pushed down the boat,—his wife's little dory,—and helped Barbara in. She slipped, and he caught her, but neither spoke: she released her hands slowly. An old fisherman stood on the beach, hauling his dirty boat, with a rasping noise, across the coarse gray sand.

"I wouldn't put up that there sail ef I was yeou," he said.

"And why not?" argued Ostrander, glad to have something to smile at just then. Avis and he had always differed about that sail: she never used it.

"You mought as well put spurs onto an angel as a sail onto a dory," observed the fisherman, dogmatically moistening his hands for another tug at his boat. "'Tain't in the natur' of a dory to stand it: there's natur' in boats likewise as there's natur' in fishes and folks. No use rowin' agin tide in none of us. A dory, now, knows what she wants done as clear as yeou do, or the lady. Ef I was yeou, I wouldn't cross her."

"I wouldn't, either," said Barbara.

So Ostrander took the oars. He rowed hard, but composedly, with the long, virile Harmouth stroke. He rowed quite into the heart of the harbor; but few boats were in sight. He drew in his oars, and they drifted beneath the blazing sky. Barbara put up the sun-umbrella, and they sat under it in a purple light. The breeze struck pleasantly across the bay, and the sun dipped. The wind lifted one of Barbara's curls, and blew it softly against his cheek. He looked at her; but she did not return his look. She sat quite still.

"I am very sorry," he began, and stopped. What in the name of reason was he to say he was sorry for? Barbara came to his aid. She turned her head: the wind was at her back, and carried all her hair forward, so that her face looked out of a soft aureola. She said,—

"Avis was very much annoyed."

"I suppose so," answered Ostrander irritably.

"Do you think," asked Barbara timidly, "that any— anything unpleasant—any harm will come?"

"Harm cannot come where there is no harm," said Os-

trander, suddenly remembering that this was the thing to
say.

"Certainly not," replied Barbara more courageously.

"The whole world is welcome to hear anything that I
have ever said to you, Miss Barbara," he went on in a confident, clear tone.

"Why, of course," said Barbara.

It seemed for the moment to make quite sure of it, that
he should say it, and that she should assent to it. He took
up the oars with a sigh of relief, and instinctively, perhaps, made toward the shore, as if it were safer to let this
scene end just where it was.

The tide, while they drifted, had turned. He rowed a
few minutes in the hot sun, laboriously, and then laid down
the oars: he came and sat under the sun-umbrella. Barbara's face looked unusually tender in the purple light.
Their eyes met. Necessarily they sat so near, that he could
perceive the agitated fluctuation of her breath.

"The man was right," he said in a low tone: "it is of no
use to row against the tide."

"Oh, hush!" said Barbara.

It is possible to say a very dangerous thing in a perfectly safe way. Ostrander's readiness both of the lip and
of the fancy at once exposed and protected him in the
possession of this perilous power. When he said, "It is of
no use to row against the tide," he certainly was not altogether thinking of the tides of Harmouth Harbor. But
when Barbara not only perceived that he was not, but
committed the mistake of letting him know that she perceived it, he fell back at once upon the literal significance
of his words. Instinctively he had provided himself with a
barricade of such significance. If one trench had failed, he
would have withdrawn to another, strictly, in his own
view at least, on terms of honorable retreat. This is one of
the accidents liable to a lithe mind, and may fasten itself
upon a nature of great delicacy; in rare cases, upon one
of real rectitude.

Ostrander regarded Barbara with a certain gentlemanly
surprise, and saying in his usual voice,—

"However, we will try again," took up the oars. But
the tide set sternly against him, and he perceived now
how far they had drifted. His friend the fisherman was
abreast of them: he sat in the sun, hauling out his nets,
still as a figure in the foreground of a marine picture.

"With your permission," said Ostrander after a few minutes' very unplatonic hard work, "I think we will put up the sail. There is not wind enough to trouble a nautilus."

He put it up, and they glided along quietly; the swifter motion at once rested and excited him. When Barbara said, How pleasant it was! his deepening voice and eyes answered,—

"I am afraid it is too pleasant." But Barbara did not say, "Oh, hush!" She knew better this time.

They were sitting so, she leaning over the gunwale like a violet, with the purple light across her white dress, when a slight stir struck the perfectly calm water, as if the feet of an unseen spirit trod across it. Then the whole bay seemed to gather her bright shoulders, and shiver a little. Then the near waves crinkled and curdled, as flesh does with fear.

Ostrander sprang to wrench the little mast out of its socket just as the dory reeled. He was too late.

As he went down, he saw the fisherman leaning, gunwale to the water's edge, the fine lines that his black net made against the sky, and the wreath of smoke from his pipe. Distinctly he thought what a good sketch Avis would make of it.

Then he thought how the bay looked like a lake of blue fire, and how he and Barbara were going into it together. The last thing that occurred to him was, "We have been struck by a white squall."

By the time that he had begun to ascend, he was not conscious of any coherent idea, except that, if he and Barbara were drowned, then and there, together, his wife would believe him a rascal to the end of her life. And then he knew that the mere fact of dying was only an incident in that supreme despair.

He struggled up, and struck out madly. Barbara was clinging to the bottom of the dory. She was calling to him. He seemed a great way off. The water between them—calm now as outworn feeling—was a cold and deadly blue. Once more he thought of the lake of fire, and of those terrible old Bible metaphors that played upon it in such a ghastly way.

He made his way rather weakly. Who would have believed that the blazing summer sea could hold so cold a heart? The fisherman was coming with long, sharp, agitated strokes: the water reeled under his blows. Ostrander's head reeled too. He was growing very cold. A paralytic thickening of the tendons, and stiffening in his muscles, had crept upon him.

"My God!" he said aloud, "am I going to have the cramp?"

Then the boat made a great leap, and recoiled on itself, like a jaguar, and snatched him up.

"You took me before the lady!" cried Ostrander, horror struck.

"The lady does very well!" said he of the sea imperturbably. "As long as they can screech, they ain't cramped. Just you stay where you be. You mought be took agin—and she's pretty solid. I'll haul her in."

Barbara was hauled in, hand over hand, like a mackerel-net; the dory was righted, and taken in tow—possibly the whole thing had taken seven minutes. The fisherman had not removed the pipe from his mouth.

Ostrander and Barbara sat awkwardly and miserably in the dirty boat. When the fish flopped in the net, and an eel, in the struggle for existence, jumped into Barbara's lap, Ostrander felt as if he were watching the blue-devils in the last act of some second-rate opera. The purple umbrella was gone. High in the western heavens the holy sun peered into their faces. His fastidious fancy revolted from this grotesque, satiric ending to a highly-wrought experience. He would have found it hard to explain why he felt as if it must be, somehow, Barbara's fault. He could not imagine his wife, for instance, in the same boat with an eel. At all events, she would not have shrieked at it. He was surprised to find how it altered Barbara's appearance to have her curls washed straight.

The fisherman took the pipe from his mouth as they grated on the solitary beach.

"Mebbe," he said, "ye'll remember next time not to hurt the feelin's of a dory. A dory's like a lady, sir. The man that slights it has to pay for it fust or last. She's tender in the feelin's a dory is."

He had landed them, as chance would have it, just off the light-house reef; and Barbara and Ostrander walked up through the divorced gorge together. Barbara did not understand the expression which his face had assumed. She thought him very cross. He, for his part, was not thinking about Barbara at all.

He and Barbara parted miserably enough, at the edge of the town. They agreed that it was better so. Barbara protested that she was not very wet, and preferred to take care of herself. When he said that he supposed it would attract less attention, she assented decidedly. She said she was sorry they went to row. She asked him if he were going to tell Avis. Barbara was thoroughly alarmed.

Ostrander went quickly home. As he passed his wife's room, she called him. The door was open. Avis sat upon the edge of the bed, partly dressed: she had thrown a thick shawl about her, and her bare feet, with which, it seemed, she had been trying her strength, hung weakly, just touching the floor. Something in her attitude—whether it were the weakness or the strength of it, its courage or despair—affected Ostrander powerfully. He stopped in the door-way, feeling disgraced and miserable. He did not cross the threshold of his wife's room. She said rapidly,—

"What has happened, Philip?"

"I was out in the dory, and got struck by a white squall. That is all, except that I had the cramp, and a mackerel-boat picked me up."

Ostrander brought the words out stolidly. He did not exactly mean to appeal to her fear or sympathy; yet he felt conscious of some disappointment that she exhibited no sign of either. She said,—

"Was Barbara with you?"

"Yes," said Ostrander doggedly. His quick sense of irritation rose. He was not going to stand and defend himself like a school-boy. There was a long silence.

"Well," he said, breaking it uneasily, "I must go and get out of these wet things."

"It will be best for both of us," said Avis in a low voice, after yet another pause, in which she had sat with her eyes upon the floor, but rising now, and slipping to her feet, "if this thing is to go on,—if you wish to indulge platonic friendships with other women,—that your wife should not be unnecessarily insulted by it; you would agree with me, I am sure, that I had better take the children, and go to father's for a while."

When he was gone, she crawled back into bed. The words of the woman Susan Jessup had dogged her thoughts that day: "He got tired of me, I thought he would get tired of every other woman." Oddly beside them stepped in that hideous old rhyme of Goethe's,—

"The false one looked for a daintier lot;
The constant one wearied me out and out."

These pursued her like the jingle on the hand-organ that
follows us seven squares away. She hated her own heart
for giving hospitality to such words.

The children were laughing in the nursery. Birds broke
their hearts for joy upon the window-ledge. She shrank as
she listened, turning wearily in bed. All sweet sounds in life
seemed to have fallen suddenly a semi-tone too high or too
low for her, so that harmony itself became an exquisite
ingenuity of discord. She seemed to herself like that afflicted musician to whose physical ear this happened; or
like that other, who stood stone deaf in the middle of his
orchestra.

How could they ever hear—she and Philip now—the
perfect music of a happy home again?

She struggled with the unique dismay which overtakes
the woman who first learns that she has married a capricious man. Avis thought, that if her husband had committed a forgery, or been brought home drunk, she should
have seen more distinctly, at least more clearly, where her
duty lay. She was sure that she should have gone on loving
him, in fierce proportion to the depth of his fall, till death
had resolved all love to elements so simple, that it knew
no code of duty, and needed no spoken bond. But then
he would have loved her. She could not spend herself
for the husband whose tone and touch had hardened
to her. She could not cast away the pearls of wifehood:
that were to commit the unpardonable sin of married
story.

But Ostrander came back presently, manfully enough,
to his wife's room. He was startled by what she had said,
and touched by the gentle dignity with which she had said
it. Then the consciousness of clean linen is in and of itself
a source of moral strength only second to that of a clean
conscience. A well-ironed collar, or a fresh glove, has
carried many a man through the emergency in which
a wrinkle or a rip would have defeated him. Ostrander
came in, looking very clean and comfortable, shut the
door, and sat down by his wife on the edge of the bed.
He leaned, putting one arm over her where there was
room to support himself, upon his hand: Avis stirred uneasily, and he removed it.

"You have given me no chance, Avis," he began, "to explain myself: I don't see but I must take it."

"What is the use?" asked Avis drearily.

"I don't understand your disinclination to discuss the matter," said Ostrander, flushing slightly.

"There is nothing to discuss," said his wife, turning her head from side to side upon the pillow. "When a man has ceased to love his wife, that is not a subject of discussion between them."

"Upon your own lips rest the shadow from those words!" he cried with an heroic air. "*I* did not utter them. I scorn to deny that I have ceased to love my wife."

"You adopt a singular method of expressing your affection," said Avis. She was terrified at her own words as soon as they were spoken. Roots of bitterness and blight seemed to be fastening upon her soul, like a fungoid disease upon the flesh.

"Well, admit then," said he with a peculiarly winning air of patient sadness, "that my love is not quite the same as it was; that it has assumed, with time, a different form and different force."

"Oh, hush!" cried Avis. She could not help it: the imperious impulse of the woman overswept her. When her husband understated in her ears that which her own voice had underscored, she felt as if she had plunged a knife into a dissolving ghost, and drawn it back, reeking with human blood. All was over now, she thought. They never could look at each other with tender fictions in their glance again. Their four lips had spoken the terrible truth: in their eyes forever would be the memory of it.

"I am sorry," continued Ostrander sadly, "that my peculiar temperament has brought you into suffering. I ought to have foreseen it; but I had more confidence in myself than events have warranted."

"Do you care for—do you love Barbara?" asked Avis abruptly. Her voice rang foreign to her own ears. The whole scene moved on dimly to her, as if they sat on some solemn historic tribunal, weighing the fate of two strangers whose life hung in their trembling hands.

"Love her? *No!*" thundered Ostrander, recoiling.

"What *is* it like, I wonder," asked Avis, "to feel as you do? I am not made so as to understand it, Philip."

"You may thank Heaven you are not," murmured Ostrander, exactly as if she had inquired of him touching the sufferings consequent upon some physical deformity.

"Is it friendship you seek?" went on Avis simply. "My husband was my friend. I needed no other."

"That is your temperament," said Ostrander: "mine is different. I am sorry it is so. I don't know what more I can say."

It is impossible to convey the absence of self-insistence and presence of gentle regret by which Ostrander contrived to transfigure these feeble words: they seemed, as he uttered them, to be the outgrowth of a delicate and forbearing reticence, in itself the index of essential strength. Avis lay for a few moments with a pathetic confusion on her worn face. Her husband made her feel as if she were dealing with an afflicted man.

"It is harder to be the subject than the object of an infirmity," he went on. "Do me the justice, Avis, to remember that I must suffer more in discovering that my affection is capable of change than you can in the consequences of such a fact."

"That will do," said Avis faintly, after a silence. "It is a waste of strength for us to talk. We do not understand each other."

"I repeat," he said more earnestly, "that I am sorry for the whole thing. You shall not be annoyed again. Don't take the children to Father's just yet!" He leaned over her, smiling; but her soul sickened within her. He had rather expected to kiss her; but the expression of her mouth deterred him. He would as soon have dared to kiss the Melian Venus.

How could he know that a great impulse came upon her to throw herself upon his heart, and sob her misery out? It seemed incredible that Philip could not help her to bear it. They had been so dear to each other—for so long! Then she thought how he would soothe her, and how she should writhe to remember it. He did not love her. He was her husband. Humiliation beyond humiliation lay forever now in his caress. She gave him her hand gravely, like a courteous acquaintance.

She thought, "I would have clung to *you!*" But she said only,—

"Well, Philip, we must make the best we can of it." After a silence she added,—

"We shall always need each other's forebearance, though"— She could not bring herself to say, "though we have lost each other's love." And then Van ran in, radiant and indescribable. He had invited Mary Ann and the kitty to a party. He had been dressing his hair—with the prepared glue.

Barbara that afternoon curled *her* hair, with cheeks hotter than the seething tongs. She had made up her mind that it would be best for her to marry before long. She thought, perhaps, she had amused herself with men about long enough. Barbara was exceedingly disconcerted at what had happened. She hoped there would be no talk: Barbara could think of nothing worse than to be talked about. She had never forgotten herself before. In Barbara's "set" in Harmouth, young ladies did not flirt with married men. Barbara had never been the least in love with Philip Ostrander. But, strictly speaking, it could not be said that she had ever quite forgiven him for not having fallen in love with herself before he married Avis. Yet she knew it was expecting too much of the masculine perception that he should understand all that.

Probably he would go to his grave supposing that she cared.

No more subtly confusing type of woman than Barbara is as yet rudimentary in the world. That man must have a keen and modest eye who will distinguish her vanity from her tenderness, or her love of his admiration from her love of himself.

Barbara thought she should marry a minister.

One day not long after, John Rose ran over to High Street. There was a poor fellow who could not get a scholarship; and Mrs. Ostrander had promised some flannels to those Pinkham babies; and Coy sent over a taste of snow-pudding; and so on. But, when he went away, he put one finger upon Ostrander's arm with a delicate yet deepening pressure. Ostrander followed him at once to the street.

"I suppose you know," began John Rose, hesitating gravely, "at least I thought I had better call your attention to the fact, that Harmouth is very much occupied just now with—that accident in the dory."

"The—mischief it is!" said Ostrander, stopping short. There was a silence, in which the two young men walked up and down in front of the gate. Avis watched them from the windows contentedly. She always liked to see her husband and John Rose together. She thought, or rather she felt, that John's must be one of the golden natures of which it would be possible to say, as was said of one of the grandest of our time—the noblest words, that can be spoken of any human life,—"There never lived a truer friend."

Ostrander put his hand upon the other's shoulder as they walked, and leaned upon it heavily.

"Seriously so, Rose?" he asked.

"Not unkindly so, I think," said Rose thoughtfully; "but there is some unnecessary and annoying gossip. It will soon blow over; but I thought—excuse me, Phil—it would be as well for you to understand it at the outset."

"John," said Ostrander, after a longer silence than before, "if it be possible,—you will help me, old fellow, I know—I hope my wife may never hear of this."

She never did.

CHAPTER XX

"Every man has experienced how feelings which end in themselves, and do not express themselves in action, leave the heart debilitated. We get feeble and sickly in character when we feel keenly, and cannot do the thing we feel."—ROBERTSON.

In September the college papers announced that Professor Philip Ostrander had resigned the assistant geological chair in Harmouth University, on account of an increasing delicacy of the lungs, in consequence of which his physicians had forbidden all brain labor, and required a change of climate. It was understood that he would sail for Havre next week to spend the winter in the south of France. His resignation was deeply regretted by the Faculty and students. The academic year opened prosperously under the hands of Professor Brown, his successor. Professor Cobin was expected to resign at the close of the winter term.

Professor Ostrander was so feeble, that he had not been present at the Senior Party kindly given by Mrs. President Hogarth at the usual time. He had been as deeply missed in the drawing-room as he would be in the class-room, both of which locations he eminently graced.

Professor Brown was understood to be the man who had recently detected the precise difference between the frontal sinuses in the white and grisly bears. A brilliant career was predicted for him.

FOOTNOTE.—A contributor adds, that he is also the discoverer of the left foramen of the third cervical vertebra of the first monkey who harmonized with the environment. It is needless to say that a Freshman bears the entire responsibility of this grave statement.

After the first strange chill was out of the lonely air, Avis was shocked to find her husband's absence a relief. He had become extremely irritable before he went away. The reaction from his college-work, and from his escapade with Barbara, had added mortification to mortification, under which he weakened petulantly. Like all untuned natures, he grew discordant under the friction of care and trouble. He became really so ill, that Avis felt that not an hour should be lost in removing him from the immediate pressure of annoyances from which she could not shield him. It was she who passed lightly over the embarrassments and economies under which the projected journey must place the family. It was she who was sure they could get along till the lease of the house was out. It was she who was confident that rest would restore him, and that a future would await him. It was she who remembered the draughts that lurked for him, shaded the sun that dazzled him, cured the headaches that tore him, went away to amuse the children when they fretted him. Philip must have the cream-whip and the sherry, and the canter across country, and Europe, though the nurse were dismissed, and the seamstress abandoned, and the rent paid—Heaven help her!—out of that locked studio to whose cold and disused walls she should creep by and by with barren brain, and broken heart, and stiffened fingers.

Avis took the emergency in her own strong hand. She planned, she hoped, she commanded, she contrived. That intelligent self-surrender which is the supreme sign of strength, expressed itself in her with the pictorial graciousness peculiar to her special gift. She brought the whole force of her professional training to bear upon the shade of dye which might renew a baby's cloak. She made the very shoes that Van wore in those days—poor little pathetic shoes, badly stitched, perhaps, but of exquisite color, and a temporary defiance to the family shoemaker. If only Papa could have beefsteak at breakfast, the omelette need not be in a nicked platter; and a flower or so on the table gave Van a swelling consciousness of hilarious domestic dissipation, which obviated the gloom of absent luxuries.

"I am sorry to have you burdened with such petty economies," Philip had said one day. But he spoke with the polite reserve which had become habitual with him. He was always polite to his wife. He noticed her domestic ingenuities with approval. He said,—

"We never thought you would turn out so comfortable a housekeeper, did we, Avis?" with an absent-minded smile. And then he asked her what she did with his passports, and if she had packed the Calasaya bark, and where was the lecture on. "Chalk," which he thought he might have a chance to deliver in England. Avis answered patiently. She thought Philip walked about like a frost-bitten man. A certain hardness in his nature, of which she could not be mistaken in fancying herself the especial object, developed itself in a delicate but freezing form, like the ice-scenery upon a window. It was with profound intellectual confusion that she remembered his first kiss. Was this the man who had wooed and won her with an idealizing gentleness which made of his incarnate love a thing divine? To admit it seemed like a challenge to the doctrine of personal identity. One day, spurred by a momentary impulse to leave no overture of wifely forgiveness and yearning unoffered, of whose omission she might think afterwards with that scorching self-rebuke in which all shallow pride shrivels to the bitterest ashes, she crept up to him and began timidly,—

"Philip, this poor old carmine shawl that you used to like so much is pretty well faded out. Do you remember the night when we first came home, when I had it on?"

"Yes, I remember," said Philip distinctly.

"We were very happy, Philip—then."

"Yes."

"Sometimes I wonder," tremulously, "if nothing in this world can ever make us feel so again."

"That," he said, regarding her with cool, distant eyes, "is entirely out of the question." The man whose unapproachable tenderness had spared the life of a dumb bird because it trusted him, could say this—to his wife. His voice had a fine, grating sound. It made Avis think of the salute of icebergs meeting and passing in the dark.

Yet we should see that, apparently, Philip Ostrander was as unconscious of cruelty as the burnt-out crater is of the snow that has sifted down its sides. It was his temperament, he reasoned, to express himself as he felt, and he certainly did not feel to his wife as he did when they first married. He saw no occasion for dwelling upon an ardor which marriage must inevitably chill. Avis's good sense must perceive this. Why should they trouble themselves? The daily annoyances and anxieties which the bond between them compelled them to share were as much, he thought, as either of them could bear just now, without adding any finer affectional subtleties to their burden. He wished with all his heart, he said, that it had been the necessary outgrowth of his nature to love with the poetic constancy natural to his wife. Events had proved that it was not. What, then, could he do? Ostrander pitied himself. He sincerely believed that he bore the heavier end of their mutual sorrow.

And now he was gone.

He had not, indeed, parted with his wife without emotion; but it was a perfectly silent one, like that of a man struggling with feelings ill defined to himself. He had hung over his boy, and clung to him, choking. He was very fond of Van.

His departure left Avis free for a space to wrestle as she might with the inevitable reaction of the last few months. In the calm of her first solitary hours she was chastened to perceive how her married story had deepened and broadened, nay, it seemed, created in her, certain quivering human sympathies. Her great love—so hardly won, so lightly cherished—withdrew upon itself in a silence through which all the saddened lovers of the world seemed to glide with outstretched hand, and minister to her,—a mighty company. Especially her heart leaned out to all denied and deserted women, to all deceived and trustful creatures. A strange kinship, too solemn for any superficial caste of the nature to blight, seemed to bind her to them all. Betrayed girls, abandoned wives, aged and neglected mothers, lived in her fancy with a new, exacting claim. To the meanest thing that trod the earth, small in all else, but large enough to love and suffer, her strong heart stooped, and said, "Thou—thou, too, art my sister."

Avis had been bred to the reticence not uncharacteristic of the New-England religion among its more cultivated, or at least, among its more studious possessors. She was one of those sincere and silent Christians with whom we must look more to the life than to the lip for the evidence of the faith that is in them. The professor's had been a home in which the religious character of his child was taken for granted, like her sense of delicacy. She was expected to be a Christian woman precisely as she was expected to be a cultivated lady: in a matter of course, abundant speech was a superfluous weakness. She had escaped the graver dangers of this training, but not its life-long influences. It was inevitable that the tragedy of her married life should result in a temporary syncope of faith, which it was equally inevitable that she should support in perfect solitude. But to dwell upon this phase of her experience would seem to copy the rude fault of those biographers that break faith with the personal confidence of the dead who can no longer protest.

With a terror for which I do not feel at liberty to find speech or language, Avis watched departing love shake the slow dust of his feet against her young life. With a dread which shook to the roots of belief, she perceived that her own slighted tenderness had now begun to chill. That Philip should cease to love her—this could be borne. There was a worse thing than that. All was hers while she yet loved him. She wrestled with her retreating affection as Jacob of old wrestled with the angel till break of day. She struggled with that which was greater and graver than the sweet ghost of a ruined home. She fought for her faith in all that makes life a privilege, or death a joy.

No argument for the immortality of the human soul seemed to her so triumphant as the faith and constancy of one single human love.

"Mamma, has Papa gone to Jerusalem?"

"No, my son. Mamma has told you a great many times where Papa has gone."

"Jesus went to Jerusalem!" said Van with a reproving smile, quite gentle, and a little sad, as if his father had been caught in the omission of some vital religious duty. "But after I got frough crying, I fought I'd like to have him go. I'd rather kiss you myself, Mamma. I don't like another man to do it. I'll have a wife of my own, when I get big enough he needn't fink!"

"There, Van; that's enough for now. Don't you see I am very busy painting? I can't kiss little boys *all* day. Run away now."

Van disappeared, not without something of the reluctance of a jealous lover drawing his first breath of bliss in the absence of his rival. Van's love for his mother was one of those select and serious passions which occasionally make the tie between son and mother an influence of complex power. She must be a woman of a rare maternal nature who will supersede in the heart of a man the mother who is capable of inspiring in the boy a love of this controlling and sensitive kind.

Scarcely had the palette-knife struck the cobalt to the Naples yellow, when the studio-door shivered, stirred, and started with a prolonged and inspiring creak. Van admitted his little nose on probation into the crack, and heaved a heart-breaking sigh.

"Mamma," very sweetly, "now *Philip* is gone, I suppose I may call you *Avis,* mayn't I?"

"Shut the door, Van."

His pretty mamma had an unhappy habit of expecting to be obeyed, which was a source of serious disorder to Van's small system of philosophy. He shut the door in— nose and all—with a filial haste and emphasis, the immediate consequences of which fell heavily upon both parties in this little domestic tragedy. When the outcry is over, and the sobbing has ceased, and the tears are kissed away, and the solid little sinner lies soothed upon the cramped and forgiving arm, where is the strength and glory of the vision? Where are the leaping fingers that quivered to do its bidding in the fresh life of the winter morning hour?

"Run away, again, Van: mother must go to work now."

"Mamma," faintly, "I've sat down on—something—soft. I'm all blue and colors, Mamma, on my sack behind. I didn't know it was your palette, Mamma. I didn't mean to. Oh! I'd rather not. I'd like a shair!"

"Mamma," presently from behind the locked door, "I want a piece o' punky-pie."

"No more pumpkin-pie, to-day, Van; and you mustn't talk to Mamma through the door any more."

"Oh!—well, Mamma, a *piece* o' punky-pie will do. I've had the sherries. I've had twenty-free or nineteen canned sherries. Me and the baby eat 'em. I eat the sherries, and she eated the stones, Mamma. I put 'em down her froat. She needn't have cried, I don't fink. So I want a piece o' punky-pie."

Silence succeeds.

"Mamma, can't you kiss little boys *all* day? Not very *dee* little boys, Mamma?"

"By and by, Van. Run to Julia now. Run and play with your little sister."

But Master Van stoutly maintained that he did not wish

the society of his little sister. He thought his little sister had bumped her head. He should expect Mamma would want to unlock the door, and find out. If he had the mucilage-bottle, and Papa's razor, and the pretty purple ink (and the kiss), he would go and find out, and never come upstairs any more.

"Mamma," by and by, "do you love my little sister best of me, or me best of my little sister? I should fink you'd rather let me in and tell me 'bout that.

"O Mamma!" once more persuasively, "I want to say my prayers."

"To-night, Van, at bed-time."

"No, I want to say 'em quick vis minute. If you'll let me in to say my prayers, I'll go straight down and see if Julia's got the cookies done."

Love in the guise of religion, as ever since the world was young, carried the yielding day before him. With despair in her heart and the palette fresh from its service as a cricket in her hand, Avis admits the little devotee. Plump upon his knees upon the drying-oil—in the unutterable background of that sack—drops Van, and thus waylays the throne of grace,—

"O Lord! please to not let boys tell lies and say he's got a jack-knife and a pistol in his pocket when he hasn't either one which a boy did to Jack Rose and me this morning O Lord Amen. . . . Mamma, I fink it was one of the Plimpton boys. *Now* will you kiss me, Mamma?"

And so, and so, and so—what art can tell us how? O golden winter morning! your coy heart is repulsed forever; and when from the depths of the house, sweeps, like a scythe upon the artist's nerves, that sound which all the woman in her shrinks to hear,—the cry of a hurt baby, —Avis with a sigh unlocks the studio-door. There is the problem of ages in that speechless sigh. Van, all paint and patience, like a spaniel lies curled upon the floor, with his lips against the studio-door. The stout little lover, faithful in exile, has lain and kissed the threshold till he has kissed himself asleep.

The rare tears filled Avis's eyes as she lifted him; and then Julia brought the baby, and the bump, and the brown paper. And there she was sitting, pinioned, with both children, patient and worn, with the bright colors of her paints around her, and the pictures, with their mute faces to the wall, about the room (there was a hand-organ, too, playing a dismal little tune somewhere down the street), when an impatient knock preceded a nervous push to the unlatched door, and, with the familiarity of art and age, her old master presented himself upon the scene.

Frederick Maynard stood still. He did not immediately speak. He looked from child to child, from both to her, from her to the barren easel. The dismal hand-organ below set up a discordant wail, the more pathetic for its discord, like all inharmonious things. The baby had pulled down Avis's pink neck-ribbon and her bright hair. The tears lay undried upon her cheek, whose color slowly stirred, and scorched her lifted, languid face.

"You see," she said, trying to smile, "how it is."

"I am not here to see anything," answered the drawing-master shortly. "What have you done this week?"

"Nothing."

"Last week? The week before?"

"Nothing at all. Only the sketch for the crayon that you see. And I have begun to give drawing lessons to Chatty Hogarth. Mr. Maynard, once a visitor came into Andrea del Sarto's studio. It was after his marriage. He was dabbling away at some little thing. He looked up and said, 'Once I worked for eternity: now I work for my kitchen.'"

"Confound the kitchen-work!" cried Maynard savagely. "Kitchen-work, indeed! Crayon portraits, I should think! Drawing-lessons if you dare! You—you! Why, I am sixty years old. I have never got a picture into the exhibition but once. There was a quarrel among the directors, and one fellow put my landscape in to spite another—but I've never thought the less of the landscape. And here are you with your sphinxes and your sphinxes—why, New York has gone wild over you in one week's time! Every studio in the city pricking up its ears, and 'The Easel' and 'The Blender' in a duel over the picture to start with. May Heaven bless them for it! Drawing-lessons, indeed!"

"Pray tell me," said Avis, growing very pale, and putting the children down, lest her faint arms should drop them,—"pray explain exactly what you mean. I do not understand. I have never heard from the picture since you sent it to New York. Has anybody noticed—will anybody buy my sphinx?"

"No," said the drawing-master with a short laugh. "I don't think anybody will buy the picture—just yet. Not immediately, that is. The trouble is, you see"—

"I expected trouble," sighed Avis patiently. "I am used to that. Don't mind telling me. I don't mind."

"Why, the only trouble is," said Frederick Maynard, "that the picture was caught up the second day out."

"Caught up?" asked Avis faintly.

"Engaged—bought—sold—paid for. The sphinx was sold before Goupil had held it forty-eight hours. Mind you don't let Goupil photograph it. You can't afford to photograph a fledgling. *You* have a future. 'The Easel' says it is a work of pure imagination. 'The Blender' says it shows signs of haste."

" 'The Blender' is right," said Avis with returning breath and color. "That child in the foreground—the Arab child looking at the sphinx with his finger on his lips, swearing her to silence—do you remember? I put in that child in one hour. It was the day"—

She checked herself. Her husband himself should never know the story of that day—he would not understand. It would not have been to him as it was to her, coming down that morning, not a month after he had sailed, to find the dun for those college debts. Avis had the blind horror and shame of most delicate women in the presence of a debt. Her stinging impulse had been to discharge this without telling Philip or her father. Upon the spot she drew up an order for the sale of some bonds of her own, upon whose proceeds the family were in part dependent for the coming year. Fortunately she had not to deal with stock or real estate, which the wife cannot sell without the husband's consent. Avis did not know this. She knew nothing, except that she was grieved and shamed, and vaguely in need of money. She flew to the studio, struck the great sphinx dumb with the uplifted finger of a child, and sent it desperately from her before the cool of her frenzy fell.

"You are to make no more portraits, you understand," said Frederick Maynard, stumbling over Van, and narrowly escaping sitting on the baby as he went out. "You'll never be a portrait-painter. You must create: you cannot copy. That is what we lack in this country. We have no imagination. The sphinx is a creation. I told Goupil so when I took it on. He bowed politely. And now he comes asking for a photograph! You—*you!*—life is before you now. And I am sixty-three years old."

But Avis put her hand in his with a patient, unresponsive smile. She looked very gentle in her falling hair. The children clung to her. The light lay gravely on the studio-floor. She could hear the faint pulse of the sea, whose mighty heart beat between her and her husband, throbbing upon the frozen shore. The hand-organ in the street wailed on.

"Life is behind me too," she said gently. "It was before my marriage that I painted the sphinx. Don't be too much disappointed in me, if there are never any more pictures. Oh, I shall try! but I do not hope—do not think. We all have our lives to bear. If I, too, were sixty-three, perhaps—there, hush, my little girl!—perhaps—I should not —mind so much"—

"It seems to me," interrupted the drawing-master, winking resolutely, "that it can't be quite right for those children to look just as they do. Isn't there something a little peculiar in their expression?

Van was ingeniously trying to cut his throat with the palette-knife, and it would have been impossible to accuse the baby of not trying to swallow the tube of Prussian blue.

The year ran fleetly. Van was ailing a great deal that spring; and in the summer her father was ill. Thus, in the old, sad, subtle ways, Avis was exiled from the studio. She could not abandon herself to it without a feminine sense of guilt, under which women less tender may thrive callously, but at whose first touch she quivered with pain. She was stunned to find how her aspiration had emaciated during her married life. Household care had fed upon it like a disease. Sometimes she thought it an accession to her misery, that still, straight forever through the famine of her lot, its heart beat on, like that of the nervous physique, which is first to yield, but last to die. Then she wished, with all the wild, hot protest of her nature, that the spirit of this gift with which God had created her— in a mood of awful infinite irony, it seemed—would return to Him who gave it, that the dust of her days might descend to the dust in peace. She wished she were like other women,—content to stitch and sing, to sweep and smile. She bowed her face on the soft hair of her children; but she could not forget that they had been bought with a great price. She thought of the husband whose love she had mislaid, and counted the cost of her marriage in the blood of her soul.

Mary Wilkins Freeman (1852–1930)

Mary Wilkins Freeman was born into an old New England family which was rapidly losing its position in the world. She completed high school in Brattleboro, Vermont in 1870 and went, for a year, to Mount Holyoke Female Seminary, which she thought paid too much attention to the students' consciences and not enough to their digestions. Returning to her family, she spent the next ten years of her life apparently drifting, seeming to prepare herself to lead a life of genteel poverty if she did not marry.

In the 1880's, however, she began to write for publication instead of just for her own amusement, as she had been doing, and in 1882 won a prize from *The Boston Sunday Budget* for one of her short stories. These stories, based on her knowledge of dying New England villages, won for her an increasing financial success and literary following, and were collected into several volumes, for example: *A Humble Romance* (1887), *A New England Nun* (1891), and *The Best Stories of Mary E. Wilkins* (1927). Freeman also wrote novels: *Pembroke* (1894) and *The Portion of Labour* (1901), both about New England milltowns: *Jerome, A Poor Man* (1897), about rural poverty; and *The Shoulders of Atlas* (1908), which she sold for a total of $20,000—an enormous sum in those days. Her later works show an increasing interest in the social conditions which produce the warped and self-sacrificing characters who dominated her fiction from the beginning.

Despite poor health and a failing marriage to an alcoholic husband, Freeman continued to write and to publish until the early 1920's. She received a medal from the American Academy of Arts and Letters and was elected to the National Institute of Arts and Letters in 1926. These awards indicate the awareness of a large and significant public that Freeman—who read Dostoevsky and who was admired by Henry James—was more than the simple regionalist she is sometimes dismissed as being.

[References: Thompson, Charles M., "Miss Wilkins: An Idealist in Masquerade." *The Atlantic Monthly*, 83 (1899), 665-75; Foster, Edward. *Mary E. Wilkins Freeman*. New

York: Hendricks House, 1956. Westbrook, Perry D. *Mary Wilkins Freeman*. New York: Twayne Publishers, 1967. Ziff, Larzer. *The American 1890's*. New York: Viking, 1966. Pp. 275-305 *passim*.]

A NEW ENGLAND NUN

It was late in the afternoon, and the light was waning. There was a difference in the look of the tree shadows out in the yard. Somewhere in the distance, cows were lowing and a little bell was tinkling; now and then a farm wagon tilted by, and the dust flew; some blue-shirted laborers with shovels over their shoulders plodded past; little swarms of flies were dancing up and down before the people's faces in the soft air. There seemed to be a gentle stir arising over everything for the mere sake of subsidence—a very premonition of rest and hush and night.

This soft diurnal commotion was over Louisa Ellis also. She had been peacefully sewing at her sitting-room window all the afternoon. Now she quilted her needle carefully into her work, which she folded precisely, and laid in a basket with her thimble and thread and scissors. Louisa Ellis could not remember that ever in her life she had mislaid one of these little feminine appurtenances, which had become, from long use and constant association, a very part of her personality.

Louisa tied a green apron round her waist, and got out a flat straw hat with a green ribbon. Then she went into the garden with a little blue crockery bowl, to pick some currants for her tea. After the currants were picked she sat on the back doorstep and stemmed them, collecting the stems carefully in her apron and afterward throwing them into the hencoop. She looked sharply at the grass beside the step to see if any had fallen there.

Louisa was slow and still in her movements; it took her a long time to prepare her tea; but when ready it was set forth with as much grace as if she had been a veritable guest to her own self. The little square table stood exactly in the center of the kitchen, and was covered with a starched linen cloth whose border pattern of flowers glis-

Published in *A New England Nun and Other Stories*. New York: Harper and Brothers, 1891.

tened. Louisa had a damask napkin on her tea tray, where were arranged a cut-glass tumbler full of teaspoons, a silver cream pitcher, a china sugar bowl, and one pink china cup and saucer. Louisa used china every day— something which none of her neighbors did. They whispered about it among themselves. Their daily tables were laid with common crockery, their sets of best china stayed in the parlor closet, and Louisa Ellis was no richer nor better bred than they. Still she would use the china. She had for her supper a glass dish full of sugared currants, a plate of little cakes, and one of light white biscuits. Also a leaf or two of lettuce, which she cut up daintily. Louisa was very fond of lettuce, which she raised to perfection in her little garden. She ate quite heartily, though in a delicate, pecking way; it seemed almost surprising that any considerable bulk of the food should vanish.

After tea she filled a plate with nicely baked thin corn cakes, and carried them out into the back yard.

"Caesar!" she called. "Caesar! Caesar!"

There was a little rush, and the clank of a chain, and a large yellow-and-white dog appeared at the door of his tiny hut, which was half hidden among the tall grasses and flowers. Louisa patted him and gave him the corn cakes. Then she returned to the house and washed the tea things, polishing the china carefully. The twilight had deepened; the chorus of the frogs floated in at the open window wonderfully loud and shrill, and once in a while a long sharp drone from a tree toad pierced it. Louisa took off her green gingham apron, disclosing a shorter one of pink-and-white print. She lighted her lamp, and sat down again with her sewing.

In about half an hour Joe Dagget came. She heard his heavy step on the walk, and rose and took off her pink-and-white apron. Under that was still another—white linen with a little cambric edging on the bottom; that was Louisa's company apron. She never wore it without her calico sewing apron over it unless she had a guest. She had barely folded the pink-and-white one with methodical haste and laid it in a table drawer when the door opened and Joe Dagget entered.

He seemed to fill up the whole room. A little yellow canary that had been asleep in his green cage at the south window woke up and fluttered wildly, beating his little yellow wings against the wires. He always did so when Joe Dagget came into the room.

"Good evening," said Louisa. She extended her hand with a kind of solemn cordiality.

"Good evening, Louisa," returned the man, in a loud voice.

She placed a chair for him, and they sat facing each other, with the table between them. He sat bolt upright, toeing out his heavy feet squarely, glancing with a good-humored uneasiness around the room. She sat gently erect, folding her slender hands in her white-linen lap.

"Been a pleasant day," remarked Dagget.

"Real pleasant," Louisa assented, softly. "Have you been haying?" she asked, after a little while.

"Yes, I've been haying all day, down in the ten-acre lot. Pretty hot work."

"It must be."

"Yes, it's pretty hot work in the sun."

"Is your mother well today?"

"Yes, Mother's pretty well."

"I suppose Lily Dyer's with her now?"

Dagget colored. "Yes, she's with her," he answered, slowly.

He was not very young, but there was a boyish look about his large face. Louisa was not quite so old as he, her face was fairer and smoother, but she gave people the impression of being older.

"I suppose she's a good deal of help to your mother," she said, further.

"I guess she is; I don't know how mother'd get along without her," said Dagget, with a sort of embarrassed warmth.

"She looks like a real capable girl. She's pretty-looking too," remarked Louisa.

"Yes, she is pretty fair looking."

Presently Dagget began fingering the books on the table. There was a square red autograph album, and a Young Lady's Gift Book which had belonged to Louisa's mother. He took them up one after the other and opened them; then laid them down again, the album on the Gift Book.

Louisa kept eyeing them with mild uneasiness. Finally she rose and changed the position of the books, putting the album underneath. That was the way they had been arranged in the first place.

Dagget gave an awkward little laugh. "Now what difference did it make which book was on top?" said he.

Louisa looked at him with a deprecating smile. "I always keep them that way," murmured she.

"You do beat everything," said Dagget, trying to laugh again. His large face was flushed.

He remained about an hour longer, then rose to take leave. Going out, he stumbled over a rug, and trying to recover himself, hit Louisa's work basket on the table, and knocked it on the floor.

He looked at Louisa, then at the rolling spools; he ducked himself awkwardly toward them, but she stopped him. "Never mind," said she; "I'll pick them up after you're gone."

She spoke with a mild stiffness. Either she was a little disturbed, or his nervousness affected her and made her seem constrained in her effort to reassure him.

When Joe Dagget was outside he drew in the sweet evening air with a sigh, and felt much as an innocent and perfectly well-intentioned bear might after his exit from a china shop.

Louisa, on her part, felt much as the kind-hearted, long-suffering owner of the china shop might have done after the exit of the bear.

She tied on the pink, then the green apron, picked up all the scattered treasures and replaced them in her work basket, and straightened the rug. Then she set the lamp on the floor and began sharply examining the carpet. She even rubbed her fingers over it, and looked at them.

"He's tracked in a good deal of dust," she murmured. "I thought he must have."

Louisa got a dustpan and brush, and swept Joe Dagget's track carefully.

If he could have known it, it would have increased his perplexity and uneasiness, although it would not have disturbed his loyalty in the least. He came twice a week to see Louisa Ellis, and every time, sitting there in her delicately sweet room, he felt as if surrounded by a hedge of lace. He was afraid to stir lest he should put a clumsy foot or hand through the fairy web, and he had always the consciousness that Louisa was watching fearfully lest he should.

Still the lace and Louisa commanded perforce his perfect respect and patience and loyalty. They were to be

married in a month, after a singular courtship which had
lasted for a matter of fifteen years. For fourteen out of
the fifteen years the two had not once seen each other, and
they had seldom exchanged letters. Joe had been all those
years in Australia, where he had gone to make his fortune, and where he had stayed until he made it. He would
have stayed fifty years if it had taken so long, and come
home feeble and tottering, or never come home at all,
to marry Louisa.

But the fortune had been made in the fourteen years,
and he had come home now to marry the woman who
had been patiently and unquestioningly waiting for him
all that time.

Shortly after they were engaged he had announced to
Louisa his determination to strike out into new fields and
secure a competency before they should be married. She
had listened and assented with the sweet serenity which
never failed her, not even when her lover set forth on
that long and uncertain journey. Joe, buoyed up as he was
by his steady determination, broke down a little at the
last, but Louisa kissed him with a mild blush, and said
good-by.

"It won't be for long," poor Joe had said, huskily; but it
was for fourteen years.

In that length of time much had happened. Louisa's
mother and brother had died, and she was all alone in
the world. But greatest happening of all—a subtle happening which both were too simple to understand—
Louisa's feet had turned into a path, smooth maybe under
a calm, serene sky, but so straight and unswerving that it
could only meet a check at her grave, and so narrow
that there was no room for anyone at her side.

Louisa's first emotion when Joe Dagget came home (he
had not apprised her of his coming) was consternation,
although she would not admit it to herself, and he never
dreamed of it. Fifteen years ago she had been in love
with him—at least she considered herself to be. Just at that
time, gently acquiescing with and falling into the natural
drift of girlhood, she had seen marriage ahead as a reasonable feature and a probable desirability of life. She
had listened with calm docility to her mother's views upon
the subject. Her mother was remarkable for her cool
sense and sweet, even temperament. She talked wisely to
her daughter when Joe Dagget presented himself, and

Louisa accepted him with no hesitation. He was the first lover she had ever had.

She had been faithful to him all these years. She had never dreamed of the possibility of marrying anyone else. Her life, especially for the last seven years, had been full of a pleasant peace; she had never felt discontented nor impatient over her lover's absence; still, she had always looked forward to his return and their marriage as the inevitable conclusion of things. However, she had fallen into a way of placing it so far in the future that it was almost equal to placing it over the boundaries of another life.

When Joe came she had been expecting him, and expecting to be married for fourteen years, but she was as much surprised and taken aback as if she had never thought of it.

Joe's consternation came later. He eyed Louisa with an instant confirmation of his old admiration. She had changed but little. She still kept her pretty manner and soft grace, and was, he considered, every whit as attractive as ever. As for himself, his stent was done; he had turned his face away from fortune seeking, and the old winds of romance whistled as loud and sweet as ever through his ears. All the song which he had been wont to hear in them was Louisa; he had for a long time a loyal belief that he heard it still, but finally it seemed to him that although the winds sang always that one song, it had another name. But for Louisa the wind had never more than murmured; now it had gone down, and everything was still. She listened for a little while with half-wistful attention; then she turned quietly away and went to work on her wedding clothes.

Joe had made some extensive and quite magnificent alterations in his house. It was the old homestead; the newly-married couple would live there, for Joe could not desert his mother, who refused to leave her old home. So Louisa must leave hers. Every morning, rising and going about among her neat maidenly possessions, she felt as one looking her last upon the faces of dear friends. It was true that in a measure she could take them with her, but, robbed of their old environments, they would appear in such new guises that they would almost cease to be themselves.

Then there were some peculiar features of her happy

solitary life which she would probably be obliged to re-
linquish altogether. Sterner tasks than these graceful but
half-needless ones would probably devolve upon her. There
would be a large house to care for; there would be company to entertain; there would be Joe's rigorous and
feeble old mother to wait upon; and it would be contrary
to all thrifty village traditions for her to keep more than
one servant.

Louisa had a litle still, and she used to occupy herself
pleasantly in summer weather with distilling the sweet and
aromatic eccences from roses and peppermint and spear-
mint. By-and-by her still must be laid away. Her store
of essences was already considerable, and there would be
no time for her to distill for the mere pleasure of it.
Then Joe's mother would think it foolishness; she had already hinted her opinion in the matter.

Louisa dearly loved to sew a linen seam, not always
for use, but for the simple, mild pleasure which she took
in it. She would have been loathe to confess how more
than once she had ripped a seam for the mere delight of
sewing it together again. Sitting at her window during long
sweet afternoons, drawing her needle gently through the
dainty fabric, she was peace itself. But there was small
chance of such foolish comfort in the future. Joe's mother, domineering, shrewd old matron that she was even in
her old age, and very likely even Joe himself, with his
honest masculine rudeness, would laugh and frown down
all these pretty but senseless old maiden ways.

Louisa had almost the enthusiasm of an artist over the
mere order and cleanliness of her solitary home. She had
throbs of genuine triumph at the sight of the windowpanes
which she had polished until they shone like jewels. She
gloated gently over her orderly bureau drawers, with their
exquisitely folded contents redolent with lavender and
sweet clover and very purity. Could she be sure of the
endurance of even this? She had visions, so startling that
she half repudiated them as indelicate, of coarse masculine
belongings strewn about in endless litter; of dust and
disorder arising necessarily from a coarse masculine presence in the midst of all this delicate harmony.

Among her forebodings of disturbance, not the least
was with regard to Caesar. Caesar was a veritable hermit
of a dog. For the greater part of his life he had dwelt
in his secluded hut, shut out from the society of his kind

and all innocent canine joys. Never had Caesar since his early youth watched at a woodchuck's hole; never had he known the delights of a stray bone at a neighbor's kitchen door. And it was all on account of a sin committed when hardly out of his puppyhood. No one knew the possible depth of remorse of which this mild-visaged, altogether innocent-looking old dog might be capable; but whether or not he had encountered remorse, he had encountered a full measure of righteous retribution. Old Caesar seldom lifted up his voice in a growl or a bark; he was fat and sleepy; there were yellow rings which looked like spectacles around his dim old eyes; but there was a neighbor who bore on his hand the imprint of several of Caesar's sharp white youthful teeth, and for that he had lived at the end of a chain, all alone in a little hut, for fourteen years. The neighbor, who was choleric and smarting with the pain of his wound, had demanded either Caesar's death or complete ostracism. So Louisa's brother, to whom the dog had belonged, had built him his little kennel and tied him up. It was now fourteen years since, in a flood of youthful spirits, he had inflicted that memorable bite, and with the exception of short excursions, always at the end of the chain, under the strict guardianship of his master or Louisa, the old dog had remained a close prisoner. It is doubtful if, with his limited ambition, he took much pride in the fact, but it is certain that he was possessed of considerable cheap fame. He was regarded by all the children in the village and by many adults as a very monster of ferocity. St. George's dragon could hardly have surpassed in evil repute Louisa Ellis's old yellow dog. Mothers charged their children with solemn emphasis not to go too near to him, and the children listened and believed greedily, with a fascinated appetite for terror, and ran by Louisa's house stealthily, with many sidelong and backward glances at the terrible dog. If perchance he sounded a hoarse bark, there was a panic. Wayfarers chancing into Louisa's yard eyed him with respect, and inquired if the chain were stout. Caesar at large might have seemed a very ordinary dog and excited no comment whatever; chained, his reputation overshadowed him, so that he lost his own proper outlines and looked darkly vague and enormous. Joe Dagget, however, with his good-humored sense and shrewdness, saw him as he was. He strode valiantly up to him and patted him on the head, in spite of Louisa's soft clamor of warning, and even attempted to set him loose. Louisa grew so alarmed that he desisted, but kept announcing his opinion in the matter quite forcibly at intervals. "There ain't a better-natured dog in town," he would say, "and it's downright cruel to keep him tied up there. Some day I'm going to take him out."

Louisa had very little hope that he would not, one of these days, when their interests and possessions should be more completely fused in one. She pictured to herself Caesar on the rampage through the quiet and unguarded village. She saw innocent children bleeding in his path. She was herself very fond of the old dog, because he had belonged to her dead brother, and he was always very gentle with her; still she had great faith in his ferocity. She always warned people not to go too near him. She fed him on ascetic fare of corn mush and cakes, and never fired his dangerous temper with heating and sanguinary diet of flesh and bones. Louisa looked at the old dog munching his simple fare, and thought of her approaching marriage and trembled. Still no anticipation of disorder and confusion in lieu of sweet peace and harmony, no forebodings of Caesar on the rampage, no wild fluttering of her little yellow canary, were sufficient to turn her a hair's-breadth. Joe Dagget had been fond of her and working for her all these years. It was not for her, whatever came to pass, to prove untrue and break his heart. She put the exquisite little stitches into her wedding garments, and the time went on until it was only a week before her wedding day. It was a Tuesday evening, and the wedding was to be a week from Wednesday.

There was a full moon that night. About nine o'clock Louisa strolled down the road a little way. There were harvest fields on either hand, bordered by low stone walls. Luxuriant clumps of bushes grew beside the wall, and trees—wild cherry and old apple trees—at intervals. Presently Louisa sat down on the wall and looked about her with mildly sorrowful reflectiveness. Tall shrubs of blueberry and meadow-sweet, all woven together and tangled with blackberry vines and horsebriers, shut her in on either side. She had a little clear space between them. Opposite her, on the other side of the road, was a spreading tree; the moon shone between its boughs, and the leaves twinkled like silver. The road was bespread with a beautiful shifting dapple of silver and shadow; the air was full of a mysterious sweetness. "I wonder if it's wild grapes?" murmured Louisa. She sat there some time. She was just thinking of rising, when she heard footsteps and low voices, and remained quiet. It was a lonely place, and she felt a little timid. She thought she would keep still in the shadow and let the persons, whoever they might be, pass her.

But just before they reached her the voices ceased, and the footsteps. She understood that their owners had also found seats upon the stone wall. She was wondering if she could not steal away unobserved, when the voice broke the stillness. It was Joe Dagget's. She sat still and listened.

The voice was announced by a loud sigh, which was as familiar as itself. "Well," said Dagget, "you've made up your mind, then, I suppose?"

"Yes," returned another voice; "I'm going day after to-morrow."

"That's Lily Dyer," thought Louisa to herself. The voice embodied itself in her mind. She saw a girl tall and full-figured, with a firm, fair face, looking fairer and firmer in the moonlight, her strong yellow hair braided in a close knot. A girl full of a calm rustic strength and bloom, with a masterful way which might have beseemed a princess. Lily Dyer was a favorite with the village folk; she had just the qualities to arouse the admiration. She was good and handsome and smart. Louisa had often heard her praises sounded.

"Well," said Joe Dagget, "I ain't got a word to say."

"I don't know what you could say," returned Lily Dyer.

"Not a word to say," repeated Joe, drawing out the words heavily. Then there was a silence. "I ain't sorry," he began at last, "that that happened yesterday—that we kind of let on how we felt to each other. I guess it's just as well we knew. Of course I can't do anything any different. I'm going right on an' get married next week. I ain't going back on a woman that's waited for me fourteen years, an' break her heart."

"If you should jilt her tomorrow, I wouldn't have you," spoke up the girl, with sudden vehemence.

"Well, I ain't going to give you the chance," said he; "but I don't believe you would, either."

"You'd see I wouldn't. Honor's honor, an' right's right. An' I'd never think anything of any man that went against 'em for me or any other girl; you'd find that out, Joe Dagget."

"Well, you'll find out fast enough that I ain't going against 'em for you or any other girl," returned he. Their voices sounded almost as if they were angry with each other. Louisa was listening eagerly.

"I'm sorry you feel as if you must go away," said Joe, "but I don't know but it's best."

"Of course it's best. I hope you and I have got common sense."

"Well, I suppose you're right." Suddenly Joe's voice got an undertone of tenderness. "Say, Lily," said he, "I'll get along well enough myself, but I can't bear to think— You don't suppose you're going to fret much over it?"

"I guess you'll find out I shan't fret much over a married man."

"Well, I hope you won't—I hope you won't, Lily. God knows I do. And—I hope—one of these days—you'll— come across somebody else—"

"I don't see any reason why I shouldn't." Suddenly her tone changed. She spoke in a sweet, clear voice, so loud that she could have been heard across the street. "No, Joe Dagget," said she, "I'll never marry any other man as long as I live. I've got good sense, an' I ain't going to break my heart nor make a fool of myself; but I'm never going to be married, you can be sure of that. I ain't that sort of a girl to feel this way twice."

Louisa heard an exclamation and a soft commotion behind the bushes; then Lily spoke again—the voice sounded as if she had risen. "This must be put a stop to," said she. "We've stayed here long enough. I'm going home."

Louisa sat there in a daze, listening to their retreating steps. After a while she got up and slunk softly home herself. The next day she did her housework methodically; that was as much a matter of course as breathing; but she did not sew on her wedding clothes. She sat at her window and meditated. In the evening Joe came. Louisa Ellis had never known that she had any diplomacy in her, but when she came to look for it that night she found it, although meek of its kind, among her little feminine weapons. Even now she could hardly believe that she had heard right, and that she would not do Joe a terrible injury should she break her troth plight. She wanted to sound him out without betraying too soon her own inclinations in

the matter. She did it successfully, and they finally came to
an understanding; but it was a difficult thing, for he was
as afraid of betraying himself as she.

She never mentioned Lily Dyer. She simply said that
while she had no cause of complaint against him, she had
lived so long in one way that she shrank from making a
change.

"Well, I never shrank, Louisa," said Dagget. "I'm going
to be honest enough to say that I think maybe it's better
this way; but if you'd wanted to keep on, I'd have stuck to
you till my dying day. I hope you know that."

"Yes, I do," said she.

That night she and Joe parted more tenderly than they
had done for a long time. Standing in the door, holding
each other's hands, a last great wave of regretful memory
swept over them.

"Well, this ain't the way we've thought it was all going
to end, is it, Louisa?" said Joe.

She shook her head. There was a little quiver on her
placid face.

"You let me know if there's ever anything I can do for
you," said he. "I ain't ever going to forget you, Louisa."
Then he kissed her, and went down the path.

Louisa, all alone by herself that night, wept a little, she
hardly knew why; but the next morning, on waking, she
felt like a queen who, after fearing lest her domain be
wrested away from her, sees it firmly insured in her possession.

Now the tall weeds and grasses might cluster around
Caesar's little hermit hut, the snow might fall on its roof
year in and year out, but he never would go on a rampage
through the unguarded village. Now the little canary might
turn itself into a peaceful yellow ball night after night, and
have no need to wake and flutter with wild terror against
its bars. Louisa could sew linen seams, and distill roses,
and dust and polish and fold away in lavender, as long as
she listed. That afternoon she sat with her needlework at
the window, and felt fairly steeped in peace. Lily Dyer,
tall and erect and blooming, went past; but she felt no
qualm. If Louisa Ellis had sold her birthright she did not
know it; the taste of the pottage was so delicious, and had
been her sole satisfaction for so long. Serenity and placid
narrowness had become to her as the birthright itself. She
gazed ahead through a long reach of future days strung

together like pearls in a rosary, every one like the others, and all smooth and flawless and innocent, and her heart went up in thankfulness. Outside was the fervid summer afternoon; the air was filled with the sounds of the busy harvest of men and birds and bees; there were halloos, metallic clatterings, sweet calls, and long hummings. Louisa sat, prayerfully numbering her days, like an uncloistered nun.

THE REVOLT OF "MOTHER"

"Father!"

"What is it?"

"What are them men diggin' over there in the field for?"

There was a sudden dropping and enlarging of the lower part of the old man's face, as if some heavy weight had settled therein; he shut his mouth tight, and went on harnessing the great bay mare. He hustled the collar on to her neck with a jerk.

"Father!"

The old man slapped the saddle upon the mare's back.

"Look here, Father, I want to know what them men are diggin' over in the field for, an' I'm goin' to know."

"I wish you'd go into the house, Mother, an' 'tend to your own affairs," the old man said then. He ran his words together, and his speech was almost as inarticulate as a growl.

But the woman understood; it was her most native tongue. "I ain't goin' into the house till you tell me what them men are doin' over there in the field," said she.

Then she stood waiting. She was a small woman, short and straight-waisted like a child in her brown cotton gown. Her forehead was mild and benevolent between the smooth curves of gray hair; there were meek downward lines about her nose and mouth; but her eyes, fixed upon the old man, looked as if the meekness had been the result of her own will, never of the will of another.

They were in the barn, standing before the wide-open doors. The spring air, full of the smell of growing grass and unseen blossoms, came in their faces. The deep yard in front was littered with farm wagons and piles of wood; on the edges, close to the fence and the house, the grass was a vivid green, and there were some dandelions.

The old man glanced doggedly at his wife as he

Published in *A New England Nun and Other Stories*. New York: Harper and Brothers, 1891.

tightened the last buckles on the harness. She looked as immovable to him as one of the rocks in his pasture land, bound to the earth with generations of blackberry vines. He slapped the reins over the horse, and started forth from the barn.

"Father!" said she.

The old man pulled up. "What is it?"

"I want to know what them men are diggin' over there in that field for."

"They're diggin' a cellar, I s'pose, if you've got to know."

"A cellar for what?"

"A barn."

"A barn? You ain't goin' to build a barn over there where we was goin' to have a house, Father?"

The old man said not another word. He hurried the horse into the farm wagon, and clattered out of the yard, jouncing as sturdily on his seat as a boy.

The woman stood a moment looking after him, then she went out of the barn across a corner of the yard to the house. The house, standing at right angles with the great barn and a long reach of sheds and outbuildings, was infinitesimal compared with them. It was scarcely as commodious for people as the little boxes under the barn eaves were for doves.

A pretty girl's face, pink and delicate as a flower, was looking out of one of the house windows. She was watching three men who were digging over in the field which bounded the yard near the road line. She turned quietly when the woman entered.

"What are they digging for, Mother?" said she. "Did he tell you?"

"They're diggin' for—a cellar for a new barn."

"Oh, Mother, he ain't going to build another barn?"

"That's what he says."

A boy stood before the kitchen glass combing his hair. He combed slowly and painstakingly, arranging his brown hair in a smooth hillock over his forehead. He did not seem to pay any attention to the conversation.

"Sammy, did you know Father was going to build a new barn?" asked the girl.

The boy combed assiduously.

"Sammy!"

He turned, and showed a face like his father's under his

smooth crest of hair. "Yes, I s'pose I did," he said, reluctantly.

"How long have you known it?" asked his mother.

" 'Bout three months, I guess."

"Why didn't you tell of it?"

"Didn't think 'twould do no good."

"I don't see what Father wants another barn for," said the girl, in her sweet, slow voice. She turned again to the window, and stared out at the digging men in the field. Her tender, sweet face was full of a gentle distress. Her forehead was as bald and innocent as a baby's, with the light hair strained back from it in a row of curl papers. She was quite large, but her soft curves did not look as if they covered muscles.

Her mother looked sternly at the boy. "Is he goin' to buy more cows?" said she.

The boy did not reply; he was tying his shoes.

"Sammy, I want you to tell me if he's goin' to buy more cows."

"I s'pose he is."

"How many?"

"Four, I guess."

His mother said nothing more. She went into the pantry, and there was a clatter of dishes. The boy got his cap from a nail behind the door, took an old arithmetic from the shelf, and started for school. He was lightly built, but clumsy. He went out of the yard with a curious spring in the hips that made his loose homemade jacket tilt up in the rear.

The girl went to the sink, and began to wash the dishes that were piled up there. Her mother came promptly out of the pantry, and shoved her aside. "You wipe 'em," said she; "I'll wash. There's a good many this mornin'."

The mother plunged her hands vigorously into the water, the girl wiped the plates slowly and dreamily. "Mother," said she, "don't you think it's too bad Father's going to build that new barn, much as we need a decent house to live in?"

Her mother scrubbed a dish fiercely. "You ain't found out yet we're womenfolks, Nanny Penn," said she. "You ain't seen enough of menfolks yet to. One of these days you'll find it out, an' then you'll know that we know only what menfolks think we do, so far as any use of it goes, an' how we'd ought to reckon menfolks in with Providence, an' not complain of what they do any more than we do of the weather."

"I don't care; I don't believe George is anything like that, anyhow," said Nanny. Her delicate face flushed pink; her lips pouted softly, as if she were going to cry.

"You wait an' see. I guess George Eastman ain't no better than other men. You hadn't ought to judge Father, though. He can't help it, 'cause he don't look at things jest the way we do. An' we've been pretty comfortable here, after all. The roof don't leak—ain't never but once —that's one thing. Father's kept it shingled right up."

"I do wish we had a parlor."

"I guess it won't hurt George Eastman any to come to see you in a nice clean kitchen. I guess a good many girls don't have as good a place as this. Nobody's ever heard me complain."

"I ain't complained either, Mother."

"Well, I don't think you'd better, a good father an' a good home as you've got. S'pose your father made you go out an' work for your livin'? Lots of girls have to that ain't no stronger an' better able to than you be."

Sarah Penn washed the frying pan with a conclusive air. She scrubbed the outside of it as faithfully as the inside. She was a masterly keeper of her box of a house. Her one living room never seemed to have in it any of the dust which the friction of life with inanimate matter produces. She swept, and there seemed to be no dirt to go before the broom; she cleaned, and one could see no difference. She was like an artist so perfect that he has apparently no art. Today she got out a mixing bowl and a board, and rolled some pies, and there was no more flour upon her than upon her daughter who was doing finer work. Nanny was to be married in the fall, and she was sewing on some white cambric and embroidery. She sewed industriously while her mother cooked; her soft milk-white hands and wrists showed whiter than her delicate work.

"We must have the stove moved out in the shed before long," said Mrs. Penn. "Talk about not havin' things, it's been a real blessin' to be able to put a stove up in that shed in hot weather. Father did one good thing when he fixed that stove pipe out there."

Sarah Penn's face as she rolled her pies had that expression of meek vigor which might have characterized one of the New Testament saints. She was making mince pies. Her husband, Adoniram Penn, liked them better than any other kind. She baked twice a week. Adoniram often liked a piece of pie between meals. She hurried this morning. It had been later than usual when she began, and she wanted to have a pie baked for dinner. However deep a resentment she might be forced to hold against her husband, she would never fail in sedulous attention to his wants.

Nobility of character manifests itself at loopholes when it is not provided with large doors. Sarah Penn's showed itself today in flaky dishes of pastry. She made the pies faithfully, while across the table she could see, when she glanced up from her work, the sight that rankled in her patient and steadfast soul—the digging of the cellar of the new barn in the place where Adoniram forty years ago had promised her their new house should stand.

The pies were done for dinner. Adoniram and Sammy were home a few minutes after twelve o'clock. The dinner was eaten with serious haste. There was never much conversation at the table in the Penn family. Adoniram asked a blessing, and they ate promptly, then rose up and went about their work.

Sammy went back to school, taking soft sly lopes out of the yard like a rabbit. He wanted a game of marbles before school, and feared his father would give him some chores to do. Adoniram hastened to the door and called after him, but he was out of sight.

"I don't see what you let him go for, Mother," said he. "I wanted him to help me unload that wood."

Adoniram went to work out in the yard unloading wood from the wagon. Sarah put away the dinner dishes, while Nanny took down her curl papers and changed her dress. She was going down to the store to buy some more embroidery and thread.

When Nanny was gone, Mrs. Penn went to the door. "Father!" she called.

"Well, what is it!"

"I want to see you jest a minute, Father."

"I can't leave this wood nohow. I've got to git unloaded an' go for a load of gravel afore two o'clock. Sammy had ought to helped me. You hadn't ought to let him go to school so early."

"I want to see you jest a minute."

"I tell ye I can't, nohow, Mother."

"Father, you come here." Sarah Penn stood in the door like a queen; she held her head as if it bore a crown; there was that patience which makes authority royal in her voice. Adoniram went.

Mrs. Penn led the way into the kitchen, and pointed to a chair. "Sit down, Father," said she; "I've got somethin' I want to say to you."

He sat down heavily; his face was quite stolid, but he looked at her with restive eyes. "Well, what is it, Mother?"

"I want to know what you're buildin' that new barn for, Father?"

"I ain't got nothin' to say about it."

"It can't be you think you need another barn?"

"I tell ye I ain't got nothin' to say about it, Mother; an' I ain't goin' to say nothin'."

"Be you goin' to buy more cows?"

Adoniram did not reply; he shut his mouth tight.

"I know you be, as well as I want to. Now, Father, look here"—Sarah Penn had not sat down; she stood before her husband in the humble fashion of a Scripture woman —"I'm goin' to talk real plain to you; I never have sence I married you, but I'm goin' to now. I ain't never complained, an' I ain't goin' to complain now, but I'm goin' to talk plain. You see this room here, Father; you look at it well. You see there ain't no carpet on the floor, an' you see the paper is all dirty an' droppin' off the walls. We ain't had no new paper on it for ten year, an' then I put it on myself, an' it didn't cost but ninepence a roll. You see this room, Father; it's all the one I've had to work in an' eat in an' sit in sence we was married. There ain't another woman in the whole town whose husband ain't got half the means you have but what's got better. It's all the room Nanny's got to have her company in; an' there ain't one of her mates but what's got better, an' their fathers not so able as hers is. It's all the room she'll have to be married in. What would you have thought, Father, if we had had our weddin' in a room no better than this? I was married in my mother's parlor, with a carpet on the floor, an' stuffed furniture, an' a mahogany card table. An' this is all the room my daughter will have to be married in. Look here, Father!"

Sarah Penn went across the room as though it were a tragic stage. She flung open a door and disclosed a tiny bedroom, only large enough for a bed and bureau, with a path between. "There, Father," said she—"there's all the room I've had to sleep in in forty year. All my children were born there—the two that died an' the two that's livin'. I was sick with a fever there."

She stepped to another door and opened it. It led into the small, ill-lighted pantry. "Here," said she, "is all the buttery I've got—every place I've got for my dishes, to set away my victuals in, an' to keep my milk pans in. Father, I've been takin' care of the milk of six cows in this place, an' now you're goin' to build a new barn, an' keep more cows, an' give me more to do in it."

She threw open another door. A narrow crooked flight of stairs wound upward from it. "There, Father," said she, "I want you to look at the stairs that go up to them two unfinished chambers that are all the places our son an' daughter have had to sleep in all their lives. There ain't a prettier girl in town nor a more ladylike one than Nanny, an' that's the place she has to sleep in. It ain't so good as your horse's stall; it ain't so warm an' tight."

Sarah Penn went back and stood before her husband. "Now, Father," said she, "I want to know if you think you're doin' right an' accordin' to what you profess. Here, where we was married, forty year ago, you promised me faithful that we should have a new house built in that lot over in the field before the year was out. You said you had money enough, an' you wouldn't ask me to live in no such place as this. It is forty year now, an' you've been makin' more money, an' I've been savin' of it for you ever since, an' you ain't built no house yet. You've built sheds an' cow houses an' one new barn, an' now you're goin' to build another. Father, I want to know if you think it's right. You're lodgin' your dumb beasts better than you are your own flesh an' blood. I want to know if you think it's right."

"I ain't got nothin' to say."

"You can't say nothin' without ownin' it ain't right, Father. An' there's another thing—I ain't complained; I've got along forty year, an' I s'pose I should forty more, if it wa'n't for that—if we don't have another house. Nanny, she can't live with us after she's married. She'll have to go somewheres else to live away from us, an' it don't seem as if I could have it so, noways, Father. She wa'n't ever strong. She's got considerable color, but there wa'n't never any backbone to her. I've always took the heft of everything off her, an' she ain't fit to keep house an' do everything herself. She'll be all worn out inside of a year. Think of her doin' all the washin' an' ironin' an' bakin' with them soft white hands an' arms, an' sweepin'! I can't have it so, noways, Father."

Mrs. Penn's face was burning; her mild eyes gleamed. She had pleaded her little cause like a Webster; she had ranged from severity to pathos; but her opponent employed that obstinate silence which makes eloquence futile with mocking echoes. Adoniram arose clumsily.

"Father, ain't you got nothin' to say?" said Mrs. Penn.

"I've got to go off after that load of gravel. I can't stan' here talkin' all day."

"Father, won't you think it over, an' have a house built there instead of a barn?"

"I ain't got nothin' to say."

Adoniram shuffled out. Mrs. Penn went into her bedroom. When she came out, her eyes were red. She had a roll of unbleached cotton cloth. She spread it out on the kitchen table, and began cutting out some shirts for her husband. The men over in the field had a team to help them this afternoon; she could hear their halloos. She had a scanty pattern for the shirts; she had to plan and piece the sleeves.

Nanny came home with her embroidery, and sat down with her needlework. She had taken down her curl papers, and there was a soft roll of fair hair like an aureole over her forehead; her face was as delicately fine and clear as porcelain. Suddenly she looked up, and the tender red flamed all over her face and neck. "Mother," said she.

"What say?"

"I've been thinking—I don't see how we're goin' to have any—wedding in this room. I'd be ashamed to have his folks come if we didn't have anybody else."

"Mebbe we can have some new paper before then; I can put it on. I guess you won't have no call to be ashamed of your belongin's."

"We might have the wedding in the new barn," said Nanny, with gentle pettishness. "Why, Mother, what makes you look so?"

Mrs. Penn had started, and was staring at her with a

curious expression. She turned again to her work, and spread out a pattern carefully on the cloth. "Nothin'," said she.

Presently Adoniram clattered out of the yard in his two-wheeled dump cart, standing as proudly upright as a Roman charioteer. Mrs. Penn opened the door and stood there a minute looking out; the halloos of the men sounded louder.

It seemed to her all through the spring months that she heard nothing but the halloos and the noises of saws and hammers. The new barn grew fast. It was a fine edifice for this little village. Men came on pleasant Sundays, in their meeting suits and clean shirt bosoms, and stood around it admiringly. Mrs. Penn did not speak of it, and Adoniram did not mention it to her, although sometimes, upon a return from inspecting it, he bore himself with injured dignity.

"It's a strange thing how your mother feels about the new barn," he said, confidentially, to Sammy one day.

Sammy only grunted after an odd fashion for a boy; he had learned it from his father.

The barn was all completed ready for use by the third week in July. Adoniram had planned to move his stock in on Wednesday; on Tuesday he received a letter which changed his plans. He came in with it early in the morning. "Sammy's been to the post office," said he, "an' I've got a letter from Hiram." Hiram was Mrs. Penn's brother, who lived in Vermont.

"Well," said Mrs. Penn, "what does he say about the folks?"

"I guess they're all right. He says he thinks if I come up country right off there's a chance to buy jest the kind of a horse I want." He stared reflectively out of the window at the new barn.

Mrs. Penn was making pies. She went on clapping the rolling pin into the crust, although she was very pale, and her heart beat loudly.

"I dun' know but what I'd better go," said Adoniram. "I hate to go off jest now, right in the midst of hayin', but the ten-acre lot's cut, an' I guess Rufus an' the others can git along without me three or four days. I can't get a horse round here to suit me, nohow, an' I've got to have another for all that wood haulin' in the fall. I told Hiram to watch out, an' if he got wind of a good horse to let me know. I guess I'd better go."

"I'll get out your clean shirt an' collar," said Mrs. Penn, calmly.

She laid out Adoniram's Sunday suit and his clean clothes on the bed in the little bedroom. She got his shaving water and razor ready. At last she buttoned on his collar and fastened his black cravat.

Adoniram never wore his collar and cravat except on extra occasions. He held his head high, with a rasped dignity. When he was all ready, with his coat and hat brushed, and a lunch of pie and cheese in a paper bag, he hesitated on the threshold of the door. He looked at his wife, and his manner was defiantly apologetic. "*If* them cows come today, Sammy can drive 'em into the new barn," said he; "an' when they bring the hay up, they can pitch it in there."

"Well," replied Mrs. Penn.

Adoniram set his shaven face ahead and started. When he had cleared the doorstep, he turned and looked back with a kind of nervous solemnity. "I shall be back by Saturday if nothin' happens," said he.

"Do be careful, Father," returned his wife.

She stood in the door with Nanny at her elbow and watched him out of sight. Her eyes had a strange, doubtful expression in them; her peaceful forehead was contracted. She went in, and about her baking again. Nanny sat sewing. Her wedding day was drawing nearer, and she was getting pale and thin with her steady sewing. Her mother kept glancing at her.

"Have you got that pain in your side this mornin'?" she asked.

"A little."

Mrs. Penn's face, as she worked, changed; her perplexed forehead smoothed; her eyes were steady, her lips firmly set. She formed a maxim for herself, although incoherently with her unlettered thoughts. "Unsolicited opportunities are the guideposts of the Lord to the new roads of life," she repeated in effect, and she made up her mind to her course of action.

"S'posin' I *had* wrote to Hiram," she muttered once, when she was in the pantry—"s'posin' I had wrote, an' asked him if he knew of any horse? But I didn't, an'

Father's goin' wa'n't none of my doin'. It looks like a providence." Her voice rang out quite loud at the last.

"What you talkin' about, mother?" called Nanny.

"Nothin'."

Mrs. Penn hurried her baking; at eleven o'clock it was all done. The load of hay from the west field came slowly down the cart track and drew up at the new barn. Mrs. Penn ran out. "Stop!" she screamed—"stop!"

The men stopped and looked; Sammy upreared from the top of the load, and stared at his mother.

"Stop!" she cried out again. "Don't you put the hay in that barn; put it in the old one."

"Why, he said to put it in here," returned one of the haymakers, wonderingly. He was a young man, a neighbor's son, whom Adoniram hired by the year to help on the farm.

"Don't you put the hay in the new barn; there's room enough in the old one, ain't there?" said Mrs. Penn.

"Room enough," returned the hired man, in his thick, rustic tones. "Didn't need the new barn, nohow, far as room's concerned. Well, I s'pose he changed his mind." He took hold of the horses' bridles.

Mrs. Penn went back to the house. Soon the kitchen windows were darkened, and a fragrance like warm honey came into the room.

Nanny laid down her work. "I thought Father wanted them to put the hay into the new barn?" she said, wonderingly.

"It's all right," replied her mother.

Sammy slid down from the load of hay, and came in to see if dinner was ready.

"I ain't goin' to get a regular dinner today, as long as Father's gone," said his mother. "I've let the fire go out. You can have some bread an' milk an' pie. I thought we could get along." She set out some bowls of milk, some bread, and a pie on the kitchen table. "You'd better eat your dinner now," said she. "You might jest as well get through with it. I want you to help me afterward."

Nanny and Sammy stared at each other. There was something strange in their mother's manner. Mrs. Penn did not eat anything herself. She went into the pantry, and they heard her moving dishes while they ate. Presently she came out with a pile of plates. She got the clothes basket out of the shed, and packed them in it. Nanny and Sammy watched. She brought out cups and saucers, and put them in with the plates.

"What you goin' to do, Mother?" inquired Nanny, in a timid voice. A sense of something unusual made her tremble, as if it were a ghost. Sammy rolled his eyes over his pie.

"You'll see what I'm goin' to do," replied Mrs. Penn. "If you're through, Nanny, I want you to go upstairs an' pack up your things; an' I want you, Sammy, to help me take down the bed in the bedroom."

"Oh, Mother, what for?" gasped Nanny.

"You'll see."

During the next few hours a feat was performed by this simple, pious New England mother which was equal in its way to Wolfe's storming of the Heights of Abraham. It took no more genius and audacity of bravery for Wolfe to cheer his wondering soldiers up those steep precipices, under the sleeping eyes of the enemy, than for Sarah Penn, at the head of her children, to move all their little household goods into the new barn while her husband was away.

Nanny and Sammy followed their mother's instructions without a murmur; indeed, they were overawed. There is a certain uncanny and superhuman quality about all such purely original undertakings as their mother's was to them. Nanny went back and forth with her light loads, and Sammy tugged with sober energy.

At five o'clock in the afternoon the little house in which the Penns had lived for forty years had emptied itself into the new barn.

Every builder builds somewhat for unknown purposes, and is in a measure a prophet. The architect of Adoniram Penn's barn, while he designed it for the comfort of four-footed animals, had planned better than he knew for the comfort of humans. Sarah Penn saw at a glance its possibilities. Those great box stalls, with quilts hung before them, would make better bedrooms than the one she had occupied for forty years, and there was a tight carriage room. The harness room, with its chimney and shelves, would make a kitchen of her dreams. The great middle space would make a parlor, by-and-by, fit for a palace. Upstairs there was as much room as down. With partitions and windows, what a house would there be! Sarah looked at the row of stanchions before the allotted space for cows, and reflected that she would have her front entry there.

At six o'clock the stove was up in the harness room, the kettle was boiling, and the table set for tea. It looked almost as homelike as the abandoned house across the yard had ever done. The young hired man milked, and Sarah directed him calmly to bring the milk to the new barn. He came gaping, dropping little blots of foam from the brimming pails on the grass. Before the next morning he had spread the story of Adoniram Penn's wife moving into the new barn all over the little village. Men assembled in the store and talked it over; women with shawls over their heads scuttled into each other's houses before their work was done. Any deviation from the ordinary course of life in this quiet town was enough to stop all progress in it. Everybody paused to look at the staid, independent figure on the side track. There was a difference of opinion with regard to her. Some held her to be insane; some, of a lawless and rebellious spirit.

Friday the minister went to see her. It was in the forenoon, and she was at the barn door shelling peas for dinner. She looked up and returned his salutation with dignity; then she went on with her work. She did not invite him in. The saintly expression of her face remained fixed, but there was an angry flush over it.

The minister stood awkwardly before her, and talked. She handled the peas as if they were bullets. At last she looked up, and her eyes showed the spirit that her meek front had covered for a lifetime.

"There ain't no use talkin', Mr. Hersey," said she. "I've thought it all over an' over, an' I believe I'm doin' what's right. I've made it the subject of prayer, an' it's betwixt me an' the Lord an' Adoniram. There ain't no call for nobody else to worry about it."

"Well, of course, if you have brought it to the Lord in prayer, and feel satisfied that you are doing right, Mrs. Penn," said the minister, helplessly. His thin gray-bearded face was pathetic. He was a sickly man; his youthful confidence had cooled; he had to scourge himself up to some of his pastoral duties as relentlessly as a Catholic ascetic, and then he was prostrated by the smart.

"I think it's right jest as much as I think it was right for our forefathers to come over from the old country 'cause they didn't have what belonged to 'em," said Mrs. Penn. She arose. The barn threshold might have been Plymouth Rock, from her bearing. "I don't doubt you mean well, Mr. Hersey," said she, "but there are things people hadn't ought to interfere with. I've been a member of the church for over forty year. I've got my own mind an' my own feet, an' I'm goin' to think my own thoughts an' go my own ways, an' nobody but the Lord is goin' to dictate to me unless I've a mind to have him. Won't you come in an' set down? How is Mis' Hersey?"

"She is well, I thank you," replied the minister. He added some more perplexed apologetic remarks; then he retreated.

He could expound the intricacies of every character study in the Scriptures; he was competent to grasp the Pilgrim Fathers and all historical innovators; but Sarah Penn was beyond him. He could deal with primal cases, but parallel ones worsted him. But, after all, although it was aside from his province, he wondered more how Adoniram Penn would deal with his wife than how the Lord would. Everybody shared the wonder. When Adoniram's four new cows arrived, Sarah ordered three to be put in the old barn, the other in the house shed where the cooking stove had stood. That added to the excitement. It was whispered that all four cows were domiciled in the house.

Toward sunset on Saturday, when Adoniram was expected home, there was a knot of men in the road near the new barn. The hired man had milked, but he still hung around the premises. Sarah Penn had supper all ready. There were brown bread and baked beans and a custard pie; it was the supper that Adoniram loved on a Saturday night. She had on a clean calico, and she bore herself imperturbably. Nanny and Sammy kept close at her heels. Their eyes were large, and Nanny was full of nervous tremors. Still there was to them more pleasant excitement than anything else. An inborn confidence in their mother over their father asserted itself.

Sammy looked out of the harness-room window. "There he is," he announced, in an awed whisper. He and Nanny peeped around the casing. Mrs. Penn kept on about her work. The children watched Adoniram leave the new horse standing in the drive while he went to the house-door. It was fastened. Then he went around to the shed.

That door was seldom locked, even when the family was away. The thought how her father would be confronted by the cow flashed upon Nanny. There was a hysterical sob in her throat. Adoniram emerged from the shed and stood looking about in a dazed fashion. His lips moved; he was saying something, but they could not hear what it was. The hired man was peeping around a corner of the old barn, but nobody saw him.

Adoniram took the new horse by the bridle and led him across the yard to the new barn. Nanny and Sammy slunk close to their mother. The barn doors rolled back, and there stood Adoniram, with the long mild face of the great Canadian farm horse looking over his shoulder.

Nanny kept behind her mother, but Sammy stepped suddenly forward, and stood in front of her.

Adoniram stared at the group. "What on airth you all down here for?" said he. "What's the matter over to the house?"

"We've come here to live, Father," said Sammy. His shrill voice quavered out bravely.

"What"—Adoniram sniffed—"what is it smells like cookin'?" said he. He stepped forward and looked in at the open door of the harness room. Then he turned to his wife. His old bristling face was pale and frightened. "What on airth does this mean, Mother?" he gasped.

"You come in here, Father," said Sarah. She led the way into the harness room and shut the door. "Now, Father," said she, "you needn't be scared. I ain't crazy. There ain't nothin' to be upset over. But we've come here to live, an' we're goin' to live here. We've got jes as good a right here as new horses an' cows. The house wa'n't fit for us to live in any longer, an' I made up my mind I wa'n't goin' to stay there. I've done my duty by you forty year, an' I'm goin' to do it now; but I'm goin' to live here. You've got to put in some windows and partitions; an' you'll have to buy some furniture."

"Why, Mother!" the old man gasped.

"You'd better take your coat off an' get washed—there's the wash basin—an' then we'll have supper."

"Why, Mother!"

Sammy went past the window, leading the new horse to the old barn. The old man saw him, and shook his head speechlessly. He tried to take off his coat, but his arms seemed to lack the power. His wife helped him. She poured some water into the tin basin, and put in a piece of soap. She got the comb and brush, and smoothed his thin gray hair after he had washed. Then she put the beans, hot bread, and tea on the table. Sammy came in, and the family drew up. Adoniram sat looking dazedly at his plate, and they waited.

"Ain't you goin' to ask a blessin', Father?" said Sarah.

And the old man bent his head and mumbled.

All through the meal he stopped eating at intervals, and stared furtively at his wife; but he ate well. The home food tasted good to him, and his old frame was too sturdily healthy to be affected by his mind. But after supper he went out, and sat down on the step of the smaller door at the right of the barn, through which he had meant his Jerseys to pass in stately file, but which Sarah designed for her front house door, and he leaned his head on his hands.

After the supper dishes were cleared away and the milk pans washed, Sarah went out to him. The twilight was deepening. There was a clear green glow in the sky. Before them stretched the smooth level of field; in the distance was a cluster of haystacks like the huts of a village; the air was very cool and calm and sweet. The landscape might have been an ideal one of peace.

Sarah bent over and touched her husband on one of his thin, sinewy shoulders. "Father!"

The old man's shoulders heaved; he was weeping.

"Why, don't do so, Father," said Sarah.

"I'll—put up the—partitions, an'—everything you—want, Mother."

Sarah put her apron up to her face; she was overcome by her own triumph.

Adoniram was like a fortress whose walls had no active resistance, and went down the instant the right besieging tools were used. "Why, Mother," he said, hoarsely, "I hadn't no idee you was so set on't as all this comes to."

ONE GOOD TIME

Richard Stone was nearly seventy-five years old when he died; his wife was over sixty, and his daughter Narcissa past middle age. Narcissa Stone had been very pretty, and would have been pretty still had it not been for those lines, as distinctly garrulous of discontent and worry as any words of mouth, which come so easily in the face of a nervous, delicate-skinned woman. They were around Narcissa's blue eyes, her firmly closed lips, her thin nose; a frown like a crying repetition of some old anxiety and indecision was on her forehead; and she had turned her long neck so much to look over her shoulder for new troubles on her track that the lines of fearful expectation had settled there. Narcissa had yet her beautiful thick hair, which the people in the village had never quite liked because it was red; her cheeks were still pink, and she stooped only a little from her slender height when she walked. Some people said that Narcissa Stone would be quite good-looking now if she had a decent dress and bonnet. Neither she nor her mother had any clothes which were not deemed shabby, even by the humbly attired women in the little mountain village. "Mis' Richard Stone, she ain't had a new silk dress since Narcissa was born," they said; "and as for Narcissa, she ain't never had anything that looked fit to wear to meeting."

When Richard Stone died, people wondered if his widow and Narcissa would not have something new. Mrs. Nathan Wheat, who was a third cousin to Richard Stone, went, the day before the funeral, a half mile down the brook road to see Hannah Turbin, the dressmaker. The road was little traveled; she walked through an undergrowth of late autumn flowers, and when she reached the Turbins' house her black Thibet gown was gold-powdered

Published in *The Love of Parson Lord and Other Stories*. New York: Harper and Brothers, 1900.

and white-flecked to the knees with pollen and winged seeds of passed flowers.

Hannah Turbin's arm, brown and wrinkled like a monkey's, in its woolen sleeve, described arcs of jerky energy past the window, and never ceased when Mrs. Wheat came up the path and entered the house. Hannah herself scarcely raised her seamy brown face from her work.

"Good afternoon," said Mrs. Wheat.

Hannah nodded. "Good afternoon," she responded then, as if words were an after-thought.

Mrs. Wheat shook her black skirts vigorously. "I'm all over dust from them yaller weeds," said she. "Well, I don't care about this old Thibet." She pulled a rocking-chair forward and seated herself. "Warm for this time of year," said she.

Hannah drew her thread through her work. "Yes, 'tis," she returned, with a certain pucker of scorn, as if the utter foolishness of allusions to obvious conditions of nature struck her. Hannah Turbin was not a favorite in the village, but she was credited with having much common sense, and people held her in somewhat distant respect.

"Guess it's Injun summer," remarked Mrs. Wheat.

Hannah Turbin said nothing at all to that. Mrs. Wheat cast furtive glances around the room as she swayed in her rocking-chair. Everything was very tidy and there were few indications of its owner's calling. A number of fashion papers were neatly piled on a bureau in the corner, and some nicely folded breadths of silk lay beside them. There was not a scrap or shred of cloth upon the floor; not a thread, even. Hannah was basting a brown silk basque. Mrs. Wheat could see nowhere the slightest evidence of what she had come to ascertain, so was finally driven to inquiry, still, however, by devious windings.

"Seems sad about Richard," she said.

"Yes," returned Hannah, with a sudden contraction of her brown face, which seemed to flash a light over a recollection in Mrs. Wheat's mind. She remembered that there was a time, years ago, when Richard Stone had paid some attention to Hannah Turbin, and people had thought he might marry her instead of Jane Basset. However, it had happened so long ago that she did not really believe that Hannah dwelt upon it, and it faded immediately from her own mind.

"Well," said she, with a sigh, "it is a happy release, after all; he's been such a sufferer so long. It's better for him, and it's better for Jane and Narcissa. He's left 'em comfortable; they've got the farm, and his life's insured, you know. Besides, I suppose Narcissa'll marry William Crane now. Most likely they'll rent the farm, and Jane will go and live with Narcissa when she's married. I want to know—"

Hannah Turbin sewed.

"I was wondering," continued Mrs. Wheat, "if Jane and Narcissa wasn't going to have some new black dresses for the funeral. They ain't got a thing that's fit to wear, I know. I don't suppose they've got much money on hand now except what little Richard saved up for his funeral expenses. I know he had a little for that because he told me so, but the life insurance is coming in, and anybody would trust them. There's a nice piece of black cashmere down to the store, a dollar a yard. I didn't know but they'd get dresses off it; but Jane she never tells me anything—anybody'd think she might, seeing as I was poor Richard's cousin; and as for Narcissa, she's as close as her mother."

Hannah Turbin sewed.

"Ain't Jane and Narcissa said anything to you about making them any new black dresses to wear to the funeral?" asked Mrs. Wheat, with desperate directness.

"No, they ain't," replied Hannah Turbin.

"Well, then, all I've got to say is they'd ought to be ashamed of themselves. There they've got fourteen if not fifteen hundred dollars coming in from poor Richard's insurance money, and they ain't even going to get decent clothes to wear to his funeral out of it. They ain't made any plans for new bonnets, I know. It ain't showing proper respect to the poor man. Don't you say so?"

"I suppose folks are their own best judges," said Hannah Turbin, in her conclusive, half-surly fashion, which intimidated most of their neighbors. Mrs. Wheat did not stay much longer. When she went home through the ghostly weeds and grasses of the country road she was almost as indignant with Hannah Turbin as with Jane Stone and Narcissa. "Never saw anybody so close in my life," said she to herself. "Needn't talk if she don't want to. Dun'no' as thar's any harm in my wanting to know if my own third cousin is going to have mourning wore for him."

Mrs. Wheat, when she reached home, got a black shawl which had belonged to her mother out of the chest, where it had lain in camphor, and hung it on the clothesline to air. She also removed a spray of bright velvet flowers from her bonnet, and sewed in its place a black ostrich feather. She found an old crêpe veil, too, and steamed it into stiffness. "I'm going to go to that funeral looking decent, if his own wife and daughter ain't," she told her husband.

"If I wa'n't along, folks would take you for the widder," said Nathan Wheat with a chuckle. Nathan Wheat was rather inclined to be facetious with his wife.

However, Mrs. Wheat was not the only person who attended poor Richard Stone's funeral in suitable attire. Hannah Turbin was black from head to foot; the material, it is true, was not of the conventional mourning kind, but the color was. She wore a black silk gown, a black ladies'-cloth mantle, a black velvet bonnet trimmed with black flowers, and a black lace veil.

"Hannah Turbin looked as if she was dressed in second mourning," Mrs. Wheat said to her husband after the funeral. "I should have thought she'd most have worn some color, seeing as some folks might remember she was disappointed about Richard Stone; but, anyway, it was better than to go looking the way Jane and Narcissa did. There was Jane in that old brown dress, and Narcissa in her green, with a blue flower in her bonnet. I think it was dreadful, and poor Richard leaving them all that money through his dying, too."

In truth, all the village was scandalized at the strange attire of the widow and daughter of Richard Stone at his funeral, except William Crane. He could not have told what Mrs. Stone wore, through scarcely admitting her in any guise into his inmost consciousness, and as for Narcissa, he admitted her so fully that he could not see her robes at all in such a dazzlement of vision.

"William Crane never took his eyes off Narcissa Stone all through the funeral; shouldn't be surprised if he married her in a month or six weeks," people said.

William Crane took Jane and Narcissa to the grave in his covered wagon, keeping his old white horse at a decorous jog behind the hearse in the little funeral procession, and people noted that. They wondered if he would go over to the Stones' that evening, and watched, but he did not. He left the mother and daughter to their closer communion of grief that night, but the next the neighbors saw him in his best suit going down the road before dark. "Must have done up his chores early to get started soon as this," they said.

William Crane was about Narcissa's age but he looked older. His gait was shuffling, his hair scanty and gray, and, moreover, he had that expression of patience which comes only from long abiding, both of body and of soul. He went through the south yard to the side door of the house, stepping between the rocks. The yard abounded in mossy slopes of half-sunken rocks, as did the entire farm. Folks often remarked of Richard Stone's place, as well as himself, "Stone by name, and stone by nature." Underneath nearly all his fields, cropping plentifully to the surface, were rock ledges. The grass could be mown only by hand. As for this south yard, it required skilful maneuvering to drive a team through it. When William Crane knocked that evening, Narcissa opened the door. "Oh, it's you!" she said. "How do you do?"

"How do you do, Narcissa?" William responded, and walked in. He could have kissed his old love in the gloom of the little entry, but he did not think of that. He looked at her anxiously with his soft, patient eyes. "How are you gettin' on?" he asked.

"Well as can be expected," replied Narcissa.

"How's your mother?"

"She's as well as can be expected."

William followed Narcissa, who led the way, not into the parlor as he had hoped, but into the kitchen. The kitchen's great interior of smoky gloom was very familiar to him, but tonight it looked strange. For one thing, the armchair to which Richard Stone had been bound with his rheumatism for the last fifteen years was vacant, and pushed away into a corner. William looked at it, and it seemed to him that he must see the crooked, stern old figure in it, and hear again the peremptory tap of the stick which he kept always at his side to summon assistance. After his first involuntary glance at the dead man's chair, William saw his widow coming forward out of her bedroom with a great quilt over her arm.

"Good evenin', William," she said, with faint melancholy, then lapsed into feeble weeping.

"Now, Mother, you said you wouldn't; you know it don't do any good, and you'll be sick," Narcissa cried out, impatiently.

"I know it, Narcissa, but I can't help it, I can't. I'm dreadful upset! Oh, William, I'm dreadful upset! It ain't his death alone—it's——"

"Mother, I'd rather tell him myself," interrupted Narcissa. She took the quilt from her mother, and drew the rocking chair toward her. "Do sit down and keep calm, Mother," said she.

But it was not easy for the older woman, in her bewilderment of grief and change, to keep calm.

"Oh, William, do you know what we're goin' to do?" she wailed, yet seating herself obediently in the rocking chair. "We're goin' to New York. Narcissa says so. We're goin' to take the insurance money, when we get it, an' we're goin' to New York. I tell her we hadn't ought to, but she won't listen to it! There's the trunk. Look at there, William! She dragged it down from the garrret this forenoon. Look at there, William!"

William's startled eyes followed the direction of Mrs. Stone's wavering index finger, and saw a great ancient trunk lined with blue-and-white wall paper, standing open against the opposite wall.

"She dragged it down from the garret this forenoon," continued Mrs. Stone, in the same tone of unfaltering tragedy, while Narcissa, her delicate lips pursed tightly, folded up the bed quilt which her mother had brought. "It bumped so hard on those garret stairs I thought she'd break it, or fall herself, but she wouldn't let me help her. Then she cleaned it, an' made some paste, an' lined it with some of the parlor paper. There ain't any key to it—I never remember none. The trunk was in this house when I come here. Richard had it when he went West before we were married. Narcissa she says she is goin' to tie it up with the clothesline. William, can't you talk to her? Seems to me I can't go to New York, nohow."

William turned then to Narcissa, who was laying the folded bed quilt in the trunk. He looked pale and bewildered, and his voice trembled when he spoke. "This ain't true, is it, Narcissa?" he said.

"Yes, it is," she replied, shortly, still bending over the trunk.

"We ain't goin' for a month," interposed her mother again; "we can't get the insurance money before then, Lawyer Maxham says; but she says she's goin' to have the trunk standin' there, an' put things in when she thinks of it, so she won't forgit nothin'. She says we'd better take one bed quilt with us, in case they don't have 'nough clothes on the bed. We've got to stay to a hotel. Oh, William, can't you say anything to stop her?"

"This ain't true, Narcissa?" William repeated, helplessly.

Narcissa raised herself and faced him. Her cheeks were red, her blue eyes glowing, her hair tossing over her temples in loose waves. She looked as she had when he first courted her. "Yes, it is, William Crane," she cried. "Yes, it is."

William looked at her so strangely and piteously that she softened a little. "I've got my reasons," said she. "Maybe I owe it to you to tell them. I suppose you were expecting something different." She hesitated a minute, looking at her mother, who cried out again:

"Oh, William, say somethin' to stop her! Can't you say somethin' to stop her?"

Then Narcissa motioned to him resolutely. "Come into the parlor, William," said she, and he followed her out across the entry. The parlor was chilly; the chairs stood as they had done at the funeral, primly against the walls glimmering faintly in the dusk with blue and white paper like the trunk lining. Narcissa stood before William and talked with feverish haste. "I'm going," said she—"I'm going to take that money and go with Mother to New York, and you mustn't try to stop me, William. I know what you've been expecting. I know, now Father's gone, you think there ain't anything to hinder our getting married; you think we'll rent this house, and Mother and me will settle down in yours for the rest of our lives. I know you ain't counting on that insurance money; it ain't like you."

"The Lord knows it ain't, Narcissa," William broke out with pathetic pride.

"I know that as well as you do. You thought we'd put it in the bank for a rainy day, in case Mother got feeble, or anything, and that is all you did think. Maybe I'd ought to. I s'pose I had, but I ain't going to. I ain't never done anything my whole life that I thought I ought not to do, but now I'm going to. I'm going to if it's wicked. I've made up my mind. I ain't never had one good time in my whole life, and now I'm going to even if I have to suffer for it afterward.

"I ain't never had anything like other women. I've never had any clothes nor gone anywhere. I've just stayed at home here and drudged. I've done a man's work on the farm. I've milked and made butter and cheese; I've waited on Father; I've got up early and gone to bed late. I've just drudged, drudged, ever since I can remember. I don't know anything about the world nor life. I don't know anything but my own old tracks, and—I'm going to get out of them for a while, whether or no."

"How long are you calculating to stay?"

"I don't know."

"I've been thinking," said William, "I'd have some new gilt paper on the sitting room at my house, and a new stove in the kitchen. I thought——"

"I know what you thought," interrupted Narcissa, still trembling and glowing with nervous fervor. "And you're real good, William. It ain't many men would have waited for me as you've done, when Father wouldn't let me get married as long as he lived. I know by good rights I hadn't ought to keep you waiting, but I'm going to, and it ain't because I don't think enough of you—it ain't that; I can't help it. If you give up having me at all, if you think you'd rather marry somebody else, I can't help it; I won't blame you——"

"Maybe you want me to, Narcissa," said William, with a sad dignity. "If you do, if you want to get rid of me, if that's it——"

Narcissa started. "That ain't it," said she. She hesitated, and added, with formal embarrassment—she had the usual reticence of a New England village woman about expressions of affection, and had never even told her lover in actual words that she loved him—"My feelings toward you are the same as they have always been, William."

It was almost dark in the parlor. They could see only each other's faces gleaming as with pale light. "It would be a blow to me if I thought they wa'n't, Narcissa," William returned, simply.

"They are."

William put his arm around her waist, and they stood

close together for a moment. He stroked back her tumbled red hair with clumsy tenderness. "You have had a hard time, Narcissa," he whispered, brokenly. "If you want to go, I ain't going to say anything against it. I ain't going to deny I'm kind of disappointed. I've been living alone so long, and I feel kind of sore' sometimes with waitin' but——"

"I shouldn't make you any kind of a wife if I married you now, without waiting," Narcissa said, in a voice at once stern and tender. She stood apart from him, and put up her hand with a sort of involuntary maiden primness to smooth her hair where his had stroked it awry. "If," she went on, "I had to settle down in your house, as I have done in Father's, and see the years stretching ahead like a long road without any turn, and nothing but the same old dog trot of washing and ironing and scrubbing and cooking and sewing and washing dishes till I drop into my grave, I should hate you, William Crane."

"I could fetch an' carry all the water for the washin', Narcissa, and I could wash the dishes," said William, with humble beseeching.

"It ain't that. I know you'd do all you could. It's— Oh, William! I've got to have a break; I've got to have one good time. I—like you, and—I liked Father; but love ain't enough sometimes when it ties anybody. Everybody has got their own feet and their own wanting to use 'em, and sometimes when love comes in the way of that, it ain't anything but a dead wall. Once we had a black heifer that would jump all the walls; we had to sell her. She always made me think of myself. I tell you, William, I've got to jump my wall, and I've got to have one good time."

William Crane nodded his gray head in patient acquiescence. His forehead was knitted helplessly; he could not in the least understand what his sweetheart meant; in her present mood she was in altogether a foreign language for him, but still the unintelligible sound of her was sweet as a song to his ears. This poor village lover had at least gained the crown of absolute faith through his weary years of waiting; the woman he loved was still a star, and her rays not yet resolved into human reachings and graspings.

"How long do you calculate to be gone, Narcissa?" he asked again.

"I don't know," she replied. "Fifteen hundred dollars is a good deal of money. I s'pose it'll take us quite a while to spend it, even if we ain't very saving."

"You ain't goin' to spend it all, Narcissa!" William gave a little dismayed gasp in spite of himself.

"Land, no! we couldn't, unless we stayed three years, an' I ain't calculating to be gone as long as that. I'm going to bring home what we don't want, and put it in the bank; but—I shouldn't be surprised if it took 'most a year to spend what I've laid out to."

" 'Most a year!"

"Yes; I've got to buy us both new clothes, for one thing. We ain't neither of us got anything fit to wear, and ain't had for years. We didn't go to the funeral lookin' decent, and I know folks talked. Mother felt bad about it, but I couldn't help it. I wa'n't goin' to lay out money foolish and get things here when I was going to New York and could have others the way they ought to be. I'm going to buy us some jewelry, too; I ain't never had a good breast-pin even; and as for Mother, Father never even bought her a ring when they were married. I ain't saying anything against him; it wa'n't the fashion so much in those days."

"I was calculatin'—" William stammered, blushing. "I always meant to, Narcissa."

"Yes, I know you have; but you mustn't lay out too much on it, and I don't care anything about a stone ring—just a plain gold one. There's another thing I'm going to have, too, an' that's a gold watch. I've wanted one all my life."

"Mebbe—" began William, painfully.

"No!" cried Narcissa, peremptorily. "I don't want you to buy me one. I ain't ever thought of it. I'm going to buy it myself. I'm going to buy Mother a real cashmere shawl, too, like the one that New York lady had that came to visit Lawyer Maxham's wife. I've got a list of things written down on paper. I guess I'll have to buy another trunk in New York to put them in."

"Well," said William, with a great sigh, "I guess I'd better be goin'. I hope you'll have as good a time as you're countin' on, Narcissa."

"It's the first good time I ever did count on, and I'd ought to," said Narcissa. "I'm going to take Mother to the theater, too. I don't know but it's wicked, but I'm going to." Narcissa fluttered out of the parlor and William shuffled after her. He would not go into the kitchen again.

"Well, good night," said Narcissa, and William also said good night, with another heavy sigh. "Look out for them rocks going out of the yard, an' don't tumble over 'em," she called after him.

"I'm used to 'em," he answered back, sadly, from the darkness.

Narcissa shut and bolted the door. "He don't like it; he feels real bad about it; but I can't help it—I'm going."

Through the next few weeks Narcissa Stone's face looked strange to those who had known her from childhood. While the features were the same, her soul informed them with a new purpose, which overlighted all the old ones of her life, and even the simple village folks saw the effect, though with no understanding. Soon the news that Narcissa and her mother were going to New York was abroad. On the morning they started, in the three-seated open wagon which served as stage to connect the little village with the railroad ten miles away, all the windows were set with furtively peering faces.

"There they go," the women told one another. "Narcissa an' her mother an' the trunk. Wonder if Narcissa's got that money put away safe? They're wearin' the same old clothes. S'pose we shan't know 'em when they get back. Heard they was goin' to stay a year. Guess old Mr. Stone would rise up in his grave if he knew it. Lizzy saw William Crane a-helpin' Narcissa h'ist the trunk out ready for the stage. I wouldn't stan' it if I was him. Ten chances to one Narcissa'll pick up somebody down to New York, with all that money. She's good-lookin', and she looks better since her father died."

Narcissa, riding out of her native village to those unknown fields in which her imagination had laid the scene of the one good time of her life, regarded nothing around her. She sat straight, her slender body resisting stiffly the jolt of the stage. She said not a word, but looked ahead with shining eyes. Her mother wept, a fold of her old shawl before her face. Now and then she lamented aloud, but softly, lest the driver hear. "Goin' away from the place where I was born an' married an' have lived ever since I knew anything, to stay a year. I can't stan' it, I can't."

"Hush, Mother! You'll have a real good time."

"No, I shan't, I shan't. Goin'—to stay a whole—year. I —can't, nohow."

"S'pose we shan't see you back in these parts for some time," the stage driver said, when he helped them out at the railroad station. He was an old man, and had known Narcissa since her childhood.

"Most likely not," she replied. Her mother's face was quite stiff with repressed emotion when the stage driver lifted her out. She did not want him to report in the village that she was crying when she started for New York. She had some pride in spite of her distress.

"Well, I'll be on the lookout for ye a year from today," said the stage driver, with a jocular twist of his face. There were no passengers for his village on the in-coming train, so he had to drive home alone through the melancholy autumn woods. The sky hung low with pale, freezing clouds; over everything was that strange hush which prevails before snow. The stage driver, holding the reins loosely over his tramping team, settled forward with elbows on his knees, and old brows bent with aimless brooding. Over and over again his brain worked the thought, like a peaceful cud of contemplation. "They're goin' to be gone a year. Narcissa Stone an' her mother are goin' to be gone a year afore I'll drive 'em home."

So little imagination had the routine of his life fostered that he speculated not, even upon the possible weather of that far-off day, or the chances of his living to see it. It was simply, "They're goin' to be gone a year afore I'll drive 'em home."

So fixed was his mind upon that one outcome of the situation that when Narcissa and her mother reappeared in less than one week—in six days—he could not for a moment bring his mind intelligently to bear upon it. The old stage driver may have grown something like his own horses through his long sojourn in their company, and his intelligence, like theirs, been given to only the halts and gaits of its first breaking.

For a second he had a bewildered feeling that time had flown fast, that a week was a year. Everybody in the village had said the travelers would not return for a year. He hoisted the ancient paper-lined trunk into his stage, then a fine new one, nailed and clamped with shining brass, then a number of packages, all the time with puzzled eyes askant upon Narcissa and her mother. He would scarcely have known them, as far as their dress was concerned. Mrs. Stone wore a fine black satin gown; her perturbed old face looked out of luxurious environments of fur and lace and rich black plumage. As for Narcissa, she was almost regal. The old stage driver backed and ducked awkwardly, as if she were a stranger, when she approached. Her flesh skirts flared imposingly and rustled with unseen silk; her slender shoulders were made shapely by the graceful spread of rich fur; her red hair shone under a hat fit for a princess, and there was about her a faint perfume of violets which made the stage driver gaze confusedly at the snowy ground under the trees when they had started on the homeward road. "Seems as if I smelt posies, but I know there ain't none hereabouts this time of year," he remarked, finally, in a tone of mild ingratiation, as if more to himself than to his passengers.

"It's some perfumery Narcissa's got on her pocket handkerchief that she bought in New York," said Mrs. Stone, with a sort of sad pride. She looked worn and bewildered, ready to weep at the sight of familiar things, and yet distinctly superior to all such weakness. As for Narcissa, she looked like a child thrilled with scared triumph at getting its own way, who rejoices even in the midst of correction at its own assertion of freedom.

"That so?" said the stage driver, admiringly. Then he added, doubtfully, bringing one white-browed eye to bear over his shoulder, "Didn't stay quite so long as you calculated on?"

"No, we didn't," replied Narcissa, calmly. She nudged her mother with a stealthy, firm elbow, and her mother understood well that she was to maintain silence.

"I ain't going to tell a living soul about it but William Crane; I owe it to him," Narcissa had said to her mother before they started on their homeward journey. "The other folks shan't know. They can guess and surmise all they want to, but they shan't know. I shan't tell; and William, he's as close-mouthed as a rock; and as for you, Mother, you always did know enough to hold your tongue when you made up your mind to it."

Mrs. Stone had compressed her mouth until it looked like her daughter's. She nodded. "Yes," said she; "I know some things that I ain't never told you, Narcissa."

The stage passed William Crane's house. He was shuffling around to the side door from the barn, with a milk pail in each hand, when they reached it.

"Stop a minute," Narcissa said to the driver. She beckoned to William, who stared, standing stockstill, holding his pails. Narcissa beckoned again imperatively. Then William set the pails down on the snowy ground and came to the fence. He looked over it, quite pale, and gaping.

"We've got home," said Narcissa.

William nodded; he could not speak.

"Come over by-and-by," said Narcissa.

William nodded.

"I'm ready to go now," Narcissa said to the stage driver. "That's all."

That evening, when William Crane reached his sweetheart's house, a bright light shone on the road from the parlor windows. Narcissa opened the door. He stared at her open-mouthed. She wore a gown the like of which he had never seen before—soft lengths of blue silk and lace trailed about her; blue ribbons fluttered.

"How do you do?" said she.

William nodded solemnly.

"Come in."

William followed her into the parlor, with a wary eye upon his feet, lest they trample her trailing draperies. Narcissa settled gracefully into the rocking chair; William sat opposite and looked at her. Narcissa was a little pale, still her face wore that look of insistent triumph.

"Home quicker'n you expected," William said, at length.

"Yes," said Narcissa. There was a wonderful twist on her red hair, and she wore a high shell comb. William's dazzled eyes noted something sparkling in the laces at her throat; she moved her hand, and something on that flashed like a point of white flame. William remembered vaguely how, often in the summertime when he had opened his house door in the sunny morning, the dewdrops on the grass had flashed in his eyes. He had never seen diamonds.

"What started you home so much sooner than you expected?" he asked, after a little.

"I spent—all the money—"

"All—that money."

"Yes."

"Fifteen hundred dollars in less'n a week?"

"I spent more'n that."

"More'n that?" William could scarcely bring out the words. He was very white.

"Yes," said Narcissa. She was paler than when he had entered, but she spoke quite decidedly. "I'm going to tell you all about it, William. I ain't going to make a long story of it. If after you've heard it you think you'd rather not marry me, I shan't blame you. I shan't have anything to say against it. I'm going to tell you just what I've been doing; then you can make up your mind.

"Today's Tuesday, and we went away last Thursday. We've been gone just six days. Mother an' me got to New York Thursday night, an' when we got out of the cars the men come round hollering this hotel an' that hotel. I picked out a man that looked as if he didn't drink and would drive straight, an' he took us to an elegant carriage, an' Mother an' me got in. Then we waited till he got the trunk an' put it up on the seat with him where he drove. Mother, she hollered to him not to let it fall off.

"We went to a beautiful hotel. There was a parlor with a red velvet carpet and red stuffed furniture, and a green sitting room and a blue one. The ceilin' had pictures on it. There was a handsome young gentleman downstairs at a counter in the room where we went first, and Mother asked him, before I could stop her, if the folks in the hotel was all honest. She'd been worrying all the way for fear somebody'd steal the money.

"The gentleman said—he was real polite—if we had any money or valuables, we had better leave them with him, and he would put them in the safe. So we did. Then a young man with brass buttons on his coat took us to the elevator and showed us our rooms. We had a parlor with a velvet carpet an' stuffed furniture and a gilt clock on the mantel shelf, two bedrooms, and a bathroom. There ain't anything in town equal to it. Lawyer Maxham ain't got anything to come up to it. The young man offered to untie the rope on the trunk, so I let him. He seemed real kind about it.

"Soon's the young man went I says to Mother, 'We ain't going down to get any tea tonight.'

" 'Why not?' says she.

" 'I ain't going down a step in this old dress,' says I, 'an' you ain't going in yours.'

"Mother didn't like it very well. She said she was faint

to her stomach, and wanted some tea, but I made her eat some gingerbread we'd brought from home, an' get along. The young man with the brass buttons come again after a while an' asked if there was anything we wanted, but I thanked him an' told him there wasn't.

"I would have asked him to bring up Mother some tea and a hot biscuit, but I didn't know but what it would put 'em out; it was after seven o'clock then. So we got along till morning.

"The next morning Mother an' me went out real early, an' went into a bakery an' bought some cookies. We ate 'em as we went down the street, just to stay our stomachs; then we went to buying. I'd taken some of the money in my purse, an' I got Mother an' me, first of all, two handsome black silk dresses, and we put 'em on as soon as we got back to the hotel, and went down to breakfast.

"You never see anythin' like the dining room, and the kinds of things to eat. We couldn't begin to eat 'em all. There were men standin' behind our chairs to wait on us all the time.

"Right after breakfast Mother an' me put our rooms to rights; then we went out again and bought things at the stores. Everybody was buying Christmas presents, an' the stores were all trimmed with evergreen—you never see anything like it. Mother an' me never had any Christmas presents, an' I told her we'd begin, an' buy 'em for each other. When the money I'd taken with us was gone, I sent things to the hotel for the gentleman at the counter to pay, the way he'd told me to. That day we bought our breastpins and this ring, an' Mother's and my gold watches, an'—I got one for you, too, William. Don't you say anything—it's your Christmas present. That afternoon we went to Central Park, an' that evenin' we went to the theater. The next day we went to the stores again, an' I bought mother a black satin dress, and me a green one. I got this I've got on, too. It's what they call a tea gown. I always wore it to tea in the hotel after I got it. I got a hat, too, an' Mother a bonnet; an' I got a fur cape, and Mother a cloak with fur on the neck an' all around it. That evening Mother an' me went to the opera; we sat in something they call a box. I wore my new green silk and breastpin, an' Mother wore her black satin. We both of us took our bonnets off. The music was splendid; but I wouldn't have young folks go to it much.

"The next day was Sunday. Mother an' me went to meeting in a splendid church, and wore our new black silks. They gave us seats way up in front, an' there was a real good sermon, though Mother thought it wa'n't very practical, an' folks got up an' sat down more'n we do. Mother an' me set still, for fear we'd get up an' down in the wrong place. That evening we went to a sacred concert. Everywhere we went we rode in a carriage. They invited us to at the hotel, an' I s'posed it was free, but it wa'n't, I found out afterward.

"The next day was Monday—that's yesterday. Mother an' me went out to the stores again. I bought a silk bed quilt, an' some handsome vases, an' some green-an-gilt teacups setting in a tray to match. I've got 'em home without breaking. We got some silk stockings, too, an' some shoes, an' some gold-bowed spectacles for Mother, an' two more silk dresses, an' Mother a real Cashmere shawl. Then we went to see some waxworks, and the pictures and curiosities in the Art Museum; then in the afternoon we went to ride again, and we were goin' to the theater in the evening; but the gentleman at the counter called out to me when I was going past an' said he wanted to speak to me a minute.

"Then I found out we'd spent all that fifteen hundred dollars, an' more, too. We owed 'em 'most ten dollars at the hotel; an' that wa'n't the worst of it—we didn't have enough money to take us home.

"Mother, she broke right down an' cried, an' said it was all we had in the world besides the farm, an' it was poor Father's insurance money, an' we couldn't get home, an' we'd have to go to prison.

"Folks come crowding round, an' I couldn't stop her. I don't know what I did do myself; I felt kind of dizzy, an' things looked dark. A lady come an' held a smelling bottle to my nose, an' the gentleman at the counter sent a man with brass buttons for some wine.

"After I felt better an' could talk steady they questioned me up pretty sharp, an' I told 'em the whole story— about Father an' his rheumatism, an' everything, just how I was situated, an' I must say they treated us like Christian folks, though, after all, I don't know as we were much beholden to 'em. We never begun to eat all there was on the list, an' we were real careful of the furniture; we didn't really get our money's worth after all was said. But they said the rest of our bill to them was no matter, an' they gave us our tickets to come home."

There was a pause. William looked at Narcissa in her blue gown as if she were a riddle whose answer was lost in his memory. His honest eyes were fairly pitiful from excess of questioning.

"Well," said Narcissa, "I've come back, an' I've spent all that money. I've been wasteful an' extravagant an'— There was a gentleman beautifully dressed who sat at our table, an' he talked real pleasant about the weather, an'— I got to thinking about him a little. Of course I didn't like him as well as you, William, for what comes first comes last with all our folks, but somehow he seemed to be kind of a part of the good time. I shan't never see him again, an' all there was betwixt us was his saying twice it was a pleasant day, an' once it was cold, an' me saying yes; but I'm going to tell you the whole. I've been an' wasted fifteen hundred dollars; I've let my thoughts wander from you; an' that ain't all. I've had a good time an' I can't say I ain't. I've had one good time, an'—I ain't sorry. You can—do just what you think best, William, an'—I won't blame you."

William Crane went over to the window. When he turned round and looked at Narcissa his eyes were full of tears and his wide mouth was trembling. "Do you think you can be contented to—stay on my side of the wall now, Narcissa?" he said, with a sweet and pathetic dignity.

Narcissa in her blue robes went over to him and put, for the first time of her own accord, an arm around his faithful neck. "I wouldn't go out again if the bars were down," said she.

OLD WOMAN MAGOUN

The hamlet of Barry's Ford is situated in a sort of high valley among the mountains. Below it the hills lie in moveless curves like a petrified ocean; above it they rise in greencresting waves which never break. It is *Barry's* Ford because one time the Barry family was the most important in the place; and *Ford* because just at the beginning of the hamlet the little turbulent Barry River is fordable. There is, however, now a rude bridge across the river.

Old Woman Magoun was largely instrumental in bringing the bridge to pass. She haunted the miserable little grocery, wherein whisky and hands of tobacco were the most salient features of the stock in trade, and she talked much. She would elbow herself into the midst of a knot of idlers and talk.

"That bridge ought to be built this very summer," said Old Woman Magoun. She spread her strong arms like wings, and sent the loafers, half laughing, half angry, flying in every direction. "If I were a *man*," said she, "I'd go out this very minute and lay the fust log. If I were a passel of lazy men layin' round, I'd start up for once in my life, I would." The men cowered visibly—all except Nelson Barry; he swore under his breath and strode over to the counter.

Old Woman Magoun looked after him majestically. "You can cuss all you want to, Nelson Barry," said she; "I ain't afraid of you. I don't expect you to lay ary log of the bridge, but I'm goin' to have it built this very summer." She did. The weakness of the masculine element in Barry's Ford was laid low before such strenuous feminine assertion.

Old Woman Magoun and some other women planned a treat—two sucking pigs, and pies, and sweet cake—for a reward after the bridge should be finished. They even

Published in *The Winning Lady and Others*. New York: Harper and Brothers, 1909.

viewed leniently the increased consumption of ardent spirits.

"It seems queer to me," Old Woman Magoun said to Sally Jinks, "that men can't do nothin' without havin' to drink and chew to keep their sperits up. Lord! I've worked all my life and never done nuther."

"Men is different," said Sally Jinks.

"Yes, they be," assented Old Woman Magoun, with open contempt.

The two women sat on a bench in front of Old Woman Magoun's house, and little Lily Barry, her granddaughter, sat holding her doll on a small mossy stone near by. From where they sat they could see the men at work on the new bridge. It was the last day of the work.

Lily clasped her doll—a poor old rag thing—close to her childish bosom, like a little mother, and her face, round which curled her long yellow hair, was fixed upon the men at work. Little Lily had never been allowed to run with the other children at Barry's Ford. Her grandmother had taught her everything she knew—which was not much, but tending at least to a certain measure of spiritual growth—for she, as it were, poured the goodness of her own soul into this little receptive vase of another. Lily was firmly grounded in her knowledge that it was wrong to lie or steal or disobey her grandmother. She had also learned that one should be very industrious. It was seldom that Lily sat idly holding her doll baby, but this was a holiday because of the bridge. She looked only a child, although she was nearly fourteen; her mother had been married at sixteen. That is, Old Woman Magoun said that her daughter, Lily's mother, had married at sixteen; there had been rumors, but no one had dared openly gainsay the old woman. She said that her daughter had married Nelson Barry and he had deserted her. She had lived in her mother's house, and Lily had been born there, and she had died when the baby was only a week old.

Lily's father, Nelson Barry, was the fairly dangerous degenerate of a good old family. Nelson's father before him had been bad. He was now the last of the family, with the exception of a sister of feeble intellect, with whom he lived in the old Barry house. He was a middle-aged man, still handsome. The shiftless population of Barry's Ford looked up to him as to an evil deity. They wondered how Old Woman Magoun dared brave him as she did. But Old

Woman Magoun had within her a mighty sense of reliance upon herself as being on the right track in the midst of a maze of evil, which gave her courage. Nelson Barry had manifested no interest whatever in his daughter. Lily seldom saw her father. She did not often go to the store which was his favorite haunt. Her grandmother took care that she should not do so.

However, that afternoon she departed from her usual custom and sent Lily to the store.

She came in from the kitchen, whither she had been to baste the roasting pig. "There's no use talkin'," said she, "I've got to have some more salt. I've jest used the very last I had to dredge over that pig. I've got to go to the store."

Sally Jinks looked at Lily. "Why don't you send her?" she asked.

Old Woman Magoun gazed irresolutely at the girl. She was herself very tired. It did not seem to her that she could drag herself up the dusty hill to the store. She glanced with covert resentment at Sally Jinks. She thought that she might offer to go. But Sally Jinks said again, "Why don't you let her go?" and looked with a languid eye at Lily holding her doll on the stone.

Lily was watching the men at work on the bridge, with her childish delight in a spectacle of any kind, when her grandmother addressed her.

"Guess I'll let you go down to the store an' git some salt, Lily," said she.

The girl turned uncomprehending eyes upon her grandmother at the sound of her voice. She had been filled with one of the innocent reveries of childhood. Lily had in her the making of an artist or a poet. Her prolonged childhood went to prove it, and also her retrospective eyes, as clear and blue as blue light itself, which seemed to see past all that she looked upon. She had not come of the old Barry family for nothing. The best of the strain was in her, along with the splendid stanchness in humble lines which she had acquired from her grandmother.

"Put on your hat," said Old Woman Magoun; "the sun is hot and you might git a headache." She called the girl to her, and put back the shower of fair curls under the rubber band which confined the hat. She gave Lily some money, and watched her knot it into a corner of her little cotton handkerchief. "Be careful you don't lose it," said she, "and don't stop to talk to anybody, for I am in a hurry for that salt. Of course, if anybody speaks to you answer them polite, and then come right along."

Lily started, her pocket handkerchief weighted with the small silver dangling from one hand, and her rag doll carried over her shoulder like a baby. The absurd travesty of a face peeped forth from Lily's yellow curls. Sally Jinks looked after her with a sniff.

"She ain't goin' to carry that rag doll to the store?" said she.

"She likes to," replied Old Woman Magoun, in a half-shamed yet defiantly extenuating voice.

"Some girls at her age is thinkin' about beaux instead of rag dolls," said Sally Jinks.

The grandmother bristled, "Lily ain't big nor old for her age," said she. "I ain't in any hurry to have her git married. She ain't none too strong."

"She's got a good color," said Sally Jinks. She was crocheting white cotton lace, making her thick fingers fly. She really knew how to do scarcely anything except to crochet that coarse lace; somehow her heavy brain or her fingers had mastered that.

"I know she's got a beautiful color," replied Old Woman Magoun, with an odd mixture of pride and anxiety, "but it comes an' goes."

"I've heard that was a bad sign," remarked Sally Jinks, loosening some thread from her spool.

"Yes, it is," said the grandmother. "She's nothin' but a baby, though she's quicker than most to learn."

Lily Barry went on her way to the store. She was clad in a scanty short frock of blue cotton; her hat was tipped back, forming an oval frame for her innocent face. She was very small, and walked like a child, with the clap-clap of little feet of babyhood. She might have been considered, from her looks, under ten.

Presently she heard footsteps behind her; she turned around a little timidly to see who was coming. When she saw a handsome well-dressed man, she felt reassured. The man came alongside and glanced down carelessly at first; then his look deepened. He smiled, and Lily saw he was very handsome indeed, and that his smile was not only reassuring but wonderfully sweet and compelling.

"Well, little one," said the man, "where are you bound, you and your dolly?"

"I am going to the store to buy some salt for Grandma," replied Lily, in her sweet treble. She looked up in the man's face, and he fairly started at the revelation of its innocent beauty. He regulated his pace by hers, and the two went on together. The man did not speak again at once. Lily kept glancing timidly up at him, and every time that she did so the man smiled and her confidence increased. Presently when the man's hand grasped her little childish one hanging by her side, she felt a complete trust in him. Then she smiled up at him. She felt glad that this nice man had come along, for just here the road was lonely.

After a while the man spoke. "What is your name, little one?" he asked, caressingly.

"Lily Barry."

The man started. "What is your father's name?"

"Nelson Barry," replied Lily.

The man whistled. "Is your mother dead?"

"Yes, sir."

"How old are you, my dear?"

"Fourteen," replied Lily.

The man looked at her with surprise. "As old as that?"

Lily suddenly shrank from the man. She could not have told why. She pulled her little hand from his, and he let it go with no remonstrance. She clasped both her arms around her rag doll, in order that her hand should not be free for him to grasp again.

She walked a little farther away from the man, and he looked amused.

"You still play with your doll?" he said, in a soft voice.

"Yes, sir," replied Lily. She quickened her pace and reached the store.

When Lily entered the store, Hiram Gates, the owner, was behind the counter. The only man besides in the store was Nelson Barry. He sat tipping his chair back against the wall; he was half asleep, and his handsome face was bristling with a beard of several days' growth and darkly flushed. He opened his eyes when Lily entered, the strange man following. He brought his chair down on all fours and he looked at the man—not noticing Lily at all—with a look compounded of defiance and uneasiness.

"Hullo, Jim!" he said.

"Hullo, old man!" returned the stranger.

Lily went over to the counter and asked for the salt, in her pretty little voice. When she had paid for it and was crossing the store, Nelson Barry was on his feet.

"Well, how are you, Lily? It is Lily, isn't it?" he said.

"Yes, sir," replied Lily, faintly.

Her father bent down and, for the first time in her life, kissed her, and the whisky odor of his breath came into her face.

Lily involuntarily started, and shrank away from him. Then she rubbed her mouth violently with her little cotton handkerchief, which she held gathered up with the rag doll.

"Damn it all! I believe she is afraid of me," said Nelson Barry, in a thick voice.

"Looks a little like it," said the other man, laughing.

"It's that damned old woman," said Nelson Barry. Then he smiled again at Lily. "I didn't know what a pretty little daughter I was blessed with," said he, and he softly stroked Lily's pink cheek under her hat.

Now Lily did not shrink from him. Heredity instincts and nature itself were asserting themselves in the child's innocent, receptive breast.

Nelson Barry looked curiously at Lily. "How old are you, anyway, child?" he asked.

"I'll be fourteen in September," replied Lily.

"But you still play with your doll?" said Barry, laughing kindly down at her.

Lily hugged her doll more tightly, in spite of her father's kind voice. "Yes, sir," she replied.

Nelson glanced across at some glass jars filled with sticks of candy. "See here, little Lily, do you like candy?" said he.

"Yes, sir."

"Wait a minute."

Lily waited while her father went over to the counter. Soon he returned with a package of the candy.

"I don't see how you are going to carry so much," he said, smiling. "Suppose you throw away your doll?"

Lily gazed at her father and hugged the doll tightly, and there was all at once in the child's expression something mature. It became the reproach of a woman. Nelson's face sobered.

"Oh, it's all right, Lily," he said; "keep your doll.

Here, I guess you can carry this candy under your arm."

Lily could not resist the candy. She obeyed Nelson's instructions for carrying it, and left the store laden. The two men also left, and walked in the opposite direction, talking busily.

When Lily reached home, her grandmother, who was watching for her, spied at once the package of candy.

"What's that?" she asked, sharply.

"My father gave it to me," answered Lily, in a faltering voice. Sally regarded her with something like alertness.

"Your father?"

"Yes, ma'am."

"Where did you see him?"

"In the store."

"He gave you this candy?"

"Yes, ma'am."

"What did he say?"

"He asked me how old I was, and—"

"And what?"

"I don't know," replied Lily; and it really seemed to her that she did not know, she was so frightened and bewildered by it all, and, more than anything else, by her grandmother's face as she questioned her.

Old Woman Magoun's face was that of one upon whom a long-anticipated blow had fallen. Sally Jinks gazed at her with a sort of stupid alarm.

Old Woman Magoun continued to gaze at her grandchild with that look of terrible solicitude, as if she saw the girl in the clutch of a tiger. "You can't remember what else he said?" she asked, fiercely, and the child began to whimper softly.

"No, ma'am," she sobbed. "I—don't know, and—"

"And what? Answer me."

"There was another man there. A real handsome man."

"Did he speak to you?" asked Old Woman Magoun.

"Yes, ma'am; he walked along with me a piece," confessed Lily, with a sob of terror and bewilderment.

"What did *he* say to you?" asked Old Woman Magoun, with a sort of despair.

Lily told, in her little, faltering, frightened voice,

all of the conversation which she could recall. It sounded harmless enough, but the look of the realization of a long-expected blow never left her grandmother's face.

The sun was getting low and the bridge was nearing completion. Soon the workmen would be crowding into the cabin for their promised supper. There became visible in the distance, far up the road, the heavily plodding figure of another woman who had agreed to come and help. Old Woman Magoun turned again to Lily.

"You go right upstairs to your own chamber now," said she.

"Good land! ain't you goin' to let that poor child stay up and see the fun?" said Sally Jinks.

"You jest mind your own business," said Old Woman Magoun, forcibly, and Sally Jinks shrank. "You go right up there now, Lily," said the grandmother, in a softer tone, "and Grandma will bring you up a nice plate of supper."

"When be you goin' to let that girl grow up?" asked Sally Jinks when Lily had disappeared.

"She'll grow up in the Lord's good time," replied Old Woman Magoun, and there was in her voice something both sad and threatening. Sally Jinks again shrank a little.

Soon the workmen came flocking noisily into the house. Old Woman Magoun and her two helpers served the bountiful supper. Most of the men had drunk as much as, and more than, was good for them, and Old Woman Magoun had stipulated that there was to be no drinking of anything except coffee during supper.

"I'll git you as good a meal as I know how," she said, "but if I see ary one of you drinkin' a drop, I'll run you all out. If you want anything to drink, you can go up to the store afterward. That's the place for you to go to, if you've got to make hogs of yourselves. I ain't goin' to have no hogs in my house."

Old Woman Magoun was implicitly obeyed. She had a curious authority over most people when she chose to exercise it. When the supper was in full swing, she quietly stole upstairs and carried some food to Lily. She found the girl, with the rag doll in her arms, crouching by the window in her little rocking-chair—a relic of her infancy, which she still used.

"What a noise they are makin', Grandma!" she said, in a terrified whisper, as her grandmother placed the plate before her on a chair.

"They've 'most all of 'em been drinkin'. They air a passel of hogs," replied the old woman.

"Is the man that was with—with my father down there?" asked Lily, in a timid fashion. Then she fairly cowered before the look in her grandmother's eyes.

"No, he ain't, and what's more, he never will be down there if I can help it," said Old Woman Magoun, in a fierce whisper. "I know who he is. They can't cheat me. He's one of them Willises—that family the Barrys married into. They're worse than the Barrys, ef they *have* got money. Eat your supper, and put him out of your mind, child."

It was after Lily was asleep, when Old Woman Magoun was alone, clearing away her supper dishes, that Lily's father came. The door was closed, and he knocked, and the old woman knew at once who was there. The sound of that knock meant as much to her as the whir of a bomb to the defender of a fortress. She opened the door, and Nelson Barry stood there.

"Good evening, Mrs. Magoun," he said.

Old Woman Magoun stood before him, filling up the doorway with her firm bulk.

"Good evening, Mrs. Magoun," said Nelson Barry again. "I ain't got no time to waste," replied the old woman, harshly. "I've got my supper dishes to clean up after them men."

She stood there and looked at him as she might have looked at a rebellious animal which she was trying to tame. The man laughed.

"It's no use," said he. "You know me of old. No human being can turn me from my way when I am once started in it. You may as well let me come in."

Old Woman Magoun entered the house, and Barry followed her.

Barry began without any preface. "Where is the child?" asked he.

"Upstairs. She has gone to bed."

"She goes to bed early."

"Children ought to," returned the old woman, polishing a plate.

Barry laughed. "You are keeping her a child a long

while," he remarked, in a soft voice which had a sting in it.

"She *is* a child," returned the old woman, defiantly.

"Her mother was only three years older when Lily was born."

The old woman made a sudden motion toward the man which seemed fairly menacing. Then she turned again to her dish washing.

"I want her," said Barry.

"You can't have her," replied the old woman, in a still stern voice.

"I don't see how you can help yourself. You have always acknowledged that she was my child."

The old woman continued her task, but her strong back heaved. Barry regarded her with an entirely pitiless expression.

"I am going to have the girl, that is the long and short of it," he said, "and it is for her best good, too. You are a fool, or you would see it."

"Her best good?" muttered the old woman.

"Yes, her best good. What are you going to do with her, anyway? The girl is a beauty, and almost a woman grown, although you try to make out that she is a baby. You can't live forever."

"The Lord will take care of her," replied the old woman, and again she turned and faced him, and her expression was that of a prophetess.

"Very well, let Him," said Barry, easily. "All the same I'm going to have her, and I tell you it is for her best good. Jim Willis saw her this afternoon, and—"

Old Woman Magoun looked at him. "Jim Willis!" she fairly shrieked.

"Well, what of it?"

"One of them Willises!" repeated the old woman, and this time her voice was thick. It seemed almost as if she were stricken with paralysis. She did not enunciate clearly. The man shrank a little. "Now what is the need of your making such a fuss?" he said. "I will take her, and Isabel will look out for her."

"Your half-witted sister?" said Old Woman Magoun.

"Yes, my half-witted sister. She knows more than you think."

"More wickedness."

"Perhaps. Well, a knowledge of evil is a useful thing.

How are you going to avoid evil if you don't know what it is like? My sister and I will take care of my daughter."

The old woman continued to look at the man, but his eyes never fell. Suddenly her gaze grew inconceivably keen. It was as if she saw through all externals.

"I know what it is!" she cried. "You have been playing cards and you lost, and this is the way you will pay him."

Then the man's face reddened, and he swore under his breath.

"Oh, my God!" said the old woman; and she really spoke with her eyes aloft as if addressing something outside of them both. Then she turned again to her dishwashing.

The man cast a dogged look at her back. "Well, there is no use talking. I have made up my mind," said he, "and you know me and what that means. I am going to have the girl."

"When?" said the old woman, without turning around.

"Well, I am willing to give you a week. Put her clothes in good order before she comes."

The old woman made no reply. She continued washing dishes. She even handled them so carefully they did not rattle.

"You understand," said Barry. "Have her ready a week from today."

"Yes," said Old Woman Magoun, "I understand."

Nelson Barry, going up the mountain road, reflected that Old Woman Magoun had a strong character, that she understood much better than her sex in general the futility of withstanding the inevitable.

"Well," he said to Jim Willis when he reached home, "the old woman did not make such a fuss as I expected."

"Are you going to have the girl?"

"Yes; a week from today. Look here, Jim; you've got to stick to your promise."

"All right," said Willis. "Go you one better."

The two were playing at cards in the old parlor, once magnificent, now squalid, of the Barry house. Isabel, the half-witted sister, entered, bringing some glasses on a tray. She had learned with her feeble intellect some tricks, like a dog. One of them was the mixing of sundry drinks. She set the tray on a little stand near the two men, and watched them with her silly simper.

"Clear out now and go to bed," her brother said to her, and she obeyed.

Early the next morning Old Woman Magoun went up to Lily's little sleeping chamber, and watched her a second as she lay asleep, with her yellow locks spread over the pillow. Then she spoke. "Lily," said she— "Lily, wake up. I am going to Greenham across the new bridge, and you can go with me."

Lily immediately sat up in bed and smiled at her Grandmother. Her eyes were still misty, but the light of awakening was in them.

"Get right up," said the old woman. "You can wear your new dress if you want to."

Lily gurgled with pleasure like a baby. "And my new hat?" said she.

"I don't care."

Old Woman Magoun and Lily started for Greenham before Barry's Ford, which kept late hours, was fairly awake. It was three miles to Greenham. The old woman said that, since the horse was a little lame, they would walk. It was a beautiful morning, with a diamond radiance of dew over everything. Her grandmother had curled Lily's hair more punctiliously than usual. The little face peeped like a rose out of two rows of golden spirals. Lily wore her new muslin dress with a pink sash, and her best hat of a fine white straw trimmed with a wreath of rosebuds; also the neatest black openwork stockings and pretty shoes. She even had white cotton gloves. When they set out, the old, heavily stepping woman, in her black gown and cape and bonnet, looked down at the little pink fluttering figure. Her face was full of the tenderest love and admiration, and yet there was something terrible about it. They crossed the new bridge—a primitive structure built of logs in a slovenly fashion. Old Woman Magoun pointed to a gap.

"Jest see that," said she. "That's the way men work."

"Men ain't very nice, be they?" said Lily, in her sweet little voice.

"No, they ain't, take them all together," replied her grandmother.

"That man that walked to the store with me was nicer

than some, I guess," Lily said, in a wishful fashion. Her grandmother reached down and took the child's hand in its small cotton glove. "You hurt me, holding my hand so tight," Lily said presently, in a deprecatory little voice.

The old woman loosened her grasp. "Grandma didn't know how tight she was holding your hand," said she. "She wouldn't hurt you for nothin', except it was to save your life, or somethin' like that." She spoke with an undertone of tremendous meaning which the girl was too childish to grasp. They walked along the country road. Just before they reached Greenham they passed a stone wall overgrown with blackberry vines, and, an unusual thing in that vicinity, a lusty spread of deadly nightshade full of berries.

"Those berries look good to eat, Grandma," Lily said. At that instant the old woman's face became something terrible to see. "You can't have any now," she said, and hurried Lily along.

"They look real nice," said Lily.

When they reached Greenham, Old Woman Magoun took her way straight to the most pretentious house there, the residence of the lawyer, whose name was Mason. Old Woman Magoun bade Lily wait in the yard for a few moments, and Lily ventured to seat herself on a bench beneath an oak tree; then she watched with some wonder her grandmother enter the lawyer's office door at the right of the house. Presently the lawyer's wife came out and spoke to Lily under the tree. She had in her hand a little tray containing a plate of cake, a glass of milk, and an early apple. She spoke very kindly to Lily; she even kissed her, and offered her the tray of refreshments, which Lily accepted gratefully. She sat eating, with Mrs. Mason watching her, when Old Woman Magoun came out of the lawyer's office with a ghastly face.

"What are you eatin'?" she asked Lily, sharply. "Is that a sour apple?"

"I thought she might be hungry," said the lawyer's wife, with loving, melancholy eyes upon the girl.

Lily had almost finished the apple. "It's real sour, but I like it; it's real nice, Grandma," she said.

"You ain't been drinkin' milk with a sour apple?"

"It was real nice milk, Grandma."

"You ought never to have drunk milk and eat a sour

apple," said her grandmother. "Your stomach was all out of order this mornin', an' sour apples and milk is always apt to hurt anybody."

"I don't know but they are," Mrs. Mason said, apologetically, as she stood on the green lawn with her lavender muslin sweeping around her. "I am real sorry, Mrs. Magoun. I ought to have thought. Let me get some soda for her."

"Soda never agrees with her," replied the old woman, in a harsh voice. "Come," she said to Lily, "it's time we were goin' home."

After Lily and her grandmother had disappeared down the road, Lawyer Mason came out of his office and joined his wife, who had seated herself on the bench beneath the tree. She was idle, and her face wore the expression of those who review joys forever past. She had lost a little girl, her only child, years ago, and her husband always knew when she was thinking about her. Lawyer Mason looked older than his wife; he had a dry, shrewd, slightly one-sided face.

"What do you think, Maria?" he said. "That old woman came to me with the most pressing entreaty to adopt that little girl."

"She is a beautiful little girl," said Mrs. Mason, in a slightly husky voice.

"Yes, she is a pretty child," assented the lawyer, looking pityingly at his wife; "but it is out of the question, my dear. Adopting a child is a serious measure, and in this case a child who comes from Barry's Ford!"

"But the grandmother seems a very good woman," said Mrs. Mason.

"I rather think she is. I never heard a word against her. But the father! No, Maria, we cannot take a child with Barry blood in her veins. The stock has run out; it is vitiated physically and morally. It won't do, my dear."

"Her grandmother had her dressed up as pretty as a little girl could be," said Mrs. Mason, and this time the tears welled into her faithful, wistful eyes.

"Well, we can't help that," said the lawyer, as he went back to his office.

Old Woman Magoun and Lily returned, going slowly along the road to Barry's Ford. When they came to the stone wall where the blackberry vines and the deadly nightshade grew, Lily said she was tired, and asked if she could not sit down for a few minutes. The strange look on her grandmother's face had deepened. Now and then Lily glanced at her and had a feeling as if she were looking at a stranger.

"Yes, you can set down if you want to," said Old Woman Magoun, deeply and harshly.

Lily started and looked at her, as if to make sure that it was her grandmother who spoke. Then she sat down on a stone which was comparatively free of the vines.

"Ain't you goin' to set down, Grandma?" Lily asked, timidly.

"No; I don't want to get into that mess," replied her grandmother. "I ain't tired. I'll stand here."

Lily sat still; her delicate little face was flushed with heat. She extended her tiny feet in her best shoes and gazed at them. "My shoes are all over dust," said she.

"It will brush off," said her grandmother, still in that strange voice.

Lily looked around. An elm tree in the field behind her cast a spray of branches over her head; a little cool puff of wind came on her face. She gazed at the low mountains on the horizon in the midst of which she lived, and she sighed, for no reason that she knew. She began idly picking at the blackberry vines; there were no berries on them; then she put her little fingers on the berries of the deadly nightshade. "These look like nice berries," she said.

Old Woman Magoun, standing stiff and straight in the road, said nothing.

"They look good to eat," said Lily.

Old Woman Magoun still said nothing, but she looked up into the ineffable blue of the sky, over which spread at intervals great white clouds shaped like wings.

Lily picked some of the deadly nightshade berries and ate them. "Why, they are real sweet," said she. "They are nice." She picked some more and ate them.

Presently her grandmother spoke. "Come," she said, "it is time we were going. I guess you have set long enough."

Lily was still eating the berries when she slipped down from the wall and followed her grandmother obediently up the road.

Before they reached home, Lily complained of being

very thirsty. She stopped and made a little cup of a leaf and drank long at a mountain brook. "I am dreadful dry, but it hurts me to swallow," she said to her grandmother when she stopped drinking and joined the old woman waiting for her in the road. Her grandmother's face seemed strangely dim to her. She took hold of Lily's hand as they went on. "My stomach burns," said Lily, presently. "I want some more water."

"There is another brook a little farther on," said Old Woman Magoun, in a dull voice.

When they reached that brook, Lily stopped and drank again, but she whimpered a little over her difficulty in swallowing. "My stomach burns, too," she said, walking on, "and my throat is so dry, Grandma." Old Woman Magoun held Lily's hand more tightly. "You hurt me, holding my hand so tight, Grandma," said Lily, looking up at her grandmother, whose face she seemed to see through a mist, and the old woman loosened her grasp.

When at last they reached home, Lily was very ill. Old Woman Magoun put her on her own bed in the little bedroom out of the kitchen. Lily lay there and moaned, and Sally Jinks came in.

"Why, what ails her?" she asked. "She looks feverish."

Lily unexpectedly answered for herself. "I ate some sour apples and drank some milk," she moaned.

"Sour apples and milk are dreadful apt to hurt anybody," said Sally Jinks. She told several people on her way home that Old Woman Magoun was dreadful careless to let Lily eat such things.

Meanwhile Lily grew worse. She suffered cruelly from the burning in her stomach, the vertigo, and the deadly nausea. "I am so sick, I am so sick, Grandma," she kept moaning. She could no longer see her grandmother as she bent over her, but she could hear her talk.

Old Woman Magoun talked as Lily had never heard her talk before, as nobody had ever heard her talk before. She spoke from the depths of her soul; her voice was as tender as the coo of a dove, and it was grand and exalted. "You'll feel better very soon, little Lily," said she.

"I am so sick, Grandma."

"You will feel better very soon, and then—"

"I am sick."

"You shall go to a beautiful place."

Lily moaned.

"You shall go to a beautiful place," the old woman went on.

"Where?" asked Lily, groping feebly with her cold little hands. Then she moaned again.

"A beautiful place, where the flowers grow tall."

"What color? Oh, Grandma, I am so sick."

"A blue color," replied the old woman. Blue was Lily's favorite color. "A beautiful blue color, and as tall as your knees, and the flowers always stay there, and they never fade."

"Not if you pick them, Grandma? Oh!"

"No, not if you pick them; they never fade, and they are so sweet you can smell them a mile off; and there are birds that sing, and all the roads have gold stones in them, and the stone walls are made of gold."

"Like the ring Grandpa gave you? I am so sick, Grandma."

"Yes, gold like that. And all the houses are built of silver and gold, and the people all have wings, so when they get tired walking they can fly, and—"

"I am so sick, Grandma."

"And all the dolls are alive," said Old Woman Magoun. "Dolls like yours can run, and talk, and love you back again."

Lily had her poor old rag doll in bed with her, clasped close to her agonized little heart. She tried very hard with her eyes, whose pupils were so dilated that they looked black, to see her grandmother's face when she said that, but she could not. "It is dark," she moaned, feebly.

"There where you are going it is always light," said the grandmother, "and the commonest things shine like that breastpin Mrs. Lawyer Mason had on today."

Lily moaned pitifully, and said something incoherent. Delirium was commencing. Presently she sat straight up in bed and raved; but even then her grandmother's wonderful compelling voice had an influence over her.

"You will come to a gate with all the colors of the rainbow," said her grandmother; "and it will open, and you will go right in and walk up the gold street, and cross the field where the blue flowers come up to your knees, until you find your mother, and she will take you home where you are going to live. She has a little white room all ready for you, white curtains at the windows, and a little white looking-glass, and when you look in it you will see—"

"What will I see? I am so sick, Grandma."

"You will see a face like yours, only it's an angel's; and there will be a little white bed, and you can lay down an' rest."

"Won't I be sick, Grandma?" asked Lily. Then she moaned and babbled wildly, although she seemed to understand through it all what her grandmother said.

"No, you will never be sick any more. Talkin' about sickness won't mean anything to you."

It continued. Lily talked on wildly, and her grandmother's great voice of soothing never ceased, until the child fell into a deep sleep, or what resembled sleep; but she lay stiffly in that sleep, and a candle flashed before her eyes made no impression on them.

Then it was that Nelson Barry came. Jim Willis waited outside the door. When Nelson entered he found Old Woman Magoun on her knees beside the bed, weeping with dry eyes and a might of agony which fairly shook Nelson Barry, the degenerate of a fine old race.

"Is she sick?" he asked, in a hushed voice.

Old Woman Magoun gave another terrible sob, which sounded like the gasp of one dying.

"Sally Jinks said that Lily was sick from eating milk and sour apples," said Barry, in a tremulous voice. "I remember that her mother was very sick once from eating them."

Lily lay still, and her grandmother on her knees shook with her terrible sobs.

Suddenly Nelson Barry started. "I guess I had better go to Greenham for a doctor if she's as bad as that," he said. He went close to the bed and looked at the sick child. He gave a great start. Then he felt of her hands and reached down under the bedclothes for her little feet. "Her hands and feet are like ice," he cried out. "Good God! why didn't you send for some one—for me—before? Why, she's dying; she's almost gone!"

Barry rushed out and spoke to Jim Willis, who turned pale and came in and stood by the bedside.

"She's almost gone," he said, in a hushed whisper.

"There's no use going for the doctor; she'd be dead before he got here," said Nelson, and he stood regarding the passing child with a strange, sad face—unutterably sad, because of his incapability of the truest sadness.

"Poor little thing, she's past suffering, anyhow," said the other man, and his own face also was sad with a puzzled, mystified sadness.

Lily died that night. There was quite a commotion in Barry's Ford until after the funeral, it was all so sudden, and then everything went on as usual. Old Woman Magoun continued to live as she had done before. She supported herself by the produce of her tiny farm; she was very industrious, but people said that she was a trifle touched, since every time she went over the log bridge with her eggs or her garden vegetables to sell in Greenham, she carried with her, as one might have carried an infant, Lily's old rag doll.

Kate O'Flaherty Chopin (1851–1904)

Born in St. Louis of an Irish father and a Creole mother, Katherine (Kate) O'Flaherty was educated at the convent of the Sacred Heart in her native city. As a young woman she was a local belle and extremely interested in music and literature. In 1870, shortly after her marriage to Oscar Chopin, she moved with him from Missouri to New Orleans. Ten years later her husband's business failed, and the couple moved with their six children to Nachitoches Parish in central Louisiana, where Oscar Chopin ran a general store until his death in 1882.

In 1883 Kate Chopin moved her family back to her mother's house in St. Louis and in 1888, three years after her mother's death, began to write professionally. In the remaining sixteen years of her life she produced two novels and a vast quantity of short stories, including "Lilacs," (1894) and "The Godmother," (1901), both reprinted here. Focusing primarily on the Creole and Acadian societies she knew in Louisiana, Kate Chopin wrote of the intricacies of marriage and of love. She read widely in both American and European literatures, and, interestingly, was an admirer of the work of Mary Wilkins Freeman and Sarah Orne Jewett.

Often referred to as a "regionalist" because of her settings and her use of local dialect, Chopin's style and concerns in fact belie this label. Her best known work, *The Awakening* (1899), is the story of a young matron who "was beginning to realize her position in the universe as a human being, and to recognize her relations as an individual to the world within and about her." The book, not surprisingly, was damned in St. Louis on the grounds that Chopin's treatment of sexuality was too explicit and her attitude towards her principal figure was not sufficiently disapproving. Kate Chopin wrote little in the years between the publication of *The Awakening* and her death, and it is possible that she was discouraged by the hostile and narrow-minded criticism the novel had received.

[References: Kate Chopin's complete works have been collected in a two-volume edition edited by Per Seyersted.

Baton Rouge: Louisiana State Univ. Press, 1969. Seyersted has also written *Kate Chopin: A Critical Biography*. Oslo and Baton Rouge: Universitetforlaget and Lousiana State Univ. Press. 1969. This includes a bibliography.]

LILACS

Mme. Adrienne Farival never announced her coming; but the good nuns knew very well when to look for her. When the scent of the lilac blossoms began to permeate the air, Sister Agathe would turn many times during the day to the window; upon her face the happy, beatific expression with which pure and simple souls watch for the coming of those they love.

But it was not Sister Agathe; it was Sister Marceline who first espied her crossing the beautiful lawn that sloped up to the convent. Her arms were filled with great bunches of lilacs which she had gathered along her path. She was clad all in brown; like one of the birds that come with the spring, the nuns used to say. Her figure was rounded and graceful, and she walked with a happy, buoyant step. The cabriolet which had conveyed her to the convent moved slowly up the gravel drive that led to the imposing entrance. Beside the driver was her modest little black trunk, with her name and address printed in white letters upon it: "Mme. A. Farival, Paris." It was the crunching of the gravel which had attracted Sister Marceline's attention. And then the commotion began.

White-capped heads appeared suddenly at the windows; she waved her parasol and her bunch of lilacs at them. Sister Marceline and Sister Marie Anne appeared, fluttered and expectant at the doorway. But Sister Agathe, more daring and impulsive than all, descended the steps and flew across the grass to meet her. What embraces, in which the lilacs were crushed between them! What ardent kisses! What pink flushes of happiness mounting the cheeks of the two women!

Once within the convent Adrienne's soft brown eyes moistened with tenderness as they dwelt caressingly upon the familiar objects about her, and noted the most

First published in the New Orleans *Times-Democrat* (Dec. 20, 1896).

trifling details. The white, bare boards of the floor had
lost nothing of their luster. The stiff, wooden chairs,
standing in rows against the walls of hall and parlor,
seemed to have taken on an extra polish since she had
seen them, last lilac time. And there was a new picture
of the Sacré-Coeur hanging over the hall table. What had
they done with Ste. Catherine de Sienne, who had occupied that position of honor for so many years? In the
chapel—it was no use trying to deceive her—she saw at
a glance that St. Joseph's mantle had been embellished
with a new coat of blue, and the aureole about his head
freshly gilded. And the Blessed Virgin there neglected!
Still wearing her garb of last spring, which looked almost
dingy by contrast. It was not just—such partiality!
The Holy Mother had reason to be jealous and to complain.

But Adrienne did not delay to pay her respects to the
Mother Superior, whose dignity would not permit her to
so much as step outside the door of her private apartments to welcome this old pupil. Indeed, she was dignity
in person; large, uncompromising, unbending. She kissed
Adrienne without warmth, and discussed conventional
themes learnedly and prosaically during the quarter of an
hour which the young woman remained in her company.

It was then that Adrienne's latest gift was brought in
for inspection. For Adrienne always brought a handsome
present for the chapel in her little black trunk. Last year
it was a necklace of gems for the Blessed Virgin, which
the Good Mother was only permitted to wear on extra
occasions, such as great feast days of obligation. The year
before it had been a precious crucifix—an ivory figure
of Christ suspended from an ebony cross, whose extremi-
ties were tipped with wrought silver. This time it was a
linen embroidered altar cloth of such rare and delicate
workmanship that the Mother Superior, who knew the
value of such things, chided Adrienne for the extravagance.

"But, dear Mother, you know it is the greatest pleasure
I have in life—to be with you all once a year, and to
bring some such trifling token of my regard."

The Mother Superior dismissed her with the rejoinder:
"Make yourself at home, my child. Sister Thérèse will see
to your wants. You will occupy Sister Marceline's bed in
the end room, over the chapel. You will share the room
with Sister Agathe."

There was always one of the nuns detailed to keep Adrienne company during her fortnight's stay at the convent. This had become almost a fixed regulation. It was only during the hours of recreation that she found herself with them all together. Those were hours of much harmless merrymaking under the trees or in the nuns' refectory.

This time it was Sister Agathe who waited for her outside of the Mother Superior's door. She was taller and slenderer than Adrienne, and perhaps ten years older. Her fair blonde face flushed and paled with every passing emotion that visited her soul. The two women linked arms and went together out into the open air.

There was so much which Sister Agathe felt that Adrienne must see. To begin with, the enlarged poultry yard, with its dozens upon dozens of new inmates. It took now all the time of one of the lay sisters to attend to them. There had been no change made in the vegetable garden, but—yes there had; Adrienne's quick eye at once detected it. Last year old Philippe had planted his cabbages in a large square to the right. This year they were set out in an oblong bed to the left. How it made Sister Agathe laugh to think Adrienne should have noticed such a trifle! And old Philippe, who was nailing a broken trellis not far off, was called forward to be told about it.

He never failed to tell Adrienne how well she looked, and how she was growing younger each year. And it was his delight to recall certain of her youthful and mischievous escapades. Never would he forget that day she disappeared; and the whole convent in a hubbub about it! And how at last it was he who discovered her perched among the tallest branches of the highest tree on the grounds, where she had climbed to see if she could get a glimpse of Paris! And her punishment afterwards!—half of the Gospel of Palm Sunday to learn by heart!

"We may laugh over it, my good Philippe, but we must remember that Madame is older and wiser now."

"I know well, Sister Agathe, the one ceases to commit follies after the first days of youth." And Adrienne seemed greatly impressed by the wisdom of Sister Agathe and old Philippe, the convent gardener.

A little later when they sat upon a rustic bench which overlooked the smiling landscape about them, Adrienne was saying to Sister Agathe, who held her hand and stroked it fondly:

"Do you remember my first visit, four years ago, Sister Agathe? and what a surprise it was to you all!"

"As if I could forget it, dear child!"

"And I! Always shall I remember that morning as I walked along the boulevard with a heaviness of heart—oh, a heaviness which I hate to recall. Suddenly there was wafted to me the sweet odor of lilac blossoms. A young girl had passed me by, carrying a great bunch of them. Did you ever know, Sister Agathe, that there is nothing which so keenly revives a memory as a perfume—an odor?"

"I believe you are right, Adrienne. For now that you speak of it, I can feel how the odor of fresh bread—when Sister Jeanne bakes—always makes me think of the great kitchen of ma tante de Sierge, and crippled Julie, who sat always knitting at the sunny window. And I never smell the sweet scented honeysuckle without living again through the blessed day of my first communion."

"Well, that is how it was with me, Sister Agathe, when the scent of the lilacs at once changed the whole current of my thoughts and my despondency. The boulevard, its noises, its passing throng, vanished from before my senses as completely as if they had been spirited away. I was standing here with my feet sunk in the green sward as they are now. I could see the sunlight glancing from that old white stone wall, could hear the notes of birds, just as we hear them now, and the humming of insects in the air. And through all I could see and could smell the lilac blossoms, nodding invitingly to me from their thick-leaved branches. It seems to me they are richer than ever this year, Sister Agathe. And do you know, I became like an *enragée;* nothing could have kept me back. I do not remember now where I was going; but I turned and retraced my steps homeward in a perfect fever of agitation: 'Sophie! my little trunk—quick—the black one! A mere handful of clothes! I am going away. Don't ask me any questions. I shall be back in a fortnight.' And every year since then it is the same. At the very first whiff of a lilac blossom, I am gone! There is no holding me back."

"And how I wait for you, and watch those lilac bushes, Adrienne! If you should once fail to come, it would be like the spring coming without the sunshine or the song of birds.

"But do you know, dear child, I have sometimes feared that in moments of despondency such as you have just described, I fear that you do not turn as you might to our Blessed Mother in heaven, who is ever ready to comfort and solace an afflicted heart with the precious balm of her sympathy and love."

"Perhaps I do not, dear Sister Agathe. But you cannot picture the annoyances which I am constantly submitted to. That Sophie alone, with her detestable ways! I assure you she of herself is enough to drive me to St. Lazare."

"Indeed, I do understand that the trials of one living in the world must be very great, Adrienne; particularly for you, my poor child, who have to bear them alone, since Almighty God was pleased to call to himself your dear husband. But on the other hand, to live one's life along the lines which our dear Lord traces for each one of us, must bring with it resignation and even a certain comfort. You have your household duties, Adrienne, and your music, to which, you say, you continue to devote yourself. And then, there are always good works—the poor—who are always with us—to be relieved; the afflicted to be comforted."

"But, Sister Agathe! Will you listen! Is it not La Rose that I hear moving down there at the edge of the pasture? I fancy she is reproaching me with being an ingrate, not to have pressed a kiss yet on that white forehead of hers. Come, let us go."

The two women arose and walked again, hand in hand this time, over the tufted grass down the gentle decline where it sloped toward the broad, flat meadow, and the limpid stream that flowed cool and fresh from the woods. Sister Agathe walked with her composed, nunlike tread; Adrienne with a balancing motion, a bounding step, as though the earth responded to her light footfall with some subtle impulse all its own.

They lingered long upon the foot-bridge that spanned the narrow stream which divided the convent grounds from the meadow beyond. It was to Adrienne indescribably sweet to rest there in soft, low converse with this gentle-faced nun, watching the approach of evening. The gurgle of the running water beneath them; the lowing of cattle approaching in the distance, were the only sounds that broke upon the stillness, until the clear tones of the angelus bell pealed out from the convent tower. At the

sound both women instinctively sank to their knees, sign-
ing themselves with the sign of the cross. And Sister
Agathe repeated the customary invocation, Adrienne responding in musical tones:

"The Angel of the Lord declared unto Mary,
    And she conceived by the Holy Ghost—"

and so forth, to the end of the brief prayer, after which
they arose and retraced their steps toward the convent.

It was with subtle and naïve pleasure that Adrienne prepared herself that night for bed. The room which she
shared with Sister Agathe was immaculately white. The
walls were a dead white, relieved only by one florid print
depicting Jacob's dream at the foot of the ladder, upon
which angels mounted and descended. The bare floors, a
soft yellow-white, with two little patches of gray carpet
beside each spotless bed. At the head of the white-
draped beds were two *bénitiers* containing holy water
absorbed in sponges.

Sister Agathe disrobed noiselessly behind her curtains
and glided into bed without having revealed, in the faint
candlelight, as much as a shadow of herself. Adrienne pat-
tered about the room, shook and folded her garments
with great care, placing them on the back of a chair as
she had been taught to do when a child at the convent.
It secretly pleased Sister Agathe to feel that her dear
Adrienne clung to the habits acquired in her youth.

But Adrienne could not sleep. She did not greatly
desire to do so. These hours seemed too precious to be
into the oblivion of slumber.

"Are you not asleep, Adrienne?"

"No, Sister Agathe. You know it is always so the first
night. The excitement of my arrival—I don't know what
—keeps me awake."

"Say your 'Hail, Mary,' dear child, over and over."

"I have done so, Sister Agathe; it does not help."

"Then lie quite still on your side and think of nothing
but your own respiration. I have heard that such induce-
ment to sleep seldom fails."

"I will try. Good night, Sister Agathe."

"Good night, dear child. May the Holy Virgin guard
you."

An hour later Adrienne was still lying with wide, wake-
ful eyes, listening to the regular breathing of Sister
Agathe. The trailing of the passing wind through the

treetops, the ceaseless babble of the rivulet were some of the sounds that came to her faintly through the night.

The days of the fortnight which followed were in character much like the first peaceful, uneventful day of her arrival, with the exception only that she devoutly heard mass every morning at an early hour in the convent chapel, and on Sundays sang in the choir in her agreeable, cultivated voice, which was heard with delight and the warmest appreciation.

When the day of her departure came, Sister Agathe was not satisfied to say good-by at the portal as the others did. She walked down the drive beside the creeping old cabriolet, chattering her pleasant last words. And then she stood—it was as far as she might go—at the edge of the road, waving good-by in response to the fluttering of Adrienne's handkerchief. Four hours later Sister Agathe, who was instructing a class of little girls for their first communion, looked up at the classroom clock and murmured: "Adrienne is at home now."

Yes, Adrienne was at home. Paris had engulfed her.

At the very hour when Sister Agathe looked up at the clock, Adrienne, clad in a charming *negligee*, was reclining indolently in the depths of a luxurious armchair. The bright room was in its accustomed state of picturesque disorder. Musical scores were scattered upon the open piano. Thrown carelessly over the backs of chairs were puzzling and astonishing-looking garments.

In a large gilded cage near the window perched a clumsy green parrot. He blinked stupidly at a young girl in street dress who was exerting herself to make him talk.

In the centre of the room stood Sophie, that thorn in her mistress's side. With hands plunged in the deep pockets of her apron, her white starched cap quivering with each emphatic motion of her grizzled head, she was holding forth, to the evident ennui of the two young women. She was saying:

"Heaven knows I have stood enough in the six years I have been with Mademoiselle; but never such indignities as I have had to endure in the past two weeks at the hands of that man who calls himself a manager! The very first day—and I, good enough to notify him at once of Mademoiselle's flight—he arrives like a lion; I tell you, like a lion. He insists upon knowing Mademoiselle's whereabouts. How can I tell him any more than the statue out there in the square? He calls me a liar! Me, me—a liar! He declares he is ruined. The public will not stand La Petite Gilberta in the role which Mademoiselle has made so famous—La Petite Gilberta, who dances like a jointed wooden figure and sings like a *traînée* of a *café chantant*. If I were to tell La Gilberta that, as I easily might, I guarantee it would not be well for the few straggling hairs which he has left on that miserable head of his!

"What could he do? He was obliged to inform the public that Mademoiselle was ill; and then began my real torment! Answering this one and that one with their cards, their flowers, their dainties in covered dishes! which, I must admit, saved Florine and me much cooking. And all the while having to tell them that the physician had advised for Mademoiselle a rest of two weeks at some watering-place, the name of which I had forgotten!"

Adrienne had been contemplating old Sophie with quizzical, half-closed eyes, and pelting her with hot-house roses which lay in her lap, and which she nipped off short from their graceful stems for that purpose. Each rose struck Sophie full in the face; but they did not disconcert her or once stem the torrent of her talk.

"Oh, Adrienne!" entreated the young girl at the parrot's cage. "Make her hush; please do something. How can you ever expect Zozo to talk? A dozen times he has been on the point of saying something! I tell you, she stupefies him with her chatter."

"My good Sophie," remarked Adrienne, not changing her attitude, "you see the roses are all used up. But I assure you, anything at hand goes," carelessly picking up a book from the table beside her. "What is this? Mons. Zola! Now I warn you, Sophie, the weightiness, the heaviness of Mons. Zola are such that they cannot fail to prostrate you; thankful you may be if they leave you with energy to regain your feet."

"Mademoiselle's pleasantries are all very well; but if I am to be shown the door for it—if I am to be crippled for it—I shall say that I think Mademoiselle is a woman without conscience and without heart. To torture a man as she does! A man? No, an angel!

"Each day he has come with sad visage and drooping mien. 'No news, Sophie?'

" 'None, Monsieur Henri.' 'Have you no idea where she has gone?' 'Not any more than the statue in the square,

Monsieur.' 'Is it perhaps possible that she may not return at all?' with his face blanching like that curtain.

"I assure him you will be back at the end of the fortnight. I entreat him to have patience. He drags himself, *désolé*, about the room, picking up Mademoiselle's fan, her gloves, her music, and turning them over and over in his hands. Mademoiselle's slipper, which she took off to throw at me in the impatience of her departure, and which I purposely left lying where it fell on the chiffonier —he kissed it—I saw him do it—and thrust it into his pocket, thinking himself unobserved.

"The same song each day. I beg him to eat a little good soup which I have prepared. 'I cannot eat, my dear Sophie.' The other night he came and stood long gazing out of the window at the stars. When he turned he was wiping his eyes; they were red. He said he had been riding in the dust, which had inflamed them. But I knew better; he had been crying.

"*Ma Foi!* in his place I would snap my finger at such cruelty. I would go out and amuse myself. What is the use of being young!"

Adrienne arose with a laugh. She went and seizing old Sophie by the shoulders shook her till the white cap wobbled on her head.

"What is the use of all this litany, my good Sophie? Year after year the same! Have you forgotten that I have come a long, dusty journey by rail, and that I am perishing of hunger and thirst? Bring us a bottle of Château Yquem and a biscuit and my box of cigarettes." Sophie had freed herself, and was retreating toward the door. "And, Sophie! If Monsieur Henri is still waiting, tell him to come up."

It was precisely a year later. The spring had come again, and Paris was intoxicated.

Old Sophie sat in her kitchen discoursing to a neighbor who had come in to borrow some trifling kitchen utensil from the old *bonne*.

"You know, Rosalie, I begin to believe it is an attack of lunacy which seizes her once a year. I wouldn't say it to everyone, but with you I know it will go no further. She ought to be treated for it; a physician should be consulted; it is not well to neglect such things and let them run on.

"It came this morning like a thunder clap. As I am sitting here, there had been no thought or mention of a journey. The baker had come into the kitchen—you know what a gallant he is—with always a girl in his eye. He laid the bread down upon the table and beside it a bunch of lilacs. I didn't know they had bloomed yet. 'For Mam'selle Florine, with my regards,' he said with his foolish simper.

"Now, you know I was not going to call Florine from her work in order to present her the baker's flowers. All the same, it would not do to let them wither. I went with them in my hand into the dining room to get a majolica pitcher which I had put away in the closet there, on an upper shelf, because the handle was broken. Mademoiselle, who rises early, had just come from her bath, and was crossing the hall that opens into the dining room. Just as she was, in her white *peignoir*, she thrust her head into the dining room, snuffling the air and exclaiming, 'What do I smell?'

"She espied the flowers in my hand and pounced upon them like a cat upon a mouse. She held them up to her, burying her face in them for the longest time, only uttering a long 'Ah!'

"Sophie, I am going away. Get out the little black trunk; a few of the plainest garments I have; my brown dress that I have not yet worn."

" 'But, Mademoiselle,' I protested, 'you forget that you have ordered a breakfast of a hundred francs for tomorrow.'

" 'Shut up!' she cried, stamping her foot.

" 'You forget how the manager will rave,' I persisted, 'and vilify me. And you will go like that without a word of adieu to Monsieur Paul, who is an angel if ever one trod the earth.'

"I tell you, Rosalie, her eyes flamed.

" 'Do as I tell you this instant,' she exclaimed, 'or I will strangle you—with your Monsieur Paul and your manager and your hundred francs!' "

"Yes," affirmed Rosalie, "it is insanity. I had a cousin seized in the same way one morning, when she smelled calf's liver frying with onions. Before night it took two men to hold her."

"I could well see it was insanity, my dear Rosalie, and I uttered not another word as I feared for my life. I simply obeyed her every command in silence. And now—whiff, she is gone! God knows where. But between us, Rosalie—I wouldn't say it to Florine—but I believe it is for no good. I, in Monsieur Paul's place, should have her watched. I would put a detective upon her track.

"Now I am going to close up; barricade the entire establishment. Monsieur Paul, the manager, visitors, all —all may ring and knock and shout themselves hoarse. I am tired of it all. To be vilified and called a liar—at my age, Rosalie!"

Adrienne left her trunk at the small railway station, as the old cabriolet was not at the moment available; and she gladly walked the mile or two of pleasant roadway which led to the convent. How infinitely calm, peaceful, penetrating was the charm of the verdant, undulating country spreading out on all sides of her! She walked along the clear smooth road, twirling her parasol; humming a gay tune; nipping here and there a bud or a waxlike leaf from the hedges along the way; and all the while drinking deep draughts of complacency and content.

She stopped, as she had always done, to pluck lilacs in her path.

As she approached the convent she fancied that a white-capped face had glanced fleetingly from a window; but she must have been mistaken. Evidently she had not been seen, and this time would take them by surprise. She smiled to think how Sister Agathe would utter a little joyous cry of amazement, and in fancy she already felt the warmth and tenderness of the nun's embrace. And how Sister Marceline and the others would laugh, and make game of her puffed sleeves! For puffed sleeves had come into fashion since last year; and the vagaries of fashion always afforded infinite merriment to the nuns. No, they surely had not seen her.

She ascended lightly the stone steps and rang the bell. She could hear the sharp metallic sound reverberate through the halls. Before its last note had died away the door was opened very slightly, very cautiously by a lay sister who stood there with downcast eyes and flaming cheeks. Through the narrow opening she thrust forward toward Adrienne a package and a letter, saying, in confused tones: "By order of our Mother Superior." After which she closed the door hastily and turned the heavy key in the great lock.

Adrienne remained stunned. She could not gather her faculties to grasp the meaning of this singular reception. The lilacs fell from her arms to the stone portico on which she was standing. She turned the note and the parcel stupidly over in her hands, instinctively dreading what their contents might disclose.

The outlines of the crucifix were plainly to be felt through the wrapper of the bundle, and she guessed, without having courage to assure herself, that the jeweled necklace and the altar cloth accompanied it.

Leaning against the heavy oaken door for support, Adrienne opened the letter. She did not seem to read the few bitter reproachful lines word by word—the lines that banished her forever from this haven of peace, where her soul was wont to come and refresh itself. They imprinted themselves as a whole upon her brain, in all their seeming cruelty—she did not dare to say injustice.

There was no anger in her heart; that would doubtless possess her later, when her nimble intelligence would begin to seek out the origin of this treacherous turn. Now, there was only room for tears. She leaned her forehead against the heavy oaken panel of the door and wept with the abandonment of a little child.

She descended the steps with a nerveless and dragging tread. Once as she was walking away, she turned to look back at the imposing façade of the convent, hoping to see a familiar face, or a hand, even, giving a faint token that she was still cherished by some one faithful heart. But she saw only the polished windows looking down at her like so many cold and glittering and reproachful eyes.

In the little white room above the chapel, a woman knelt beside the bed on which Adrienne had slept. Her face was pressed deep in the pillow in her efforts to smother the sobs that convulsed her frame. It was Sister Agathe.

After a short while, a lay sister came out of the door with a broom, and swept away the lilac blossoms which Adrienne had let fall upon the portico.

THE GODMOTHER

I

Tante Elodie attracted youth in some incomprehensible way. It was seldom there was not a group of young people gathered about her fire in winter or sitting with her in summer, in the pleasant shade of the live-oaks that screened the gallery.

There were several persons forming a half circle around her generous chimney early one evening in February. There were Madame Nicolas' two tiny little girls who sat on the floor and played with a cat the whole time; Madame Nicolas herself; who only came for the little girls and insisted on hurrying away because it was time to put the children to bed, and who, moreover, was expecting a caller. There was a fair, blonde girl, one of the younger teachers at the Normal school. Gabriel Lucaze offered to escort her home when she got up to go, after Madame Nicolas' departure. But she had already accepted the company of a silent, studious looking youth who had come there in the hope of meeting her. So they all went away but young Gabriel Lucaze, Tante Elodie's godson, who stayed and played cribbage with her. They played at a small table on which were a shaded lamp, a few magazines and a dish of *pralines* which the lady took great pleasure in nibbling during the reflective pauses of the game. They had played one game and were nearing the end of the second. He laid a queen upon the table.

"Fifteen-two" she said, playing a five.

"Twenty, and a pair."

"Twenty-five. Six points for me."

"Its a 'go.' "

"Thirty-one and out. That is the second game I've won. Will you play another rubber, Gabriel?"

"Not much, Tante Elodie, when you are playing in such luck. Besides, I've got to get out, it's half-past-eight." He had played recklessly, often glancing at the bronze

First published in the St. Louis *Mirror* (Dec. 12, 1901).

clock which reposed majestically beneath its crystal globe on the mantle-piece. He prepared at once to leave, going before the gilt-framed, oval mirror to fold and arrange a silk muffler beneath his great coat.

He was rather good looking. That is, he was healthy looking; his face a little florid, and hair almost black. It was short and curly and parted on one side. His eyes were fine when they were not bloodshot, as they sometimes were. His mouth might have been better. It was not disagreeable or unpleasant, but it was unsatisfactory and drooped a little at the corners. However, he was good to look at as he crossed the muffler over his chest. His face was unusually alert. Tante Elodie looked at him in the glass.

"Will you be warm enough, my boy? It has turned very cold since six o'clock."

"Plenty warm. Too warm."

"Where are you going?"

"Now, Tante Elodie," he said, turning, and laying a hand on her shoulder; he was holding his soft felt hat in the other. "It is always 'where are you going?' 'Where have you been?' I have spoiled you. I have told you too much. You expect me to tell you everything; consequently, I must sometimes tell you fibs. I am going to confession. There! are you satisfied?" and he bent down and gave her a hearty kiss.

"I am satisfied, provided you go to the right priestess to confession; not up the hill, mind you!"

"Up the hill" meant up at the Normal School with Tante Elodie. She was a very conservative person. "The Normal" seemed to her an unpardonable innovation, with its teachers from Minnesota, from Iowa, from God-knows-where, bringing strange ways and manners to the old town. She was one, also, who considered the emancipation of slaves a great mistake. She had many reasons for thinking so and was often called upon to enumerate this in her wordy arguments with her many opponents.

II

Tante Elodie distinctly heard the Doctor leave the Widow Nicolas' at a quarter past ten. He visited the

handsome and attractive young woman two evenings in
the week and always left at the same hour. Tante Elodie's
double glass doors opened upon the wide upper gallery.
Around the angle of the gallery were the apartments
of Madame Nicolas. Anyone visiting the widow was
obliged to pass Tante Elodie's door. Beneath was a store
occasionally occupied by some merchant or other, but
oftener vacant. A stairway led down from the porch to
the yard where two enormous live-oaks grew and cast a
dense shade upon the gallery above, making it an agreeable retreat and resting place on hot summer afternoons. The high, wooden yard-gate opened directly upon
the street.

A half hour went by after the Doctor passed her door.
Tante Elodie played "solitaire." Another half hour followed and still Tante Elodie was not sleepy nor did she
think of going to bed. It was very near midnight when
she began to prepare her night toilet and to cover the
fire.

The room was very large with heavy rafters across
the ceiling. There was an enormous bed over in the
corner; a four-posted mahogany covered with a lace
spread which was religiously folded every night and laid
on a chair. There were some old ambrotypes and photo-
graphs about the room; a few comfortable but simple
rocking chairs and a broad fireplace in which a big log
sizzled. It was an attractive room for anyone, not because
of anything that was in it except Tante Elodie herself.
She was far past fifty. Her hair was still soft and brown
and her eyes bright and vivacious. Her figure was slender
and nervous. There were many lines in her face, but it
did not look care-worn. Had she her youthful flesh, she
would have looked very young.

Tante Elodie had spent the evening in munching *pralines* and reading by lamp-light some old magazines that
Gabriel Lucaze had brought her from the club.

There was a romance connected with her early days.
Romances serve but to feed the imagination of the
young; they add nothing to the sum of truth. No one
realized this fact more strongly than Tante Elodie herself. While she tacitly condoned the romance, perhaps
for the sake of the sympathy it bred, she never thought
of Justin Lucaze but with a feeling of gratitude towards
the memory of her parents who had prevented her mar-

rying him thirty-five years before. She could have no connection between her deep and powerful affection for young Gabriel Lucaze and her old-time, brief passion for his father. She loved the boy above everything on earth. There was none so attractive to her as he; none so thoughtful of her pleasures and pains. In his devotion there was no trace of a duty-sense; it was the spontaneous expression of affection and seeming dependence.

After Tante Elodie had turned down her bed and undressed, she drew a grey flannel *peignoir* over her night-gown and knelt down to say her prayers; kneeling before a rocker with her bare feet turned to the fire. Prayers were no trifling matter with her. Besides those which she knew by heart, she read litanies and invocations from a book and also a chapter of "The Following of Christ." She had said her *Notre Père,* her *Salve Marie* and *Je crois en Dieu* and was deep in the litany of the blessed Virgin when she fancied she heard footsteps on the stairs. The night was breathlessly still; it was very late.

"*Vierge des Vierges: Priez pour nous. Mère de Dieu: Priez—*"

Surely there was a stealthy step upon the gallery, and now a hand at her door, striving to lift the latch. Tante Elodie was not afraid. She felt the utmost security in her home and had no dread of mischievous intruders in the peaceful old town. She simply realized that there was someone at her door and that she must find out who it was and what they wanted. She got up from her knees, thrust her feet into her slippers that were near the fire and, lowering the lamp by which she had been reading her litanies, approached the door. There was the very softest rap upon the pane. Tante Elodie unbolted and opened the door the least bit.

"*Qui est là?*" she asked.

"Gabriel." He forced himself into the room before she had time to fully open the door to him.

III

Gabriel strode past her towards the fire, mechanically taking off his hat, and sat down in the rocker before which she had been kneeling. He sat on the prayer books she had left there. He removed them and laid them upon the table. Seeming to realize in a dazed way that it was not their accustomed place, he threw the two books on a nearby chair.

Tante Elodie raised the lamp and looked at him. His eyes were bloodshot, as they were when he drank or experienced any unusual emotion or excitement. But he was pale and his mouth drooped excessively, and twitched with the effort he made to control it. The top button was wrenched from his coat and his muffler was disarranged. Tante Elodie was grieved to the soul, seeing him thus. She thought he had been drinking.

"Gabriel, w'at is the matter?" she asked imploringly. "Oh, my poor child, w'at is the matter?" He looked at her in a fixed way and passed a hand over his head. He tried to speak, but his voice failed, as with one who experiences stage fright. Then he articulated, hoarsely, swallowing nervously between the slow words:

"I—killed a man—about an hour ago—yonder in the old Nigger-Luke Cabin." Tante Elodie's two hands went suddenly down to the table and she leaned heavily upon them for support.

"You did not; you did not," she panted. "You are drinking. You do not know w'at you are saying. Tell me, Gabriel, who 'as been making you drink? Ah! they will answer to me! You do not know w'at you are saying. *Boute!* how can you know!" she clutched him and the torn button that hung in the button-hole fell to the floor.

"I don't know why it happened," he went on, gazing into the fire with unseeing eyes, or rather with eyes that saw what was pictured in his mind and not what was before them.

"I've been in cutting scrapes and shooting scrapes that never amounted to anything, when I was just as crazy mad as I was to-night. But I tell you, Tante Elodie, he's dead. I've got to get away. But how are you going to get out of a place like this, when every dog and cat"—His effort had spent itself, and he began to tremble with a nervous chill; his teeth chattered and his lips could not form an utterance.

Tante Elodie, stumbling rather than walking, went over to a small buffet and pouring some brandy into a glass, gave it to him. She took a little herself. She looked much older in the *peignoir* and the handkerchief tied around her head. She sat down beside Gabriel and took his hand. It was cold and clammy.

"Tell me everything," she said with determination, "everything; without delay; and do not speak so loud. We shall see what must be done. Was it a Negro? Tell me everything."

"No, it was a white man, you don't know, from Conshotta, named Everson. He was half-drunk; a hulking bully as strong as an ox, or I could have licked him. He tortured me until I was frantic. Did you ever see a cat torment a mouse? The mouse can't do anything but lose its head. I lost my head, but I had my knife; that big hornhandled knife."

"Where is it?" she asked sharply. He felt his back pocket.

"I don't know." He did not seem to care, or to realize the importance of the loss.

"Go on; make haste; tell me the whole story. You went from here—you went—go on."

"I went down the river a piece," he said, throwing himself back in the chair and keeping his eyes fixed upon one burning ember on the hearth, "down to Symund's store where there was a game of cards. A lot of the fellows were there. I played a little and didn't drink anything, and stopped at ten. I was going"—He leaned forward with his elbows on his knees and his hands hanging between. "I was going to see a woman at eleven o'clock; it was the only time I could see her. I came along and when I got by the old Nigger-Luke Cabin I lit a match and looked at my watch. It was too early and it wouldn't do to hang around. I went into the cabin and started a blaze in the chimney with some fine wood I found there. My feet were cold and I sat on an empty soap-box before the fire to dry them. I remember I kept looking at my watch. It was twenty-five minutes to eleven when Everson came into the cabin. He was half-drunk and his face was red and looked like a beast. He had left the game and had followed me. I hadn't spoken of where I was going. But he said he knew I was off for a lark and he wanted to go along. I said he couldn't go where I was going, and there was no use talking. He kept it up. At a quarter to eleven I wanted to go, and he went and stood in the doorway.

" 'If I don't go, you don't go', he said, and he kept it

up. When I tried to pass him he pushed me back like I was a feather. He didn't get mad. He laughed all the time and drank whiskey out of a bottle he had in his pocket. If I hadn't got mad and lost my head, I might have fooled him or played some trick on him—if I had used my wits. But I didn't know any more what I was doing than the day I threw the inkstand at old Dainean's head when he switched me and made fun of me before the whole school.

"I stooped by the fire and looked at my watch; he was talking all kinds of foolishness I can't repeat. It was eleven o'clock. I was in a killing rage and made a dash for the door. His big body and his big arm were there like an iron bar, and he laughed. I took out my knife and stuck it into him. I don't believe he knew at first that I had touched him, for he kept on laughing; then he fell over like a pig, and the old cabin shook."

Gabriel had raised his clinched hand with an intensely dramatic movement when he said, "I stuck it into him." Then he let his head fall back against the chair and finished the concluding sentences of his story with closed eyes.

"How do you know he is dead?" asked Tante Elodie, whose voice sounded hard and monotonous.

"I only walked ten steps away and went back to see. He was dead. Then I came here. The best thing is to go give myself up, I reckon, and tell the whole story like I've told you. That's about the best thing I can do if I want any peace of mind."

"Are you crazy, Gabriel! You have not yet regained your senses. Listen to me. Listen to me and try to understand what I say."

Her face was full of a hard intelligence he had not seen there before; all the soft womanliness had for the moment faded out of it.

"You 'ave not killed the man Everson," she said deliberately. "You know nothing about 'im. You do not know that he left Symund's or that he followed you. You left at ten o'clock. You came straight in town, not feeling well. You saw a light in my window, came here; rapped on the door; I let you in and gave you something for cramps in the stomach and made you warm yourself and lie down on the sofa. Wait a moment. Stay still there."

She got up and went shuffling out the door, around

the angle of the gallery and tapped on Madame Nicolas' door. She could hear the young woman jump out of bed bewildered, asking, "Who is there? Wait! What is it?"

"It is Tante Elodie." The door was unbolted at once.

"Oh! how I hate to trouble you, *cherie*. Poor Gabriel 'as been at my room for hours with the most severe cramps. Nothing I can do seems to relieve 'im. Will you let me 'ave the morphine which Doctor left with you for old Betsy's rheumatism? Ah! thank you. I think a quarter of a grain will relieve 'im. Poor boy! Such suffering! I am so sorry dear, to disturb you. Do not stand by the door, you will take cold. Good night."

Tante Elodie persuaded Gabriel, if the club were still open, to look in there on his way home. He had a room in a relative's house. His mother was dead and his father lived on a plantation several miles from town. Gabriel feared that his nerve would fail him. But Tante Elodie had him up again with a glass of brandy. She said that he must get the fact lodged in his mind that he was innocent. She inspected the young man carefully before he went away, brushing and arranging his toilet. She sewed the missing button on his coat. She had noticed some blood upon his right hand. He himself had not seen it. With a wet towel she washed his face and hands as though he were a little child. She brushed his hair and sent him away with a thousand reiterated precautions.

IV

Tante Elodie was not overcome in any way after Gabriel left her. She did not indulge in a hysterical moment, but set about accomplishing some purpose which she had evidently had in her mind. She dressed herself again; quickly, nervously, but with much precision. A shawl over her head and a long, black cape across her shoulders made her look like a nun. She quitted her room. It was very dark and very still out of doors. There was only a whispering wail among the live-oak leaves.

Tante Elodie stole noiselessly down the steps and out the gate. If she had met anyone, she intended to say she was suffering with toothache and was going to the doctor or druggist for relief.

But she met not a soul. She knew every plank, every uneven brick of the sidewalk; every rut of the way, and might have walked with her eyes closed. Strangely enough she had forgotten to pray. Prayer seemed to belong to her moments of contemplation; while now she was all action; prompt, quick, decisive action.

It must have been near upon two o'clock. She did not meet a cat or a dog on her way to the Nigger-Luke Cabin. The hut was well out of town and isolated from a group of tumbled-down shanties some distance off, in which a lazy set of Negroes lived. There was not the slightest feeling of fear or horror in her breast. There might have been, had she not already been dominated and possessed by the determination that Gabriel must be shielded from ignominy—maybe, worse.

She glided into the low cabin like a shadow, hugging the side of the open door. She would have stumbled over the dead man's feet if she had not stepped so cautiously. The embers were burning so low that they gave but a faint glow in the sinister cabin with its obscure corners, its black, hanging cobwebs and the dead man lying twisted as he had fallen with his face on his arm.

Once in the cabin the woman crept towards the body on her hands and knees. She was looking for something in the dusky light; something she could not find. Crawling towards the fire over the uneven, creaking boards, she stirred the embers the least bit with a burnt stick that had fallen to one side. She dared not make a blaze. Then she dragged herself once more towards the lifeless body. She pictured how the knife had been thrust in; how it had fallen from Gabriel's hand; how the man had come down like a felled ox. Yes, the knife could not be far off, but she could not discover a trace of it. She slipped her fingers beneath the body and felt all along. The knife lay up under his arm pit. Her hand scraped his chin as she withdrew it. She did not mind. She was exultant at getting the knife. She felt like some other being, possessed by Satan. Some fiend in human shape, some spirit of murder. A cricket began to sing on the hearth.

Tante Elodie noticed the golden gleam of the murdered man's watch chain, and a sudden thought invaded her. With deft, though unsteady fingers, she unhooked the watch and chain. There was money in his pockets.

She emptied them, turning the pockets inside out. It was difficult to reach his left hand pockets, but she did so. The money, a few bank notes and some silver coins, together with the watch and knife she tied in her handkerchief. Then she hurried away, taking a long stride across the man's body in order to reach the door.

The stars were like shining pieces of gold upon dark velvet. So Tante Elodie thought as she looked up at them an instant.

There was the sound of disorderly voices away off in the Negro shanties. Clasping the parcel close to her breast she began to run. She ran, ran, as fast as some fleet fourfooted creature, ran, panting. She never stopped till she reached the gate that let her in under the live-oaks. The most intent listener could not have heard her as she mounted the stairs; as she let herself in at the door; as she bolted it. Once in the room she began to totter. She was sick to her stomach and her head swam. Instinctively she reached out towards the bed, and fell fainting upon it, face downward.

The gray light of dawn was coming in at her windows. The lamp on the table had burned out. Tante Elodie groaned as she tried to move. And again she groaned with mental anguish, this time as the events of the past night came back to her, one by one, in all their horrifying details. Her labor of love, begun the night before, was not yet ended. The parcel containing the watch and money were there beneath her, pressing into her bosom. When she managed to regain her feet the first thing which she did was to rekindle the fire with splinters of pine and pieces of hickory that were at hand in her wood box. When the fire was burning briskly, Tante Elodie took the paper money from the little bundle and burned it. She did not notice the denomination of the bills, there were five or six, she thrust them into the blaze with the poker and watched them burn. The few loose pieces of silver she put in her purse, apart from her own money; there was sixty-five cents in small coin. The watch she placed between her mattresses; then, seized with misgiving, took it out. She gazed around the room, seeking a safe hiding place and finally put the watch into a large, strong stocking which she pinned securely around her waist beneath her clothing. The knife she washed carefully, drying it with pieces of newspaper which she burned. The water in which she had washed it she also threw in a corner of the large fireplace upon a heap of ashes. Then she put the knife into the pocket of one of Gabriel's coats which she had cleaned and mended for him; it was hanging in her closet.

She did all this slowly and with great effort, for she felt very sick. When the unpleasant work was over it was all she could do to undress and get beneath the covers of her bed.

She knew that when she did not appear at breakfast Madame Nicolas would send to investigate the cause of her absence. She took her meals with the young widow around the corner of the gallery. Tante Elodie was not rich. She received a small income from the remains of what had once been a magnificent plantation adjoining the lands which Justin Lucaze owned and cultivated. But she lived frugally, with a hundred small cares and economies and rarely felt the want of extra money except when the generosity of her nature prompted her to help an afflicted neighbor, or to bestow a gift upon some one of whom she was fond. It often seemed to Tante Elodie that all the affection of her heart was centered upon her young protégé, Gabriel; that what she felt for others was simply an emanation—rays, as it were, from this central sun of love that shone for him alone.

In the midst of twinges, of nervous tremors, her thoughts were with him. It was impossible for her to think of anything else. She was filled with unspeakable dread that he might betray himself. She wondered what he had done after he left her: what he was doing at that moment? She wanted to see him again alone, to insist anew upon the necessity of his self-assertion of innocence.

As she expected, Mrs. Wm. Nicolas came around at the breakfast hour to see what was the matter. She was an active woman, very pretty and fresh looking, with willing, deft hands and the kindest voice and eyes. She was distressed at the spectacle of poor Tante Elodie extended in bed with her head tied up, and looking pale and suffering.

"Ah! I suspected it!" she exclaimed, "coming out in the cold on the gallery last night to get morphine for

Gabriel; *ma foi!* as if he could not go to the drugstore
for his morphine! Where have you pain? Have you any
fever, Tante Elodie?"

"It is nothing, *chérie.* I believe I am only tired and
want to rest for a day in bed."

"Then you must rest as long as you want. I will look
after your fire and see that you have what you need.
I will bring your coffee at once. It is a beautiful day;
like spring. When the sun gets very warm I will open
the window."

V

All day long Gabriel did not appear, and she dared not
make inquiries about him. Several persons came in to
see her, learning that she was sick. The midnight murder
in the Nigger-Luke Cabin seemed to be the favorite subject of conversation among her visitors. They were not
greatly excited over it as they might have been were the
man other than a comparative stranger. But the subject
seemed full of interest, enhanced by the mystery surround-
ing it. Madame Nicolas did not risk to speak of it.

"That is not a fit conversation for a sick-room. Any
doctor—anybody with sense will tell you. For Mercy's
sake! change the subject."

But Fifine Delonce could not be silenced.

"And now it appears," she went on with renewed ani-
mation, "it appears he was playing cards down at Symund's store. That shows how they pass their time—
those boys! It's a scandal! But nobody can remember
when he left. Some say at nine, some say it was past
eleven. He sort of went away like he didn't want them
to notice."

"Well, we didn't know the man. My patience! there
are murders every day. If we had to keep up with
them, *ma foi!* Who is going to Lucie's card party to-
morrow? I hear she did not invite her cousin Claire.
They have fallen out again it seems." And Madame Nicolas, after speaking, went to give Tante Elodie a drink
of *Tisane.*

"Mr. Ben's got about twenty darkies from Niggerville,
holding them on suspicion," continued Fifine, dancing
on the edge of her chair. "Without doubt the man was

enticed to the cabin and murdered and robbed there. Not a picayune left in his pockets! only his pistol—that they didn't take, all loaded, in his back pocket, that he might have used, and his watch gone! Mr. Ben thinks his brother in Conshotta, that's very well off, is going to offer a big reward."

"What relation was the man to you, Fifine?" asked Madame Nicolas, sarcastically.

"He was a human being, Amelia; you have no heart, no feeling. If it makes a woman that hard to associate with a doctor, then thank God—well—as I was saying, if they can catch those two strange section hands that left town last night—but you better bet they're not such fools to keep that watch. But old Uncle Marte said he saw little footprints like a woman's, early this morning, but no one wanted to listen to him or pay any attention, and the crowd tramped them out in little or no time. None of the boys want to let on; they don't want us to know which ones were playing cards at Symund's. Was Gabriel at Symund's, Tante Elodie?"

Tante Elodie coughed painfully and looked blankly as though she had only heard her name and had been inattentive to what was said.

"For pity sake leave Tante Elodie out of this! it's bad enough she has to listen, suffering as she is. Gabriel spent the evening here, on Tante Elodie's sofa, very sick with cramps. You will have to pursue your detective work in some other quarter, my dear."

A little girl came in with a huge bunch of blossoms. There was some bustle attending the arrangement of the flowers in vases, and in the midst of it, two or three ladies took their leave.

"I wonder if they're going to send the body off tonight, or if they're going to keep it for the morning train," Fifine was heard to speculate, before the door closed upon her.

Tante Elodie could not sleep that night. The following day she had some fever and Madame Nicolas insisted upon her seeing the doctor. He gave her a sleeping draught and some fever drops and said she would be all right in a few days; for he could find nothing alarming in her condition.

By a supreme effort of the will she got up on the third day hoping in the accustomed routine of her daily life to get rid, in part, of the uneasiness and unhappiness that possessed her.

The sun shone warm in the afternoon and she went and stood on the gallery watching for Gabriel to pass. He had not been near her. She was wounded, alarmed, miserable at his silence and absence; but determined to see him. He came down the street, presently, never looking up, with his hat drawn over his eyes.

"Gabriel!" she called. He gave a start and glanced around.

"Come up; I want to see you a moment."

"I haven't time now, Tante Elodie."

"Come in!" she said sharply.

"All right, you'll have to fix it up with Morrison," and he opened the gate and went in. She was back in her room by the time he reached it, and in her chair, trembling a little and feeling sick again.

"Gabriel, if you 'ave no heart, it seems to me you would 'ave some intelligence; a moment's reflection would show you the folly of altering your 'abits so suddenly. Did you not know I was sick? did you not guess my uneasiness?"

"I haven't guessed anything or known anything but a taste of hell," he said, not looking at her. Her heart bled afresh for him and went out to him in full forgiveness. "You were right," he went on, "it would have been horrible to say anything. There is no suspicion. I'll never say anything unless someone should be falsely accused."

"There will be no possible evidence to accuse anyone," she assured him. "Forget it, forget it. Keep on as though it was something you had dreamed. Not only for the outside, but within yourself. Do not accuse yourself of that act, but the actions, the conduct, the ungovernable temper that made it possible. Promise me it will be a lesson to you, Gabriel; and God, who reads men's hearts, will not call it a crime, but an accident which your unbridled nature invited. I will forget it. You must forget it. 'Ave you been to the office?"

"To-day; not yesterday. I don't know what I did yesterday, but look for the knife—after they—I couldn't go while he was there—and I thought every minute someone was coming to accuse me. And when I realized they weren't—I don't know—I drank too much, I think. Reading law! I might as well have been reading Hebrew. If Morrison thinks —See here Tante Elodie, are there any spots on this coat? Can you see anything here in the light?"

"There are no spots anywhere. Stop thinking of it, I implore you." But he pulled off the coat and flung it across a chair. He went to the closet to get his other coat which he knew hung there. Tante Elodie, still feeble and suffering, in the depths of her chair, was not quick enough, could think of no way to prevent it. She had at first put the knife in his pocket with the intention of returning it to him. But now she dreaded to have him find it, and thus discover the part she had played in the sickening dream.

He buttoned up his coat briskly and started away.

"Please burn it," he said, looking at the garment on the chair, "I never want to see it again."

VI

When it became distinctly evident that no slightest suspicion would be attached to him for the killing of Everson; when he plainly realized that there was no one upon whom the guilt could be fastened, Gabriel thought he would regain his lost equilibrium. If in no other way, he fancied he could reason himself back into it. He was suffering, but he someway had no fear that his present condition of mind would last. He thought it would pass away like a malignant fever. It would have to pass away or it would have to kill him.

From Tante Elodie's he went over to Morrison's office where he was reading law. Morrison and his partner were out of town and he had the office to himself. He had been there all morning. There was nothing for him to do now but to see anyone who called on business, and to go on with his reading. He seated himself and spread his book before him, but he looked into the street through the open door. Then he got up and shut the door. He again fastened his eyes upon the pages before him, but his mind was traveling other ways. For the hundredth time he was going over every detail of the fatal night, and trying to justify himself in his own heart.

If it had been an open and fair fight there would have been no trouble in squaring himself with his conscience; if the man had shown the slightest disposition to do him bodily harm, but he had not. On the other hand, he asked himself, what constituted a murder? Why, there was Morrison himself, who had once fired at Judge Filips on that very street. His ball had gone wide of the mark, and subsequently he and Filips had adjusted their difficulties and become friends. Was Morrison any less a murderer because his weapon had missed?

Suppose the knife had swerved, had penetrated the arm, had inflicted a harmless scratch or flesh wound, would he be sitting there now, calling himself names? But he would try to think it all out later. He could not bear to be there alone, he never liked to be alone, and now he could not endure it. He closed the book without the slightest recollection of a line his eyes had followed. He went and gazed up and down the street, then he locked the office and walked away.

The fact of Everson having been robbed was very puzzling to Gabriel. He thought about it as he walked along the street.

The complete change that had taken place in his emotions, his sentiments, did not astonish him in the least: we accept such phenomena without question. A week ago—not so long as that—he was in love with the fair-haired girl up at the Normal. He was undeniably in love with her. He knew the symptoms. He wanted to marry her and meant to ask her whenever his position justified him in doing so.

Now, where had that love gone? He thought of her with indifference. Still, he was seeking her at that moment, through habit, without any special motive. He had no positive desire to see her; to see anyone; and yet he could not endure to be alone. He had no desire to see Tante Elodie. She wanted him to forget and her presence made him remember.

The girl was walking under the beautiful trees, and she stood and waited for him, when she saw him mounting the hill. As he looked at her, his fondness for her and his intentions toward her, appeared now, like child's play. Life was something terrible of which she had no conception. She seemed to him as harmless, as innocent, as insignificant as a little bird.

"Oh! Gabriel," she exclaimed. "I had just written you a note. Why haven't you been here? It was foolish to get offended. I wanted to explain: I couldn't get out of it the other night, at Tante Elodie's, when he asked me. You know I couldn't, and that I would rather have come with you." Was it possible he would have taken this seriously a week ago?

"Delonce is a good fellow; he's a decent fellow. I don't blame you. That's all right." She was hurt at his easy complaisance. She did not wish to offend him, and here she was grieved because he was not offended.

"Will you come indoors to the fire?" she asked.

"No; I just strolled up for a minute." He leaned against a tree and looked bored, or rather, preoccupied with other things than herself. It was not a week ago that he wanted to see her every day; when he said the hours were like minutes that he passed beside her. "I just strolled up to tell you that I am going away."

"Oh! going away?" and the pink deepened in her cheeks, and she tried to look indifferent and to clasp her glove tighter. He had not the slightest intention of going away when he mounted the hill. It came to him like an inspiration.

"Where are you going?"

"Going to look for work in the city."

"And what about your law studies?"

"I have no talent for the law; it's about time I acknowledged it. I want to get into something that will make me hustle. I wouldn't mind—I'd like to get something to do on a railroad that would go tearing through the country night and day. What's the matter?" he asked, perceiving the tears that she could not conceal.

"Nothing's the matter," she answered with dignity, and a sense of seeming proud.

He took her word for it and, instead of seeking to console her, went rambling on about the various occupations in which he should like to engage for a while.

"When are you going?"

"Just as soon as I can."

"Shall I see you again?"

"Of course. Good-bye. Don't stay out here too long; you might take cold." He listlessly shook hands with her and descended the hill with long rapid strides.

He would not intentionally have hurt her. He did

not realize that he was wounding her. It would have been as difficult for him to revive his passion for her as to bring Everson back to life. Gabriel knew there could be fresh horror added to the situation. Discovery would have added to it; a false accusation would have deepened it. But he never dreamed of the new horror coming as it did, through Tante Elodie, when he found the knife in his pocket. It took a long time to realize what it meant; and then he felt as if he never wanted to see her again. In his mind, her action identified itself with his crime, and made itself a hateful, hideous part of it, which he could not endure to think of, and of which he could not help thinking.

It was the one thing which had saved him, and yet he felt no gratitude. The great love which had prompted the deed did not soften him. He could not believe that any man was worth loving to such length, or worth saving at such a price. She seemed, to his imagination, less a woman than a monster, capable of committing, in cold-blood, deeds, which he himself could only accomplish in blind rage. For the first time, Gabriel wept. He threw himself down upon the ground in the deepening twilight and wept as he never had before in his life. A terrible sense of loss overpowered him; as if someone dearer than a mother had been taken out of the reach of his heart; as if a refuge had gone from him. The last spark of human affection was dead within him. He knew it as he was losing it. He wept at the loss which left him alone with his thoughts.

VII

Tante Elodie was always chilly. It was warm for the last of April, and the women at Madame Nicolas' wedding were all in airy summer attire. All but Tante Elodie, who wore her black silk, her old silk with a white lace fichu, and she held an embroidered handkerchief and a fan in her hand.

Fifine Delonce had been over in the morning to take up the seams in the dress, for, as she expressed herself, it was miles too loose for Tante Elodie's figure. She appeared to be shrivelling away to nothing. She had not again been sick in bed since that little spell in February; but she was plainly wasting and was very feeble. Her eyes, though, were as bright as ever; sometimes they looked as hard as flint. The doctor, whom Madame Nicolas insisted upon her seeing occasionally, gave a name to her disease; it was a Greek name and sounded convincing. She was taking a tonic especially prepared for her, from a large bottle, three times a day.

Fifine was a great gossip. When and how she gathered her news nobody could tell. It was always said she knew ten times more than the weekly paper would dare to print. She often visited Tante Elodie, and she told her news of everyone; among others of Gabriel.

It was she who told that he had abandoned the study of the law. She told Tante Elodie when he started for the city to look for work and when he came back from the fruitless search.

"Did you know that Gabriel is working on the railroad, now? Fireman! Think of it! What a comedown from reading law in Morrison's office. If I were a man, I'd try to have more strength of character than to go to the dogs on account of a girl; an insignificant somebody from Kansas! Even if she is going to marry my brother, I must say it was no way to treat a boy— leading him on, especially a boy like Gabriel, that any girl would have been glad—Well, it's none of my business; only I'm sorry he took it like he did. Drinking himself to death, they say."

That morning, as she was taking up the seams of the silk dress, there was fresh news of Gabriel. He was tired of the railroad, it seemed. He was down on his father's place herding cattle, breaking in colts, drinking like a fish.

"I wouldn't have such a thing on my conscience! Goodness me! I couldn't sleep at nights if I was that girl."

Tante Elodie always listened with a sad, resigned smile. It did not seem to make any difference whether she had Gabriel or not. He had broken her heart and he was killing her. It was not his crime that had broken her heart; it was his indifference to her love and his turning away from her.

It was whispered about that Tante Elodie had grown indifferent to her religion. There was no truth in it. She had not been to confession for two months; but oth-

erwise she followed closely the demands made upon her;
redoubling her zeal in church work and attending mass
each morning.

At the wedding she was holding quite a little reception of her own in the corner of the gallery. The air
was mild and pleasant. Young people flocked about her
and occasionally the radiant bride came out to see if she
were comfortable and if there was anything she wanted
to eat or drink.

A young girl leaning over the railing suddenly exclaimed *"Tiens!* someone is dead. I didn't know anyone was sick." She was watching the approach of a man
who was coming down the street, distributing, according to
the custom of the country, a death notice from door to
door.

He wore a long black coat and walked with a measured tread. He was as expressionless as an automaton; handing the little slips of paper at every door; not
missing one. The girl, leaning over the railing, went to
the head of the stairs to receive the notice when he entered Tante Elodie's gate.

The small, single sheet, which he gave her, was bordered in black and decorated with an old-fashioned wood
cut of a weeping willow beside a grave. It was an announcement on the part of Monsieur Justin Lucaze of
the death of his only son, Gabriel, who had been instantly killed, the night before, by a fall from his horse.

If the automaton had had any sense of decency, he
might have skipped the house of joy, in which there was
a wedding feast, in which there was the sound of laughter, the click of glasses, the hum of merry voices, and
a vision of sweet women with their thoughts upon love
and marriage and earthly bliss. But he had no sense
of decency. He was as indifferent and relentless as
Death, whose messenger he was.

The sad news, passed from lip to lip, cast a shadow
as if a cloud had flitted across the sky. Tante Elodie
alone stayed in its shadow. She sank deeper down into
the rocker, more shrivelled than ever. They all remembered Tante Elodie's romance and respected her grief.

She did not speak any more, or even smile, but wiped
her forehead with the old lace handkerchief and sometimes closed her eyes. When she closed her eyes she pictured Gabriel dead, down there on the plantation, with

his father watching beside him. He might have betrayed himself had he lived. There was nothing now to betray him. Even the shining gold watch lay deep in a gorged ravine where she had flung it when she once walked through the country alone at dusk.

She thought of her own place down there beside Justin's, all dismantled, with bats beating about the eaves and Negroes living under the falling roof.

Tante Elodie did not seem to want go indoors again. The bride and groom went away. The guests went away, one by one, and all the little children. She stayed there alone in the corner, under the deep shadow of the oaks while the stars came out to keep her company.

Mary Hunter Austin (1868–1934)

Perhaps the most exotic of the authors in this collection, Mary Hunter Austin was born in Carlinville, Illinois, but travelled widely during her life and knew well many of the most prominent artistic and intellectual figures of her day, including Jack London, George Bernard Shaw, W. B. Yeats, Joseph Conrad, H. G. Wells, D. H. Lawrence, Mabel Dodge Luhan, Charlotte Perkins Gilman, and Willa Cather, who wrote *Death Comes for the Archbishop* in Austin's New Mexico adobe.

At an early age she demonstrated her intelligence as well as her interests in religion, mysticism, and literature. Educated at a local college, she received a B.S. in 1888, then went with her family to California where she met Stafford Wallace Austin, whom she married in 1891. The marriage was blighted by her husband's financial failures and by the birth of a severely retarded child. The couple was finally divorced.

California, however, opened up to Austin a new world of travel, independence, experience, and nature. Enraptured by the American desert and passionately interested in the lives and cultures of native Americans, Mary Austin began to write and, in 1903 published a collection of fourteen sketches entitled *The Land of Little Rain*. Other publications swiftly followed: a book of Paiute Indian legends, *The Basket Woman* (1904); *Isidro* (1905), a romantic account of California life during the mission days; *The Flock* (1909), a narrative detailing the lives of sheep herders in her adopted countryside. Interested in the folk literature, myths, and oral traditions of the peoples of the Far West and Southwest, Austin was also involved in some of the radical political movements of her time and was an active supporter of the causes of feminism, birth control, and socialism. *A Woman of Genius* (1912), excerpted here, is a clear reflection of these latter concerns.

[References: The papers of Mary Austin are in the Huntington Library, San Marino, California, and the best published biographies are her own *Earth Horizon*. New

York: Houghton Mifflin, 1932, and an autobiographical sketch published in Overton, Grant. *The Women Who Make Our Novels.* rev. ed., 1928; rpt. Freeport, New York: Books for Libraries Press, 1967, pp. 164-169.]

A WOMAN OF GENIUS

BOOK II

CHAPTER I

The first notion of an obligation I had in writing this part of my story, was that if it is to be serviceable, no lingering sentiment should render it less than literal, and none of that egotism turned inside out which makes a kind sanctity of the personal experience, prevent me from offering it whole. And the next was that the only way in which it could be made to appear in its complete pitiableness, would be to write it from the point of view of Tommy Bettersworth. For after all, I have emerged—retarded, crippled in my affectional capacities, bodily the worse, but still with wings to spread and some disposition toward flying. And when I think of the dreams Tommy had, how he must have figured in them to himself, large between me and all misadventure, adored, dependable; and then how he blundered and lost himself in the mazes of unsuitability, I find bitterness augmenting in me not on my account but his. The amazing pity of it was that it might all have turned out very well if I had been what I seemed to him and to my family at the time when I let him engage himself to me to save me from imminent embarrassment.

My mother, though she took on for the occasion an appropriate solemnity, was frankly relieved to have me so well disposed. Tommy had been brought up in the church, had no bad habits, and was earning a reasonable salary with Burton Brothers, Tailors and Outfitters.

There was nobody whose business it was to tell me that I did not love Tommy enough to marry him. I have often wondered, supposing a medium of communication had been established between my mother and me, if I had told her how much more that other kiss had meant to me than Tommy's mild osculation, she would have understood or made a fight for me? I am afraid she would only have

From *A Woman of Genius*. Garden City, New York. Doubleday, Page & Co., 1912.

seen in it evidence of an infatuation for an undesirable young man, one who smoked and drove rakishly about town in red neckties on Sunday morning. But in fact I liked Tommy immensely. The mating instinct was awake; all our world clapped us forward to the adventure.

If you ask what the inward monitor was about on this occasion, I will say that it is always and singularly inept at human estimates. If, often in search of companionship, its eye is removed from the Mark, to fix upon the personal environment, it is still unfurnished to divine behind which plain exterior lives another like itself! I took Tommy's community of interest for granted on the evidence of his loving me, though, indeed, after all these years I am not quite clear why he, why Forester and Pauline couldn't have walked in the way with me toward the Shining Destiny. I was not conscious of any private advantage; certainly so far as our beginnings were concerned, none showed, and I should have been glad of their company . . . and here at the end I am walking in it alone.

About a month after my engagement, Henry Mills proposed to Pauline, and she began preparations to be married the following June. Tommy's salary not being thought to justify it so soon, the idea of my own marriage had not come very close to me until I began to help Pauline work initials on table linen.

The chief difference between Pauline and me had been that she had lived all her life, so to speak, at home; nothing exigent to her social order had ever found her "out"; but Olivia seemed always to be at the top of the house or somewhere in the back garden, to whom the normal occasions presented themselves as a succession of cards under the door. I do not mean to say that I actually missed any of these appointed visitors, but all my early life comes back to me as a series of importunate callers whose names I was not sure of, and who distracted me frightfully from something vastly more pleasant and important that I wanted very much to do, without knowing very well what it was. But it was in the long afternoons when Pauline and I sat upstairs together sewing on our white things that I began to take notice of the relation of what happened to me to the things that went on inside, and to be intrigued away from the Vision by the possibility of turning it into facts of line and colour and suitability. It was the beginning of my realizing what came afterward to be such a bitter and engrossing need with me, the need of money.

Much that had struck inharmoniously on me in the furnishings of Taylorville, had identified itself so with the point of view there, that I had come to think of the one as being the natural and inevitable expression of the other; now, with the growing appreciation of a home of my own as a medium of self-realization, I accepted its possibility of limitation by the figure of my husband's income without being entirely daunted thereby. For I was still of the young opinion that getting rich involved no more serious matter than setting about it. As I saw it then, Men's Tailoring and Outfitting did not appear an unlikely beginning; if Tommy had achieved the magnificence I planned for him, it wouldn't have been on the whole more remarkable than what has happened. What I had to reckon with later was the astonishing fact that Tommy liked plush furniture, and liked it red for choice.

I do not know why it should have taken me by surprise to find him in harmony with his bringing up; there was no reason for the case being otherwise except as I seemed to find one in his being fond of me. His mother's house was not unlike other Taylorvillian homes, more austerely kept; the blinds were always pulled down in the best room, and they never opened the piano except when there was company, or for the little girls to practise their music lessons. Mrs. Bettersworth was a large, fair woman with pale, prominent eyes, and pale hair pulled back from a corrugated forehead, and his sisters, who were all younger than Tommy, were exactly like her, their eyes if possible more protruded, which you felt to be owing to their hair being braided very tightly in two braids as far apart as possible at the corners of their heads.

They treated me always with the greatest respect. If there had been anybody who could have thrown any light on the situation it would have been Mr. Bettersworth. He was a dry man, with what passed in Taylorville for an eccentric turn of mind. He had, for instance, been known to justify himself for putting Tommy to the Men's Outfitters rather than to his own business of building and contracting, on the ground that Tommy wanted the imagination for it. Just as if an imagination could be of use to anybody!

"So you are going to undertake to make Tommy happy?" he said to me on the occasion of my taking supper with the family as a formal acknowledgment of my engagement.

"Don't you think I can do it?" He was looking at me rather quizzically, and I really wished to know.

"Oh! I was wondering," he said, "what you would do with what you had left over." But it was years before I understood what he meant by that.

About the time I was bridesmaid for Pauline, Tommy had an advantageous offer that put our marriage almost immediately within reach. Burton Brothers was a branch house, one of a score with the Head at Chicago, to whom Tommy had so commended himself under the stimulus of being engaged, that on the establishment of a new store in Higgleston they offered him the sales department. There was also to be a working tailor and a superintendent visiting it regularly from Chicago, which its nearness to the metropolis allowed.

All that we knew of Higgleston was that it was a long settled farming community, which, having discovered itself at the junction of two railway lines that approached Chicago from the southeast, conceived itself to have arrived there by some native superiority, and awoke to the expectation of importance.

It lay, as respects Taylorville, no great distance beyond the flat horizon of the north, where the prairie broke into wooded land again, far enough north not to have been fanned by the hot blast of the war and the spiritual struggle that preceded it, and so to have missed the revitalizing processes that crowded the few succeeding years. Whatever difference there was between it and Taylorville besides population, was just the difference between a community that has fought whole-heartedly and one that stood looking on at the fight.

It was not far enough from Taylorville to have struck out anything new for itself in manners or furniture, but the necessity of going south two or three hours to change cars, and north again several hours more, set up an illusion of change which led to a disappointment in its want of variety. Tommy went out in July, and in a month wrote me that he would be able to come for me as soon as I was ready, and hoping it would not be long. If I had looked, as in the last hesitancies of girlhood I believe I did, for my mother to have raised an objection to my going so far from home, I found myself, instead, almost with the feeling of being pushed out of the nest. It seemed as if in hastening me out of the family she would be the sooner free to give herself without reproach to a new and extraordinary scheme of Forester's. What I guess now to have been in part the motive, was that she already had been touched by the warning of that disorder which finally carried her off, which, with the curious futility of timid women, she hoped, by not mentioning, to postpone.

For a long time now Forester had found himself in the situation of having grown beyond his virtues. That assumption of mannishness which sat so prettily on his nonage was rendered inconspicuous by his majority. People who had forgotten that he had never had any boyhood, found nothing especially commendable in the mild soberness of twenty-three. I have a notion, too, that the happy circumstance of my marriage lit up for him some personal phases which he could hardly have regarded with complacence, for by this time he had passed, in his character of philanderer, from being hopefully regarded as reclaimable to constancy, to a sort of public understudy in the practice of the affections. However it had come about, the young ladies who still took on Forester at intervals, no longer looked on him so much as privileged but as eminently safe; and the number of girls in a given community who can be counted on for such a performance, is limited. That summer before I was married, after Belle Endsleigh had run away from home with a commercial traveller who disappointed the moral instance by making her a very good husband afterward, my brother found himself, as regards the young people's world, in a situation of uneasy detachment. And there was no doubt that the Coöperative, where he had been seven years, bored him excessively. It was then he conceived the idea of reinstating himself in the atmosphere of importance by setting himself up in business.

Adjacent to Niles's Ice Cream Parlours, there was a small stationery and news agency which might be bought and enlarged to creditable proportions. There was, I believe, actually nothing to be urged against this as a matter of business; the difficulty was that to accomplish it my mother would be obliged to hypothecate the whole of her small capital. What my mother really thought about her property was that she held it in trust for the family interest, and that, with the secret intimation of her end which I surmise must have reached her by this time, she believed to be served by Forester's plan. It was so much the general view that by marrying I took myself out of the family altogether, that I felt convinced that she meant, so soon as that was accomplished, to undertake what, in the face of my protesting attitude, she had not the courage to begin. I remember how shocked she was at my telling her that this tying up of the two ends of life in a monetary obligation, would put her and Forester very much in the situation of a young man married to a middle-aged woman. I mention this here because the implication that grew out of it, of my marriage being looked forward to as a relief, had much to do with the failure out of my life at this juncture, of informing intimacy.

A great deal of necessary information had come my way through Pauline's marriage, through the comment set free by Belle Endsleigh's affair, through the natural awakening of my mind toward the intimations of books. Marriage I began to perceive as an engulfing personal experience. Until now I hadn't been able to think of it except as a means of providing pleasant companionship on the way toward that large and shining world for which I felt myself forever and unassailably fit. It began to exhibit now, through vistas that allured, the aspect of a vast inhuman grin. Somewhere out of this prospect of sympathy and understanding, arose upon you the tremendous inundation of Life. Dimly beyond the point of Tommy's joyous possession of me, I was aware of an incalculable Force by which the whole province of my being was assailed, very different from the girlish prevision of motherhood which had floated with the fragrance of orris root from Aunt Alice's bureau drawer in the Allingham's spare room.

I don't say this is the way all girls feel about the approach of maternity, but I saw it then like the wolf in the fairy tale, which as soon as its head was admitted, thrust in a shoulder and so came bodily into the room and devoured the protestant. Long afterward, when I was in a position to know something of the private experience of trapeze performers, I learned that they came to a point sometimes in mid-spring when the body apprised them of inadequacy, a warning sure to be followed in no long time by disaster. I have thought sometimes that what reached

me then was the advice of a body instinctively aware of
being unequal to the demands about to be imposed upon
it.

I hardly know now by what road I arrived at the
certainty that some women, Pauline for instance, were
able to face this looming terror of childbearing by making
terms with it. Life, it appeared, waited at their doors with
respect, modified the edge of its inevitableness to their
convenience. If Pauline had been accessible—but she was
living in Chicago with Henry Mills, going out a great deal,
and writing me infrequent letters of bright complacency.
It was only in the last frightened gasp I fixed upon my
mother. You must imagine for yourself from what you
know of nice girls thirty years ago, how inarticulate the
whole business was; the most I can do is to have you
understand my desperate need to know, to interpose between marriage and maternity never so slight an interval
in which to collect myself and leave off shrinking.

About a week before my wedding we were sitting together at the close of the afternoon; my mother had taken
up her knitting, as her habit was when the light failed.
Something in the work we had been doing, putting the
last touches to my wedding dress, led her to speak of her
own, and of my father as a young man. The mention
pricked me to notice what I recall now as characteristic
of Taylorville women, that, with all she had been through,
the war, her eight children, so many graves, there was
still in her attitude, toward all these, a kind of untutored
virginity. It made, my noticing it then and being touched
by it, a sort of bridge by which it seemed for the moment
she might be drawn over to my side. On the impulse I
spoke.

"Mother," I said, "I want to know . . . ?"

It seemed a natural sort of knowledge to which any
woman had a right. Almost before the question was out I
saw the expression of offended shock come over my
mother's reminiscent softness, the nearly animal rage of
terror with which the unknown, the unaccustomed,
assailed her.

"Olivia! Olivia!" She stood up, her knitting rigid in her
hands, the ball of it speeding away in the dusk of the floor
on some private terror of its own. "Olivia, I'll not hear of
such things! You are not to speak of them, do you understand! I'll have nothing to do with them!"

"I wanted to know," I said. "I thought you could tell me . . . ."

I went over and stood by the window; a little dry snow was blowing—it was the first week in November—beginning to collect on the edges of the walks and along the fences; the landscape showed sketched in white on a background of neutral gray. I heard a movement in the room behind me; my mother came presently and stood looking out with me. She was very pale, scared but commiserating. Somehow my question had glanced in striking the dying nerve of long since encountered dreads and pains. We faced them together there in the cold twilight.

"I'm sorry, daughter"—she hesitated—"I can't help you. I don't know . . . I never knew myself."

CHAPTER II

It is no doubt owing to the habit of life in Higgleston being so little differentiated from Taylorville that I was never able to get any other impression of it than as a place one put up at on the way to some other; always it bore to my mind the air of a traveller's room in one of those stops where it is necessary to open the trunks but not worthwhile to unpack them. Nor do I think it was altogether owing to what I left there that my recollection of it centres paganly about the cemetery. In Taylorville, love and birth, though but scantily removed from the savour of impropriety, were still the salient facts of existence, but in Higgleston a funeral was your real human occasion. It was as if the rural fear of innovation had thrown them back for a pivotal centre upon the point of continuity with their past.

It was a generous rolling space set aside for the dead, abutting on two sides on the boardwalks of the town, stretching back by dips and hollows to the wooded pastures. Near the gates which opened from the walk, it was divided off in single plots and family allotments, scattering more and more to the farthest neglected mounds that crept obscurely under the hazel thickets and the sapling oaks, happiest when named the least, assimilated quickest to their native earth. It was this that rendered the pagan touch, for though nearly all Higgleston was church-going and looked forward to a hymn-book heaven, they seemed to me never quite dissevered from the untutored pastures to which their whole living and dying was a process of being reabsorbed.

Higgleston, until this junction of railroads occurred, had been a close settled farming community, and a vague notion of civic improvement had ripped through the centre of its wide old yards and comfortable, country looking dwellings, a shadeless, unpaved street lined with what were known as business blocks, with a tendency to run mostly to front and a general placarded state of being to let, or about to be opened on these premises.

Beyond the railway station there was a dingy region devoted to car shops and cheap lodgings, known locally as

Track Town, whose inhabitants were forever at odds with the older rural population, withdrawing itself into a kind of aristocracy of priority and propriety; and between these an intermediary group, self styled, "the leading businessmen of the town," forever and trivially busy to reconcile the two factions in the interests of trade. That Tommy was by reason of his position as managing salesman of Burton Brothers, generically of this class, might have had something to do with my never having formed any vital or lasting relations with either community; and it might have been for quite other reasons. For in the very beginning of my stay there, Life had seized me; that bubbling, frothing Force, working forever to breach the film of existence. I was used by it, I was abused by it. For what does Life care what it does to the tender bodies of women?

My baby was born within ten months of my marriage and most of that time I was wretchedly, depressingly ill. All my memories of my early married life are of Olivia, in the mornings still with frost, cowering away from the kitchen sights and smells, or gasping up out of ingulfing nausea to sit out the duty calls of the leading ladies of Higgleston in the cold, disordered house; of Tommy gulping unsuitable meals of underdone and overdone things, and washing the day's accumulation of dishes after business hours, patient and portentously cheerful, with Olivia in a wrapper, half hysterical with weakness—all the young wife's dreams gone awry! And Tommy too, he must have had visions of himself coming home to a well-kept house, of delicious little dinners and long hours in which he should appear in his proper character as the adored, achieving male. Not long ago I read a book of a man's life written by a man, in which he justified himself of unfaithfulness because his wife appeared before him habitually in curl papers—and there were days when I couldn't even do my hair!

In the beginning we had taken, in respect to Tommy's position among those same live business men, a house rather too large for us, and we hadn't counted on the wages of a servant. Now with the necessity upon us of laying by money for the Great Expense, we felt less justified in it than ever. This pinch of necessity was of the quality of corrosion on what must have been meant for the consummate experience. I have to dwell on it here because in this practical confusion of my illness, was laid the foundation of our later failure to come together on any working basis. We hadn't, in fact, time to find it; no time to understand, none whatever in which to explore the use of passion and react into that superunion of which the bodily relation is the overt sign—young things we were, who had not fairly known each other as man and woman before we were compelled to trace in one another lineaments of parents, all attention drawn away from the imperative business of framing a common ideal, to centre on the child.

What this precipitance accomplished was, that, instead of being drawn insensibly to find in the exigencies of marriage the natural unfolding of that inward vitality, always much stronger in me than any exterior phase, I was by the shock of too early maternity driven apart from the usual, and I still believe the happier, destiny of women.

With all this we were spared the bitterness of the unwelcoming thought. Little homely memories swim up beyond the pains and depressions to mark, like twigs and leafage on a freshet, the swelling of the new affection: Effie at Montecito, overruling all my mother's shocked suggestions as to her supposed obliviousness of my condition, sitting up nights to sew for me . . . the dress I tried to make myself . . . the bureau drawer from which I used to take the little things every night to look at them . . . the smell of orris.

"See, Tommy; I've done *so* much to-day. Isn't it pretty?"

"My dear, you've shown that to me at least forty times and I've always said so."

"Yes, but isn't it? . . . the little sleeves . . . did you think anything *could* be so small? Tommy, don't you wish it would *come?*"

We had to make what we could of these moments of thrilled expectancy, of tender brooding curiosity.

I scarcely recall now all the reasons why it was thought best for me to go back to my mother in August, and to the family physician, but I find it all pertinent to my subject. Whatever was done there was mostly wrong, though I was years finding it out. I mean that whatever chance I had of growing up into the competent mother of a family was probably lost to me through the inexactitudes of country practice. We hadn't then arrived at the realization that the well or ill going of maternity is a matter of sceptics rather than sentiment. Taylorville was a town of ten thousand inhabitants, but at that time no one had heard of such a thing as a trained nurse; the business of midwifery was given over in general to a widow so little attractive that she was thought not to have a chance of marrying again, and by the circumstance of having had two or three children of her own, believed to be eminently fit. To Olivia's first encounter with the rending powers of Life, there went any amount of affectionate consideration and much old wives' lore of an extraordinary character. It seems hardly credible now, but in the beginning of things going wrong, there were symptoms concealed from the doctor on the ground of delicacy.

My baby, too, poor little man, was feeble from birth, a bottle baby; the best that could have been done would hardly have been a chance for him. Lying there in the hot, close room, all the air shut out with the light, in the midst of pains, I made a fight for him, tried to interpose such scraps of better knowledge as had come to me through reading, but they made no headway against my mother's confidential, "Well, I ought to know, I've buried five," and against Forester, who by the added importance of having invested all her fortune, had gained such way with my mother that she listened respectfully to his explication of what should be done for the baby. It was Forester who overbore with ridicule my suggestion that he should be fed at regular hours, for which I never forgave him. But I had enough to do to fortify my racked body against the time when I should be obliged to get up and go on again, as it seemed privately I never should be able.

And they were all so fond and proud of my little Thomas Henry—he was named so for his father and mine—Effie simply adored him; the wonder of his smallness, the way in which he moved his limbs and opened and shut his eyes; quite as if there had never been one born before. The way they hung over him, and the wrong things they did! Even Cousin Lydia drove into church the first Sunday after, for the purpose of holding him for a quarter of an hour in her large, silk poplin arms, at the end of which time she had softened almost to the point of confidence.

"I thought I was going to have one once," she admitted, "but somehow I couldn't seem to manage it." She looked over to where Cousin Judd sat with my mother. "He was always fond of young ones. . . ." It occurred to me then that Cousin Lydia was probably a much misunderstood woman.

Of the next six months at Higgleston after I returned to it with a three months' old baby I have scarcely any recollection that is not mixed up with bodily torment for myself and anxiety for the child. I think it probable that most of that time my husband found the house badly kept, the meals irregular and his wife hysterical. I hadn't anything to spare with which to consider what figure I might have cut in the eyes of the onlooker. Tommy shines out for me in that period by reason of the unwearying patience and cheerfulness with which he successfully ignored the general unsatisfactoriness of his home, and at times for a certain exasperation I had with him, as if by being somehow less quiescent he might have opposed a better front to the encroachments of distress. We did try help in the kitchen after our finances had a little recovered from the strain of my confinement, a Higgleston girl of no very great competence and a sort of back-door visiting acquaintance with two thirds of the community. Her chief accomplishments while she stayed with us, were concocted out of the scraps and fag ends of our private conversations. I could always tell that Ida had overheard something by the alacrity with which she banged the pots about in the kitchen in order that she might get through with her work and go out and tell somebody. In the end Tommy said that when it came to a choice between getting his own meals and losing his best customers he preferred the former.

All this time I did not know how ill I was because of the consuming anxiety for the baby. I remember times in the night—the dreadful momentary revolt of my body rousing to this new demand upon it, before the mind waked to the selfless consideration; and the failure of composure which was as much weakness as fear; the long watching, the walking to and fro, and the debates as to whether we ought or ought not to venture on the expense of the doctor. And for long years afterward what is the bitterest of bitterness, finding out that we had done the wrong thing. To this day I cannot come across any notices of the more competent methods for the care of delicate children, without a remembering pang.

All the time this was going on I was aware by a secondary detached sort of self, that there was a point somewhere beyond this perplexity of pain, at which the joyful possession of my son should begin. I was anxious to get at him, to have speech with him, to realize his identity—any woman will understand—and along about the time the blue flags and the live-for-evers and the white bridal wreaths were at their best in the cemetery, it came upon me terrifyingly that I might, after all, have to let him go without it. We were walking there that day, the first we had thought it safe to take the baby out, for it was customary to walk in the cemetery on Sunday and almost obligatory to your social standing. The oaks were budding, and the wind in the irises and the shadow of them on the tombstones, and the people all in their Sunday best, walking in the warm light, gave an effect of more aliveness than the sombre yards of the town could afford.

Tommy had taken the baby from me, for, though I could somehow never get enough of the feel of him, his head in the hollow of my shoulder, his weight against my arm, I was so little strong myself that I was glad to pretend that it was because he was really getting heavy, and just then we passed a little mound, so low, where a new headboard had been set up with the superscription, "Only son of ——— and ——— aged eight months," and it was the age, and the little mound was just the length of my boy. I think there was a rush of tears to cover that, the realization by a kind of prevision that it was just to that he was to come, tears checked in mid-course by the swift up-rush of the certainty, of the reality, of the absoluteness of human experience. For by whatever mystery or magic he had come to identity through me, he was my son as I knew, and not even death could so unmake him.

I dwell upon this and one other incident which I shall relate in its proper place, as all that was offered to me of the traditional compensation for what women are supposed to be. If a sedulous social ideal has kept them from the world touch through knowledge and achievement, it has been because, sincerely enough, they have not been supposed to be prevented from world processes so much as directed to find them in a happier way. This would be reasonable if they found them. What society fails to understand, or dishonesty fails to admit, is that marriage as an act is not invariably the stroke that ushers in the experience of being married.

Whatever proportions the change in my life had assumed to the outward eye, it was only by the imagined pain of loss that I began to perceive that I could never be quite in the same relation to things again, and to identify my experience with the world adventure. I had become, by the way of giving life and losing it, a link in the chain that leads from dark to dark; I had touched for the moment a reality from which the process of self-realization could be measured. It was the most and the best I was to know of the incident called maternity, that whether it were most bitter or most sweet it was irrevocable.

I suppose, though he was always so inarticulate, that Tommy must have caught something of my mood from me. He didn't seem to see anything ridiculous in my holding on to a fold of the baby's skirt all the way home; and when we had come into the house and the boy was laid in his crib again, so wan and so little, I sat on my young husband's knee and cried with my face against his, and he did not ask me what it was about.

I think, though, that we had not yet appreciated how near we were to losing him until my mother came to visit us along in the middle of the summer. She was quite excited, as she walked up from the station with Tommy, and for her, almost gay with the novelty of spending a month with a married daughter, and then as soon as she had sight of the child, I saw her checked and startled inquiry travel from me to Tommy and back to the child's meagre little features, and a new and amazing tenderness in all her manner to me. That night after I was in bed she came in her night-dress and kissed me without saying anything, and I was too surprised to make any motion of response. That was the first time I remember my mother having kissed me on anything less than an official occasion . . . but she had buried five herself.

Notwithstanding, my mother's coming and the care she took of the baby, seemed to make me, if anything, less prepared for the end. There were new remedies of my mother's to be tried which appeared hopeful. I recovered composure, thought of him as improving, when in fact it was only I who was stronger for a few nights' uninterrupted sleep. Then there was a day on which he was very quiet and she scarcely put him down from her lap at all. I do not know what I thought of that, nor of the doctor coming twice that day, unsummoned. I suppose my sensibilities must have been blunted by the strain, for I recall thinking when Tommy came home in the middle of the afternoon, how good it was we could all have this quiet time together. It was the end of June. I remember the blinds half drawn against the sun and the smell of lawns newly cut and the damask rose by the window; I was going about putting fresh flowers in the vases, a thing I had of late little time to do . . . suddenly I noticed Tommy crying. He sat close to my mother trying to make the boy's poor little claws curl round his finger, and at the failure tears ran down unwiped. I had never seen Tommy cry. I put down my roses uncertain if I ought to go to him . . . and all at once my mother called me.

CHAPTER III

Very closely on the loss of my baby, of which I have spared you as much as possible, came crowding the opening movement of my artistic career. Within a month I was in a hospital in Chicago, recovering from the disastrous termination of another expectancy that had come, scarcely regarded in the obsession of anxiety and overwork during the last weeks of my boy's life, and had failed to sustain itself under the shock of his death. And after the hospital there was a month of convalescence at Pauline's. It was the first time I had seen her since her marriage.

I found her living in one of those curious, compressed city houses, one room wide and three deep, which, after the rambling, scattered homes of Higgleston, induced a feeling of cramp, until I discovered a kind of spaciousness in the life within. It was really very little else than relief from the accustomed inharmonies of rurality, a sort of scenic air and light that answered perfectly so long as you believed it real. Pauline's wall papers were soft, unpatterned, with wide borders; her windows were hung with plain scrim and the furniture coverings were in tone with the carpets. When ladies called in the afternoon, Pauline gave them tea which she made in a brass kettle over a spirit lamp. You can scarcely understand what that kettle stood for in my new estimate of the graciousness of living: a kind of sacred flame, round which gathered unimagined possibilities for the dramatization of that eager inward life which, now that the strictures of bodily pain were loosed, began to press toward expression. It rose insistently against the depressing figure my draggled and defeated condition must have cut in the face of Pauline's bright competency and the quality of assurance in her choice of the things among which she moved. Whatever her standards of behaviour or furniture, they were always present to the eye, not sunk below the plane of consciousness like mine, and she could always name you the people who practised them or the places where they could be bought and at what price. My expressed interest in the teakettle, led at once to the particular department store where I saw rows of them shining in the ticketed inaccessibility of seven dollars and ninety-eight cents. From point to point of such eminent practicability I was pricked to think of preëmpting some of these new phases of suitability for myself, finding myself debarred by the flatness of my purse. The effect of it was to throw me back into the benumbing sense of personal neglect with which the city had burst upon me. From the first, as I began to go about still in my half-invalided condition, I had been tremendously struck with the plentitude of beauty. Here was every article of human use made fair and fit so that nobody need have lacked a portion of it, save for an inexplicable error in the means of distribution. I, for instance, who had within me the witness of heirship, had none of it.

That I should have felt it so, was no doubt a part of that Taylorvillian fallacy in which I had been reared, that all that was precious and desirable was shed as the natural flower and fruit of goodness. Here confronted with the concrete preciousness of the shop windows, I realized that if there had been anything originally sound in that proposition, I had at least missed the particular kind of goodness to which it was chargeable. I wanted, I absurdly wanted just then to collect my arrears of privilege and consideration in terms of hardwood furniture and afternoon teakettles, in graceful, feminine leisure, all the traditional sanctity and enthronement of women, for which I had paid with my body, with maternal anxieties and wifely submission. What glimmered on my horizon was the realization that it was not in such appreciable coin the debt was paid, the beginning of knowledge that seldom, except by accident, is it paid at all. What I learned from Pauline was that most of it came by way of the bargain counter. Not even the Shining Destiny was due to arrive merely by reason of your own private conviction of being fit, but demanded something to be laid down for it; though if you had ~ed the whole price to me at that juncture, I should have efused to pay.

Besides all this, the most memorable thing that came of my visit to Pauline was that I went to the theatre. It was Henry's suggestion; he thought I wanted cheering. Pauline was not going out much that season and her reluctance to claim my attention, in the face of my bereavement, to her own approaching Event, threw at times a shadow of constraint on our quiet evenings. Henry had fallen into a way of taking me out for timid and Higglestonian glimpses of the night sights of the city, but I am not sure it was the obligation of hospitality which led him to propose the theatre. I recall that he displayed a particular knowingness about what he styled "the attractions." What surprised me most was that I discovered no qualms in myself over a proceeding so at variance with my bringing up; and the piece, a broad comedy of Henry's selection, made no particular impression on me other than the singular one of having known a great deal about it before. My criticism of the acting brought Pauline around with a swing from the City Cousin attitude in which she had initiated the experience for me, to one aesthetically sympathetic.

"The things men choose, my dear—and to anybody who has been saturated in Shakespeare as you have! You really must see Modjeska; it will be an inspiration to you. Henry, you must take her to see Modjeska."

I had not yet made up my mind as to whether I liked Henry Mills, but I was willing to go and see Modjeska with him; we had orchestra seats and Pauline insisted on my wearing her black silk wrap. On the way, Henry told me a great deal about Madam Modjeska with that same air of knowingness which fitted so oddly with his assumption of the model husband. I had accustomed myself to think of Henry as an attorney, which in Taylorville meant a man who could be trusted with the administration of widows' property and Fourth of July orations. Henry, it transpired, was a sort of junior partner in one of those city firms whose concern is not with people who have broken the law, but with those who are desirous to sail as close to the wind as possible without breaking it. They had a great deal to do with stock companies, in connection with which Henry had found some personal advantage. He always referred to it as "our office" so that I am in doubt still as to the exact nature of his connection with it; its only relation to his private life was to lead to his habitually appearing in what is known as a business suit, and an air of shrewd reliability. If in the beginning he had any notions of his own as to what a husband ought to be, he had discarded them in favour of Pauline's, and if as early as that he had devised any system of paying himself off for his complicity in her ideals, I didn't discover it.

I saw Modjeska with Henry, in "Romeo and Juliet," and afterward stole away to a matinee by myself and saw her as Rosalind. I do not know now if she was the great artist she seemed, it is so long since I have seen her, but she sufficed. I had no words in which to express my extraordinary sense of possession in her, the profound, excluding intimacy of her art. Long after Henry Mills had gone to his connubial pillow I remained walking up and down in my room in a state of intense, inarticulate excitement. I did not think concretely of the stage nor of acting; what I had news of, was a country of large impulses and satisfying movement. I felt myself strong, had I but known the way, to set out for it. When I found sleep at last, it was to dream, not of the theatre, but of Helmeth Garrett. I was made aware of him first by a sense of fulness about my heart, and then I came upon him looking as he had looked last in the Willesden woods, writing at a table, a pale blur about him of the causeless light of dreams. I recognized the carpet underfoot as a favourite Taylorvillian selection, but overhead, red boughs of sycamore and oak depended through the dream-fogged atmosphere. I stood and read over his shoulder what he wrote, and though the words escaped me, the meaning of them put all straight between us. He turned as he wrote and looked at me with a look that set us back in the wrapt intimacy of the flaming forest . . . . somehow we had got there and found it softly dark! In the interval between my dream and morning, that kiss which had been the source of so much secret blame and secret exultation was somehow accounted for: it was a waif out of the country of Rosalind and Juliet. The sense of a vital readjustment remained with me all that day; there had been after all, in the common phrase, "something between us." But I explained the recrudescence of memory on the basis that it was from Helmeth Garrett that I had first heard of Chicago and Modjeska.

I came back to Higgleston reasonably well, with some fine points of achievement twinkling ahead of me, to have my new-found sense of direction put all at fault by the trivial circumstance of Tommy's having papered the living room. The walls when we took the house, had been finished hard and white, much in need of renewing, from the expense of which our immediate plunge into the cares of a family had prevented us. Casting about for any way of ridding it against my return, of the sadness of association, Tommy had hit upon the idea of papering the room himself in the evenings after closing hours, and by way of keeping it a pleasant surprise, had chosen the paper of his own taste. Any one who kept house in the early 80's will recall a type of paper then in vogue, of large unintelligent arabesques of a liverish bronzy hue, parting at regular intervals upon Neapolitan landscapes of pronounced pinks and blues. Tommy's landscapes achieved the added atrocity of having Japanese ladies walking about in them, and though the room wanted lighting, the paper was very dark. It must have cost him something too! From the amount of his salary which he had remitted for my hospital expenses he could hardly have left himself money to pay for his meals at Higgleston's one doubtful restaurant. The appearance of the kitchen, indeed, suggested that he had made most of them on crackers and tinned ham.

I was glad to have discovered this before I said to him how much better it would have been for him to send me the money and let me select the paper in Chicago. What leaped upon me as he waved the lamp about to show me how cleverly he had matched the borders, was the surprising, the confounding certainty that after all our shared sorrow and anxiety we hadn't in the least come together. I had lived in the house with him for two years, had borne him a child and lost it, and he had chosen this moment of heartrending return, to give me to understand that he couldn't even know what I might like in the way of wall papers.

I suppose all this time when the surface of my attention was taken up with the baby, I had been making unconscious estimates of my husband, but that night just as we had come from the station, the moment of calculating that on a basis of necessary economy, I should have to live at least three years with the evidence of his ineptitude, was the first of my regarding him critically as the instrument of my destiny. And I hadn't primarily selected him for that purpose. I do not know now exactly why I married Tommy, except that marriage seemed a natural sort of experience and I had taken to it as readily as though it had been something to eat, something to nourish and sustain. I hadn't at any rate thought of it as entangling. I did not then; but certainly it occurred to me that for the enlarged standard of living I had brought home with me, a man of Tommy's taste was likely to prove an unsuitable tool.

Slight as the incident of the wall paper was, it served to check my dawning interest in domesticity, and set my hungering mind looking elsewhere for sustenance. We were still a little in arrears on account of the funeral expenses and my illness, and no more improvements were to be thought of; Tommy and I were of one mind in that we had the common Taylorvillian horror of debt. There were other things which seemed to put off my conquest of the harmonious environment, things every woman who has lost a child will understand . . . starting awake at night to the remembered cry . . . the blessed weight upon the arm that failed and receded before returning consciousness. I recall going into the bedroom once where a shawl had been dropped on the pillow, like . . . so like . . . and the memories of infinitesimal neglects that began to show now preposterously blamable.

In my first year at Higgleston I had been rather driven apart from the community by the absorption of my condition and the intimation that instead of being the crown of life it merely saved itself by not being mentioned. Now, in my desperate need of the social function, I began to imagine, for want of any other likeness between us, a community of lack. I thought of Higgleston as aching for life as I ached, and began to wonder if we mightn't help one another.

As the colder weather shut me more into the haunted rooms, Tommy thought it might be a good thing if I took an interest in the entertainment which the I.O.O.F., of which he was a Fellow, was undertaking for the benefit of their new hall. As the sort of service counted on from the wives of prominent members, it might also be beneficial to trade. On this understanding I did take an interest, with the result that the entertainment was an immense success. It led naturally to my being put in charge of the annual Public School Library theatricals and a little later to my being connected with what was the acute dramatic crisis of the Middle West.

There should be a great many people still who remember a large, loose melodrama called "The Union Spy," or "The Confederate Spy," accordingly as it was performed north or south of Mason and Dixon's line, participated in by the country at large; a sort of localized Passion play lifted by its tremendous personal interest free of all theatrical taint. There was a Captain McWhirter who went about with the scenery and accessories, casting the parts and conducting rehearsals, sharing the profits with the local G.A.R. The battle scenes were invariably executed by the veterans of the order, with horrid realism. Effie wrote me that there had been three performances in Taylorville and Cousin Judd had been to every one of them.

With the reputation I had acquired in Higgleston, it came naturally when the town, by its slighter hold on the event, achieved a single performance, for me to be cast for the principal part, unhindered by any convention on behalf of my recent mourning. Rather, so close did the subject lie to the community feeling, there was an instinctive sense of dramatic propriety in my sorrow in connection with the anguish of war-bereaved women. One can imagine such a sentiment operating in the choice of players at Oberammergau. In addition to my acting, I began very soon to take a large share of the responsibility of rehearsals.

I do not know where I got the things I put into that business. Where, in fact, does Gift come from, and what is the nature of it? I found myself falling back on my studies with Professor Winter, on slight amateurish incidents of Taylorville, on my brief Chicago contact even, to account to Higgleston for insights, certainties, that they would not have accepted without some such obvious backing. Nevertheless the thing was there, the aptitude to seize and carry to its touching, its fruitful expression, the awkward eagerness of the community to relive its most moving actualities. Never in America have we been so near the democratic drama.

In the final performance I surprised Tommy and myself with my success, most of all I surprised Captain McWhirter. He was arranging a production of "The

Spy" at the twin towns of Newton and Canfield, about two hours south of us, and asked me to go down there for him and attend to alternate rehearsals. Tommy was immensely flattered, pleased to have me forget my melancholy, and the money was a consideration. I saw the captain through with two performances in each town, and three at Waterbury. All this time I had not thought of the stage professionally. I returned to Tommy and the wall paper after the final performance with a vague sense of flatness, to try to pull together out of Higgleston's unwilling materials the stuff of a satisfying existence.

Suddenly in April came a telegram and a letter from Captain McWhirter at Kincade, to say that on the eve of production, his leading lady had run away to be married, and could I, would I, come down and see him through. The letter contained an enclosure for travelling expenses, and a substantial offer for my time. No reasonable objection presenting itself, I went down to him by Monday's train.

CHAPTER V

Understand that up to this time I had not yet thought of the stage as a career for myself. I hadn't yet needed it. I had not then realized that the insight and passion which have singled me out among women of my profession couldn't be turned to render the mere business of living beautiful and fit. I hardly understand it now. Why should people pay night after night to see me loving, achieving, suffering, in a way they wouldn't think of undertaking for themselves? Life as I saw it was sufficiently dramatic: charged, wonderful. I at least felt at home in the great moments of kings, the tender hours of poets, and I hadn't thought of my participation in these things rendering me in any way superior to Higgleston or even different. If I had, I shouldn't have settled there in the first place. If I had glimpsed even at Tommy's exclusion from all that mattered passionately to me, I shouldn't have married him. It was because I had not yet begun to be markedly dissatisfied with either of them that I presently got myself the reputation of having trampled both Tommy and Higgleston underfoot. I must ask your patience for a little until I show you how wholly I offered myself to them both and how completely they wouldn't have me.

The point of departure was of course that I didn't accept the Higglestonian reading of married obligations to mean that my whole time was to be taken up with just living with Tommy. It was as natural, and in view of the scope it afforded for individual development, a more convenient arrangement than living with my mother, but not a whit more absorbing. I couldn't, anyway, think of just living as an end, and accordingly I looked about for a more spacious occupation; I thought I had found it in the directing of that submerged spiritual passion which I had felt in the sustaining drama of the war. I had a notion there might be a vent for it in the shape of a permanent dramatic society by means of which all Higgleston, and I with them, could escape temporarily from its commonness into the heroic movement. It was all very clear in my own mind but it failed utterly in communication.

I began wrongly in the first place by asking the Higgleston ladies to tea. Afternoon tea was unheard of in Higgleston, and I had forgotten, or perhaps I had never learned, that in Higgleston you couldn't do anything different without implying dissatisfaction with things as they were. You were likely on such occasions to be visited by the inquiry as to whether the place wasn't good enough for you. As a matter of fact afternoon tea was almost as unfamiliar to me as to the rest of them, but I had read English novels and I knew how it ought to be done. I knew for instance, that people came and went with a delightful informality and had tea made fresh for them, and were witty or portentous as the occasion demanded. My invitations read from four to five, and the Higgleston ladies came solidly within the minute and departed in phalanxes upon the stroke of five. They all wore their best things, which, from the number of black silks included, and black kid gloves not quite pulled on at the finger tips, gave the affair almost a funereal atmosphere. They had most of them had their tea with their midday meal, and Mrs. Dinkelspiel said openly that she didn't approve of eating between meals. They sat about the room against the wall and fairly hypnotized me into getting up and passing things, which I knew was not the way tea should be served. In Higgleston, the only occasion when things were handed about, were Church sociables and the like, when the number of guests precluded the possibility of having them all at your table; and by the time I got once around, the tea was cold and I realized how thin my thin bread and butter and chocolate wafers looked in respect to the huge, soft slabs of layer cake, stiffened by frosting and filling, which, in Higgleston went by the name of light refreshments. The only saving incident was the natural way in which Mrs. Ross, our attorney's wife who visited East every summer and knew how things were done, asked for "two lumps, please," and came back a second time for bread and butter. I think they were all tremendously pleased to be asked, though they didn't intend to commit themselves to the innovation by appearing to have a good time. And that was the occasion I chose for broaching my great subject, without, I am afraid, in the least grasping their incapacity to share in my joyous discovery of the world of Art which I so generously held out to them.

It hadn't been possible to keep my professional adventure from the townspeople, nor had I attempted it. What I really felt was that we were to be congratulated as a community in having one among us privileged to experience it, and I honestly think I should have felt so of anyone to whom the adventure had befallen. But I suspect I must have given the impression of rather flaunting it in their faces.

I put my new project on the ground that though we were dissevered by our situation, there was no occasion for our being out of touch with the world of emotion, not, at least, so long as we had admission to it through the drama; and it wasn't in me to imagine that the world I prefigured to them under those terms was one by their standards never to be kept sufficiently at a distance.

Mrs. Miller put the case for most of them with the suggestion thrown out guardedly that she didn't "know as she held with plays for church members"; she was a large, tasteless woman, whose husband kept the lumber yard and derived from it an extensive air of being in touch with the world's occupations. "And I don't know," she went on relentlessly, "that I ever see any good come of play acting to them that practise it."

Mrs. Ross, determined to live up to her two lumps, came forward gallantly with:

"Oh, but, Mrs. Miller, when our dear Mrs. Bettersworth——"

"That's what I was thinking of," Mrs. Miller put it over her.

"Well for my part," declared Mrs. Dinkelspiel, with the air of not caring who knew it, "I don't want my girls to sell tickets or anything; it makes 'em too forward." Mrs. Harvey, whose husband was in hardware, began to tell discursively about a perfectly lovely entertainment they had had in Newton Centre for the missionary society, which Mrs. Miller took exception to on the ground of its frivolity.

"I don't know," she maintained, "if the Lord's work ain't hindered by them sort of comicalities as much as it's helped."

I am not sure where this discussion mightn't have landed us if the general attention had not been distracted just then by my husband, an hour before his time, coming through the front gate and up the walk. He had evidently forgotten my tea party, for he came straight to me, and

backed away precipitately through the portières as soon
as he saw the assembled ladies sitting about the wall. It
was not that which disturbed us; any Higgleston male
would have done the same, but it was plain in the brief
glimpse we had of him that he looked white and stricken.
A little later we heard him in the back of the house
making ambiguous noises such as not one of my guests
could fail to understand as the precursor of a domestic
crisis. I could see the little flutter of uneasiness which
passed over them, between their sense of its demanding
my immediate attention and the fear of leaving before
the expressed time. Fortunately the stroke of five released
them. The door was hardly shut on the last silk skirt when
I ran out and found him staring out of the kitchen window.

"Well?" I questioned.

"I thought they would never go," he protested. "Come
in here." He led the way to the living room as if somehow
he found it more appropriate to the gravity of what he had
to impart, and yet failed to make a beginning with his
news. He shut the door and leaned against it with his
hands behind him for support.

"Has anything happened?"

"Happened? Oh, I don't know. I've lost my job."

"Lost? Burton Brothers?" I was all at sea.

He nodded. "They're closing out; the manager's in town
to-day. He told us . . . " By degrees I got it out of him.
Burton Brothers thought they saw hard times ahead, they
were closing out a number of their smaller establishments,
centering everything on their Chicago house. Suddenly my
thought leaped up.

"But couldn't they give you something there . . . in
Chicago?" I was dizzy for a moment with the wild hope of
it. Never to live in Higgleston any more—but Tommy cut
me short.

"They've men who have been with them longer than I
have to provide for . . . I asked."

"Oh, well, no matter. The world is full of jobs." Looking for one appealed to me in the light of an adventure,
but because I saw how pale he was I went to him and
began to kiss him softly. By the way he yielded himself to
me I grasped a little of his lost and rudderless condition,
once he found himself outside the limits of a salaried em-

ployment. I began to question him again as the best way of getting the extent of our disaster before us.

"What does Mr. Rathbone say?" Rathbone was our working tailor, a thin, elderly, peering man of a sort you could scarcely think of as having any existence apart from his shop. He used to come sidling down the street to it and settle himself among his implements with the air of a brooding hen taking to her nest; the sound of his machine was a contented clucking.

"He was struck all of a heap. They're better fixed than we are." Tommy added this as an afterthought as likely to affect the tailor's attitude when he came to himself. "They" were old Rathbone and his daughter, one of those conspicuously blond and full-breasted women who seem to take to the dressmaking and millinery trades by instinct. As she got herself up on Sunday in her smart tailoring, with a hat "from the city," and her hair amazingly pompadoured, she was to some of the men who came to our church, very much what the brass teakettle was to me, a touch of the unattainable but not unappreciated elegancies of life. Tommy admired her immensely and was disappointed that I did not have her at the house oftener.

"They've got her business to fall back on," Tommy suggested now with an approach to envy. He had never seen Miss Rathbone as I had, professionally, going about with her protuberant bosom stuck full of pins, a tape line draped about her collarless neck, and her skirt and belt never quite together in the back, so he thought of her establishment as a kind of stay in affliction.

"And I have the stage," I flourished. It was the first time I had thought of it as an expedient, but I glanced away from the thought in passing, for to say the truth I didn't in the least know how to go about getting a living by it. I creamed some chipped beef for Tommy's supper, a dish he was particularly fond of, and opened a jar of quince marmalade, and all the time I wasn't stirring something or setting the table, I had my arms around him, trying to prop him against what I did not feel so much terrifying as exciting. We talked a little about his getting his old place back in Taylorville, and just as we were clearing away the supper things we saw Miss Rathbone, with her father tucked under her arm, pass the square of light raying out into the spring dusk from our window, and a moment later they knocked at our door. It was one of the things that I felt bound to like Miss Rathbone for, that she took such care of her father; she did everything for him, it was said, even to making up his mind for him, and this evening by the flare of the lamp Tommy held up to welcome them, it was clear she had made it up to some purpose. It must have been what he saw in her face that made my husband put the lamp back on the table from which the white cloth had not yet been removed, as if the clearing up was too small a matter to consort with the occasion.

I was relieved to have my husband take charge of the visit, especially as he made no motion to invite them into the front room where the remains of the bread and butter and the chairs against the wall would have apprised Miss Rathbone of my having entertained company on an occasion to which she had not been invited. It was part of Tommy's sense of social obligation that we ought never to neglect Mr. Rathbone, whom, though his connection with the business was as slight as my husband's, he insisted on regarding as in some sort a partner. So we sat down rather stiffly about the table still shrouded in its white cloth, as though upon it were about to be laid out the dead enterprise of Burton Brothers, and looked, all of us, I think, a little pleased to find ourselves in so grave a situation.

Miss Rathbone, who had always a great many accessories to her toilet, bags and handkerchiefs and scarves and things, laid them on the table as though they were a kind of insignia of office, and made a poor pretence to keep up with me the proper feminine detachment from the business which had brought them there. We neither of us, Miss Rathbone and I, had the least idea what the other might be thinking about or presumably interested in, though I think she made the more gallant effort to pretend that she did. On this evening I could see that she was full of the project for which she had primed her father, and was nervously anxious lest he shouldn't go off at the right moment or with the proper pyrotechnic.

I remember the talk that went on at first, because it was so much in the way of doing business in Higgleston, and impressed me even then with its factitious shrewdness, based very simply on the supposition that Capitalists —it was under that caption that Burton Brothers figured

—never meant what they said. Capitalists were always talking of hard times; it was part of their deep laid perspicacity. Burton Brothers wished to sell out the business; was it reasonable to suppose they would think it good enough to sell and not good enough to go on with?

"Father thinks," said Miss Rathbone, and I am sure he had done so dutifully at her instigation, "that they couldn't ask no great price after talking about hard times the way they have."

It was not in keeping with what was thought to be woman's place, that she should go on to the completed suggestion. In fact, so far as I remember it never was completed, but was talked around and about, as if by indirection we could lessen the temerity of the proposal that old Rathbone and Tommy should buy out the shop on such favorable terms as Burton Brothers, in view of their own statement of its depreciation, couldn't fail to make.

"You could live over the store," Miss Rathbone let fall into the widening rings of silence that followed her first suggestion; "your rent would be cheaper, and it would come into the business."

I felt that she made it too plain that the chief objection that my husband could have was the lack of money for the initial adventure; but because I realized that much of my instinctive resistance to a plan that tied him to Higgleston as to a stake, was due to her having originated it, I kept it to myself. I had a hundred inarticulate objections, chief of which was that I couldn't see how any plan that was acceptable to the Rathbones, could get me on toward the Shining Destiny, but when you remember that I hadn't yet been able to put that concretely to myself, you will see how impossible it was that I should have put it to my husband. In the end Tommy was talked over. I believe the consideration of going on in the same place and under the same circumstances without the terrifying dislocation of looking for a job, had more to do with it than Miss Rathbone's calculation of the profits. We wrote home for the money; Effie wrote back that everything of mother's was involved in the stationery business, which was still on the doubtful side of prosperity, but Tommy's father let us have three hundred dollars.

The necessity of readjusting our way of life to Tommy's new status of proprietor, and moving in over the store, kept my plans for the dramatic exploitation of Higgleston in abeyance. It seemed however by as much as I was now bound up with the interest of the community, to put me on a better footing for beginning it, and on Decoration Day, walking in the cemetery under the bright boughs, between the flowery mounds, the Gift stirred in me, played upon by this touching dramatization of common human pain and loss. I recalled that it was just such solemn festivals of the people that I had had in mind to lay hold on and make the medium of a profounder appreciation. And the next one about to present itself as an occasion was the Fourth of July.

I detached myself from Tommy long enough to make my way around to two or three of the ladies who usually served on the committee.

"We ought to have a meeting soon now," I suggested; "it will take all of a month to get the children ready."

"That's what we thought," agreed Mrs. Miller heavily. "They was to our house Thursday——" She went on to tell me who was to read the Declaration and who deliver the oration.

"But," I protested, "that's exactly what they've had every Fourth these twenty years!"

"Well, I guess," said Mrs. Harvey, "if Higgleston people want that kind of a celebration, they've a right to have it."

"I guess they have," Mrs. Miller agreed with her.

They had always rather held it out against me at Higgleston that I had never taken the village squabbles seriously, that I was reconciled too quickly for a proper sense of their proportions, and they must have reckoned without this quality in me now, for I was so far from realizing the deliberateness of the slight, that I thought I would go around on the way home and see our minister; perhaps he could do something. It appeared simply ridiculous that Higgleston shouldn't have the newest of this sort of thing when it was there for the asking.

I found him raking the garden in his third best suit and the impossible sort of hat affected by professional men in their more human occasions. The moment I flashed out at him with my question about the committee, he fell at once into a manner of ministerial equivocation—the air of being man enough to know he was doing a mean thing without being man enough to avoid doing it. Er . . . yes, he believed there had been a meeting . . . he hadn't realized that I was expecting to be notified. I wasn't a regular member, was I?

"No," I admitted, "but last year——" The intention of the slight began to dawn on me.

"You see, the programme is usually made up from the children of the united Sunday schools. . ."

"I know, of course, but what has that? . . ." He did know how mean it was; I could see by the dexterity with which he delivered the blow.

"A good many of the mothers thought they'd rather not have them exposed to . . . er . . . professional methods." As an afterthought he tried to give it the cast of a priestly remonstrance which he must have seen didn't in the least impose on me.

I suppose it was the fear of how I might put it to one of his best paying parishioners that led him to go around to the store the next morning and make matters worse by explaining to Tommy that though the children weren't to be contaminated by my professionalism, it could probably be arranged for me to "recite something." To do Tommy justice, he was as mad as a hatter. Being so much nearer to village-mindedness himself, I suppose my husband could better understand the mean envy of my larger opportunity, but his obduracy in maintaining that I had been offended led to the only real initiative he ever showed in all the time I was married to him.

"I'd just like to *show* them!" he kept sputtering. All at once he cheered up with a snort. "*I'll* show them!" He was very busy all the evening with letters which he went out on purpose to post, with the result that when a few days later he made his contribution to the fireworks fund, he made it a little larger, as became a live business man, on the ground that he wouldn't be able to participate as his wife had "accepted an invitation to take charge of the programme at Newton Centre." Newton Centre was ten miles away, and though I couldn't do much on account of the difficulty of rehearsals, I managed to make the announcement of it in the county paper convey to them that what they had missed wasn't quite to be sicklied over with Mrs. Miller's asseveration of a notable want of moral particularity at Newton Centre. The very first time I went out to a Sunday-school social thereafter it was made plain to me that if I wanted to take up the annual Library entertainment, it was open to me.

"And I always will say," Mrs. Miller conceded, "that there's nobody can make your children seem such a credit to you as Mrs. Bettersworth."

"It's a regular talent you have," Mrs. Harvey backed her up, "like a person in the Bible." This scriptural reference came in so aptly that I could see several ladies nodding complacently. Mrs. Ross sailed quite over them and landed on the topmost peak of approbation.

"I've always believed," she asserted, "that a Christian woman on the stage would have an uplifting influence."

But by this time my ambition had slacked under the summer heat and the steady cluck of old Rathbone's machine and the mixed smell of damp woollen under the iron, and creosote shingle stains. There had been no loss of social standing in our living over the store; such readjustments in Higgleston went by the name of bettering yourself, and were commendable. But somehow I could never ask ladies to tea when the only entrance was by way of a men's furnishing store. The four rooms, opening into one another so that there was no way of getting from the kitchen to the parlour except through the bedroom, I found quite hopeless as a means of expressing my relation to all that appealed to me as inspiring, dazzling. Because I could not go out without making a street toilet, I went out too little, and suffered from want of tone. And suddenly along in September came a letter from O'Farrell offering me a place in his company, and a note from Sarah begging me to accept it. If up to that time I had not thought of the stage as a career, now at the suggestion the desire of it ravened in me like a flame.

CHAPTER VI

"And you never seem to think I might not *want* my wife to go on the stage?"

I do not know what unhappy imp prompted Tommy to take that tone with me; but whenever I try to fix upon the point of reprehensibleness which led on from my writing to O'Farrell that I would join him in ten days in Chicago, to the tragic termination of my marriage, I found myself whirled about this attitude of his in the deep-seated passionate Why of my life. Why should love be tied to particular ways of doing things? What was this horror of human obligation that made it necessary, since Tommy and I were so innocently fond of one another, that one of us should be made unhappy by it? Why should it be so accepted on all sides that it should be I? For my husband's feeling was but a single item in the total of social prejudice by which, once my purpose had gone abroad by way of the Rathbones, I found myself driven apart from the community interest as by a hostile tide, across which Higgleston gazed at me with strange, begrudging eyes. I recall how the men looked at me the first time I went out afterward, a little aslant, as though some ineradicable taint of impropriety attached in their minds to any association with the stage.

Whatever attitude Tommy finally achieved in the necessity of sustaining the situation he had created for himself by his backing of my first professional venture, was no doubt influenced by the need of covering his hurt at realizing, through my own wild rush to embrace the present opportunity, how far I was from accepting life gracefully at his hands, the docile creature of his dreams. Little things come back to me . . . words, looks . . . sticks and straws of his traditions made wreckage by the wind of my desire, which my resentment at his implication in the general attitude, prevented me from fully estimating. My mother too, to whom I wrote my decision as soon as I had arrived at it, in a long letter designed to convince me that a wife's chief duty and becomingness lay in seeing that nothing of her lapped over the bounds prescribed by her husband's capacity, contributed to the exasperated sense I had of having every step toward the fulfilment of my natural gift dragged at by loving hands. Poor Mother, I am afraid I never quite realized what a duckling I turned out to her, nor with what magnanimity she faced it.

"But I suppose you think you are doing right," she wrote at the end, and then in a postscript, "I read in the papers there is a church in New York that gives communion to actors, but I don't expect you will get as far as that."

It was finally Miss Rathbone who relieved the situation by pulling Tommy over to a consenting frame of mind in consideration of the neat little plumlet she extracted from it for herself by making me a travelling dress in three days. She brought it down to the house for me to try on, and it was pathetic to see the way my husband hung upon the effect she made for him of turning me out in a way that was a credit to them both.

"You'll see," she seemed to be saying to him by nothing more explicit than an exclamation full of pins and a clever way of squinting at the hang of my skirt, "that when we two take a hand at the affairs of the great world we can come up to the best of them." And all the time I could hear the Higgleston ladies drumming up trade for her out of Newton Centre with their "Stylish? Oh, very. She makes all her clothes for Mrs. Bettersworth—Olivia Lattimore, the actress, you know."

Just at the end though, when we were lying in bed the last morning, afraid to go to sleep again lest we shouldn't get up early enough to catch the train, I believe if Tommy had risen superior to his traditional objection to a married woman having interests outside her home, and claimed me by some strong personal need of his own, I should have answered it gladly. The trouble with my husband's need of me was that it left too much over.

"But of course," he reminded me at the station, "you can give it up any minute if you want to." I think quite to the last he hoped I would rise to some such generous pretence and come back to him, but we neither of us had much notion of the nature of a player's contract.

I had arranged to stay with Pauline until I could look about me, and from the little that I had been able to tell her of my affairs I could see she was in a flutter what to think of me. During the five days I was in her house I watched her swing through a whole arc of possible attitudes, to settle with truly remarkable instinct on the one which her own future permitted her most consistently to maintain.

"You dear, ridiculous child," she hovered over the point with indulgent patronage, "what will you think of next?"

Pauline herself was going through a phase at the time. They had moved out to a detached house at Evanston on account of its being better for the baby, and there was a visible diminution of her earlier effect of housewifely efficiency, in view of Henry's growing prosperity. You could see all Pauline's surfaces like a tulip bed in February, budding toward a new estimate of her preciousness in terms of her husband's income. When she took me by the shoulders, holding me off from her to give play to the pose of amused, affectionate bewilderment, I could see just where the consciousness of a more acceptable femininity as evinced by her being provided with a cook and a housemaid, prompted her to this gracious glossing over of my not being in quite so fortunate a case. I was to be the Wonder, the sport on the feminine bush, dear and extenuated, made adorably not to feel my excluding variation; an attitude not uncommon in wives of well-to-do husbands toward women who work. It was an attitude successfully kept up by Pauline Mills for as long as I provided her the occasion. Just at first I suspect I rather contributed to it by my own feeling of its being such a tremendous adventure for me, Olivia Lattimore, with Taylorville, Hadley's pasture and the McGee children behind me, to be going on the stage. How I exulted in it all, the hall bedroom where I finally settled across from Sarah Croyden, the worry of rehearsals, the baked smell of the streets bored through by the raw lake winds, the beckoning night lights—the vestibule of doors opening on the solemn splendour of the world.

At the rehearsals I met Cecelia Brune, if anything prettier than before, and quite perceptibly harder, and Jimmy Vantine, still in love with her, still with his bald crown not quite clean and the same objectionable habit of sidling about, fingering one's dress, laying hands on one as he talked. I met Manager O'Farrell, not a whit altered, and Miss Laurine Dean. I liked and I didn't like her. She drew by a certain warm charm of personality that repelled in closer quarters by its odours of sickliness. There was a quality in her beauty as of a flower kept too long in its glass, not so much withered as ready to fall apart. She had small appealing hands, such as moved one to take them up and handle them, and served somehow to mitigate a subtle impression of impropriety conveyed by her slight sidewise smile. She was probably good-natured by temperament and peevish through excessive use of cigarettes. She made a point of always speaking well of everybody, but it was a long time before I learned that no sort of blame was so deadly as her commendation. "Such a beautiful woman Miss Croyden is," she would say, "isn't it a pity about her nose," and though I had never thought of Sarah's nose as mitigating against her perfection, I found myself after that thinking of it. You could see that magnanimity, which was her chosen attitude, was often a strain to her. I do not think she had any gift at all, but she had a perception of it that had enabled her to produce a very tolerable imitation of acting and kept her, in a covert way, inordinately jealous of the gift in others. She was jealous of mine.

It was not all at once I discovered it. In the beginning, because I never detected her in any of the obvious snatchings of lines and positions that went on at rehearsals, but even making a stand for me against incursions into my part which I was too unaccustomed to forestall, I thought of her as being of rather better strain than most of the company. I was probably the only member of it unaware of her deliberate measures not to permit me such a footing as might lead to my supplanting her with Manager O'Farrell, toward whom I began to find myself in what, for me, was an interesting and charming relation. It was a relation I should have been glad to maintain with any member of the company, but it was only O'Farrell who found himself equal to it. I was full and effervescing with the joy of creation; night by night as I felt the working of the living organism we should have been, transmitting supernal energies of emotion to the audience, who by the very communicating act became a part of us, I felt myself also warming toward my fellow players. I was so charged I should have struck a spark from any one of them when we met, but for the fact that by degrees I discovered that they presented to me the negative pole.

I was aware of such communicating fluid between particular pairs of them. I saw it spark from eye to eye, heard it break in voices; it flashed like sheet lightning about our horizons on occasions of great triumph; but I was distinctly alive to the fact that the medium by which it was accomplished was turned from me. At times I was brushed by the wing of a suspicion that among the men, there was something almost predetermined in their denial of what was for me, the sympathetic, creative impulse. I was a little ashamed for them of the gaucherie of withholding what seemed so important to our common success, and yet I seemed always to be surprising all of them at it, except Jimmy Vantine and the manager. I couldn't of course, on account of his propensity for laying hands on one, take it from Jimmy, but between Mr. O'Farrell and me it ran with a pleasant, profitable warmth. I was conscious always of acting better the scenes I had with him. The thrill of them was never quite broken in off-the-stage hours. I felt myself sustained by it. For one thing the man had genuine talent, and I think besides Sarah Croyden and Jimmy Vantine, no one else in the company had very much. Jimmy had a gift, besmeared and discredited by his own cheapness, but O'Farrell had a real flowing genius and a degree of personal vitality that sketched him out as by fire from the flat Taylorville types I had known. We used to talk together about my own possibilities and I had many helpful hints from him, but in spite of this friendliness I never made any way with him against Miss Dean. Not that I tried, but by degrees I found that suggestions made and favours asked, were granted or accepted on the basis of their non-interference with our leading lady. I was not without intimations, which I usually disregarded because I found their conclusions impossible to maintain, that she even triumphed over me in little matters too inconsiderable to have been taken into account except on the understanding that we were pitted in a deliberate rivalry. I was hurt and amazed at times to discover that we presented this aspect to the rest of the company. I felt that I was being judged by my conduct of a business in which I was not engaged.

The situation, however, had not developed to such a pitch by the time we played in Kincade, that it could affect my pleasure in the visit Tommy paid me there; I was overjoyed to have the arms of my own man about me again; I was proud of his pride in my success as *Polly Eccles*, and pleased to have him and Sarah pleased with one another. I thought then that if I could only have Tommy and my work I should ask no more of destiny; I do not now see why I couldn't, but I like best to think of him as he seemed to me then, wholesome and good, raised by his joy of our reunion almost to my excited plane, generous in his sharing of my triumphs. It seemed for the moment to put my feet quite on solid ground. I knew at last where I was.

It was about a month after this that I began to find myself pitted against Miss Dean in a struggle for some dimly grasped advantage, with the dice cogged against me. I saw myself in the general estimate, convinced of handling my game badly, and could form no guess even at the expected moves. I smarted under a sense that Manager O'Farrell was not backing up the friendliness of our relations, and I remember saying to Sarah Croyden once that I suspected Miss Dean was using her sex attraction against me, but I missed the point of Sarah's slow, commiserating smile. At the time we were all more or less swamped by the discomforts of our wintry flights from town to town, execrable hotels, irregular and unsatisfying meals. One and another of us went down with colds, and finally toward the end of February, I was taken with a severe neuralgia. It reached its acutest stage the first night we played at Louisville.

I had hurried home from the theatre the moment I was released from my part, to find relief from it in rest, but an hour or two later, still suffering and discovering that I had taken all my powders, I decided to go down to Sarah's room on the lower floor to ask for some that I knew she had. I slipped on my shoes and a thick gray dressing gown, and taking the precaution of wrapping my head in a shawl against the draughty halls, I went down to her. I was returning with the box of powders in my hand when I was startled by the sound of a door lifting carefully on the latch. The hotel was

built in the shape of a capital T, with the stair half-
way of the stem. I was almost at the foot of it facing
the cross hall that gave me a view of the door of Miss
Dean's room, and I saw now that it was slightly ajar.
I shrank instinctively into the shadow of the recess where
the stair began, for I was unwilling that anybody should
see the witch I looked in my dressing gown and shawl.
In the interval before the door widened I heard the
tick of a tin-faced clock just across from me. Part of
the enamel was fallen away from the face of it so that
it looked as if eaten upon by discreditable sores; a chandelier holding two smoky kerosene lamps hung slightly
awry at the crossing of the T, and cast a tipsy shadow.
The door swung back slightly, it opened into the room,
and a man came out of it and crossed directly in front
of me, probably to his room in the other arm of the
T.

Once out of the door it snapped softly to behind
him, and the man fell instantly into a manner that dis-
connected him with it to a degree that could only have
been possible to an accomplished actor. If I had not
seen him come out of it, I should have supposed him
abroad upon such a casual errand as my own.

But there was no mistaking that it was Manager O'Farrell. By the tin-faced clock it was a quarter past one.
And he would have been home from the theatre more
than an hour!

I got up to my room somehow; I think my neuralgia
must have left me with the shock; I can't remember
feeling it any more after that. You have to remember
that this was my first actual contact with sin of any
sort. Generations of the stock of Methodism revolted in
me. I had liked the man, I had thought of our relation
as something precious, to be kept intact because it
nourished the quality of our art, and I had all the conventional woman's horror of being brought in touch with
looseness. It was part of the admitted business of the
men of my class to keep their women from such con-
tacts, and Manager O'Farrell had allowed me to enter into
a sort of rivalry with a shameless woman—with his mistress.

I have always been what the country people in Ohianna call a knowledgable woman. I have not much faculty of getting news of a situation through the facts as

they present themselves, but I have instincts which under the stimulus of emotion work with extraordinary celerity and thoroughness. Now suddenly the half-apprehended suggestion of the last few months took fire from the excitement of my mind, and exploded into certainties. I sensed all at once intolerable things, the withholden eyes, the covert attention fixed on my relations with the manager and Miss Dean. I lay on the bed and shuddered with dry sobs; other times I lay still, awake and blazing. About daylight Sarah came up to inquire how my neuralgia did. She found me with the unopened box clutched tightly in my hand. She turned up the smoky gas and noted the dark circles under my eyes.

"What has happened? Something, I know," she insisted gently. I blurted it out.

"Mr. O'Farrell . . . I saw him come out of Miss Dean's room . . . at a quarter of one. He was . . . oh, Sarah . . . he was! . . ." I relapsed again into the horror of it.

"Oh!" she said. She turned out the light and came and forced me gently under the covers and got into bed beside me.

"Didn't you know?" she questioned.

"Did you?"

"No one really knows these things. I didn't want to be the first to suggest it to you."

"Do the others know?"

"As much as we do. It has been going on a long time."

"And you put up with it—you go about with them?" I was astonished at the welling up of disgust in me. Sarah felt for my hand and held it.

"My dear, in our business you have to learn to take no notice. It is not that these things are so much worse with actors, but it is more difficult to keep them covered up. You must know that a great many people do such things."

"I know—*wicked* people. I never thought of its being done by anybody you liked."

"Oh, yes"; she was perfectly simple. "You can like them, you can like them greatly." I remembered that I oughtn't to have said that to Sarah Croyden.

"You mustn't think Mr. O'Farrell such a bad man. He

is probably fond of her. In some respects he is a very
good man. When I was—left, without a penny, he might
have made terms with me. Some managers would. But
he gave me a living salary and left me to myself. He has
been very kind to me."

"But she——" I choked back my sick resentment to
get at what had been tearing its way through my consciousness for the last three hours. "She must have
thought that *that* was what I wanted of him. . . ."

"Well, it is natural she should be anxious, with other
women about. She is in love with him."

"Did you think so? About me, I mean?"

"No," said Sarah. "No, I didn't think so."

It was light enough now to show the outline of the
drifts along the sills and the fine gritty powder which
the wind dashed intermittently against the panes; the
filter of day under the scant blinds brought out in the
affair streaks of vulgarity as evident as the pattern of
the paper on the wall. It seemed to borrow cheapness
from the broken castor of the bureau, as from my recollection of the eaten face of the clock and the leaning
chandelier. I sat up in the bed and laid hold of Sarah
in my eagerness to get clear of what by my mere knowledge of it, seemed an unbearable complicity.

"I had a feeling for him," I admitted. "I could act
better with him; but it was different from that—you
know it was different."

"Yes," said Sarah, "I know. I know because I am
that way myself; it is *like* that, but it isn't that." I
was still, holding my breath while she considered; we were
very close upon the twined roots of sex and art.

"There's a feeling that goes with acting, with other
sorts of things, painting and music, maybe, a feeling of
your wanting to get *through* to something and lay hold of
it, and your not being able to leaves you . . . aching
somehow, and you think if there's a particular person
. . . I think O'Farrell would understand . . . it is being
able to act makes you know the difference I suppose. He
really can act you know, and you can, but Dean wouldn't
understand, nor the others. My—Mr. Lawrence didn't
understand!" It was the first time she had ever mentioned him to me. "Sometimes I think they might have
felt the difference just at first, but nobody told them and

they got used to thinking it is . . . the other thing."
She drew me down into the bed again and covered me.
"You mustn't take it too hard . . . we all go through it
once . . . and you are safe so long as you know."

"But I can't go on with it." I was positive on that
point. "Sarah, Sarah, don't say I have to go on with it."

"I know you can't. But you just have to."

"I should never be able to face either of them again
without showing that I know."

"And then the others will know and they will think . . ."

I threw out my arms, seeing how I was trapped. I
wanted to cry out on them; to despise the woman openly. "And they will think that I am jealous . . . that I
wanted it myself. . . ."

I rolled in the bed and bit my hands with shame and
anger. Sarah caught me in her arms and held me until
the paroxysm passed. I was quieted at last from exhaustion.

"You can stay in your room to-day," she suggested.
"I can bring your meals up to you; this neuralgia will
give you an excuse, and you needn't see any one until
you go to the theatre. That will give you one day. Maybe by to-morrow . . ."

But I had no confidence that to-morrow would bring
me any sensible relief. The moral shock was tremendous.
All my pride was engaged on the side of never letting
anybody know; to have been misunderstood in the quality of my disgust would have been the intolerable last
thing. Sarah brought up my breakfast before she had her
own; she reported nobody about yet except Jimmy Vantine who had inquired for me. About half an hour later
she came softly in again with a yellow envelope open in
her hand. I saw by her face that it was for me and
that the news it contained put the present situation out
of question.

"Is it from my husband?" I demanded. I hardly
knew what I hoped or expected, a possibility of release
flashed up in me.

"It has been forwarded." She sat down on the bed
beside me. "My poor Olivia . . . you must try to think
of it as anything but a way out. Mr. O'Farrell will let
you go for this . . . ." If it had to happen it couldn't
have happened better.

"Give it to me——"

"Remember it is a way out."
I read it hastily:

> Mother had a stroke. Come at once.
> Signed: FORESTER.

CHAPTER VII

It was a common practice in Taylorville never to send for the doctor until you knew what was the matter with you. So long as the symptoms failed to align themselves with any known disorder, they were supposed to be amenable to neighbourly advice, to the common stock of medical misinformation, to the almanac or some such repository of science; and though this practice led on too many occasions to the disease getting past the curable stages before the physician was called, I never remember to have heard it questioned.

"You see," people remarked to one another at the funeral, "they didn't know what was the matter with her until it was too late," and it passed for all extenuation. It was natural then that my mother should have kept any premonitory symptoms of her indisposition even from Forester; close as they were in their affections she would have thought it indelicate to have spoken to him of her health. The first determinate stroke of it came upon her sitting quietly in her usual place at prayer meeting on a Wednesday evening.

It had been Forester's habit to close the shop a little early on that evening, going around to the church to walk home with her, getting in before the last hymn to save his face with the minister by a show of regular attendance. But on this evening customers detained him beyond his usual hour, so that by the time he reached the corner opposite the church, he saw the people dribbling out by twos and threes, across the lighted doorway, and noted that my mother was not with them. He thought she might have slipped out earlier and gone around to the shop for him as occasionally happened, but seeing the lights did not go out at once in the church, he looked in to make sure, and saw her still sitting in her accustomed place. The sexton and the organist, who were fussing together about a broken pedal, appeared not to have observed her there, and one of them was reaching up to put out the light when Forester touched her on the shoulder. She started and seemed to come awake with an effort, and on the way home she stumbled once or twice in a manner that led him, totally unaccustomed as he was to think of my mother as ill in any sort, to get a little entertainment out of it by gentle rallying, which was dropped when he discovered that it caused her genuine, pained embarrassment. The following Tuesday he came home to the midday meal to find her lying on the floor, inarticulate and hardly conscious. There must have been two strokes in close succession, for she had managed after falling, to get a cushion from the worn sitting-room lounge under her head and to pull a shawl partly over her. Effie, who was at Montecito, was summoned home, and that evening, by the doctor's advice, the telegram was sent which separated me so opportunely from the Shamrocks. By the time I reached her, speech had returned in a measure, and by the end of a fortnight she was able to be lifted into the chair which she never afterward left.

I remember as if it were yesterday, the noble outline of her face and of her head against the pillows, the smooth hair parted Madonna-wise and brought low across her ears, the blue of her eyes looking out of the dark, swollen circles, for all her fifty-two years, with the un-awakened clarity of a girl's. Stricken as I was from my first realizing contact with sin, and my identification with it through the assumed passions of the stage, it grew upon me during the days of my mother's illness that there was a kind of intrinsic worth in her which I, with all my powers, must forever and inalienably miss. With it there came a kind of exasperation, never quite to leave me, of the certainty of not choosing my own values, but of being driven with them aside and apart.

It was responsible in part for a feeling I had of being somehow less related to my mother's house than many of her distant kin who were continually arriving out of all quarters, in wagons and top buggies, to express a continuity of interest and kind which had the effect of constituting me definitely outside the bond.

The situation was furthered no doubt, by the whisper of my connection with the stage which got about and set up in them an attitude of circumspection, out of which I caught them at times regarding me with a curiosity unmixed with any human sympathy. Yet I recall how keen an appetite I had for what this illness of my mother's had thrown into relief, the web of passionate human interactions, bone and body of the spirituality that went clothed as gracelessly in the routine of their daily lives as the figures of the men under the unyielding ugliness of store clothing. It came out in the talk of the women sitting about the base burner at night with their skirts folded back carefully across their knees, in the watches we found it necessary to keep for the first fortnight or so. I remember one of these occasions as the particular instance by which my mother emerged for me from her condition of parenthood, to the common plane of humanity, by way of an old romance of her's with Cousin Judd. Cousin Lydia sat up with her that night and Almira Jewett, a brisk, country clad woman of the Skaldic temperament who from long handling of the histories of her clan had acquired an absolute art of it. She was own sister to the woman who married my mother's half-brother, and the Saga of the Judds and the Wilsons and the Jewetts and the Lattimores ran off the points of her bright needles as she sat with her feet on the fender, with a click and a spark. Cousin Lydia never knitted; she sat with her hands folded in her large lap and time seemed to rest with her.

"It will be hard on Judd," Almira offered to the unspoken reference forever in the air, as to the possible fatal termination of my mother's illness.

"Yes, it'll be hard on him." A faint, so faint nuance of assent in Cousin Lydia's voice seemed to admit the succeeding comment, shorn of impertinence. I guessed that the several members of the tribe were relieved rather than constrained to drop their intimate concerns into Almira Jewett's impartial histories.

"I never," Almira invited, "did get the straight of that. Sally was engaged to him, warn't she?"

"Not to say engaged," Cousin Lydia paused for just the right shade of relation, "but so as to want to be. Judd set store by her; he'd have had it that way anyway, but Sally couldn't make up her mind to it on account of their being own cousins."

"I reckon she had the right of it; the Lord don't seem no way pleased with kin marrying."

"I don't know, I don't know"; Cousin Lydia dropped the speculation into the pit of her own experience. "It looks like He wouldn't have made 'em to care about it then. But being as she saw it that way, they couldn't have done different. Not that Judd didn't see it in the light of his duty, too." There was evidently nothing in the annals of the Judds and the Lattimores which allowed a violation of the inward monitor.

"Well, I must say, he has turned it into grace, if ever a man has. Not to say but what you've helped him to it." It was in the manner of Almira's concession of naught in the matter, that Cousin Judd had chosen Lydia chiefly for her capacity not to offer any distraction to his profounder passion, and nothing in Cousin Lydia's comment to deny it. From the room beyond we could hear the inarticulate, half-conscious notice of my mother's pain. Cousin Lydia moved to attend her.

"All those years," I whispered to Almira, "she has loved him and he has loved my mother!" I was pierced through with the pure sword of the spirit which had divided them. But Almira was more practical.

"She was better off," Almira insisted. "Lydia hadn't no knack with men folk ever. She knew Judd wouldn't have loved her, but so long as he loved your mother she was safe. They got a good deal out of it, her knowing and sympathizing. She could sympathize, you see, for she knew how it was herself, loving Judd that way. It was no more than right they should get what they could out of it. It was the only thing they had between them."

"All those years!" I said again. I felt myself immeasurably lifted out of the mists and mires of the Shamrocks into clear and aching atmospheres.

"I will say this for Lydia," extenuated the Skald, "that though she hadn't no gift to draw a man to her, she knew how to hold her hand off and let him go his own thought. It was religion kept your mother and Judd apart, and yet it was in religion they comforted one another. Lydia never put herself forward like she might, claiming it was her religion too. And she was one that appreciated church privileges."

But I wondered where my father came in. It had been, I knew, a passionate attachment.

"Like a new house," said Almira, "built up where the old one has been, but the cellars of it don't change. Real loving is never really got over." I felt the phrase sounding in some subterranean crypt of my own.

With this new light on it, it came out for me wonderfully in my mother's face, as I watched her through the anxious days, how much her life had been stayed in renunciations. I suppose my new appreciation must have shone out for her as well, for I could see rising out of her disorder, like a drowned person out of the sea, a bond of our common experience. We were two women, together at last, my mother and I, and could have speech with one another.

Something no doubt contributed to this new understanding by an affair of Forester's which, as I began to be acquainted with the incidents preceding it, I believed to be partly responsible for my mother's stroke. I have already sketched to you how Forester had grown up in the need of finding himself always at the centre of feminine interest without the opportunity of satisfying it normally by marriage, and how the too early stimulation of sentiment and affection had led to his being handed about from girl to girl in the attempt to gratify his need without transgressing any of the lines marked out by his profession as an eminently nice young man. It came naturally out of the mere circumstance of there being a limited number of girls at hand whom he might conceivably court without the intention of marrying, for him to fall into the society of others whom he might not court but who might nevertheless find it much to their advantage to marry him.

I do not know how and when it came to my mother's ears that he was calling frequently at the Jastrows; very likely they brought it to her notice themselves. They were a poor, pushing sort, forever exposing themselves to the slights arising from their own undesirability, which they forever tearfully attributed to an undeserved and paraded poverty. They paraded it now as the insuperable bar to all that they might have done for my mother, all that they actually had it in their hearts to do on their assumption of a right of being interested, an assumption which, even in her weakness, before she could trust herself to talk very much, I felt her dumbly imploring me to deny. The girl—Lily they called her—was not without a certain appeal to the senses; and knowing rather more of my brother's methods, I did not find Mrs. Jastrow's pretension to a community of interest in what might be expected to come of his attention, altogether unjustified.

But in view of mother's condition and what Effie told me of the way business was going—rather was not going at all—any kind of marriage would have been out of the question. It was the way I put the finality of that into my dealings with Mrs. Jastrow, that drew mother over into the only relation of normal human interdependence I was ever to have with her. Whenever Mrs. Jastrow would come to call with that air she had, in her dress and manner, of being pulled together and made the best of, I could see my mother's fears signalling to me from the region of tremors and faintness in which she had sunk, and I would set my wits up as a defence against what, considering all there was against her, was a really gallant effort on Mrs. Jastrow's part to make out of Forester's philanderings a basis for a family intimacy. It was plain that neither my mother nor Mrs. Jastrow dared put the question to Forester, but rested their case on such mutual admissions of it as they could wring from one another.

I could never make out on my mother's part, whether she was really afraid of the issue, or if in the preoccupation of their affection both she and Forester had overlooked his young man's right to a woman and a life of his own. Through all her dumb struggle against it, never but once did my mother openly face the ultimate possibility of his marriage with Lily Jastrow.

It was about the third week of her illness, and Mrs. Jastrow, making one of her interminable calls, had been brought so nearly to the point of tears by my imperiousness, that Effie had been obliged to draw her off into the kitchen to have her opinion about a recipe for a mince meat such as she knew the Jastrows couldn't afford to be instructed in, and so had gotten her out of the side door and started down the walk before the situation could come to a head. My mother watched her go.

"Do you think," she hazarded suddenly, "that Forester really is engaged to her?"

"To Lily? Oh, no; Forester doesn't get engaged to girls, he just—dangles." It was characteristic of my mother's partiality that even damaging insinuations such as this, slid off from it as too far from the possibility to be even entertained. Perhaps a trace of my old exasperation with the whole situation, and the glimpse I had of

Mrs. Jastrow letting herself out of our gate with her assumption of being as good as anybody still to the fore but a little awry, prompted me to add:

"And it is only natural for her mother to make the most of it. She's looking out for her own, just as you are."

"A mother has a right to do that"; she protested, "to keep them from making themselves miserable. It is no more than her duty."

"Yes," I said; the remark had the effect of a challenge.

"Young people don't know how to choose for themselves; they make mistakes." She revolved something in her mind. "You, now . . . you're unhappy, aren't you, Olivia?"

"Yes; oh, yes." I had not thought of myself as being so particularly, but I did not see my way to deny it.

"I've been afraid . . . sometimes . . . since you wrote me about going on the stage, maybe you weren't exactly . . . satisfied. But it isn't that, is it?"

"No, Mother, it isn't that."

"There! You see!" She shook off her weakness with the conviction. "And you mightn't have been if I hadn't looked out for you a little."

"Why, Mother, what could you possibly—" She triumphed.

"You remember that Garrett boy that was visiting at his uncle's? He called that night; the night you were engaged to Tommy."

"Yes, I remember. You sent him away?"

"He wasn't suitable at all . . . smoking, and driving about on Sunday that way . . . ." Her tone was defensive. "He left a letter that night—"

"Mother! You didn't tell me!"

"I was thinking it over . . . I had a right . . . you were too young!"

"Mother . . . did you read it?"

"I . . . looked at it. You hadn't met him but once and I had a right to know; and that night you were engaged. I took it for a sign."

"And the letter?" It seemed all at once an immeasurable and irreparable loss.

"I sent it back . . . and, anyway, it turned out all right." I was possessed for the moment with the conviction that it was all dreadfully, despairingly wrong.

"I couldn't have borne for you to marry anybody but a Christian, Olivia!" I thought of Tommy's exceedingly slender claim to that distinction and I laughed.

"Tommy smokes," I said; "he says he has to do it with the customers."

"Oh, but not as a habit, Olivia." I overrode that.

"Tell me what became of him—of Mr. Garrett. Did you ever hear?"

"He went West," she recollected; "I asked his aunt. He quarrelled with them because his uncle wouldn't send him to school. At his age they thought it wasn't suitable. I wouldn't have wanted you to go West, Olivia."

I took her worn hands in mine. "It's all right, Mother. I'm not going West. And I'm not going on the stage any more. I'm done with it." I felt so, passionately, at the time. We sat quietly for a time in that assurance and listened to Effie singing in the kitchen.

"Olivia," she began timidly at last, "aren't you ever going to have any more children?"

"Oh, I hope so, Mother. I haven't been strong, you know, since the first one. We didn't think it advisable."

"Well, if you can manage it that way . . ." There was a trace in her tone of the woman who hadn't been able to manage. I wished to reassure her.

"When I was in the hospital the doctor told me . . ." I could see the deep flush rising over her face and neck; there were some things which her generation had never faced. I let them fall with her hands and sat gazing at the red core of the base burner, waiting until she should take up her thought again.

"I used to think those things weren't right, Olivia, but I don't know. Sometimes I think it isn't right, either, to bring them into the world when there is no welcome for them." She struggled with the admission. "You and I, Olivia, we never got on together."

"But that's all past now, Mother." She clung to me for a while for reassurance.

"I hope so, I hope so; but still there are things I've always wanted to tell you. When you wrote me about going on the stage . . . there are wild things in you, Olivia, things I never looked for in a daughter of mine, things I can't understand nor account for unless—unless it was I turned you against life . . . my kind of life . . . before you were born. Many's the time I've seen you hating it and I've been harsh with you; but I wanted you should know I was being harsh with myself . . ."

"Mother, dear, is it good for you to talk so?"

"Yes, yes, I've wanted to. You see it was after your father came home from the war and we were all broken up. Forester was sickly, and there was the one that died. So when I knew you were coming, I—hated you, Olivia. I wanted things different. I hated you . . . until I heard you cry. You cried all the time when you were little, Olivia, and it was I that was crying in you. I've expected some punishment would come of it."

"Oh, hush, hush Mother! I shouldn't have liked it either in your place. Besides, they say—the scientists—that it isn't so that things before you are born can affect you as much as that." She moved her head feebly on the pillows in deep-rooted denial.

"They can say that, but we've never got on. There's things in you that aren't natural for any daughter of mine. They can say that, Olivia, but we—we know."

"Yes, Mother, we know."

I took her hands again and nursed them against my cheek; after a time tears began to drip down her flaccid cheeks and I wiped them away for her.

"Don't, Mother, don't! We get along now, anyway! And as for the things in me which are different, do you know, Mother, I'm getting to know that they are the best things in me."

I honestly thought so; and after all these years I think so now.

I wheeled her into the bedroom presently, where she fell into the light slumber of the feeble, and seemed afterward hardly to remember, but I was glad then to have talked it all out with her, for though she lived nearly two years after, before I saw her again another stroke had deprived her of articulateness.

CHAPTER VIII

I went home to my husband after it began to seem certain that my mother's condition would not change for some time, but I knew in the going that neither Tommy nor Higgleston could ever present themselves to me again in the aspect of an absolute destiny. By the incidents of the past few weeks I had been pulled free from the obsession of inevitableness with which my life had clothed itself until now; I stood outside of it and questioned it in the light of what it might have been, what it might yet become. Suppose I had received Helmeth Garrett's letter; suppose my interest in Mr. O'Farrell had wavered a hair's breadth out of the community of work into that more personal and particular passion——?

I quaked in the cold blasts which blew on me out of unsuspected doors opening on my life.

And still I went back to Higgleston. There seemed nothing else to do. I think I deceived myself with the notion that there was something in Tommy's resistance to a more acceptable destiny, that could be resolved and dissipated by the proper stimulus. But I knew, in fact, that he and Higgleston suited one another admirably. To my husband, that he should keep a clothing store in a town of five thousand inhabitants was part of the great natural causation. The single change to which our condition was liable was that the business might take a turn which would enable us to move out of the store into a house of our own. It had not occurred to Tommy to take a turn himself. The Men's Tailors and Outfitters lay like most business in Higgleston, in the back water, rocking at times in the wake of the world traffic, but never moving with it. There was a vague notion of progress abroad which resulted in our going through the motions of the main current. The Live Business Men organized a Board of Trade and rented a room to hold meetings in, but I do not remember that when they had met, anything came of it. The great tides of trade went about the world and our little fleet rocked up and down. If I had ever had any hope that Tommy and I might make out of our common stock, somehow hoist sail and make a way out of it, in that spring and summer I completely lost it.

I believe Tommy thought we were perfectly happy. Considering how things turned out, I am glad to have it so; but the fact is, there was not between us so much as a common taste in furniture. In the five years of married life, our home had filled up with articles which by colour and line and unfitness jarred on every sense. Tommy had what he was pleased to call an ear for music, and if the warring discords of our furnishings could have been translated into sound he would have gone distracted with it; being as it was he bought me a fire screen for my birthday. Miss Rathbone hand-painted it for the Baptist bazaar, and Tommy had bought it at three times what we could have afforded for a suitable ornament. It was his notion of our relations that we and the Rathbones should do things like that by one another. I suppose you can find the like of that fire screen at some county fair still in Ohianna, but you will find nothing more atrocious. Tommy liked to have it sitting well out in the room where he could admire it. He would remark upon it sometimes with complacency, evenings after the store was shut up, before he sat down in his old coat and slippers to read the paper. Occasionally I read to him out of a magazine or a play I had picked up, in the intervals of which I used to catch him furtively keeping up with his newspaper out of the tail of his eye.

Now and then we went out to a sociable or to the Rathbones for supper. Less frequently we had them to a meal with us. It was characteristic of business partnerships in Higgleston that they involved you in obligations of chicken salad and banana cake and the best tablecloth. Tommy enjoyed these occasions, and if he had allowed himself to criticise me at all, it would have been for my ineptitude at the happy social usage. Things went on so with us month after month.

And if you ask me why I didn't take the chance life offers to women to justify themselves to the race, I will say that though the hope of a child presents itself sentimentally as opportunity, it figures primarily in the calculation of the majority, as a question of expense. The hard times foreseen by Burton Brothers hung black-winged in the air. We had not, in fact, been able to do more than keep up the interest on what was still due on the stock and fixtures. Nor had I even quite recovered the bodily equilibrium disturbed by my first encounter with the rending powers of life. There was a time when the spring came on in a fulness, when the procreant impulse stirred awake. I saw myself adequately employed shaping men for it . . . maybe . . . but the immediate deterring fact was the payment to be made in August.

I went on living in Higgleston where human intercourse was organized on the basis that whatever a woman has of intelligence and worth, over and above the sum of such capacity in man, is to be excised as a superfluous growth, a monstrosity. Does anybody remember what the woman's world was like in small towns before the days of woman's clubs? There was a world of cooking and making over; there was a world of church-going and missionary societies and ministerial coperation, half grudged and half assumed as a virtue which, since it was the only thing that lay outside themselves, was not without extenuation. And there was another world which underlay all this, coloured and occasioned it, sicklied over with futility; it was a world all of the care and expectancy of children overshadowed by the recurrent monthly dread, crept about by whispers, heretical but persistent, of methods of circumventing it, of a secret practice of things openly condemned. It was a world that went half the time in faint-hearted or unwilling or rebellious anticipation, and half on the broken springs of what as the subject of the endless, objectionable discussions, went by the name of "female complaints."

In all this there was no room for Olivia. Somehow the ordering of our four rooms over the store didn't appear to me as a justification of existence, and I didn't care to undertake again matching the adventures of my neighbours in the field of domestic economy with mine in the department of self-expression. Let any one who disbelieves it try if he can assure the acceptance of his art on its merit as work, free of the implication of egotism. You may talk about a new frosting for cake, or an aeroplane you have invented, but you must not speak of a new verse form or a plastic effect.

All this time, in spite of my recent revulsion from it, I was consumed with the desire of acting. My new-found faculty ached for use. It woke me in the night and wasted me; I had wild thoughts such as men have in the grip of an unjustifiable passion. All my imaginings at that time were of events, untoward, fantastic, which should somehow throw me back upon the stage without the necessity on my part, of a moral conclusion. Sarah Croyden, to whom I wrote voluminously, could not understand why I resisted it; there was after all no actual opposition except what lay inherent in my traditions. Sarah had such a way of accepting life; she used it and her gift. Mine used me. I saw that it might even abuse me. She went, by nature, undefended and unharmed from the two-edged sword that keeps the gates of Creative Art, but me it pierced even to the dividing of soul and spirit. My husband stood always curiously outside the consideration. I think he was scarcely aware of what went on in me; if any news of my tormented state reached him, he would have seen, except as it was mollified by affection, what all Higgleston saw in it, the restlessness of vanity, a craving for excitement, for praise, and a vague taint of irregularity. He was sympathetic to the point of admitting that Higgleston was dull; he thought we might join the Chatauqua Society.

"Or you might get up a class," he suggested hopefully; "it would give you something to think about."

"Teach," I cried; "TEACH! when I'm just aching to learn!"

"Well, then," he achieved a triumph of reasonableness, "if you don't know enough to teach in Higgleston, how are you going to succeed on the stage?"

It was not Tommy, however, but a much worse man who made up my mind for me. He had been brought out from Chicago during my absence, to set up in Higgleston's one department store, that factitious air of things being done, which passed for the evidence of modernity. He had, in the set of his clothes, the way he made the most of his hair and the least of the puffiness about his eyes, the effect of having done something successfully for himself, which I believe was the utmost recommendation he had for the place. He preferred himself to my favour on the strength of having seen more than a little of the theatre. Very soon after my return, he took to dropping into my husband's store which, in view of its being patronized by men who were chiefly otherwise occupied during the day, was kept open rather late in the evenings. From sheer loneliness I had fallen

into the habit of going down after supper to wait on
a stray customer while Tommy made up the books.
Mr. Montague, who went familiarly about town by the
name of Monty, would come in then and loll across the
counter chatting to me, while Tommy sat at his desk
with a green shade over his eyes, and Mr. Rathbone,
who never came more than a step or two out of his character as working tailor, clattered about with his irons
in the back, half screened by the racks of custom made
"Nobby suits, $9.98," which made up most of our stock
in trade.

I had already, without paying much attention to it,
become accustomed to the shifting of men's interest in
me the moment my connection with the stage became
known: a certain speculation in the eye, a freshening of
the wind in the neighbourhood of adventure; but by degrees it began to work through my preoccupations that
Mr. Montague's attention had the quality of settled expectation, the suggestion of a relation apart from the
casual social contact, which it wanted but an opportunity
to fulfill. It took the form very early, when Tommy
would look up from his entries and adding up to make his
cheerful contribution to the conversation, of an attempt
to include me in a covert irritation at the interruption.
If by any chance he found me alone, his response to the
potential impropriety of the occasion, awoke in me the
plain vulgar desire to box his ears. But no experience
so far served to reveal the whole offensiveness of the
man's assurance.

The week that Tommy went up to Chicago to do his
summer buying, we made a practice of closing rather
early in the long, enervating evenings, since hardly any
customer could have been inveigled into the store on any
account. I found it particularly irritating then, to have
Mr. Montague leaning across the counter to me with a
manner that would have caused the dogs in the street
to suspect him of intrigue. The second or third time
this happened I made a point of slipping around to Mr.
Rathbone with the suggestion that if he would shut up
and go home I would take the books upstairs with me
and attend them.

I was indifferent whether or not Mr. Montague
should hear me, but I judged he had not, for far from
accepting it as a hint that I wished to get rid of him,

that air he had of covert understanding appeared to have increased in him like a fever. He made no attempt to resume the conversation, but stood tapping his boot with a small cane he affected, a flush high up under the puffy eyes, the corners of his mouth loosened, every aspect of the man fairly bristling with an objectionable maleness. I made believe to be busy putting stock in order, and in a minute more I could hear old Rathbone come puttering out of his corner to draw the dust cloths over the racks of ready-made suits and, after what seemed an interminable interval, fumbling at the knobs of the safe.

"Oh," I snatched at the opportunity, "I changed the combination; let me show you." I was around beside him in a twinkling.

"Good-night," I called to Montague over my shoulder.

"Good-night," he said; the tone was charged. The fumbling of the locks covered the sound of his departure. I got Mr. Rathbone out at the door at last, and locked it behind him. I turned back to lower the flame of the acetylene lamp and in the receding flare of it between the shrouded racks I came face to face with Mr. Montague. He stood at the outer ring of the light and in the shock of amazement I gave the last turn of the button which left us in a sudden blinding dark. I felt him come toward me by the sharp irradiation of offensiveness.

"Oh, you clever little joker, you!" The tone was fatuous.

I dodged by instinct and felt for the button again to throw on the flood of light; it caught him standing square in the middle of the aisle in plain sight from the street; almost unconsciously he altered his attitude to one less betraying, but the response of his mind to mine was not so rapid.

"I'm going to shut up the store." I was very quiet about it. "You'll oblige me by going——"

"Oh, come now; what's the use? I thought you were a woman of the world."

I got behind the counter, past him toward the door.

"You an actress . . . you don't mean to say! By Jove, I'm not going to be made a fool of after such an encouragement! I'm not going without——"

"Mr. Montague," I said, "Tillie Hemingway is coming

to stay with me nights; she will be here in a few minutes; you'd better not let her find you here." I unbarred the door and threw it wide open.

"Oh, come now——" He struggled for some footing other than defeat. "Of course, if you can't meet me like a woman of the world——you're a nice actress, you are!" I looked at him; the steps and voices of passersby sounded on the pavement; he went out with his tail between his legs. I locked the door after him and double locked it.

I climbed up to my room and locked myself in that. The boiling of my blood made such a noise in my ears that I could not hear Tillie Hemingway when she came knocking, and the poor girl went away in tears. After a long time I got to bed and sat there with my arms about my knees. I did not feel safe there; I knew I should never be safe again except in that little square of the world upon which the footlights shone, from which the tightening of the reins of the audience in my hands, should justify my life to me. I was sick with longing for it, aching like a woman abandoned for the arms of her beloved. I fled toward it with all my thought from illicit solicitation, but it was not the husband of my body I thought of in that connection, but the choice of my soul.

People wonder why sensitive, self-respecting women are not driven away from the stage by the offences that hedge it; they are driven deeper and farther into its enfoldment. There is nothing to whiten the burning of its shames but the high whiteness of its ultimate perfection. It is so with all art, not back in the press of life, but forward on some over-topping headland, one loses behind the yelping pack and eases the sting of resentment. I did not agree in the beginning to make you understand this. I only tell you that it is so. All that night I sat with my head upon my knees and considered how I might win back to it.

I tried, when my husband came home, to put the incident to him in a way that would stand for my newfound determination. I did not get so far with it. I saw him shrink from the mere recital with a man's timorousness.

"Oh, come—he couldn't have meant so bad as that." His male dread of a "situation" pleaded with me not to insist upon it. "And he went just as soon as you told him to. Of course if he had tried to force you . . . but you say yourself he went quietly."

He was seeing and shrinking from what Higgleston would get out of the incident in the way of vulgar entertainment if I insisted on his taking it up; by the code there, I shouldn't have been subject to such if I hadn't invited it.

"Of course," he enforced himself, "you did right to turn him down, but I don't believe he'll try it again."

"He won't have a chance. I'm going back on the stage so soon"; the implication of my tone must have got through even Tommy's unimaginativeness; he said the only bitter thing that I ever heard from him.

"Well, if you hadn't gone on the stage in the first place it probably wouldn't have happened."

He came round to the situation in another frame when he learned that I had written to Sarah putting matters in train for an engagement.

"You will probably be away all winter," he said. "It seems to me, Olivia, that you don't take any account of the fact that I am fond of you." We were sitting on a little shelf of a back balcony we had, for the sake of coolness, and I went and sat on his knee.

"I'm fond of you, Tommy, ever so. But I can't stand the life here; it smothers me. And we don't do anything; we don't get anywhere."

"I don't know what you mean, Olivia; we're building up quite a business; we'll be able to make a payment this year, and as the town improves——"

"Oh, Tommy, come away; come away into the world with me. Let us go out and do things; let us be part of things."

"Higgleston's good enough for me. We're building up trade, and everybody says the town is sure to go ahead——"

"Oh, Tommy, Tommy, what do I care about a business here if we lose the whole world—and we'll be old and gray before we get the business paid for. Oh, it isn't because I don't care about you, Tommy, because I am not satisfied with you; it is the glory of the world I want, and the wonder of Art, and great deeds going up and down in it! I want us to have that, Tommy; to have it together . . . you and I, and not another.

It's all there in the world, Tommy, all the colour and the splendour . . . great love and great work . . . let us go out and take it; let us go . . ." I had slipped down from his knees to my own as I talked, pleading with him, and I saw, by the light of the lamp from within, his face, charged with pained bewilderment, settle into lines of habitual resistance to the unknown, the unknowable. My voice trailed out into sobbing.

"Of course, Olivia, I don't want to keep you if you are not happy here, but I have to stay myself." His voice was broken but determined, with the determination of a little man not seeing far ahead of him. "I have to keep the business together."

I went, as it was foredoomed I should, about the middle of September. Sarah and I had been so fortunate as to get engagements together. My going, upheaving as it had been in respect to my own adjustments, made hardly a ripple in the life around me. Even Miss Rathbone failed to rise to her former heights, but was obliged to piece out her interest with her customary dressmaker's manner of having temporarily overlaid her absorption in your affair with an unwilling distraction.

The rest of Higgleston received the announcement with the air of not supposing it to be any of their business, but that in any case they couldn't approve of it. Mrs. Harvey put a common feminine view of it very aptly.

"I shouldn't think," she said, "your husband would let you." It was not a view that was likely to have a deterrent effect upon me.

CHAPTER IX

We had the good fortune that year, Sarah and I, to be with a manager who redeemed many O'Farrells. The Hardings—for his wife, under her stage name of Estelle Manning, played with him and was the better half of all his counsels—were of the sort of actor-managers to whom, if the American stage ever arrives at anything commensurate with its opportunity, it will owe much. They were not either of them of the stripe of genius, but up to the limit of their endowment, sound, sincere and able to interpret life to the people through the virtue of being so humanly of the people themselves. It was very good for me to be with them, not only for the stage craft they taught me, but for the healing of my mind against the contagion of irresponsibility. The Hardings taught me my way about the professional world, the management of my gift, its market value, but I am not sure I do not owe much more to the fact that they loved one another quite simply and devotedly, and to the certainty which they seemed to make for us all that loyalty, truth, and forbearance were part of the natural order of things.

I was aware, when I was with the Shamrocks, of a subconscious current against which any mention of my husband appeared a kind of gaucherie; it was wholesome for me then, to find it expected of me by the Hardings that I should act better after I had received a long, affectionate letter from Tommy, and to be able to refer to it quite unaffectedly. Everybody in the company took the greatest interest in his coming on at Christmas to spend four days with me.

We had a carefully chosen company, and clean, straightforward plays which met with gratifying success. At the end of February, when traffic was tied up during the great ice storm, I was near enough to get home to Taylorville and spend a week there.

Tommy came to meet me and we were all happy together, Mother sitting nearly inarticulate in her chair, pleased as a child to see me doing all the parts in our repertory, and Effie reading my press notices to whoever

could be got to listen to them. I seemed to have found
the groove in which the wheels of my life went round
smoothly; I was justified of much that in my girlhood
I had been made to feel so sorely, set me reprehen-
sibly apart. I remember Forester telling how he had
heard Charlie Gowers retailing the incident of my having slapped him when he tried to kiss me, getting a kind
of reflected glory out of the incident being so much
to my credit.

I went back to Higgleston in May and was happier than
I had been in the six years of my married life. I had my
work and my husband; all that I wanted now was to
bring the two into closer relation; it seemed not unlikely
of accomplishment. With what I had saved of my salary,
Tommy was able to make quite a payment on the business, and with the release of that pressure the whole grip
of Higgleston seemed to be loosed from him. When I
suggested that I might get permanent engagements in
Chicago or St. Louis, where he could establish himself,
he was disposed to view it as not unthinkable in connection with what might be expected from a live business
man.

I had to leave home early in the autumn for rehearsals,
and to leave Tommy, by some chance of the weather a
trifle under it. I felt I shouldn't have been able to do so if
my husband and Miss Rathbone hadn't been eminently on
those terms that fulfilled Tommy's ideal in respect to the
women-folk of his partner. Very likely, as she maintained,
it was a feeling of caste that rendered her professional
affectionateness offensive to me. One had to admit that
when she applied it to her shuffling, peering old father,
with red-lidded eyes and a nose that occasionally wanted
wiping, it was every way commendable. At any rate I was
glad on this occasion to take what she did for old Rathbone
as an assurance that if Tommy fell ill, or anything untoward, he wouldn't lack for anything a woman might do
for him.

That winter Mr. Harding starred me, and what a wonderful winter it was! Sarah says, taking account of the cold
and the condition of the roads, it was rather a hard one,
but I was floated clear of all such considerations on the
crest of success. Nothing whatever seemed to have gone
wrong with it except that Tommy failed me at Christmas.
He was to have spent a week, but wired me at the last

moment that he could not leave before Wednesday, and then when he came stayed only until Saturday. He had something to say about the pressure of the holiday trade in neckties and cuff links such as the ladies of Higgleston habitually invested in, on behalf of their masculine members, and all the time he was with me, wore that efflorescence of appreciation which I have long since learned to recognize as the overt sign of male delinquency.

If I thought of it at all in that connection, it was clean swept out of my mind by meeting early in January with Mr. Eversley and hearing him first apply to myself that phrase which I have chosen for the title to this writing. Mark Eversley, the greatest modern actor! So we all believed. He had been an old friend of Mr. Harding's; they had had their young struggles together; we crowded around our manager to hear him tell of them; struggles which, in so far as they identified themselves with our own, seemed to bring us by implication within reach of his present fame. Eversley played in St. Louis while we were there, and having an evening to spare, in spite of all the eager social appeal, chose to spend it with the Hardings. They had had dinner together, and as Mr. Harding did not come on until the second act, the great tragedian sat with him in his dressing room, visiting together between the cues like two boys in a dormitory. That was how Eversley happened to be standing in the wings in my great third act, and as I came out between gusts of applause after it, he was very kind to me.

"You will go far, little lady," said he, his lean face alive with kindliness, "you will go farther and have to come back and pick up some dropped stitches, but in the end you will get where you are bound." It was not for me to tell him how the mere consciousness of his presence had carried me that night to the utmost pitch of my capacity; I stood and blushed with confusion while he fumbled for his card.

"I will hear of you again," he said; "I am bound to hear of you; in the meantime here is my permanent address. It may be that I can be of use to you when you come to the bad places."

"Oh," said Mrs. Harding, whose failure to win any conspicuous distinction for herself had not embittered her, "she seems to have cleared most of the hard places at a bound."

"My dear young lady," Eversley appealed to me with a charming whimsicality, "whatever you do, don't let them put that into your head; you will indeed need me if you get to thinking that. You are, I suspect, a woman of genius, and in that case there will always be bad places ahead of you—you are doomed, you are driven; they will never let up on you."

Well, he should know; he was a man of genius. I hope it might be true about me, but I was afraid. For to be a genius is no such vanity as you imagine. It is to know great desires and to have no will of your own toward fulfilment; it is to feed others, yourself unfed; it is to be broken and plied as the Powers determine; it is to serve, and to serve, and to get nothing out of it beyond the joy of serving. And to know if you have done that acceptably you have to depend on the plaudits of the crowd; the Powers give no sign; many have died not knowing.

There is no more vanity in calling yourself a woman of genius if you know what genius means, than might be premised of one of the guinea pigs set aside for experimentation in a laboratory; but the guinea pigs who run free in the garden impute it to us. I wrote my mother and Tommy what Eversley had said, but I knew they would see nothing more in it than that he had paid me a compliment which it would not be modest to make much of in public.

The successes of that year prolonged the season by a month, and by the time I got home to Higgleston the leaves were all out on the maples and the wide old yards smelled of syringa. I came back to it full of the love of the world, alive in every fibre of my being, and the first thing I noticed was that it caused my husband some embarrassment. There was a shyness in his resumption of our relations more than could be accounted for by the native Taylorvillian gaucheries of emotion.

"My dear," I protested, "you don't seem a bit glad to see me."

"You are away so much," he excused. "You're getting to seem almost a stranger."

"Getting? I should say I am. This morning it seemed to me almost as if I waked up in another woman's house." I meant no more than to suggest how little the walls of it, the furniture, the draperies, expressed my new mood of creative power, but suddenly I saw my husband colour a deep, embarrassed red.

"You never did take any interest in our life here . . . in the business . . . in me." He seemed to be making out a case against me.

"Don't say in you, Tommy; but the life here, yes; there is so little to it. Another year and Mr. Harding says I could hope to stay in Chicago." My husband pushed away his plate; we were at breakfast the second morning.

"Higgleston's good enough for me," he protested. He got up and stood at the window with his back to me, looking out at the side street and the tardy traffic of the town beginning to stir in it. "When you hate it so," he said, "I wonder you come back to it." But my mood was proof against even this.

"Oh, Thomas, Thomas!" I got my hands about his arm and snuggled my head against it. "And you can't even guess why I come back?" He looked at me, vaguely troubled by the caress, but not responding to it.

"Do you care so much?"

"Ever and ever so." I thought he was in need of reassurance.

I hardly know when I began to get an inkling of what was wrong with him; it trickled coldly to me from dropped words, inflections, sidelong glances. Whenever I went out I was aware of all Higgleston watching, watching like a cat at a mouse-hole for something to come out. What? Reports of my success had reached them through the papers. Were they looking for some endemic impropriety to break out on me as a witness to what a popular actress must inevitably become? By degrees it worked through to me that all Higgleston knew things about my situation that were held from me. What they expected to see come out in my behaviour was the stripe of chastisement.

When I had been at home four or five days it occurred to me Miss Rathbone had not yet run in to see me with that quasi-familiarity which had grown out of the business association of our men. Old Rathbone had said that she had the trousseau of one of the Harvey girls in hand, but I knew that if the courtesy had been due from me, I couldn't have neglected it without the risk of being thought what Miss Rathbone herself would have called uppish. So the very next afternoon, having fallen in with some Higgleston ladies strolling the long street that led through the town from countryside to countryside, passing her gate, it struck me that here was an excellent opportunity to run in and exchange a greeting with her. I said as much to Mrs. Ross and Mrs. Harvey, as I swung the picket gate out across the boardwalk; there was something in their way of standing back from it that gave them the air of sheering off from any implication in the incident. They looked at the sidewalk and their lips were a little drawn; I should have known that look very well by that time. I threw out against it just that degree of impalpable resistance that was demanded by my official relation to the women of my husband's business partner, and clinched it with the click of the gate swinging to behind me, but as I went up the peony-bordered walk I wondered what Miss Rathbone would possibly have done to get herself talked about.

I was let into the workroom by Tillie Hemingway, in the character of a baster, with her mouth full of threads; Miss Rathbone came hurrying from a fitting, and in the brief moment of crossing my half of the room to meet her I was aware that she had turned a sickly hue of fear. She must have seen me coming up the street with the other women, I surmised, and guessed that I knew. I felt a kind of compulsion on me to assure her by an extra graciousness that I did not know, and that it wouldn't make any difference if I did. She was not changed at all except perhaps as to a trifle more abundance of bosom and a greater insensibility to the pins with which she bristled. There was the same effect of modishness in the blond coiffure with the rats showing, and the well-cut, half-hooked gown, but she seemed to know so little what to do with my visit that I was glad to cut it short and get away into the wide, overflowing day. I went on under the maples in leafage full and tender, following the faint scent of the first cutting of the meadows, quite to the end of the village and a mile or two into the country road, feeling the working of the Creative Powers in me, much as it seemed the sentiment earth must feel the summer, a warm, benignant process. I was at one with the soul of things and knew myself fruitful. At last when the dust of the roadway disturbed by the homing teams, collected in layers of the cooler air, and the bats were beginning, I tore myself away from the fair day as from a lover and went back to Tommy waiting patiently for his supper. While I was getting it on the table I recalled Miss Rathbone.

"What," I said, "has she been doing to get herself talked about?" Suddenly there whipped out on his face the counterpart of the flinching which I had noted in the dressmaker.

"Who said she had been talked about? What have they been telling you? A pack of lying old cats!"

"So she *has* been talked about?" I put down a pile of plates the better to account to myself for his excitement.

"I might have known somebody would get at you. Why can't they come to me."

"Tommy! Has Miss Rathbone been talked about with *you?* Oh, my dear!" I meant it for commiseration. Tommy went sullen all at once.

"I don't want to talk about it. I won't talk about it!"

"You needn't. And as for what the others say, you don't suppose I am going to believe it?" He turned visibly sick at the assurance.

"I'll tell you about it after supper," he protested. "I meant to tell you." I kept my mind turned deliberately away from the subject until it was night and I heard the last tardy customer depart, then the shutters go up, and after a considerable interval my husband's foot upon the stairs.

I hope I have made you understand how good he was, with what simple sort of goodness, not meant to stand the strain of the complexity in which he found himself. He wanted desperately to get out of it, to get in touch again with straight and simple lines of living. As he stood before me then his face was streaked red and white with the stress of the situation, like a man after a great bodily exertion. I was moved suddenly to spare him—after all what was the village dressmaker to us? Tommy flared out at me.

"She is as good as you are . . . she's as pure . . . as kind-hearted. It's as much your fault as anybody's. You were away; you were always away." His voice trailed out into extenuation. There fell a long pause in which several things became clear to me.

"Tell me," I said at last.

Tommy sat down on the red plush couch. He had taken

off his coat downstairs, for the evening was warm. There was pink in his necktie and the freckles stood out across his nose. I was taken with a wild sense of the ridiculous. Miss Rathbone, I knew, was six years my husband's senior.

"I went there a good deal last winter," he began. "I never meant any harm . . . my business partner . . . it was lonesome here. Of course I ought to have known people would talk. Nobody told me. She was brave, she bore it a long time, and then I saw that something was the matter. I didn't know until she told me, how fond of her I was—"

"Tommy, Tommy!" Strangely, it was I crying out. "Fond of her? Fond of *her?*"

"I was fond of her," he insisted dully. "She suffered a lot on account of me." The words dropped to me through immeasurable cold space. I believe there were more explanations, excusings. I was aware of being wounded in some far, unreachable place. I sat stunned and watched the widening rings of pain and amazement spread toward me. By and by tears came; I cried long and quietly. I got down on the floor at my husband's knees and put my arms about his body, crying. After a time I remember his helping me to undress and we got into bed. We had but the one. I know it now for the sign that I never loved my husband as wives should love, that I felt no offence in this; sex jealousy was not awake in me. We lay in bed with our arms around one another and cried for the pain and bewilderment of what had happened to us.

CHAPTER X

As if the attraction Miss Rathbone had for my husband had been a spell, the mere naming of which dissipated it, we spent the ensuing three or four days in the glow of renewal. It was Miss Rathbone herself who drew us out of that excluding intimacy; set us apart where we could feel the cold stiffness of our hurts and the injury we had inflicted each on the other.

Whatever there had been between them, and I never knew very clearly what, they had failed to reckon on the recrudescence of the interest I had always had for my husband, and the tie of association. At any rate Miss Rathbone failed. I must suppose that she loved Tommy, that she was hungering for the sight of him, needing desperately to feel again the pressure of whatever bond had been between them. She came into the store on the fourth evening after my husband's admission of it, on one of the excuses she could so easily make out of her father's being there. I was sitting upstairs with some sewing when she came and neither saw nor heard her, but the unslumbering instinct, before I was half aware of it, had drawn me to the head of the stair.

As I came down it, still in the shadow of the upper landing, I saw her leaning across the counter with that factious air of modishness which was so large a part of her stock in trade with Higgleston. She had on all her newest things, and I think she was rouged a little. Even with the width of the counter between them she had the effect of enveloping my husband with that manner of hers as with a net; to set up in him the illusion of all that I was in fact; mystery, passion, the air of the great world. I was pierced through with the realization that with men it is not so much being that counts, as seeming. There was a touch of the fatuous in the way Tommy submitted to the implication of her attitude as she took a flower from her breast and pinned it in his coat. The foot of the stair came almost to the end of the counter where they stood, and a trick of the light falling from the hanging lamp threw the upper half of it in shadow. I stood just within it with my hand upon the rail. Something in the avidity of yielding in my husband's manner was like a call in me; I moved involuntarily a step downward.

They heard and then they saw me; they stopped frozen in their places and the thing that froze them was the consciousness of guilt. They stood confessed of a disloyalty. I turned full in their sight and walked back up the stair. It was very late that night when Tommy came up to me.

"If that is going on in the house," I notified him, "you can't expect me to stay."

"I dare say you'd be glad of a chance to leave."

"Is that why you are offering it to me?"

It was by such degrees we covered the distance between our situation and the open question of divorce. But there were lapses of tenderness and turning back upon the trail.

"I don't want anybody but you, Olivia," Tommy would protest. "If you would only stay with me!"

"Oh, Tommy, if you would only come away with me!"

If either of these things had been possible for us, I think Tommy would have recovered from his infatuation and been the happier for it. Or even if Miss Rathbone had kept away from him. But that is what she couldn't or wouldn't do. She might have thought that by being seen coming in and out of the store, she could stave off criticism by the appearance of being on good terms with us. At any rate she came. I think her coming caused my husband some embarrassment, and, manlike, he made her pay for it. As I think of it now, I realize that I really did not know what went on in her; whether she had set a trap for my husband or yielded to an unconquerable passion. In any case she had imagination enough to see that unless she could maintain the tragic status, she cut rather a ridiculous figure. Sometimes I think people are drawn into these affairs not so much by the hope of happiness as the need, the deep-seated, desperate need of emotion, any kind of emotion. I think if we had taken her note, had had it out on the world-without-end basis, she would have been almost as well satisfied by a recognized romantic loss as by success. But I never knew exactly. She was equally in the dark about me. Now and then I had a glimpse of the figure I was in her eyes, in some stricture of my husband's on my behaviour—some criticism which bore the stamp of her suggestion; it was as if he was being dragged from me by an invisible creature of which

I knew nothing but an occasional scraping of its claws. I try to do her the justice in my mind, of thinking that the situation which she had built up out of Tommy's loneliness was as real for her as it was for him. Nobody in Higgleston had ever taken my natural alienation from the people there as anything but deliberate and despising. To her, my husband was the victim of a cold, neglectful wife, and to him she contrived to be a figure of romance.

"I owe her a lot," Tommy insisted; "she has suffered on account of me." He went back to that phrase again, "I owe her a lot."

"What do you owe her that you can't pay?"

"Well, I couldn't marry as long as you——"

"You want to marry her?" I cried. "You want to marry *her?*"

"I couldn't expect you to appreciate her." Tommy was sullen again. "You're so full of yourself." I held on to a graver matter.

"You want us to be divorced?" I can hear that sounding hollowly in a great space out of which all other interests in life seemed suddenly to shrink and shrivel. I had learned to talk of divorce in the great world, but to me my marriage was one of the incontrovertible things.

"We might as well be," I heard my husband say; "you are never at home any more." Then the reaction set in. "Stay with me, Olivia. I don't want anybody but you; just stay with me!"

"You want me to give up the stage and live here in Higgleston *forever?*" The unfairness of this overcame me.

"Well, why not, if you're married to me?"

I believe he would have done it. He would have wasted me like that and thought little of it. I was married, and not altogether to Tommy, but to Higgleston and the clothing business. The condition he demanded of me was not of loving and being faithful, but of living over the store. Until now, though I knew I did not love my husband as life had taught me men could be loved, I had never given up expecting to. Somewhere, somehow, but I was certain it was not in Higgleston, the transmuting touch should find him which would turn my husband into the Lord of Life. Now I discovered myself pulled over into another point of view. He had become a man capable of being interested in the village dressmaker. The farther she drew him from me the more the stripe of Higgleston came out in him.

I had planned to go up to Chicago for a week in August; to consult with Mr. Harding about the plays he was to produce the next season. I had not signed with him yet, but I knew that I should, that I could no more dissever myself from that connection than I could voluntarily surrender my own breath; I might try, but after the few respirations withheld, nature would have her way with me. It was not that I came to a decision about it; the whole matter appeared to lie in that region of finality that made the assumption of a decision ridiculous. I do not know if I expected to divorce my husband or if he or Miss Rathbone expected it. I think we were all a little scared by the situation we had evoked, as children might be at a dog they let loose. We felt the shames of publicity yelping at our heels.

The day before I left, I went to see Miss Rathbone; I had to have a skirt shortened. It was absurd, of course, but there was really no one else to go to. If there had been I shouldn't have dared; all Higgleston would have known of it and drawn its own conclusion. As it was, Higgleston was extremely dissatisfied with the affair. It did not know whom properly to blame, me for neglecting my husband or Miss Rathbone for snapping him up; they felt balked of the moral conclusion.

I hardly know what Miss Rathbone thought of my coming to her. I think she had braved herself for some sort of emotional struggle sharp enough to drown the whisper of reprobation. My quiet acceptance of the situation left her somehow toppling over her own defences. Sometimes I think the emotionalism which the attitude of that time demanded to be worked up over a divorce, drew people to it with that impulse which leads them to rush toward a fire or hurl themselves from precipices. Miss Rathbone must have been aching to fling out at me, to justify her own position by abuse of mine, and here she was down on the floor with her mouth full of pins squinting at the line of my skirt. It was then that I told her what I was going to Chicago for. "You'll be away from home all winter, then?" The question was a challenge.

"I don't know, I haven't signed yet." For the life of me I couldn't have foreborne that; it was exactly the kind of an advantage she would have taken of me. If I chose not to sign for the next winter, where was she? She stood up blindly at last. "I guess I can do the rest without you," she said. Some latent instinct of fairness flashed up in me.

"But I think I shall sign," I admitted. "I couldn't stand a winter in Higgleston." I was glad afterward that I had said that; it gave her leave for the brief time that was left to them, to think of him as being given into her hands.

I was greatly relieved to get away, even for a week, from the cold curiosity of Higgleston which, without saying so, had made me perfectly aware that I showed I had been crying a great deal lately. But no sooner was I freed from the pull of affection than I began to feel a deep resentment against Tommy. His attempt to charge his lapse of loyalty, on my art, on that thing in me which, as I read it, constituted my sole claim upon consideration, appeared a deeper indignity than his interest in the dressmaker. It was all a part of that revelation which sears the path of the gifted woman as with a flame, that no matter what her value to society, no man will spare her anything except as she pleases him. At the first summer heat of it I felt my soul curl at the edges. His repudiation of me as an actress began to appear a slight upon all that world of fineness which Art upholds, a thing not to be tolerated by any citizen of it. In its last analysis it seemed that my husband had deserted me in favour of Higgleston quite as much as I had deserted him, and it was for me to say whether I should consent to it. In that mood I met Mr. Harding and signed with him for the ensuing season, and then quite unaccountably, ten days before I was expected, I found myself pulled back to Higgleston. I had wired Tommy, and was surprised to have Mr. Ross meet me at the station.

"Mr. Bettersworth is not very well," he explained, as he put me into Higgleston's one omnibus. "It came on him rather suddenly. Some kind of a seizure," he admitted, though I did not gather from his manner that it was particularly serious until the 'bus, instead of stopping at our store, drove straight on up the one wide street.

"I thought you'd want to see him immediately," the attorney interposed to my arresting gesture. "You see he was taken at his partner's house." He seemed to avoid some unpleasant implication by not mentioning Rathbone's name.

I scarcely remember what other particulars he gave me at the time; my next sharp impression was of my husband lying white and breathing heavily in the bed in the Rathbone's front room, the drapery of which had been torn

hastily down to make room for him, regardless of the
finished pieces of Miss Harvey's trousseau still crowding the
chairs upon which they had been hastily thrust. Empty
sleeves hung down and vaguely seemed to reach for what
they could not clasp; strangely I was aware in them of an
aching lack and loss which must have sprung in my bosom.
I took my husband's hand and it dropped back from my
clasp, waxlike and nerveless. I think I had been kneeling
by the bed for some time, talk had been going on whisper-
ingly around me; finally the light faded and I discovered
that the doctor had gone. The beribboned bridal garments
hung limply still on the chairs and mocked me with their
empty arms. Presently I was aware that Miss Rathbone
had come in with a lamp. She stood there on the other
side of the bed and we looked at him and at one another.

"How long?" I asked her.

"Two or three days maybe, the doctor says."

"Will he know me again."

"The doctor says not."

"Oh, Tommy, Tommy!" I began to shake with suppressed sobbing. Miss Rathbone looked at me with cold
resentment.

"You can cry as much as you like, it won't disturb
him," she said.

She seemed to have taken the fact that she wasn't to
cry herself, as final. In a few minutes old Rathbone shuffled
in from the shop and stood peering at Tommy with his
little red-lidded eyes, wiping them furtively. I believe the
old man was fond of his partner and it was not strange to
him that Tommy should be lying ill at his home. Miss
Rathbone came and took him by the shoulders as one does
to a grieving child and turned his face to her bosom. She
was a head taller than he, and as she looked across him
to me there was compulsion in her look and pleading.

"He is never to know," the look said, and I looked
back, "Never."

It was then that I realized how genuine her affection
was for the feeble, snuffling old man; she would suffer at
being lessened in his eyes.

Someone came and took me away for a while, and
by degrees I got to know the story. It had been the night
before, just about the time I was taken with that strange
impulse to return, that Tommy had shut up the store and
gone over to the half-furnished room belonging to the

Board of Trade, which had become a sort of club for the soberer men of the community. A great deal of talk went on there which gave them the agreeable impression of something being done, though there must have been much of it of the character of that which was going on in a group around Montague when Tommy came in at the door. He came in very quietly, blinded by the light, and they had their backs to him, shaking with the loose laughter which punctuates a ribald description. Then Montague's voice took it up again.

"Rathbone'll get him," he said. "She's got the goods. The other one has probably got somebody on the side; these actresses are all alike."

There was a word or two more to that before Tommy's fist in his jaw stopped him. Montague struck back, he was a heavier man than my husband, but in a minute the others had rushed in between them. They were drawn back and held; Tommy's nose bled profusely, he appeared dazed, and accepted Montague's forced apology without a word. The men were all scared and yet excited; some of them were ashamed of themselves. They suspected it was not the sort of thing that should go on at a Board of Trade, and agreed it ought to be kept out of the papers. Someone walked home with my husband, and on the way he was seized with a violent fit of vomiting.

"Who was it hit me?" he asked at the door, and seemed but vaguely to remember what it was about. The next morning he opened the store as usual and appeared quite himself to old Rathbone, who came shuffling and sidestepping in to his nest at the accustomed hour. About half-past ten the tailor was made aware by the rapping of a customer on the deserted counter, that Tommy had gone out without a word. He must have gone straight to Miss Rathbone; those who met him on the street recalled that his gait was unsteady. She must have been greatly concerned to have him there at that hour, for people were moving about the streets and customers beginning to come in, and in the presence of Tillie Hemingway he could offer her no adequate explanation.

She was desperately revolving the risk of taking him into the front room to have out of him what his distraut presence half declared, when he was taken with a momentary retching; she went into the next room to fetch him a glass of water and a moment after her back was turned she heard him pitch forward on the floor.

When Rathbone had sent for me by the wire that passed me on the way home, he sent also to Tommy's father, who got in before noon the next day. I remember him as a quizzical sort of man always with his hands in his pockets, and a bristling brown moustache cut off square with his upper lip, and a better understanding of the situation than he had any intention of admitting. I had by some unconscious means derived from him that though he was fond of Tommy, he never had much opinion of his capacity. I think now it must have been his presence there and his manner of being likely to do the most unexpected thing, that pulled those same live business men who had stood listening in loose-mouthed relish of Monty's ribaldry, out of the possibility of entertainment in the case that might be made out of his implication in my husband's death, to the consideration of the town's repute as a place where such things could not possibly happen. By the time Forester came on, a covert discretion had supplied the event with its sole consoling circumstance of secrecy. Not even my family got to know what led up to that blow which had precipitated an unsuspected weakness. It was quite in accordance with what they believed of the life I had chosen, that my husband's death in a brawl should be among its contingencies. Poor Tommy's end took on a tinge of theatricality.

It was toward the end of the second day that he began to respond to the stimulants the doctor had been pouring into him. He opened his eyes and looked at us, conscious, but out of all present time. Feebly his glance roved over the figures by the bed, and fell at last on me.

"Ollie," he whispered, "Ollie!" It was a name he had not called for a long time.

"Oh, my dear, my dear!" I took his hand again and felt a faint pressure. Miss Rathbone hardly dared to look at him with the others standing about. I whispered her name to him, and his partner's, but he did not so much as turn his eyes in their direction. I could see him studying me out of half-shut glances; there would be an appreciable interval before the sense of what he saw penetrated the dulled brain; I thought I knew the very moment when the significance of our standing all about his bed crying, took hold of him. All at once he spoke out clearly:

"Is my Father here?" I fancied he must have hit on that question as a confirmation; but before there could be any talk between them he slid off again into the deeps of insensibility. At the end of half an hour or so he started up almost strongly.

"Ollie!" he demanded, "where is the baby?"

"Asleep," I told him.

"Then I will sleep too," and in a little while it was so.

The Odd Fellows took charge of my husband's funeral, his body was moved from the Rathbones', to their hall and did not go back again to the rooms over the store. Miss Rathbone made up my crepe for me. I believe it gave her a little comfort to do so. Forester came and settled up my husband's affairs; he was rather inclined to resent what he felt was an effort of the Rathbones to claim a larger share in the business than the books showed, but he thought my indifference natural to my grief. He was shocked a little at my determination to go on with my engagement; we were not so poor he thought, that I could not afford a little retirement to my widowhood. But in that strange renewal of communion after death, I felt my husband nearer than before. He would go with me at last out of Higgleston. Strangely. I wanted to see Miss Rathbone, but she kept away from me. That was as it should have been in Higgleston. She had tried to get my husband, she had been, in a way, the death of him. It was hardly expected that I could bear the sight of her, though it would have been Christian to forgive her.

I did see her, however, the night before I went away. It was the dusk of the first of September. There was a moon coming up, large and dulled at the edges by the haze, and that strange earthy smell with the hint of decay in it, kept in by the banded mists that lay below the moon. The darkness crept close along the earth and spread upward like an exhalation into the sky where almost the full day halted. I had slipped out down a side street and across an open lot to the cemetery. I would have that hour with my dead free from observation.

I went between the white head stones and the flower borders. As I neared my husband's grave, something moved upon it. It arose out of the low mound as I approached; for one heart-riving second I stopped, speechless; it moved again and showed a woman.

"Miss Rathbone!" I called. "Henrietta!" I had not used her name before; I have just now remembered it.

"You might have left me this," she said. I saw that she had covered the mound with flowers, and I was glad I had not brought any.

"I am leaving," I answered. "I am going tomorrow . . . where my work is."

"Yes, *you* can go. But I have to stay . . . where my work is. I stay with him. You can go . . . you always wanted to go. And I, I have been talked about and I daren't even cry for him, not even at night, for my father hears me." She was crying now, deeply, bitterly. "You never cared for him," she insisted, "and now he knows it; he knows and has come back to me . . . to *me*."

"He comes back," I admitted. I was stricken suddenly with the futility of all human conviction. Moving about the house that day I had been conscious of him beside me then, and now, lying there beside my boy, touching him . . . mine . . . sealed to me in the certainty of death. And he had come back to *her*. I did not know even now what she and my husband had been to one another.

It swept over me somehow, drowningly, that this was the secret that the dead know, how to belong to all of us. They had no bond, how could they be unfaithful? For a moment I was caught up by the thought to nobility.

"Look here, Henrietta, if you feel that way, I'll leave it to you. I'll not come here any more." I did not know what else I could do about it.

"It's the least you *can* do." She was accepting it as her right. Any woman will understand how I wanted to lay my hand there, above his breast. She must really have believed I did not love him. I turned back across the borders.

"Good-bye, Henrietta." She made a nearly inarticulate sound. The last I saw of her in the dusk she was tucking her flowers into the fresh sod as one tucks a coverlet about a child. He had been, I suppose, both man and child to her.

Dorothy Canfield Fisher (1879–1958)

Most often associated with Vermont, where her family had lived for many generations, Dorothy Canfield was actually born in Kansas and raised in the Midwest. She was named Dorothea by her mother, Flavia, an artist who was a great admirer of *Middlemarch*. Her father, to whom she was devoted, was a college professor and president, and their home was full of books, music, people, and political discussion. She began travelling early, acting as interpreter for her mother who first took her to Europe when she was only a child.

In 1899 she graduated from Ohio State and spent several years in Europe studying languages and philology, returning to America to earn a Ph.D. from Columbia in 1904. In 1907 she married John Fisher, and they went to live in Vermont, planning to support themselves as free-lance writers. They had two children and seem to have had an exceptionally close and happy marriage which provided a model for those in her books.

She was enormously productive during her life-time, producing novels, short stories, essays on education, memoirs of Vermont, France, the Basque country, children's fiction, reviews, and articles on widely varied subjects. Included among her works are: *The Squirrel Cage* (1912), *Mothers and Children* (1914), *The Bent Twig* (1915), *Understood Betsy* (1917), *The Home-Maker* (1924), *Basque People* (1931), *Fables for Parents* (1937), and *A Harvest of Stories* (1956). In them she expresses her interest in family life and in finding ways to stretch conventional habits so that peoples' lives can express necessary human values.

[References: An early assessment of Fisher's work occurs in Overton, Grant. *The Women Who Make Our Novels*. rev. ed., 1928; rpt. Freeport, New York: Books for Libraries Press, 1967. Yates, Elizabeth. *The Lady from Vermont: Dorothy Canfield Fisher's Life and World*. Brattleboro, Vermont: The Stephen Green Press, 1958 provides a biographical and literary account and includes a bibliography of primary and secondary materials.]

A DROP IN THE BUCKET

There is no need to describe in detail the heroine of this tale, because she represents a type familiar to all readers of the conventional New-England-village dialect story. She was for a long time the sole inhabitant of Hillsboro, who came up to the expectations of our visiting friends from the city, on the lookout for Mary Wilkins characters. We always used to take such people directly to see Cousin Tryphena, as dwellers in an Italian city always take their foreign friends to see their one bit of ruined city wall or the heap of stones which was once an Inquisitorial torture chamber, never to see the new waterworks or the modern, sanitary hospital.

On the way to the other end of the street, where Cousin Tryphena's tiny, two-roomed house stood, we always laid bare the secrets of her somnolent, respectable, unprofitable life; we always informed our visitors that she lived and kept up a social position on two hundred and fifteen dollars a year, and that she had never been further from home than to the next village. We always drew attention to her one treasure, the fine Sheraton sideboard that had belonged to her great-grandfather, old Priest Perkins; and, when we walked away from the orderly and empty house, we were sure that our friends from the city would always exclaim with great insight into character, "What a charmingly picturesque life! Isn't she perfectly delicious!"

Next door to Cousin Tryphena's minute, snow-white house is a forlorn old building, one of the few places for rent in our village, where nearly everyone owns his own shelter. It stood desolately idle for some time, tumbling to pieces almost visibly, until, one day, two years ago, a burly, white-bearded tramp stopped in front of it, laid down his stick and bundle, and went to inquire at the

From *Hillsboro People*. New York: Grosset & Dunlap, 1915.

neighbor's if the place were for rent, then moved in with his stick and bundle and sent away for the rest of his belongings, that is to say, an outfit for cobbling shoes. He cut a big wooden boot out of the side of an empty box, painted it black with axle-grease and soot, hung it up over the door, and announced himself as ready to do all the cobbling and harness-repairing he could get . . . and a fine workman he showed himself to be.

We were all rather glad to have this odd new member of our community settle down among us . . . all, that is, except Cousin Tryphena, who was sure, for months afterward, that he would cut her throat some night and steal away her Sheraton sideboard. It was an open secret that Putnam, the antique-furniture dealer in Troy, had offered her two hundred and fifty dollars for it. The other women of the village, however, not living alone in such dangerous proximity to the formidable stranger, felt reassured by his long, white beard, and by his great liking for little children.

Although, from his name, as from his strong accent, it was evident that old Jombatiste belonged, by birth, to our French-Canadian colony, he never associated himself with that easy-going, devoutly Catholic, law-abiding, and rather unlettered group of our citizens. He allied himself with quite another class, making no secret of the fact that he was an out-and-out Socialist, Anti-clerical, Syndicalist, Anarchist, Nihilist. . . . We in Hillsboro are not acute in distinguishing between the different shades of radicalism, and never have been able exactly to place him, except that, beside his smashing, loudly-voiced theories, young Arthur Robbins' Progressivism sounds like old Martin Pelham's continued jubilation over the Hayes campaign.

The central article of Jombatiste's passionately held creed seemed to be that everything was exactly wrong, and that, while the Socialist party was not nearly sweeping enough in its ideas, it was, as yet, the best means for accomplishing the inevitable, righteous overturning of society. Accordingly, he worked incessantly, not only at his cobbling, but at any odd job he could find to do, lived the life of an anchorite, went in rags, ate mainly crackers and milk, and sent every penny he could save to the Socialist Headquarters. We knew about this not only through his own trumpeting of the programme of his life, but because Phil Latimer, the postmaster, is cousin to us all and often told us about the money-orders, so large that they must have represented almost all the earnings of the fanatical old shoemaker.

And yet he was never willing to join in any of our charitable enterprises, although his ardent old heart was evidently as tender as it was hot. Nothing threw him into such bellowing fury as cruelty. He became the terror of all our boys who trapped rabbits, and, indeed, by the sole influence of his whirlwind descents upon them, and his highly illegal destruction of their traps, he practically made that boyish pastime a thing of the past in Hillsboro. Somehow, though the boys talked mightily about how they'd have the law of dirty, hot-tempered old Jombatiste, nobody cared really to face him. He had on tap a stream of red-hot vituperation astonishingly varied for a man of his evident lack of early education. Perhaps it came from his incessant reading and absorption of Socialist and incendiary literature.

He took two Socialist newspapers, and nobody knows how many queer little inflammatory magazines from which he read aloud selections to anyone who did not run away.

Naturally enough, from his point of view, he began with his neighbor, fastidious Cousin Tryphena.

What Cousin Tryphena did not know about the way the world outside of Hillsboro was run would have made a complete treatise on modern civilization. She never took a newspaper, only borrowing, once in a while, the local sheet to read the news items from Greenford, where she had some distant cousins; and, though she occasionally looked at one of the illustrated magazines, it was only at the pictures.

It is therefore plain that old Jombatiste could not have found a worse listener for his bellowed statements that ninety per cent of the money of this country was in the hands of two per cent of the population; that the franchise was a farce because the government was controlled by a Wall Street clique; and that any man who could not earn a good living for his family had a moral right to shoot a millionaire. For the most part, Cousin Tryphena counted her tatting stitches and paid not the least attention to her malcontent neighbor. When she did listen, she did not believe a word he said. She had lived in Hillsboro for fifty-five years and she knew what made people poor. It was shiftlessness. There was always plenty of work to be had at the brush-back factory for any man who had the sense and backbone to keep at it. If they *would* stop work in deer-week to go hunting, or go on a spree Town-meeting day, or run away to fish, she'd like to know what business they had blaming millionaires because they lost their jobs. She did not expound her opinions of these points to Jombatiste because, in the first place, she despised him for a dirty Canuck, and, secondly, because opinions seemed shadowy and unsubstantial things to her. The important matters were to make your starch clear and not to be late to church.

It is proverbial that people who are mostly silent often keep for some time a reputation for more wisdom than is theirs. Cousin Tryphena unconsciously profited in the estimation of her neighbor by this fact of psychology. Old Jombatiste had thundered his per cents of the distribution of capital for many months before he discovered that he was on the wrong track.

Then, one winter day, as Cousin Tryphena was hanging out her washing, he ran over to her, waving his favorite magazine. He read her a paragraph from it, striking the paper occasionally for emphasis with his horny, blackened, shoemaker's hand, and following her as she moved along the clothes-lines——

"And it is thus definitely *proved*," he shouted in conclusion, "that Senator Burlingame was in the pay of J. D. Darby, when he held up the Rouse Workingman's Bill in the Senate Committee. . . ." He stopped and glared triumphantly at his neighbor. A rare impulse of perversity rose in Cousin Tryphena's unawakened heart. She took a clothes-pin out of her mouth and asked with some exasperation, "Well, what *of* it!" a comment on his information which sent the old man reeling back as though she had struck him.

In the conversation which followed, old Jombatiste, exploring at last Cousin Tryphena's mind, leaned giddily over the abyss of her ignorance of political economy and sociology, dropping one exploring plummet after another into its depths, only to find them fathomless. He went shakily back to his own house, silenced for once.

But, although for the first time he neglected work to do

it, he returned to the attack the next day with a new weapon. He made no more remarks about industrial slavery, nor did he begin, as was his wont, with the solemnly enunciated axiom, "Wealth comes from labor alone!" He laid down, on the Sheraton sideboard, an armful of his little magazines, and settled himself in a chair, observing with a new comprehension how instinctively Cousin Tryphena reached for her tatting as he began to read aloud. He read the story of a man who was burned to death in molten steel because his employers did not install a rather expensive safety device, and who left a young widow and three children. These tried to earn their livings by making artificial flowers. They could earn, all of them working together, three cents an hour. When the last dollar of the dead father's savings was used up, and there was talk of separating the family so that the children could be put in an asylum, the mother drowned the three little ones and herself after them. Cousin Tryphena dropped her tatting, her country-bred mind reeling. "Didn't she have any *folks* to help her out?"

Jombatiste explained that she came from East Poland, so that her folks, if indeed she had any, were too far away to be of use. He struck one fist inside his palm with a fierce gesture, such as he used when he caught a boy trapping, and cried, " . . . and that in a country that produces three times the food it consumes." For the first time, a statistical statement awoke an echo in Cousin Tryphena's atrophied brain.

Old Jombatiste read on, this time about a girl of seventeen, left by her parents' death in charge of a small brother. She had been paid twenty cents for making crocheted lace which sold for a dollar and a half. By working twelve hours a day, she had been able to make forty-seven cents. Seeing her little brother grow pale from lack of food, she had, in desperation, taken the first, the awfully decisive first step downward, and had almost at once thereafter vanished, drawn down by the maelstrom of vice. The little brother, wild with grief over his sister's disappearance, had been taken to an orphan asylum where he had since twice tried to commit suicide.

Cousin Tryphena sat rigid, her tatting fallen to the floor, her breath coming with difficulty. It is impossible for the average modern mind, calloused by promiscuous reading, to conceive the effect upon her primitive organism of this attack from the printed page. She not only did not dream that these stories might not be true, they seemed as real to her as though she had seen the people. There was not a particle of blood in her haggard face.

Jombatiste read on . . . the story of a decent, ambitious man, employed in a sweatshop tailoring establishment, who contracted tuberculosis from the foul air, and who dragged down with him, in his agonizing descent to the very depths of misery, a wife and two children. He was now dead, and his wife was living in a corner of a moldy, damp basement, a pile of rags the only bed for her and her children, their only heat what fire the mother could make out of paper and rubbish picked up on the streets.

Cousin Tryphena's horrified eyes fell on her well-blacked stove, sending out the aromatic breath of burning white-birch sticks. She recoiled from it with a shudder.

Jombatiste read on, the story of the woman who, when her three sons died in an accident due to negligence on their employer's part . . . he read no more that day, for Cousin Tryphena put her gray head down on the center-table and wept as she never had done in her life. Jombatiste rose softly and tiptoed out of the room.

The tap-tap-tap of his hammer rang loud and fast the rest of that day. He was exulting over having aroused another bourgeois from the sleep of greasy complacency. He had made a convert. To his dire and utter penniless-ness, Cousin Tryphena's tiny income seemed a fortune. He had a happy dream of persuading her to join him in his weekly contributions to the sacred funds! As he stood at midnight, in the open door, for the long draught of fresh air he always took before turning in on his pile of hay, he heard in the wood on the hill back of the house the shrill shriek of a trapped rabbit. He plowed furiously out through the deep snow to find it, gave the tortured animal a merciful death, carried the trap back to the river and threw it in with a furious splash. He strode home under the frosty stars, his dirty shirt open over his corded, old neck, his burning heart almost content. He had done a good day's work.

Early the next morning, his neighbor came to his door, very white, very hollow-eyed, evidently with a sleepless night back of her, and asked him for the papers he had read from. Jombatiste gave them to her in a tactful silence. She took them in one shaking hand, drawing her shawl around her wrinkled face with the other, and went back through the snow to her own house.

By noon that day, everyone in the village was thrilling with wild surmise. Cousin Tryphena had gone over to Graham and Sanders', asked to use their long-distance telephone and had telephoned to Putnam to come and get her sideboard. After this strange act, she had passed Albert Graham, then by chance alone in the store, with so wild a mien that he had not ventured to make any inquiries. But he took pains to mention the matter to everyone who happened to come in, that morning; and, by dinner-time, every family in Hillsboro was discussing over its pie the possibility that the well-known *queer streak*, which had sent several of Cousin Tryphena's ancestors to the asylum, was suddenly making its appearance in her.

I was detained, that afternoon, and did not reach her house until nearly four; and I was almost the last to arrive. I found Cousin Tryphena very silent, her usually pale face very red, the center of a group of neighbors who all at once began to tell me what had happened. I could make nothing out of their incoherent explanations. . . . "Trypheny was crazy . . . she'd ought to have a guardeen . . . that Canuck shoemaker had addled her brains . . . there'd ought to be a law against that kind of newspaper . . . Trypheny was goin' like her great-aunt, Lucilly, that died in the asylum. . . ." I appealed directly to Cousin Tryphena for information as to what the trouble was.

"There ain't any trouble's I know of," she answered in a shaking voice. "I've just heard of a widow-woman, down in the city, who's bringin' up her two children in the corner of a basement where the green mold stands out on the wall, and I'm goin' down to fetch her an' the children up here to live with me . . . them an' a little orphan boy as don't like the 'sylum where they've put him——"

Somebody broke in on her to cry, "Why, Trypheny, you simple old critter, that's four people! Where you goin' to put 'em in this little tucked-up place?"

Cousin Tryphena answered doggedly and pointedly,

"Your own grandmother, Rebecca Mason, brought up a family of seven in a house no bigger than this, and no cellar."

"But how, . . ." another voice exclaimed, "air you goin' to get enough for 'em to eat? You ain't got but barely enough for yourself!"

Cousin Tryphena paled a little, "I'm a good sewer, I could make money sewing . . . and I could do washings for city-folks, summer-times. . . ." Her set mouth told what a price she paid for this voluntary abandonment of the social standing that had been hers by virtue of her idleness. She went on with sudden spirit, "You all act as though I was doin' it to spite you and to amuse myself! I don't *want* to! When I think of my things I've kept so nice always, I'm *wild* . . . but how can I help it, now I know about 'em! I didn't sleep a wink last night. I'll go clean crazy if I don't do something! I saw those three children strugglin' in the water and their mother a-holdin' on 'em down, and then jumpin' in herself—— Why, I give enough milk to the *cat* to keep a baby . . . what else can I do?"

I was touched, as I think we all were, by her helpless simplicity and ignorance, and by her defenselessness against this first vision of life, the vision which had been spared her so long, only to burst upon her like a forest-fire. I had an odd fancy that she had just awakened after a sleep of half a century.

"Dear Cousin Tryphena," I said as gently as I could, "you haven't had a very wide experience of modern industrial or city conditions and there are some phases of this matter which you don't take into consideration." Then I brought out the old, wordy, eminently reasonable arguments we all use to stifle the thrust of self-questioning: I told her that it was very likely that the editor of that newspaper had invented, or at least greatly exaggerated those stories, and that she would find on investigation that no such family existed.

"I don't see how that lets me out of *lookin'* for them," said Cousin Tryphena.

"Well, at least," I urged, "don't be in such a hurry about it. Take time to think it over! Wait till——"

"Wait!" cried Cousin Tryphena. "Why, another one may

be jumpin' in the river this minute! If I'd ha' had the money, I'd ha' gone on the noon train!"

At this point, the man from Putnam's came with a team from our livery to carry away the Sheraton sideboard. Cousin Tryphena bore herself like a martyr at the stake, watching, with dry eyes, the departure of her one certificate to dear gentility and receiving with proud indifference the crisp bills of a denomination most of us had never seen before.

"You won't need all that just to go down to the city," I remonstrated.

She stopped watching the men load her shining old treasure into the wagon and turned her anguished eyes to me. "They'll likely be needing clothes and things."

I gave up. She had indeed thought it all out.

It was time for us to go home to prepare our several suppers and we went our different ways, shaking our heads over Tryphena's queerness. I stopped a moment before the cobbler's open door, watched him briskly sewing a broken halter and telling a folk-tale to some children by his knee. When he finished, I said with some acerbity, "Well, Jombatiste, I hope you're satisfied with what you've done to poor old Miss Tryphena . . . spoiling the rest of her life for her!"

"Such a life, Madame," said Jombatiste dryly, "ought to be spoiled, the sooner the better."

"She's going to start for the city to-morrow," I said, supposing of course that he had heard the news.

Jombatiste looked up very quickly. "For what goes she to the city?"

"Why . . . she's gone daft over those bogie-stories of yours . . . she's looked the list over and picked out the survivors, the widow of the man who died of tuberculosis, and so on, and she's going to bring them back here to share her luxurious life."

Jombatiste bounded into the air as if a bomb had exploded under him, scattering his tools and the children, rushing past me out of the house and toward Cousin Tryphena's. . . . As he ran, he did what I have never seen anyone do, out of a book; he tore at his bushy hair and scattered handfuls in the air. It seemed to me that some sudden madness had struck our dull little village, and I hastened after him to protect Cousin Tryphena.

She opened the door in answer to his battering knocks, frowned, and began to say something to him, but was fairly swept off her feet by the torrent of his reproaches. . . . "How dare you take the information I give you and use it to betray your fellow-man! How do you *dare* stand there, so mealy-mouthed, and face me, when you are planning a cowardly attack on the liberty of your country! You call yourself a nurse . . . what would you think of a mother who hid an ulcer in her child's side from the doctor because it did not look pretty! What *else* are you planning to do? What would you think of a nurse who put paint and powder on her patient's face, to cover up a filthy skin disease? What else are you planning to do . . . you with your plan to put court-plaster over one pustule in ten million and thinking you are helping cure the patient! You are planning simply to please yourself, you cowardly . . . and you are an idiot too . . ." he beat his hands on the door-jambs, . . . if you had the money of forty millionaires, you couldn't do anything in that way . . . how many people are you thinking to help . . . two, three . . . maybe four! But there are hundreds of others . . . why, I could read you a thousand stories of worse——"

Cousin Tryphena's limit had been reached. She advanced upon the intruder with a face as excited as his own. . . . "Jombatiste Ramotte, if you ever dare to read me another such story, I'll go right out and jump in the Necronsett River!"

The mania which had haunted earlier generations of her family looked out luridly from her eyes.

I felt the goose-flesh stand out on my arms, and even Jombatiste's hot blood was cooled. He stood silent an instant.

Cousin Tryphena slammed the door in his face.

He turned to me with a bewilderment almost pathetic, so tremendous was it. . . . "Did you hear that . . . what sort of logic do you call——"

"Jombatiste," I counseled him, "if you take my advice, you'll leave Miss Tryphena alone after this."

Cousin Tryphena started off on her crack-brained expedition, the very next morning, on the six-thirty train. I happened to be looking out sleepily and saw her trudging wearily past our house in the bleak gray of our mountain dawn, the inadequate little, yellow flame of her old-fashioned lantern like a glowworm at her side. It seemed somehow symbolical of something, I did not know what.

It was a full week before we heard from her, and we had begun really to fear that we would never see her again, thinking that perhaps, while she was among strangers, her unsettled mind might have taken some new fancy which would be her destruction.

That week Jombatiste shut the door to his house. The children reported that he would not even let them in, and that they could see him through the window stitching away in ominous silence, muttering to himself.

Eight days after Cousin Tryphena had gone away, I had a telegram from her, which read, "Build fires in both my stoves to-morrow afternoon."

The dark comes early in the mountains, and so, although I dare say there was not a house in the village without a face at the pane after the late evening train came up, none of us saw anything but our usual impenetrable December darkness. That, too, seemed, to my perhaps overwrought consciousness of the problem, highly suggestive of the usual course of our lives. At least, I told myself, Cousin Tryphena had taken her absurd little lantern and gone forth.

The next morning, soon after breakfast, I set off for the other end of the street. Cousin Tryphena saw me coming and opened the door. She did not smile, and she was still very pale, but I saw that she had regained her self-control. "Come right in," she said, in rather a tense voice, and, as I entered she added, in our rustic phrase for introduction, "Make you 'quainted with my friend, Mrs. Lindstrom. She's come up from the city to stay with me. And this is her little boy, Sugurd, and this is the baby."

Blinking somewhat, I shook hands with a small, stoop-shouldered woman, in a new, ready-made dress, with abundant yellow hair drawn back from the thinnest, palest, saddest little face I had ever seen. She was holding an immaculately clean baby, asleep, its long golden lashes lying on cheeks as white and sunken as her own. A sturdily built boy of about six scrambled up from where he lay on the floor, playing with the cat, and gave me a hand shyly, hanging down his head. His mother had glanced up at me with a quick, shrinking look of fright, the tears starting to her eyes.

Cousin Tryphena was evidently afraid that I would not take her cue and sound the right note, for she went on hastily, "Mrs. Lindstrom has been real sick and kind o' worried over the baby, so's she's some nervous. I tell her Hillsboro air is thought very good for people's nerves. Lots of city folks come here in summer time, just for that. Don't you think Sigurd is a real big boy for only six and a half? He knows his letters too! He's goin' to school as soon as we get settled down. I want you should bring over those alphabet blocks that your Peggy doesn't use any more——"

The other woman was openly crying now, clinging to her benefactress' hand and holding it against her cheek as she sobbed.

My heroic old cousin patted her hair awkwardly, but kept on talking in her matter-of-fact manner, looking at me sternly as though defying me to show, by look or word, any consciousness of anything unusual in the situation; and we fell at once, she and I, into a commonplace conversation about the incidents of the trip up.

When I came away, half an hour later, Cousin Tryphena slipped a shawl over her head and came down the walk with me to the gate. I was much affected by what seemed to me the dramatically fitting outcome of my old kinswoman's Quixotism. I saw Cousin Tryphena picturesquely as the Happy Fool of old folk-lore, the character who, through his very lack of worldy wisdom, attains without effort all that self-seeking folks try for in vain. The happy ending of her adventure filled me with a cheerful wonder at the ways of Providence, which I tried to pass on to her in the exclamation, "Why, Cousin Tryphena, it's like a story-book! You're going to *enjoy* having those people. The woman is as nice as she can be, and that's the brightest little boy! He's as smart as a whip!"

I was aware that the oddness of Cousin Tryphena's manner still persisted even now that we were alone. She sighed heavily and said, "I don't sleep much better nights now I've done it!" Then facing me, "I hadn't ought to have brought them up here! I just did it to please myself! Once I saw 'em . . . I wanted 'em!"

This seemed to me the wildest possible perversion of

the Puritan instinct for self-condemnation and, half-vexed, I attempted some expostulation.

She stopped me with a look and gesture Dante might have had, "You ain't seen what I've seen."

I was half-frightened by her expression but tried to speak coolly. "Why, was it as bad as that paper said?" I asked.

She laid her hand on my arm, "Child, it was nothing like what the paper said . . . it was so much worse!"

"Oh . . ." I commented inadequately.

"I was five days looking for her . . . they'd moved from the address the paper give. And, in those five days, I saw so many others . . . *so many others* . . ." her face twitched. She put one lean old hand before her eyes. Then, quite unexpectedly, she cast out at me an exclamation which made my notion of the pretty picturesqueness of her adventure seem cheap and trivial and superficial. "Jombatiste is right!" she cried to me with a bitter fierceness: "Everything is wrong! Everything is wrong! If I can do anything, I'd ought to do it to help them as want to smash everything up and start over! What good does it do for me to bring up here just these three out of all I saw. . ." Her voice broke into pitiful, self-excusing quavers, "but when I saw them . . . the baby was so sick . . . and little Sigurd is so cunning . . . he took to me right away, came to me the first thing . . . this morning he wouldn't pick up his new rubbers off the floor for his mother, but, when I asked him, he did, right off . . . you ought to have seen what he had on . . . such rags . . . such dirt . . . and 'twan't her fault either! She's . . . why she's like *any*body . . . like a person's cousin they never happened to see before . . . why, they were all *folks!*" she cried out, her tired old mind wandering fitfully from one thing to another.

"You didn't find the little boy in the asylum?" I asked.

"He was dead before I got there," she answered.

"Oh . . . !" I said again, shocked, and then tentatively, "Had he . . . ?"

"I don't know whether he had or not," said Cousin Tryphena, "I didn't ask. I didn't want to know. I know too much now!" She looked up fixedly at the mountain line, high and keen against the winter sky, "Jombatiste is right," she said again unsparingly, "I hadn't ought to be enjoying them . . . their father ought to be alive and with them. He was willing to work all he could, and yet he . . . here I've lived for fifty-five years and never airned my salt a single day. What was I livin' on? The stuff these folks ought to ha' had to eat . . . them and the Lord only knows how many more besides! Jombatiste is right . . . what I'm doin' now is only a drop in the bucket!"

She started from her somber reverie at the sound of a childish wail from the house. . . . "That's Sigurd . . . I *knew* that cat would scratch him!" she told me with instant, breathless agitation, as though the skies were falling, and darted back. After a moment's hesitation I, too, went back and watched her bind up with stiff, unaccustomed old fingers the little scratched hand, watched the frightened little boy sob himself quiet on her old knees that had never before known a child's soft weight, saw the expression in her eyes as she looked down at the sleeping baby and gazed about the untidy room so full of life, which had always been so orderly and so empty.

She lifted the little boy up higher so that his tousled yellow hair rested against her bosom. He put an arm around her neck and she flushed with pleasure like a girl; but, although she held him close to her with a sudden wistful tenderness, there was in her eyes a gloomy austerity which forbade me to sentimentalize over the picture she made.

"But, Cousin Tryphena," I urged, "it *is* a drop in the bucket, you know, and that's something!"

She looked down at the child on her knee, she laid her cheek against his bright hair, but she told me with harsh, self-accusing rigor, " 'Tain't right for me to be here alive enjoying that dead man's little boy."

That was eighteen months ago. Mrs. Lindstrom is dead of consumption; but the two children are rosy and hearty and not to be distinguished from the other little Yankees of the village. They are devotedly attached to their Aunt Tryphena and rule her despotically.

And so we live along, like a symbol of the great world, bewildered Cousin Tryphena toiling lovingly for her adopted children, with the memory of her descent into hell still darkening and confusing her kind eyes; Jombatiste clothing his old body in rags and his soul in flaming indignation as he batters hopefully at the ramparts of intrenched unrighteousness . . . and the rest of us doing nothing at all.

Susan Keating Glaspell (1876?–1948)

Journalist, short story writer, novelist, playwright, and—with her husband, George Cram Cook—co-founder of the Provincetown Playhouse, Susan Keating Glaspell was born and raised in Davenport, Iowa. She received a Ph.B. from Drake College in Des Moines in 1899, publishing both journalistic pieces and stories while still an undergraduate. For the next two years she worked for the *Des Moines Daily News,* covering local and state politics and writing human interest stories, but in 1901 returned to Davenport to devote herself full-time to writing fiction.

This attempt was successful: between 1901 and 1922, when she stopped writing them, she produced, approximately, forty published short stories—thirteen of which were collected in *Lifted Masks* (1912); she published her first novel, *The Glory of the Conquered* in 1909, and wrote nine more between that date and 1945; in 1915, after she had married and moved to the East coast, she began to write plays, publishing a collection of one-acts in 1920, *The Verge,* a drama concerned with feminism and with the "new woman" in 1921-22, and *Alison's House,* for which she received a Pulitzer Prize in 1931. Although best known for her plays and for her work with the Provincetown Players, her non-dramatic fiction is also of interest for its serious consideration of the problems of small-town conformity, and its exploration of the discrepancy between idealistic commitment and the demands of social rules. "A Jury of Her Peers," reprinted here, was included in *The Best Short Stories of 1917,* ed. E. J. O'Brien (Boston: Small, Maynard, and Co., 1918).

[References. Waterman, Arthur E. *Susan Glaspell.* New York:Twayne Publishers, Inc., 1966 is the only full-length study and includes a bibliography of primary and secondary materials.]

A JURY OF HER PEERS

When Martha Hale opened the storm-door and got a cut of the north wind, she ran back for her big woolen scarf. As she hurriedly wound that round her head her eye made a scandalized sweep of her kitchen. It was no ordinary thing that called her away—it was probably farther from ordinary than anything that had ever happened in Dickson County. But what her eye took in was that her kitchen was in no shape for leaving: her bread all ready for mixing, half the flour sifted and half unsifted.

She hated to see things half done; but she had been at that when the team from town stopped to get Mr. Hale, and then the sheriff came running in to say his wife wished Mrs. Hale would come too—adding, with a grin, that he guessed she was getting scarey and wanted another woman along. So she had dropped everything right where it was.

"Martha!" now came her husband's impatient voice. "Don't keep folks waiting out here in the cold."

She again opened the storm-door, and this time joined the three men and the one woman waiting for her in the big, two-seated buggy.

After she had the robes tucked around her she took another look at the woman who sat beside her on the back seat. She had met Mrs. Peters the year before at the county fair, and the thing she remembered about her was that she didn't seem like a sheriff's wife. She was small and thin and didn't have a strong voice. Mrs. Gorman, sheriff's wife before Gorman went out and Peters came in, had a voice that somehow seemed to be backing up the law with every word. But if Mrs. Peters didn't look like a sheriff's wife, Peters made it up in looking like a sheriff. He was to a dot the kind of man who could get himself elected sheriff—a heavy man with a big voice, who was particularly genial with the law-abiding, as if to make

First published in *Everyweek* (March 5, 1917).

it plain that he knew the difference between criminals and non-criminals. And right there it came into Mrs. Hale's mind, with a stab, that this man who was so pleasant and lively with all of them was going to the Wrights' now as a sheriff.

"The country's not very pleasant this time of year," Mrs. Peters at last ventured, as if she felt they ought to be talking as well as the men.

Mrs. Hale scarcely finished her reply, for they had gone up a little hill and could see the Wright place now, and seeing it did not make her feel like talking. It looked very lonesome this cold March morning. It had always been a lonesome-looking place. It was down in a hollow, and the poplar trees around it were lonesome-looking trees. The men were looking at it and talking about what had happened. The county attorney was bending to one side of the buggy, and kept looking steadily at the place as they drew up to it.

"I'm glad you came with me," Mrs. Peters said nervously, as the two women were about to follow the men in through the kitchen door.

Even after she had her foot on the door-step, her hand on the knob, Martha Hale had a moment of feeling she could not cross that threshold. And the reason it seemed she couldn't cross it now was simply because she hadn't crossed it before. Time and time again it had been in her mind. "I ought to go over and see Minnie Foster"— she still thought of her as Minnie Foster, though for twenty years she had been Mrs. Wright. And then there was always something to do and Minnie Foster would go from her mind. But *now* she could come.

The men went over to the stove. The women stood close together by the door. Young Henderson, the county attorney, turned around and said, "Come up to the fire, ladies."

Mrs. Peters took a step forward, then stopped. "I'm not —cold," she said.

And so the two women stood by the door, at first not even so much as looking around the kitchen.

The men talked for a minute about what a good thing it was the sheriff had sent his deputy out that morning to make a fire for them, and then Sheriff Peters stepped back from the stove, unbuttoned his outer coat, and leaned his hands on the kitchen table in a way that seemed to mark the beginning of official business. "Now, Mr. Hale," he said in a sort of semi-official voice, "before we move things about, you tell Mr. Henderson just what it was you saw when you came here yesterday morning."

The county attorney was looking around the kitchen.

"By the way," he said, "has anything been moved?" He turned to the sheriff. "Are things just as you left them yesterday?"

Peters looked from cupboard to sink; from that to a small worn rocker a little to one side of the kitchen table.

"It's just the same."

"Somebody should have been left here yesterday," said the county attorney.

"Oh—yesterday," returned the sheriff, with a little gesture as of yesterday having been more than he could bear to think of. "When I had to send Frank to Morris Center for that man who went crazy—let me tell you, I had my hands full *yesterday*. I knew you could get back from Omaha by to-day, George, and as long as I went over everything here myself—"

"Well, Mr. Hale," said the county attorney, in a way of letting what was past and gone go, "tell just what happened when you came here yesterday morning."

Mrs. Hale, still leaning against the door, had that sinking feeling of the mother whose child is about to speak a piece. Lewis often wandered along and got things mixed up in a story. She hoped he would tell this straight and plain, and not say unnecessary things that would just make things harder for Minnie Foster. He didn't begin at once, and she noticed that he looked queer—as if standing in that kitchen and having to tell what he had seen there yesterday morning made him almost sick.

"Yes, Mr. Hale?" the county attorney reminded.

"Harry and I had started to town with a load of potatoes," Mrs. Hale's husband began.

Harry was Mrs. Hale's oldest boy. He wasn't with them now, for the very good reason that those potatoes never got to town yesterday and he was taking them this morning, so he hadn't been home when the sheriff stopped to stay he wanted Mr. Hale to come over to the Wright place and tell the county attorney his story there, where he could point it all out. With all Mrs. Hale's other emotions came the fear now that maybe Harry wasn't dressed warm enough—they hadn't any of them realized how that north wind did bite.

"We come along this road," Hale was going on, with a motion of his hand to the road over which they had just come, "and as we got in sight of the house I says to Harry, 'I'm goin' to see if I can't get John Wright to take a telephone.' You see," he explained to Henderson, "unless I can get somebody to go in with me they won't come out this branch road except for a price *I* can't pay. I'd spoke to Wright about it once before; but he put me off, saying folks talked too much anyway, and all he asked was peace and quiet—guess you know about how much he talked himself. But I thought maybe if I went to the house and talked about it before his wife, and said all the women-folks liked the telephones, and that in this lonesome stretch of road it would be a good thing—well, I said to Harry that that was what I was going to say—though I said at the same time that I didn't know as what his wife wanted made much difference to John—"

Now, there he was!—saying things he didn't need to say. Mrs. Hale tried to catch her husband's eye, but fortunately the county attorney interrupted with:

"Let's talk about that a little later, Mr. Hale. I do want to talk about that, but I'm anxious now to get along to just what happened when you got here."

When he began this time, it was very deliberately and carefully:

"I didn't see or hear anything. I knocked at the door. And still it was all quiet inside. I knew they must be up —it was past eight o'clock. So I knocked again, louder, and I thought I heard somebody say, 'Come in.' I wasn't sure—I'm not sure yet. But I opened the door—this door," jerking a hand toward the door by which the two women stood, "and there, in that rocker"—pointing to it—"sat Mrs. Wright."

Everyone in the kitchen looked at the rocker. It came into Mrs. Hale's mind that that rocker didn't look in the least like Minnie Foster—the Minnie Foster of twenty years before. It was a dingy red, with wooden rungs up the back, and the middle rung was gone, and the chair sagged to one side.

"How did she—look?" the county attorney was inquiring.

"Well," said Hale, "she looked—queer."

"How do you mean—queer?"

As he asked it he took out a notebook and pencil. Mrs. Hale did not like the sight of that pencil. She kept her eye fixed on her husband, as if to keep him from saying unnecessary things that would go into that notebook and make trouble.

Hale did speak guardedly, as if the pencil had affected him too.

"Well, as if she didn't know what she was going to do next. And kind of—done up."

"How did she seem to feel about your coming?"

"Why, I don't think she minded—one way or other. She didn't pay much attention. I said, 'Ho' do, Mrs. Wright? It's cold, ain't it?' And she said, 'Is it?'—and went on pleatin' at her apron.

"Well, I was surprised. She didn't ask me to come up to the stove, or to sit down, but just set there, not even lookin' at me. And so I said: 'I want to see John.'

"And then she—laughed. I guess you would call it a laugh.

"I thought of Harry and the team outside, so I said, a little sharp, 'Can I see John?' 'No,' says she—kind of dull like. 'Ain't he home?' says I. Then she looked at me. 'Yes,' says she, 'he's home.' 'Then why can't I see him?' I asked her, out of patience with her now. ''Cause he's dead,' says she, just as quiet and dull—and fell to pleatin' her apron. 'Dead?' says I, like you do when you can't take in what you've heard.

"She just nodded her head, not getting a bit excited, but rockin' back and forth.

" 'Why—where is he?' says I, not knowing *what* to say.

"She just pointed upstairs—like this"—pointing to the room above.

"I got up, with the idea of going up there myself. By this time I—didn't know what to do. I walked from there to here; then I says: 'Why, what did he die of?'

" 'He died of a rope round his neck,' says she; and just went on pleatin' at her apron."

Hale stopped speaking, and stood staring at the rocker, as if he were still seeing the woman who had sat there the morning before. Nobody spoke; it was as if every one were seeing the woman who had sat there the morning before.

"And what did you do then?" the county attorney at last broke the silence.

"I went out and called Harry. I thought I might—need help. I got Harry in, and we went upstairs." His voice fell almost to a whisper. "There he was—lying over the—"

"I think I'd rather have you go into that upstairs," the county attorney interrupted, "where you can point it all out. Just go on now with the rest of the story."

"Well, my first thought was to get that rope off. It looked—"

He stopped, his face twitching.

"But Harry, he went up to him, and he said, 'No, he's dead all right, and we'd better not touch anything.' So we went downstairs.

"She was still sitting that same way. 'Has anybody been notified?' I asked. 'No,' says she, unconcerned.

" 'Who did this, Mrs. Wright?' said Harry. He said it businesslike, and she stopped pleatin' at her apron. 'I don't know,' she says. 'You don't *know*?' says Harry. 'Weren't you sleepin' in the bed with him?' 'Yes,' says she, 'but I was on the inside.' 'Somebody slipped a rope round his neck and strangled him, and you didn't wake up?' says Harry. 'I didn't wake up,' she said after him.

"We may have looked as if we didn't see how that could be, for after a minute she said, 'I sleep sound.'

"Harry was going to ask her more questions, but I said maybe that weren't our business; maybe we ought to let her tell her story first to the coroner or the sheriff. So Harry went fast as he could over to High Road—the Rivers' place, where there's a telephone."

"And what did she do when she knew you had gone for the coroner?" The attorney got his pencil in his hand all ready for writing.

"She moved from that chair to this one over here"—Hale pointed to a small chair in the corner—"and just sat there with her hands held together and looking down. I got a feeling that I ought to make some conversation, so I said I had come in to see if John wanted to put in a telephone; and at that she started to laugh, and then she stopped and looked at me—scared."

At sound of a moving pencil the man who was telling the story looked up.

"I dunno—maybe it wasn't scared," he hastened; "I wouldn't like to say it was. Soon Harry got back, and then Dr. Lloyd came, and you, Mr. Peters, and so I guess that's all I know that you don't."

He said that last with relief, and moved a little, as if relaxing. Everyone moved a little. The county attorney walked toward the stair door.

"I guess we'll go upstairs first—then out to the barn and around there."

He paused and looked around the kitchen.

"You're convinced there was nothing important here?" he asked the sheriff. "Nothing that would—point to any motive?"

The sheriff too looked all around, as if to re-convince himself.

"Nothing here but kitchen things," he said, with a little laugh for the insignificance of kitchen things.

The county attorney was looking at the cupboard—a peculiar, ungainly structure, half closet and half cupboard, the upper part of it being built in the wall, and the lower part just the old-fashioned kitchen cupboard. As if its queerness attracted him, he got a chair and opened the upper part and looked in. After a moment he drew his hand away sticky.

"Here's a nice mess," he said resentfully.

The two women had drawn nearer, and now the sheriff's wife spoke.

"Oh—her fruit," she said, looking to Mrs. Hale for sympathetic understanding. She turned back to the county attorney and explained: "She worried about that when it turned so cold last night. She said the fire would go out and her jars might burst."

Mrs. Peters' husband broke into a laugh.

"Well, can you beat the woman! Held for murder, and worrying about her preserves!"

The young attorney set his lips.

"I guess before we're through with her she may have

something more serious than preserves to worry about."

"Oh, well," said Mrs. Hale's husband, with good-natured superiority, "women are used to worrying over trifles."

The two women moved a little closer together. Neither of them spoke. The county attorney seemed suddenly to remember his manners—and think of his future.

"And yet," said he, with the gallantry of a young politician, "for all their worries, what would we do without the ladies?"

The women did not speak, did not unbend. He went to the sink and began washing his hands. He turned to wipe them on the roller towel—whirled it for a cleaner place.

"Dirty towels! Not much of a housekeeper, would you say, ladies?"

He kicked his foot against some dirty pans under the sink.

"There's a great deal of work to be done on a farm," said Mrs. Hale stiffly.

"To be sure. And yet"—with a little bow to her—"I know there are some Dickson County farm houses that do not have such roller towels." He gave it a pull to expose its full length again.

"Those towels get dirty awful quick. Men's hands aren't always as clean as they might be."

"Ah, loyal to your sex, I see," he laughed. He stopped and gave her a keen look. "But you and Mrs. Wright were neighbors. I suppose you were friends, too."

Martha Hale shook her head.

"I've seen little enough of her of late years. I've not been in this house—it's more than a year."

"And why was that? You didn't like her?"

"I liked her well enough," she replied with spirit. "Farmers' wives have their hands full, Mr. Henderson. And then—" She looked around the kitchen.

"Yes?" he encouraged.

"It never seemed a very cheerful place," said she, more to herself than to him.

"No," he agreed; "I don't think any one would call it cheerful. I shouldn't say she had the home-making instinct."

"Well, I don't know as Wright had, either," she muttered.

"You mean they didn't get on very well?" he was quick to ask.

"No; I don't mean anything," she answered, with decision. As she turned a little away from him, she added: "But I don't think a place would be any the cheerfuler for John Wright's bein' in it."

"I'd like to talk to you about that a little later, Mrs. Hale," he said. "I'm anxious to get the lay of things upstairs now."

He moved toward the stair door, followed by the two men.

"I suppose anything Mrs. Peters does'll be all right?" the sheriff inquired. "She was to take in some clothes for her, you know—and a few little things. We left in such a hurry yesterday."

The county attorney looked at the two women whom they were leaving alone there among the kitchen things.

"Yes—Mrs. Peters," he said, his glance resting on the woman who was not Mrs. Peters, the big farmer woman who stood behind the sheriff's wife. "Of course Mrs. Peters is one of us," he said, in a manner of entrusting responsibility. "And keep your eye out, Mrs. Peters, for anything that might be of use. No telling; you women might come upon a clue to the motive—and that's the thing we need."

Mr. Hale rubbed his face after the fashion of a show man getting ready for a pleasantry.

"But would the women know a clue if they did come upon it?" he said; and, having delivered himself of this, he followed the others through the stair door.

The women stood motionless and silent, listening to the footsteps, first upon the stairs, then in the room above them.

Then, as if releasing herself from something strange, Mrs. Hale began to arrange the dirty pans under the sink, which the county attorney's disdainful push of the foot had deranged.

"I'd hate to have men comin' into my kitchen," she said testily—"snoopin' round and criticizin'."

"Of course it's no more than their duty," said the sheriff's wife, in her manner of timid acquiescence.

"Duty's all right," replied Mrs. Hale bluffly; "but I guess that deputy sheriff that come out to make the fire might have got a little of this on." She gave the roller towel a pull. "Wish I'd thought of that sooner! Seems mean to talk about her for not having things slicked up, when she had to come away in such a hurry."

She looked around the kitchen. Certainly it was not "slicked up." Her eye was held by a bucket of sugar on a low shelf. The cover was off the wooden bucket, and beside it was a paper bag—half full.

Mrs. Hale moved toward it.

"She was putting this in there," she said to herself—slowly.

She thought of the flour in her kitchen at home—half sifted, half not sifted. She had been interrupted, and had left things half done. What had interrupted Minnie Foster? Why had that work been left half done? She made a move as if to finish it,—unfinished things always bothered her,—and then she glanced around and saw that Mrs. Peters was watching her—and she didn't want Mrs. Peters to get that feeling she had got of work begun and then—for some reason—not finished.

"It's a shame about her fruit," she said, and walked toward the cupboard that the county attorney had opened, and got on the chair, murmuring: "I wonder if it's all gone."

It was a sorry enough looking sight, but "Here's one that's all right," she said at last. She held it toward the light. "This is cherries, too." She looked again. "I declare I believe that's the only one."

With a sigh, she got down from the chair, went to the sink, and wiped off the bottle.

"She'll feel awful bad, after all her hard work in the hot weather. I remember the afternoon I put up my cherries last summer."

She set the bottle on the table, and, with another sigh, started to sit down in the rocker. But she did not sit down. Something kept her from sitting down in that chair. She straightened—stepped back, and, half turned away, stood looking at it, seeing the woman who had sat there "pleatin' at her apron."

The thin voice of the sheriff's wife broke in upon her: "I must be getting those things from the front room closet." She opened the door into the other room, started in; stepped back. "You coming with me, Mrs. Hale?" she asked nervously. "You—you could help me get them."

They were soon back—the stark coldness of that shut-up room was not a thing to linger in.

"My!" said Mrs. Peters, dropping the things on the table and hurrying to the stove.

Mrs. Hale stood examining the clothes the woman who was being detained in town had said she wanted.

"Wright was close!" she exclaimed, holding up a shabby black skirt that bore the marks of much making over. "I think maybe that's why she kept so much to herself. I s'pose she felt she couldn't do her part; and then, you don't enjoy things when you feel shabby. She used to wear pretty clothes and be lively—when she was Minnie Foster, one of the town girls, singing in the choir. But that—oh, that was twenty years ago."

With a carefulness in which there was something tender, she folded the shabby clothes and piled them at one corner of the table. She looked up at Mrs. Peters, and there was something in the other woman's look that irritated her.

"She don't care," she said to herself. "Much difference it makes to her whether Minnie Foster had pretty clothes when she was a girl."

Then she looked again, and she wasn't so sure; in fact, she hadn't at any time been perfectly sure about Mrs. Peters. She had that shrinking manner, and yet her eyes looked as if they could see a long way into things.

"This all you was to take in?" asked Mrs. Hale.

"No," said the sheriff's wife; "she said she wanted an apron. Funny thing to want," she ventured in her nervous little way, "for there's not much to get you dirty in jail, goodness knows. But I suppose just to make her feel more natural. If you're used to wearing an apron—. She said they were in the bottom drawer of this cupboard. Yes—here they are. And then her little shawl that always hung on the stair door."

She took the small gray shawl from behind the door leading upstairs, and stood a minute looking at it.

Suddenly Mrs. Hale took a quick step toward the other woman.

"Mrs. Peters!"

"Yes, Mrs. Hale?"

"Do you think she—did it?"

A frightened look blurred the other thing in Mrs. Peters' eyes.

"Oh, I don't know," she said, in a voice that seemed to shrink away from the subject.

"Well, I don't think she did," affirmed Mrs. Hale stoutly. "Asking for an apron, and her little shawl. Worryin' about her fruit."

"Mr. Peters says—." Footsteps were heard in the room above; she stopped, looked up, then went on in a lowered voice: "Mr. Peters says—it looks bad for her. Mr. Henderson is awful sarcastic in a speech, and he's going to make fun of her saying she didn't—wake up."

For a moment Mrs. Hale had no answer. Then, "Well, I guess John Wright didn't wake up—when they was slippin' that rope under his neck," she muttered.

"No, it's *strange*," breathed Mrs. Peters. "They think it was such a—funny way to kill a man."

She began to laugh; at sound of the laugh, abruptly stopped.

"That's just what Mr. Hale said," said Mrs. Hale, in a resolutely natural voice. "There was a gun in the house. He says that's what he can't understand."

"Mr. Henderson said, coming out, that what was needed for the case was a motive. Something to show anger—or sudden feeling."

"Well, I don't see any signs of anger around here," said Mrs. Hale. "I don't—"

She stopped. It was as if her mind tripped on something. Her eye was caught by a dish-towel in the middle of the kitchen table. Slowly she moved toward the table. One half of it was wiped clean, the other half messy. Her eyes made a slow, almost unwilling turn to the bucket of sugar and the half empty bag beside it. Things begun—and not finished.

After a moment she stepped back, and said, in that manner of releasing herself:

"Wonder how they're finding things upstairs? I hope she had it a little more red up there. You know,"—she paused, and feeling gathered,—"it seems kind of *sneaking*: locking her up in town and coming out here to get her own house to turn against her!"

"But, Mrs. Hale," said the sheriff's wife, "the law is the law."

"I s'pose 'tis," answered Mrs. Hale shortly.

She turned to the stove, saying something about that fire not being much to brag of. She worked with it a minute, and when she straightened up she said aggressively:

"The law is the law—and a bad stove is a bad stove. How'd you like to cook on this?"—pointing with the poker to the broken lining. She opened the oven door and started to express her opinion of the oven; but she was swept into her own thoughts, thinking of what it would mean, year after year, to have that stove to wrestle with. The thought of Minnie Foster trying to bake in that oven —and the thought of her never going over to see Minnie Foster—.

She was startled by hearing Mrs. Peters, say: "A person gets discouraged—and loses heart."

The sheriff's wife had looked from the stove to the sink—to the pail of water which had been carried in from outside. The two women stood there silent, above them the footsteps of the men who were looking for evidence against the woman who had worked in that kitchen. That look of seeing into things, of seeing through a thing to something else, was in the eyes of the sheriff's wife now. When Mrs. Hale next spoke to her, it was gently:

"Better loosen up your things, Mrs. Peters. We'll not feel them when we go out."

Mrs. Peters went to the back of the room to hang up the fur tippet she was wearing. A moment later she exclaimed, "Why, she was piecing a quilt," and held up a large sewing basket piled high with quilt pieces.

Mrs. Hale spread some of the blocks out on the table. "It's log-cabin pattern," she said, putting several of them together. "Pretty, isn't it?"

They were so engaged with the quilt that they did not hear the footsteps on the stairs. Just as the stair door opened Mrs. Hale was saying:

"Do you suppose she was going to quilt it or just knot it?"

The sheriff threw up his hands.

"They wonder whether she was going to quilt it or just knot it!"

There was a laugh for the ways of women, a warming of hands over the stove, and then the county attorney said briskly:

"Well, let's go right out to the barn and get that cleared up."

"I don't see as there's anything so strange," Mrs. Hale said resentfully, after the outside door had closed on the three men—"our taking up our time with little things while we're waiting for them to get the evidence. I don't see as it's anything to laugh about."

"Of course they've got awful important things on their minds," said the sheriff's wife apologetically.

They returned to an inspection of the block for the quilt. Mrs. Hale was looking at the fine, even sewing, and preoccupied with thoughts of the woman who had done that sewing, when she heard the sheriff's wife say, in a queer tone:

"Why, look at this one."

She turned to take the block held out to her.

"The sewing," said Mrs. Peters, in a troubled way. "All the rest of them have been so nice and even—but—this one. Why, it looks as if she didn't know what she was about!"

Their eyes met—something flashed to life, passed between them; then, as if with an effort, they seemed to pull away from each other. A moment Mrs. Hale sat there, her hands folded over that sewing which was so unlike all the rest of the sewing. Then she had pulled a knot and drawn the threads.

"Oh, what are you doing, Mrs. Hale?" asked the sheriff's wife, startled.

"Just pulling out a stitch or two that's not sewed very good," said Mrs. Hale mildly.

"I don't think we ought to touch things," Mrs. Peters said, a little helplessly.

"I'll just finish up this end," answered Mrs. Hale, still in that mild, matter-of-fact fashion.

She threaded a needle and started to replace bad sewing with good. For a little while she sewed in silence. Then, in that thin, timid voice, she heard:

"Mrs. Hale!"

"Yes, Mrs. Peters?"

"What do you suppose she was so—nervous about?"

"Oh, *I* don't know," said Mrs. Hale, as if dismissing a thing not important enough to spend much time on. "I don't know as she was—nervous. I sew awful queer sometimes when I'm just tired."

She cut a thread, and out of the corner of her eye looked up at Mrs. Peters. The small, lean face of the sheriff's wife seemed to have tightened up. Her eyes had that look of peering into something. But next moment she moved, and said in her thin, indecisive way:

"Well, I must get those clothes wrapped. They may be through sooner than we think. I wonder where I could find a piece of paper—and string."

"In that cupboard, maybe," suggested Mrs. Hale, after a glance around.

One piece of the crazy sewing remained unripped. Mrs. Peters' back turned, Martha Hale now scrutinized that piece, compared it with the dainty, accurate sewing of the other blocks. The difference was startling. Holding this block made her feel queer, as if the distracted thoughts of the woman who had perhaps turned to it to try and quiet herself were communicating themselves to her.

Mrs. Peters' voice roused her.

"Here's a bird-cage," she said. "Did she have a bird, Mrs. Hale?"

"Why, I don't know whether she did or not." She turned to look at the cage Mrs. Peters was holding up. "I've not been here in so long." She sighed. "There was a man round last year selling canaries cheap—but I don't know as she took one. Maybe she did. She used to sing real pretty herself."

Mrs. Peters looked around the kitchen.

"Seems kind of funny to think of a bird here." She half laughed—an attempt to put up a barrier. "But she must have had one—or why would she have a cage? I wonder what happened to it."

"I suppose maybe the cat got it," suggested Mrs. Hale, resuming her sewing.

"No; she didn't have a cat. She's got that feeling some people have about cats—being afraid of them. When they brought her to our house yesterday, my cat got in the room, and she was real upset and asked me to take it out."

"My sister Bessie was like that," laughed Mrs. Hale.

The sheriff's wife did not reply. The silence made Mrs. Hale turn round. Mrs. Peters was examining the bird-cage.

"Look at this door," she said slowly. "It's broke. One hinge has been pulled apart."

Mrs. Hale came nearer.

"Looks as if someone must have been—rough with it."

Again their eyes met—startled, questioning, apprehensive. For a moment neither spoke nor stirred. Then Mrs. Hale, turning away, said brusquely:

"If they're going to find any evidence, I wish they'd be about it. I don't like this place."

"But I'm awful glad you came with me, Mrs. Hale." Mrs. Peters put the bird-cage on the table and sat down. "It would be lonesome for me—sitting here alone."

"Yes, it would, wouldn't it?" agreed Mrs. Hale, a certain determined naturalness in her voice. She had picked up the sewing, but now it dropped in her lap, and she murmured in a different voice: "But I tell you what I *do* wish, Mrs. Peters. I wish I had come over sometimes when she was here. I wish—I had."

"But of course you were awful busy, Mrs. Hale. Your house—and your children."

"I could've come," retorted Mrs. Hale shortly. "I stayed away because it weren't cheerful—and that's why I ought to have come. I"—she looked around— "I've never liked this place. Maybe because it's down in a hollow and you don't see the road. I don't know what it is, but it's a lonesome place, and always was. I wish I had come over to see Minnie Foster sometimes. I can see now—" She did not put it into words.

"Well, you mustn't reproach yourself," counseled Mrs. Peters. "Somehow, we just don't see how it is with other folks till—something comes up."

"Not having children makes less work," mused Mrs. Hale, after a silence, "but it makes a quiet house—and Wright out to work all day—and no company when he did come in. Did you know John Wright, Mrs. Peters?"

"Not to know him. I've seen him in town. They say he was a good man."

"Yes—good," conceded John Wright's neighbor grimly.

"He didn't drink, and kept his word as well as most, I guess, and paid his debts. But he was a hard man, Mrs. Peters. Just to pass the time of day with him——." She stopped, shivered a little. "Like a raw wind that gets to the bone." Her eye fell upon the cage on the table before her, and she added, almost bitterly: "I should think she would've wanted a bird!"

Suddenly she leaned forward, looking intently at the cage. "But what do you s'pose went wrong with it?"

"I don't know," returned Mrs. Peters; "unless it got sick and died."

But after she said it she reached over and swung the broken door. Both women watched it as if somehow held by it.

"You didn't know—her?" Mrs. Hale asked, a gentler note in her voice.

"Not till they brought her yesterday," said the sheriff's wife.

"She—come to think of it, she was kind of like a bird herself. Real sweet and pretty, but kind of timid and—fluttery. How—she—did—change."

That held her for a long time. Finally, as if struck with a happy thought and relieved to get back to everyday things, she exclaimed:

"Tell you what, Mrs. Peters, why don't you take the quilt in with you? It might take up her mind."

"Why, I think that's a real nice idea, Mrs. Hale," agreed the sheriff's wife, as if she too were glad to come into the atmosphere of a simple kindness. "There couldn't possibly be any objection to that, could there? Now, just what will I take? I wonder if her patches are in here—and her things."

They turned to the sewing basket.

"Here's some red," said Mrs. Hale, bringing out a roll of cloth. Underneath that was a box. "Here, maybe her scissors are in here—and her things." She held it up. "What a pretty box! I'll warrant that was something she had a long time ago—when she was a girl."

She held it in her hand a moment; then, with a little sigh, opened it.

Instantly her hand went to her nose.

"Why—!"

Mrs. Peters drew nearer—then turned away.

"There's something wrapped up in this piece of silk," faltered Mrs. Hale.

"This isn't her scissors," said Mrs. Peters, in a shrinking voice.

Her hand not steady, Mrs. Hale raised the piece of silk. "Oh, Mrs. Peters!" she cried. "It's—"

Mrs. Peters bent closer.

"It's the bird," she whispered.

"But, Mrs. Peters!" cried Mrs. Hale. *"Look* at it! It's *neck*—look at its neck! It's all—other side to."

She held the box away from her.

The sheriff's wife again bent closer.

"Somebody wrung its neck," said she, in a voice that was slow and deep.

And then again the eyes of the two women met—this time clung together in a look of dawning comprehension, of growing horror. Mrs. Peters looked from the dead bird to the broken door of the cage. Again their eyes met. And just then there was a sound at the outside door.

Mrs. Hale slipped the box under the quilt pieces in the basket, and sank into the chair before it. Mrs. Peters stood holding to the table. The county attorney and the sheriff came in from outside.

"Well, ladies," said the county attorney, as one turning from serious things to little pleasantries, "have you decided whether she was going to quilt it or knot it?"

"We think," began the sheriff's wife in a flurried voice, "that she was going to—knot it."

He was too preoccupied to notice the change that came in her voice on that last.

"Well, that's very interesting, I'm sure," he said tolerantly. He caught sight of the bird-cage. "Has the bird flown?"

"We think the cat got it," said Mrs. Hale in a voice curiously even.

He was walking up and down, as if thinking something out.

"Is there a cat?" he asked absently.

Mrs. Hale shot a look up at the sheriff's wife.

"Well, not *now*," said Mrs. Peters. "They're superstitious, you know; they leave."

She sank into her chair.

The county attorney did not heed her. "No sign at all

of anyone having come in from the outside." he said to Peters, in the manner of continuing an interrupted conversation. "Their own rope. Now let's go upstairs again and go over it, piece by piece. It would have to have been someone who knew just the—"

The stair door closed behind them and their voices were lost.

The two women sat motionless, not looking at each other, but as if peering into something and at the same time holding back. When they spoke now it was as if they were afraid of what they were saying, but as if they could not help saying it.

"She liked the bird," said Martha Hale, low and slowly. "She was going to bury it in that pretty box."

"When I was a girl," said Mrs. Peters, under her breath, "my kitten—there was a boy took a hatchet, and before my eyes—before I could get there—" She covered her face an instant. "If they hadn't held me back I would have"—she caught herself, looked upstairs where footsteps were heard, and finished weakly—"hurt him."

Then they sat without speaking or moving.

"I wonder how it would seem," Mrs. Hale at last began, as if feeling her way over strange ground—"never to have had any children around?" Her eyes made a slow sweep of the kitchen, as if seeing what that kitchen had meant through all the years. "No, Wright wouldn't like the bird," she said after that—"a thing that sang. She used to sing. He killed that too." Her voice tightened.

Mrs. Peters moved uneasily.

"Of course we don't know who killed the bird."

"I knew John Wright," was Mrs. Hale's answer.

"It was an awful thing was done in this house that night, Mrs. Hale," said the sheriff's wife. "Killing a man while he slept—slipping a thing round his neck that choked the life out of him."

Mrs. Hale's hand went out to the bird-cage.

"His neck. Choked the life out of him."

"We don't *know* who killed him," whispered Mrs. Peters wildly. "We don't *know*."

Mrs. Hale had not moved. "If there had been years and years of—nothing, then a bird to sing to you, it would be awful—still—after the bird was still."

It was as if something within her not herself had spoken,

and it found in Mrs. Peters something she did not know
as herself.

"I know what stillness is," she said, in a queer, monotonous voice. "When we homesteaded in Dakota, and my
first baby died—after he was two years old—and me with
no other then—"

Mrs. Hale stirred.

"How soon do you suppose they'll be through looking
for the evidence?"

"I know what stillness is," repeated Mrs. Peters, in just
that same way. Then she too pulled back. "The law has
got to punish crime, Mrs. Hale," she said in her tight little
way.

"I wish you'd seen Minnie Foster," was the answer,
"when she wore a white dress with blue ribbons, and
stood up there in the choir and sang."

The picture of that girl, the fact that she had lived
neighbor to that girl for twenty years, and had let her die
for lack of life, was suddenly more than she could bear.

"Oh, I *wish* I'd come over here once in a while!" she
cried. "That was a crime! That was a crime! Who's going
to punish that?"

"We mustn't take on," said Mrs. Peters, with a
frightened look toward the stairs.

"I might 'a' *known* she needed help! I tell you, it's
queer, Mrs. Peters. We live close together, and we live
far apart. We all go through the same things—it's all
just a different kind of the same thing! If it weren't—why
do you and I *understand?* Why do we *know*—what we
know this minute?"

She dashed her hand across her eyes. Then, seeing the
jar of fruit on the table, she reached for it and choked
out:

"If I was you I wouldn't *tell* her her fruit was gone!
Tell her it *ain't*. Tell her it's all right—all of it. Here
—take this in to prove it to her! She—she may never
know whether it was broke or not."

She turned away.

Mrs. Peters reached out for the bottle of fruit as if she
were glad to take it—as if touching a familiar thing, having something to do, could keep her from something else.
She got up, looked about for something to wrap the fruit

in, took a petticoat from the pile of clothes she had brought from the front room, and nervously started winding that round the bottle.

"My!" she began, in a high, false voice, "it's a good thing the men couldn't hear us! Getting all stirred up over a little thing like a—dead canary." She hurried over that. "As if that could have anything to do with—with— My, wouldn't they *laugh*?"

Footsteps were heard on the stairs.

"Maybe they would," muttered Mrs. Hale—"maybe they wouldn't."

"No, Peters," said the county attorney incisively; "it's all perfectly clear, except the reason for doing it. But you know juries when it comes to women. If there was some definite thing—something to show. Something to make a story about. A thing that would connect up with this clumsy way of doing it."

In a covert way Mrs. Hale looked at Mrs. Peters. Mrs. Peters was looking at her. Quickly they looked away from each other. The outer door opened and Mr. Hale came in.

"I've got the team round now," he said. "Pretty cold out there."

"I'm going to stay here awhile by myself," the county attorney suddenly announced. "You can send Frank out for me, can't you?" he asked the sheriff. "I want to go over everything. I'm not satisfied we can't do better."

Again, for one brief moment, the two women's eyes found one another.

The sheriff came up to the table.

"Did you want to see what Mrs. Peters was going to take in?"

The county attorney picked up the apron. He laughed.

"Oh, I guess they're not very dangerous things the ladies have picked out."

Mrs. Hale's hand was on the sewing basket in which the box was concealed. She felt that she ought to take her hand off the basket. She did not seem able to. He picked up one of the quilt blocks which she had piled on to cover the box. Her eyes felt like fire. She had a feeling that if he took up the basket she would snatch it from him.

But he did not take it up. With another little laugh, he turned away, saying:

"No; Mrs. Peters doesn't need supervising. For that matter, a sheriff's wife is married to the law. Ever think of it that way, Mrs. Peters?"

Mrs. Peters was standing beside the table. Mrs. Hale shot a look up at her; but she could not see her face. Mrs. Peters had turned away. When she spoke, her voice was muffled.

"Not—just that way," she said.

"Married to the law!" chuckled Mrs. Peters' husband. He moved toward the door into the front room, and said to the county attorney:

"I just want you to come in here a minute, George. We ought to take a look at these windows."

"Oh—windows," said the county attorney scoffingly.

"We'll be right out, Mr. Hale," said the sheriff to the farmer, who was still waiting by the door.

Hale went to look after the horses. The sheriff followed the county attorney into the other room. Again—for one final moment—the two women were alone in that kitchen.

Martha Hale sprang up, her hands tight together, looking at that other woman, with whom it rested. At first she could not see her eyes, for the sheriff's wife had not turned back since she turned away at that suggestion of being married to the law. But now Mrs. Hale made her turn back. Her eyes made her turn back. Slowly, unwillingly, Mrs. Peters turned her head until her eyes met the eyes of the other woman. There was a moment when they held each other in a steady, burning look in which there was no evasion nor flinching. Then Martha Hale's eyes pointed the way to the basket in which was hidden the thing that would make certain the conviction of the other woman—that woman who was not there and yet who had been there with them all through that hour.

For a moment Mrs. Peters did not move. And then she did it. With a rush forward, she threw back the quilt pieces, got the box, tried to put it in her handbag. It was too big. Desperately she opened it, started to take the bird out. But there she broke—she could not touch the bird. She stood there helpless, foolish.

There was the sound of a knob turning in the inner door. Martha Hale snatched the box from the sheriff's wife, and got it in the pocket of her big coat just as the sheriff and the county attorney came back into the kitchen.

"Well, Henry," said the county attorney facetiously, "at least we found out that she was not going to quilt it. She was going to—what is it you call it, ladies?"

Mrs. Hale's hand was against the pocket of her coat.

"We call it—knot it, Mr. Henderson."

Jessie Redmon Fauset (1885–1961)

Jessie Fauset was the daughter of a prosperous and literary, black Philadelphia family. Her sister as a child wrote romances, her brother later wrote books on black history and folklore, and she herself began writing poetry when she was a child. She was educated at Cornell, where she majored in French, and earned an M.A. at the University of Pennsylvania. She did not marry until 1929, when she married Herbert Harris.

Because she could never earn enough by her writing to support herself, she taught classical languages and French in high school in Washington, D. C. and New York. From 1919 to 1926 she was literary editor of *The Crisis,* the journal of the NAACP, at a time when W. E. B. Du Bois was Chief Editor. She was one of those who participated in the birth of the Harlem Renaissance, first as the encourager of literature in others, and then as a writer herself. Although never herself "radical" or "bohemian" she was friendly with those who were, as well as with members of socially prominent and highly-educated black families.

Her published works include four novels: *There Is Confusion* (1924), *Plum Bun* (1929, part of which appears here), *The Chinaberry Tree* (1931), and *Comedy: American Style* (1934). She also wrote a few short stories, poems, reviews, essays, and translations. She began writing novels out of the impulse to present a side of black life, that of the socially and intellectually ambitious middle class, which was being ignored by white publishers and audiences because it was insufficiently dramatic. Her subjects are ordinary people, whose lives are warped and frustrated by the problem of their blackness. While sympathizing with the aspirations of the black bourgeoisie, however, she realizes the potential sterility and destructiveness of their overwhelming concern with whiteness and respectability. Her main characters, even those who are tempted by the possibility of "passing," always come to cherish their blackness because in it Fauset sees a unique and indestructible potential for warmth and courage.

[References: There is very little written on Fauset. The most useful are: Sato, Hiroko. "Under the Harlem Shadow:

A Study of Jessie Fauset and Nella Larsen," in *The Harlem Renaissance Remembered,* ed. Arna Bontemps. New York: Dodd, Mead, 1972. and Starkey, Marion L. "Jessie Fauset." *The Southern Workman,* 61 (1932), 217-20.]

PLUM BUN

"HOME"

CHAPTER I

Opal Street, as streets go, is no jewel of the first water. It is merely an imitation, and none too good at that. Narrow, unsparkling, uninviting, it stretches meekly off from dull Jefferson Street to the dingy, drab market which forms the north side of Oxford Street. It has no mystery, no allure, either of exclusiveness or of downright depravity; its usages are plainly significant,—an unpretentious little street lined with unpretentious little houses, inhabited for the most part by unpretentious little people.

The dwellings are three stories high, and contain six boxes called by courtesy, rooms—a "parlour," a midget of a dining-room, a larger kitchen and, above, a front bedroom seemingly large only because it extends for the full width of the house, a mere shadow of a bathroom, and another back bedroom with windows whose possibilities are spoiled by their outlook on sad and diminutive backyards. And above these two, still two others built in similar wise.

In one of these houses dwelt a father, a mother and two daughters. Here, as often happens in a home sheltering two generations, opposite, unevenly matched emotions faced each other. In the houses of the rich the satisfied ambition of the older generation is faced by the overwhelming ambition of the younger. Or the elders may find themselves brought in opposition to the blank indifference and ennui of youth engendered by the realization that there remain no more worlds to conquer; their fathers having already taken all. In houses on Opal Street these niceties of distinction are hardly to be found; there is a more direct and concrete contrast. The satisfied ambition of maturity is a foil for the restless despair of youth.

Affairs in the Murray household were advancing towards this stage; yet not a soul in that family of four

From *Plum Bun*. New York: Frederick A. Stokes Co.: 1929.

could have foretold its coming. To Junius and Mattie Murray, who had known poverty and homelessness, the little house on Opal Street represented the *ne plus ultra* of ambition; to their daughter Angela it seemed the dingiest, drabbest chrysalis that had ever fettered the wings of a brilliant butterfly. The stories which Junius and Mattie told of difficulties overcome, of the arduous learning of trades, of the pitiful scraping together of infinitesimal savings, would have made a latter-day Iliad, but to Angela they were merely a description of a life which she at any cost would avoid living. Somewhere in the world were paths which lead to broad thoroughfares, large, bright houses, delicate niceties of existence. Those paths Angela meant to find and frequent. At a very early age she had observed that the good things of life are unevenly distributed; merit is not always rewarded; hard labour does not necessarily entail adequate recompense. Certain fortutious endowments, great physical beauty, unusual strength, a certain unswerving singleness of mind,—gifts bestowed quite blindly and disproportionately by the forces which control life,—these were the qualities which contributed toward a glowing and pleasant existence.

Angela had no high purpose in life; unlike her sister Virginia, who meant some day to invent a marvellous method for teaching the pianoforte, Angela felt no impulse to discover, or to perfect. True she thought she might become eventually a distinguished painter, but that was because she felt within herself an ability to depict which as far as it went was correct and promising. Her eye for line and for expression was already good and she had a nice feeling for colour. Moreover she possessed the instinct for self-appraisal which taught her that she had much to learn. And she was sure that the knowledge once gained would flower in her case to perfection. But her gift was not for her the end of existence; rather it was an adjunct to a life which was to know light, pleasure, gaiety and freedom.

Freedom! That was the note which Angela heard oftenest in the melody of living which was to be hers. With a wildness that fell just short of unreasonableness she hated restraint. Her father's earlier days as coachman in a private family, his later successful, independent years as boss carpenter, her mother's youth spent as maid to a famous actress, all this was to Angela a manifestation of the sort of thing which happens to those enchained it might be by duty, by poverty, by weakness or by colour.

Colour or rather the lack of it seemed to the child the one absolute prerequisite to the life of which she was always dreaming. One might break loose from a too hampering sense of duty; poverty could be overcome; physicians conquered weakness; but colour, the mere possession of a black or a white skin, that was clearly one of those fortuitous endowments of the gods. Gratitude was no strong ingredient in this girl's nature, yet very often early she began thanking Fate for the chance which in that household of four had bestowed on her the heritage of her mother's fair skin. She might so easily have been, like her father, black, or have received the mélange which had resulted in Virginia's rosy bronzeness and her deeply waving black hair. But Angela had received not only her mother's creamy complexion and her soft cloudy, chestnut hair, but she had taken from Junius the aquiline nose, the gift of some remote Indian ancestor which gave to his face and his eldest daughter's that touch of chiselled immobility.

It was from her mother that Angela learned the possibilities for joy and freedom which seemed to her inherent in mere whiteness. No one would have been more amazed than that same mother if she could have guessed how her daughter interpreted her actions. Certainly Mrs. Murray did not attribute what she considered her happy, busy, sheltered life on tiny Opal Street to the accident of her colour; she attributed it to her black husband whom she had been glad and proud to marry. It is equally certain that that white skin of hers had not saved her from occasional contumely and insult. The famous actress for whom she had worked was aware of Mattie's mixed blood and, boasting temperament rather than refinement, had often dubbed her "white nigger."

Angela's mother employed her colour very much as she practised certain winning usages of smile and voice to obtain indulgences which meant much to her and which took nothing from anyone else. Then, too, she was possessed of a keener sense of humour than her daughter; it amused her, when by herself, to take lunch at an exclusive restaurant whose patrons would have been panic-stricken if they had divined the presence of a "coloured" woman no matter how little her appearance differed from theirs. It was with no idea of disclaiming her own that she sat in orchestra seats which Philadelphia denied to coloured patrons. But when Junius or indeed any other dark friend accompanied her she was the first to announce that she liked to sit in the balcony or gallery, as indeed she did; her infrequent occupation of orchestra seats was due merely to a mischievous determination to flout a silly and unjust law.

Her years with the actress had left their mark, a perfectly harmless and rather charming one. At least so it seemed to Junius, whose weakness was for the qualities known as "essentially feminine." Mrs. Murray loved pretty clothes, she liked shops devoted to the service of women; she enjoyed being even on the fringe of a fashionable gathering. A satisfaction that was almost ecstatic seized her when she drank tea in the midst of modishly gowned women in a stylish tea-room. It pleased her to stand in the foyer of a great hotel or of the Academy of Music and to be part of the whirling, humming, palpitating gaiety. She had no desire to be of these people, but she liked to look on; it amused and thrilled and kept alive some unquenchable instinct for life which thrived within her. To walk through Wanamaker's on Saturday, to stroll from Fifteenth to Ninth Street on Chestnut, to have her tea in the Bellevue Stratford, to stand in the lobby of the St. James' fitting on immaculate gloves; all innocent, childish pleasures pursued without malice or envy contrived to cast a glamour over Monday's washing and Tuesday's ironing, the scrubbing of kitchen and bathroom and the fashioning of children's clothes. She was endowed with a humorous and pungent method of presentation; Junius, who had had the wit not to interfere with these little excursions and the sympathy to take them at their face value, preferred one of his wife's sparkling accounts of a Saturday's adventure in "passing" to all the tall stories told by cronies at his lodge.

Much of this pleasure, harmless and charming though it was, would have been impossible with a dark skin.

In these first years of marriage, Mattie, busied with the house and the two babies, had given up those excursions.

Later, when the children had grown and Junius had reached the stage where he could afford to give himself a half-holiday on Saturdays, the two parents inaugurated a plan of action which eventually became a fixed programme. Each took a child, and Junius went off to a beloved but long since suspended pastime of exploring old Philadelphia, whereas Mattie embarked once more on her social adventures. It is true that Mattie accompanied by brown Virginia could not move quite as freely as when with Angela. But her maternal instincts were sound; her children, their feelings and their faith in her meant much more than the pleasure which she would have been first to call unnecessary and silly. As it happened the children themselves quite unconsciously solved the dilemma; Virginia found shopping tiring and stupid, Angela returned from her father's adventuring worn and bored. Gradually the rule was formed that Angela accompanied her mother and Virginia her father.

On such fortuities does life depend. Little Angela Murray, hurrying through Saturday morning's scrubbing of steps in order that she might have her bath at one and be with her mother on Chestnut Street at two, never realized that her mother took her pleasure among all these pale people because it was there that she happened to find it. It never occurred to her that the delight which her mother obviously showed in meeting friends on Sunday morning when the whole united Murray family came out of church was the same as she showed on Chestnut Street the previous Saturday, because she was finding the qualities which her heart craved, bustle, excitement and fashion. The daughter could not guess that if the economic status or the racial genius of coloured people had permitted them to run modish hotels or vast and popular department stores her mother would have been there. She drew for herself certain clearly formed conclusions which her subconscious mind thus codified:

First, that the great rewards of life—riches, glamour, pleasure,—are for white-skinned people only. Secondly, that Junius and Virginia were denied these privileges because they were dark; here her reasoning bore at least an element of verisimilitude but she missed the essential fact that her father and sister did not care for this type of pleasure. The effect of her fallaciousness was to cause her to feel a faint pity for her unfortunate relatives and also to feel that coloured people were to be considered fortunate only in the proportion in which they measured up to the physical standards of white people.

One Saturday excursion left a far-reaching impression. Mrs. Murray and Angela had spent a successful and interesting afternoon. They had browsed among the contents of the small exclusive shops in Walnut Street; they had had soda at Adams' on Broad Street and they were standing finally in the portico of the Walton Hotel deciding with fashionable and idle elegance what they should do next. A thin stream of people constantly passing threw an occasional glance at the quietly modish pair, the well-dressed, assured woman and the refined and no less assured daughter. The door-man knew them; it was one of Mrs. Murray's pleasures to proffer him a small tip, much appreciated since it was uncalled for. This was the atmosphere which she loved. Angela had put on her gloves and was waiting for her mother, who was drawing on her own with great care, when she glimpsed in the laughing, hurrying Saturday throng the figures of her father and of Virginia. They were close enough for her mother, who saw them too, to touch them by merely descending a few steps and stretching out her arm. In a second the pair had vanished. Angela saw her mother's face change—with trepidation she thought. She remarked: "It's a good thing Papa didn't see us, you'd have had to speak to him, wouldn't you?" But her mother, giving her a distracted glance, made no reply.

That night, after the girls were in bed, Mattie, perched on the arm of her husband's chair, told him about it. "I was at my old game of play-acting again to-day, June, passing you know, and darling, you and Virginia went by within arm's reach and we never spoke to you. I'm so ashamed."

But Junius consoled her. Long before their marriage he had known of his Mattie's weakness and its essential harmlessness. "My dear girl, I told you long ago that where no principle was involved, your passing means nothing to me. It's just a little joke; I don't think you'd be ashamed to acknowledge your old husband anywhere if it were necessary."

"I'd do that if people were mistaking me for a queen," she assured him fondly. But she was silent, not quite satisfied. "After all," she said with her charming frankness, "it isn't you, dear, who make me feel guilty. I really am ashamed to think that I let Virginia pass by without a word. I think I should feel very badly if she were to know it. I don't believe I'll ever let myself be quite as silly as that again."

But of this determination Angela, dreaming excitedly of Saturdays spent in turning her small olive face firmly away from peering black countenances was, unhappily, unaware.

She was very kind to him in the car; she was so sorry for him, suddenly conscious of the pain which must be his at being stripped before the girl he loved of his masculine right to protect, to appear the hero.

She let him open the two doors for her but stopped him in the box of a hall. "I think I'll say good-night now, Matthew; I'm more tired than I realized. But,—but it was an adventure, wasn't it?"

His eyes adored her, his hand caught hers: "Angela, I'd have given all I hope to possess to have been able to prevent it; you know I never dreamed of letting you in for such humiliation. Oh how are we ever going to get this thing straight?"

"Well, it wasn't your fault." Unexpectedly she lifted her delicate face to his, so stricken and freckled and woebegone, and kissed him, lifted her hand and actually stroked his reddish, stiff, "bad" hair.

Like a man in a dream he walked down the street wondering how long it would be before they married.

Angela, waking in the middle of the night and reviewing to herself the events of the day, said aloud: "This is the end," and fell asleep again.

The little back room was still Jinny's, but Angela, in order to give the third story front to Hetty Daniels, had moved into the room which had once been her mother's. She and Virginia had placed the respective head-boards of their narrow, virginal beds against the dividing wall so that they could lie in bed and talk to each other through the communicating door-way, their voices making a circuit from speaker to listener in what Jinny called a hair-pin curve.

Angela called in as soon as she heard her sister moving, "Jinny, listen. I'm going away."

Her sister, still half asleep, lay intensely quiet for another second, trying to pick up the continuity of this dream. Then her senses came to her.

"What'd you say, Angela?"

"I said I was going away. I'm going to leave Philadelphia, give up school teaching, break away from our loving friends and acquaintances, and bust up the whole shooting match."

"Haven't gone crazy, have you?"

"No, I think I'm just beginning to come to my senses. I'm sick, sick, sick of seeing what I want dangled right before my eyes and then of having it snatched away from me and all of it through no fault of my own."

"Darling, you know I haven't the faintest idea of what you're driving at."

"Well, I'll tell you." Out came the whole story, an accumulation of the slights, real and fancied, which her colour had engendered throughout her lifetime; though even then she did not tell of that first hurt through Mary Hastings. That would always linger in some remote, impenetrable fastness of her mind, for wounded trust was there as well as wounded pride and love. "And these two last happenings with Matthew and Mr. Shields are just too much; besides they've shown me the way."

"Shown you what way?"

Virginia had arisen and thrown an old rose kimono around her. She had inherited her father's thick and rather coarsely waving black hair, enhanced by her mother's softness. She was slender, yet rounded; her cheeks were flushed with sleep and excitement. Her eyes shone. As she sat in the brilliant wrap, cross-legged at the foot of her sister's narrow bed, she made the latter think of a striking dainty, colourful robin.

"Well you see as long as the Shields thought I was white they were willing to help me to all the glories of the promised land. And the doorman last night,—he couldn't tell what I was, but he could tell about Matthew, so he put him out; just as the Shields are getting ready in another way to put me out. But as long as they didn't know, it didn't matter. Which means it isn't being coloured that makes the difference, it's letting it be known. Do you see?

"So I've thought and thought. I guess really I've had it in my mind for a long time, but last night it seemed to stand right out in my consciousness. Why should I shut myself off from all the things I want most,—clever people, people who do things, Art,—" her voice spelt it with a capital,—"travel and a lot of things which are in the world for everybody really but which only white people, as far as I can see, get their hands on. I mean scholarships and special funds, patronage. Oh Jinny, you don't know, I don't think you can understand the things I want to see and know. You're not like me——"

"I don't know why I'm not," said Jinny looking more like a robin than ever. Her bright eyes dwelt on her sister. "After all, the same blood flows in my veins and in the same proportion. Sure you're not laying too much stress on something only temporarily inconvenient?"

"But it isn't temporarily inconvenient; it's happening to me every day. And it isn't as though it were something that I could help. Look how Mr. Shields stressed the fact that I hadn't told him I was coloured. And see how it changed his attitude toward me; you can't think how different his manner was. Yet as long as he didn't know, there was nothing he wasn't willing and glad, glad to do for me. Now he might be willing but he'll not be glad though I need his assistance more than some white girl who will find a dozen people to help her just because she is white." Some faint disapproval in her sister's face halted her for a moment. "What's the matter? You certainly don't think I ought to say first thing: 'I'm Angela Murray. I know I look white but I'm coloured and expect to be treated accordingly!' Now do you?"

"No," said Jinny, "of course that's absurd. Only I don't think you ought to mind quite so hard when they do find out the facts. It seems sort of an insult to yourself. And then, too, it makes you lose a good chance to do something for—for all of us who can't look like you but who really have the same combination of blood that you have."

"Oh that's some more of your and Matthew Henson's philosophy. Now be practical, Jinny; after all, I am both white and Negro and look white. Why shouldn't I declare for the one that will bring me the greatest happiness, prosperity and respect?"

"No reason in the world except that since in this country public opinion is against any infusion of black blood it would seem an awfully decent thing to put yourself, even in the face of appearances, on the side of black blood and say: 'Look here, this is what a mixture of black and white really means!' "

Angela was silent and Virginia, feeling suddenly very young, almost childish in the presence of this issue, took a turn about the room. She halted beside her sister.

"Just what is it you want to do, Angela? Evidently you have some plan."

She had. Her idea was to sell the house and to divide the proceeds. With her share of this and her half of the insurance she would go to New York or to Chicago, certainly to some place where she could by no chance be known, and launch out "into a freer, fuller life."

"And leave me!" said Jinny astonished. Somehow it had not dawned on her that the two would actually separate. She did not know what she had thought, but certainly not that. The tears ran down her cheeks.

Angela, unable to endure either her own pain or the sight of it in others, had all of a man's dislike for tears.

"Don't be absurd, Jinny! How could I live the way I want to if you're with me. We'd keep on loving each other and seeing one another from time to time, but we might just as well face the facts. Some of those girls in the art school used to ask me to their homes; it would have meant opportunity, a broader outlook, but I never dared accept because I knew I couldn't return the invitation."

Under that Jinny winced a little, but she spoke with spirit. "After that, Angela dear, I'm beginning to think that you *have* more white blood in your veins than I, and it was that extra amount which made it possible for you to make that remark." She trailed back to her room and when Hetty Daniels announced breakfast she found that a bad headache required a longer stay in bed.

For many years the memory of those next few weeks lingered in Virginia's mind beside that other tragic memory of her mother's deliberate submission to death. But Angela was almost tremulous with happiness and anticipation. Almost as though by magic her affairs were arranging themselves. She was to have the three thousand dollars and Jinny was to be the sole possessor of the house. Junius had paid far less than this sum for it, but it had undoubtedly increased in value. "It's a fair enough investment for you, Miss Virginia," Mr. Hallowell remarked gruffly. He had disapproved heartily of this summary division, would have disapproved more thoroughly and openly if he had had any idea of the reasons behind it. But the girls had told no one, not even him, of their plans. "Some sisters' quarrel, I suppose," he commented to his wife. "I've never seen any coloured people yet, relatives that is, who could stand the joint possession of a little money."

A late Easter was casting its charm over the city when Angela trim, even elegant, in her conventional tailored suit, stood in the dining-room of the little house waiting for her taxi. She had burned her bridges behind her, had resigned from school, severed her connection with the Academy, and had permitted an impression to spread that she was going West to visit indefinitely a distant cousin of her mother's. In reality she was going to New York. She had covered her tracks very well, she thought; none of her friends was to see her off; indeed, none of them knew the exact hour of her departure. She was even leaving from the North Philadelphia station so that none of the porters of the main depôt, friends perhaps of the boys who came to her house, and, through some far flung communal instinct familiar to coloured people, acquainted with her by sight, would be able to tell of her going. Jinny, until she heard of this, had meant to accompany her to the station, but Angela's precaution palpably scotched this idea; she made no comment when Virginia announced that it would be impossible for her to see her sister off. An indefinable steeliness was creeping upon them.

Yet when the taxi stood rumbling and snorting outside, Angela, her heart suddenly mounting to her throat, her eyes smarting, put her arm tightly about her sister who clung to her, frankly crying. But she only said: "Now, Jinny, there's nothing to cry about. You'll be coming to New York soon. First thing I know you'll be walking up to me: 'Pardon me! Isn't this Mrs. Henrietta Jones?'"

Virginia tried to laugh, "And you'll be saying: 'Really

you have the advantage of me.' Oh, Angela, don't leave me!"

The cabby was honking impatiently. "I must, darling. Good-bye, Virginia. You'll hear from me right away."

She ran down the steps, glanced happily back. But her sister had already closed the door.

PLUM BUN

"MARKET"

CHAPTER I

Fifth Avenue is a canyon; its towering buildings dwarf the importance of the people hurrying through its narrow confines. But Fourteenth Street is a river, impersonally flowing, broad-bosomed, with strange and devious craft covering its expanse. To Angela the famous avenue seemed but one manifestation of living, but Fourteenth Street was the rendezvous of life itself. Here for those first few weeks after her arrival in New York she wandered, almost prowled, intent upon the jostling shops, the hurrying, pushing people, above all intent upon the faces of those people with their showings of grief, pride, gaiety, greed, joy, ambition, content. There was little enough of this last. These men and women were living at a sharper pitch of intensity than those she had observed in Philadelphia. The few coloured people whom she saw were different too; they possessed an independence of carriage, a purposefulness, an assurance in their manner that pleased her. But she could not see that any of these people, black or white, were any happier than those whom she had observed all her life.

But *she* was happier; she was living on the crest of a wave of excitement and satisfaction which would never wane, never break, never be spent. She was seeing the world, she was getting acquainted with life in her own way without restrictions or restraint; she was young, she was temporarily independent, she was intelligent, she was white. She remembered an expression "free, white and twenty-one,"—this was what it meant then, this sense of owning the world, this realization that other things being equal, all things were possible. "If I were a man," she said, "I could be president," and laughed at herself for the "if" itself proclaimed a limitation. But that inconsistency bothered her little; she did not want to be a man. Power, greatness, authority, these were fitting and proper for men; but there were sweeter, more beautiful gifts for

women, and power of a certain kind too. Such a power
she would like to exert in this glittering new world, so
full of mysteries and promise. If she could afford it she
would have a salon, a drawing-room where men and wom-
en, not necessarily great, but real, alive, free and un-
trammelled in manner and thought, should come and pour
themselves out to her sympathy and magnetism. To accomplish this she must have money and influence; indeed
since she was so young she would need even protection;
perhaps it would be better to marry . . . a white man.
The thought came to her suddenly out of the void; she
had never thought of this possibility before. If she were to
do this, do it suitably, then all that richness, all that fullness of life which she so ardently craved would be doubly
hers. She knew that men had a better time of it than
women, coloured men than coloured women, white men
than white women. Not that she envied them. Only it
would be fun, great fun to capture power and protection
in addition to the freedom and independence which she
had so long coveted and which now lay in her hand.

But, she smiled to herself, she had no way of approaching these ends. She knew no one in New York; she could
conceive of no manner in which she was likely to form
desirable acquaintances; at present her home consisted of
the four walls of the smallest room in Union Square Hotel.
She had gone there the second day after her arrival, having spent an expensive twenty-four hours at the Astor.
Later she came to realize that there were infinitely cheaper
habitations to be had, but she could not tear herself away
from Fourteenth Street. It was Spring, and the Square
was full of rusty specimens of mankind who sat on the
benches, as did Angela herself, for hours at a stretch, as
though they thought the invigorating air and the mellow
sun would work some magical burgeoning on their garments such as was worked on the trees. But though these
latter changed, the garments changed not nor did their
owners. They remained the same, drooping, discouraged
down and outers. "I am seeing life," thought Angela, "this
is the way people live," and never realized that some of
these people looking curiously, speculatively at her wondered what had been her portion to bring her thus early
to this unsavoury company.

"A great picture!" she thought. "I'll make a great picture of these people some day and call them 'Fourteenth Street types'." And suddenly a vast sadness invaded her; she wondered if there were people more alive, more sentient to the joy, the adventure of living, even than she, to whom she would also be a "type." But she could not believe this. She was at once almost irreconcilably too concentrated and too objective. Her living during these days was so intense, so almost solidified, as though her desire to live as she did and she herself were so one and the same thing that it would have been practically impossible for another onlooker like herself to insert the point of his discrimination into her firm panoply of satisfaction. So she continued to browse along her chosen thoroughfare, stopping most often in the Square or before a piano store on the same street. There was in this shop a player-piano which was usually in action, and as the front glass had been removed the increased clearness of the strains brought a steady, patient, apparently insatiable group of listeners to a standstill. They were mostly men, and as they were far less given, Angela observed, to concealing their feelings than women, it was easy to follow their emotional gamut. Jazz made them smile but with a certain wistfulness—if only they had time for dancing now, just now when the mood was on them! The young woman looking at the gathering of shabby pedestrians, worn business men and ruminative errand boys felt for them a pity not untinged with satisfaction. *She* had taken what she wanted while the mood was on her. Love songs, particularly those of the sorrowful ballad variety brought to these unmindful faces a strained regret. But there was one expression which Angela could only half interpret. It drifted on to those listening countenances usually at the playing of old Irish and Scottish tunes. She noticed then an acuter attitude of attention, the eyes took on a look of inwardness of utter remoteness. A passer-by engrossed in thought caught a strain and at once his gait and expression fell under the spell. The listeners might be as varied as fifteen people may be, yet for the moment they would be caught in a common, almost cosmic nostalgia. If the next piece were jazz that particular crowd would disperse, its members going on their meditative ways, blessed or

cursed with heaven knew what memories which must not
to be disturbed by the strident jangling of the latest popular song.

"Homesick," Angela used to say to herself. And she
would feel so, too, though she hardly knew for what,—
certainly not for Philadelphia and that other life which
now seemed so removed as to have been impossible. And
she made notes in her sketch book to enable her some
day to make a great picture of these "types" too.

Angela was visual minded. She saw the days of the
week, the months of the year in little narrow divisions of
space. She saw the past years of her life falling into
separate, uneven compartments whose ensemble made up
her existence. Whenever she looked back on this period
from Christmas to Easter she saw a bluish haze beginning
in a white mist and flaming into something red and terrible; and across the bluish haze stretched the name:
Roger.

Roger! She had never seen anyone like him: so gay,
so beautiful, like a blond, glorious god, so overwhelming,
so persistent. She had not liked him so much at first except
as one likes the sun or the sky or a singing bird, anything
jolly and free. There had been no touching points for
their minds. He knew nothing of life except what was
pleasurable; it is true his idea of the pleasurable did not
always coincide with hers. He had no fears, no restraints,
no worries. Yes, he had one; he did not want to offend
his father. He wanted ardently and unswervingly his father's money. He did not begrudge his senior a day, an hour,
a moment of life; about this he had a queer, unselfish
sincerity. The old financial war horse had made his fortune
by hard labour and pitiless fighting. He had given Roger
his being, the *entrée* into a wonderful existence. Already
he bestowed upon him an annual sum which would have
kept several families in comfort. If Roger had cared to
save for two years he need never have asked his father
for another cent. With any kind of luck he could have built
up for himself a second colossal fortune. But he did not
care to do this. He did not wish his father one instant's
loss of life or of its enjoyment. But he did want final
possession of those millions.

Angela liked him best when he talked about "my dad";

he never mentioned the vastness of his wealth, but by now she could not have helped guessing even without Paulette's aid that he was a wealthy man. She would not take jewellery from him, but there was a steady stream of flowers, fruit, candy, books, fine copies of the old masters. She was afraid and ashamed to express a longing in his presence. And with all this his steady, constant attendance. And an odd watchfulness which she felt but could not explain.

"He must love me," she said to herself, thinking of his caresses. She had been unable to keep him from kissing her. Her uneasiness had amused and charmed him: he laughed at her Puritanism, succeeded in shaming her out of it. "Child, where have you lived? Why there's nothing in a kiss. If I didn't kiss you I couldn't come to see you. And I have to see you, Angèle!" His voice grew deep; the expression in his eyes made her own falter.

Yet he did not ask her to marry him. "But I suppose it's because he can see I don't love him yet." And she wondered what it would be like to love. Even Jinny knew more about this than she, for she had felt, perhaps still did feel, a strong affection for Matthew Henson. Well, anyway, if they married she would probably come to love him; most women learned to love their husbands. At first after her conversation with Paulette about Roger she had rather expected a diminution at any time of his attention, for after all she was unknown; from Roger's angle she would be more than outside the pale. But she was sure now that he loved and would want to marry her, for it never occurred to her that men bestowed attentions such as these on a passing fancy. She saw her life rounding out like a fairy tale. Poor, coloured—coloured in America; unknown, a nobody! And here at her hand was the forward thrust shadow of love and of great wealth. She would do lots of good among coloured people; she would see that Miss Powell, for instance, had her scholarship. Oh she would hunt out girls and men like Seymour Porter,— she had almost forgotten his name,—or was it Arthur Sawyer?—and give them a taste of life in its fullness and beauty such as they had never dreamed of.

To-night she was to go out with Roger. She wore her flame-coloured dress again; a pretty green one was also hanging up in her closet, but she wore the flame one because it lighted her up from within—lighted not only her lovely, fine body but her mind too. Her satisfaction with her appearance let loose some inexplicable spring of gaiety and merriment and simplicity so that she seemed almost daring.

Roger, sitting opposite, tried to probe her mood, tried to gauge the invitation of her manner and its possibilities. She touched him once or twice, familiarly; he thought almost possessively. She seemed to be within reach now if along with that accessibility she had recklessness. It was this attribute which for the first time to-night he thought to divine within her. If in addition to her insatiable interest in life—for she was always asking him about people and places,—she possessed this recklessness, then indeed he might put to her a proposal which had been hanging on his lips for weeks and months. Something innocent, pathetically untouched about her had hitherto kept him back. But if she had the requisite daring! They were dining in East Tenth Street in a small *café*—small contrasted with the Park Avenue Hotel to which he had first taken her. But about them stretched the glitter and perfection of crystal and silver, of marvellous napery and of obsequious service. Everything, Angela thought, looking about her, was translated. The slight odour of food was, she told Roger, really an aroma: the mineral water which he was drinking because he could not help it and she because she could not learn to like wine, was nectar; the bread, the fish, the courses, were ambrosia. The food, too, in general was to be spoken of as viands.

"Vittles, translated," she said laughing.

"And you, you, too, are translated. Angèle, you are wonderful, you are charming," his lips answered but his senses beat and hammered. Intoxicated with the magic of the moment and the surroundings, she turned her smiling countenance a little nearer, and saw his face change, darken. A cloud over the sun.

"Excuse me," he said and walked hastily across the room back of her. In astonishment she turned and looked after him. At a table behind her, three coloured people (under the direction of a puzzled and troubled waiter,) were about to take a table. Roger went up and spoke to the headwaiter authoritatively, even angrily. The latter glanced about the room, nodded obsequiously and crossing, addressed the little group. There was a hasty, slightly acrid discussion. Then the three filed out; past Angela's table this time, their heads high.

She turned back to her plate, her heart sick. For her the evening was ended. Roger came back, his face flushed, triumphant, "Well I put a spoke in the wheel of those 'coons'! They forget themselves so quickly, coming in here spoiling white people's appetites. I told the manager if they brought one of their damned suits I'd be responsible. I wasn't going to have them here with you, Angèle. I could tell that night at Martha Burden's by the way you looked at that girl that you had no time for darkies. I'll bet you'd never been that near to one before in your life, had you? Wonder where Martha picked that one up."

She was silent, lifeless. He went on recounting instances of how effectively he had "spoked the wheel" of various coloured people. He had black-balled Negroes at Harvard, aspirants for small literary or honour societies. "I'd send 'em all back to Africa if I could. There's been a darkey up in Harlem's got the right idea, I understand; though he must be a low brute to cave in on his race that way; of course it's merely a matter of money with him. He'd betray them all for a few thousands. Gosh, if he could really pull it through I don't know but what I'd be willing to finance it."

To this tirade there were economic reasons to oppose, tenets of justice, high ideals of humanity. But she could think of none of them. Speechless, she listened to him, her appetite fled.

"What's the matter, Angèle? Did it make you sick to see them?"

"No, no not that. I—I don't mind them; you're mistaken about me and that girl at Martha Burden's. It's you, you're so violent. I didn't know you were that way!"

"And I've made you afraid of me? Oh, I don't want to do that." But he was flattered to think that he had affected her. "See here, let's get some air. I'll take you for a spin around the Park and then run you home."

But she did not want to go to the Park; she wanted to go home immediately. His little blue car was outside; in fifteen minutes they were at Jayne Street. She would not permit him to come inside, not even in the vestibule; she barely gave him her hand.

"But Angèle, you can't leave me like this; why what have I done? Did it frighten you because I swore a little? But I'd never swear at you. Don't go like this."

She was gone, leaving him staring and nonplussed on the sidewalk. Lighting a cigarette, he climbed back in his car. "Now what the devil!" He shifted his gears. "But she likes me. I'd have sworn she liked me to-night. Those damn niggers! I bet she's thinking about me this minute."

He would have lost his bet. She was thinking about the coloured people.

She could visualize them all so plainly; she could interpret their changing expressions as completely as though those changes lay before her in a book. There were a girl and two men, one young, the other the father perhaps of either of the other two. The fatherly-looking person, for so her mind docketed him, bore an expression of readiness for any outcome whatever. She knew and understood the type. His experiences of surprises engendered by this thing called prejudice had been too vast for them to appear to him as surprises. If they were served this was a lucky day; if not he would refuse to let the incident shake his stout spirit.

It was to the young man and the girl that her interest went winging. In the mirror behind Roger she had seen them entering the room and she had thought: "Oh, here are some of them fighting it out again. Oh God! please let them be served, please don't let their evening be spoiled." She was so happy herself and she knew that the reception of fifty other *maîtres d' hôtel* could not atone for a rebuff at the beginning of the game. The young fellow was nervous, his face tense,—thus might he have looked going to meet the enemy's charge in the recent Great War; but there the odds were even; here the cards were already stacked against him. Presently his expression would change for one of grimness, determination and despair. Talk of a lawsuit would follow; apparently did follow; still a lawsuit at best is a poor substitute for an evening's fun.

But the girl, the girl in whose shoes she herself might so easily have been! She was so clearly a nice girl, with all that the phrase implies. To Angela watching her intently and yet with the indifference of safety she recalled Virginia, so slender, so appealing she was and so brave.

So very brave! Ah, that courage! It affected at first a gay hardihood: "Oh I know it isn't customary for people like us to come into this café, but everything is going to be all right." It met Angela's gaze with a steadiness before which her own quailed, for she thought: "Oh, poor thing! perhaps she thinks that I don't want her either." And when the blow had fallen the courage had had to be translated anew into a comforting assurance. "Don't worry about me, Jimmy," the watching guest could just hear her. "Indeed, indeed it won't spoil the evening, I should say not; there're plenty of places where they'd be all right. We just happened to pick a lemon."

The three had filed out, their heads high, their gaze poised and level. But the net result of the evening's adventure would be an increased cynicism in the elderly man, a growing bitterness for the young fellow, and a new timidity in the girl, who, even after they had passed into the street, could not relieve her feelings, for she must comfort her baffled and goaded escort.

Angela wondered if she had been half as consoling to Matthew Henson,—was it just a short year ago? And suddenly, sitting immobile in her arm-chair, her evening cloak slipping unnoticed to the floor, triumph began to mount in her. Life could never cheat her as it had cheated that coloured girl this evening, as it had once cheated her in Philadelphia with Matthew. She was free, free to taste life in all its fullness and sweetness, in all its minutest details. By exercising sufficient courage to employ the unique weapon which an accident of heredity had placed in her grasp she was able to master life. How she blessed her mother for showing her the way! In a country where colour or the lack of it meant the difference between freedom and fetters how lucky she was!

But, she told herself, she was through with Roger Fielding.

CHAPTER V

Now it was Spring, Spring in New York. Washington Square was a riot of greens that showed up bravely against the great red brick houses on its north side. The Arch viewed from Fifth Avenue seemed a gateway to Paradise. The long deep streets running the length of the city invited an exploration to the ends where pots of gold doubtless gleamed. On the short crosswise streets the April sun streamed in splendid banners of deep golden light.

In two weeks Angela had seen Roger only once. He telephoned every day, pleading, beseeching, entreating. On the one occasion when she did permit him to call there were almost tears in his eyes. "But, darling, what did I do? If you'd only tell me that. Perhaps I could explain away whatever it is that's come between us." But there was nothing to explain she told him gravely, it was just that he was harder, more cruel then she had expected; no, it wasn't the coloured people, she lied and felt her soul blushing, it was that now she knew him when he was angry or displeased, and she could see how ruthless, how determined he was to have things his way. His willingness to pay the costs of the possible lawsuit had filled her with a sharp fear. What could one do against a man, against a group of men such as he and his kind represented who would spend time and money to maintain a prejudice based on a silly, time-worn tradition?

Yet she found she did not want to lose sight of him completely. The care, the attention, the flattery with which he had surrounded her were beginning to produce their effect. In the beautiful but slightly wearying balminess of the Spring she missed the blue car which had been constantly at her call; eating a good but homely meal in her little living-room with the cooking odours fairly overwhelming her from the kitchenette, she found herself longing unconsciously for the dainty food, the fresh Spring delicacies which she knew he would be only too glad to procure for her. Shamefadedly she had to acknowledge that the separation which she was so rigidly enforcing meant a difference in her tiny exchequer, for it had now been many months since she had regularly taken her main meal by herself and at her own expense.

To-day she was especially conscious of her dependence upon him, for she was to spend the afternoon in Van Cortlandt Park with Anthony. There had been talk of subways and the Elevated. Roger would have had the blue car at the door and she would have driven out of Jayne Street in state. Now it transpired that Anthony was to deliver some drawings to a man, a tricky customer, whom it was best to waylay if possible on Saturday afternoon. Much as he regretted it, he would probably be a little late. Angela, therefore, to save time must meet him at Seventy-second Street. Roger would never have made a request like that; he would have brought his lawyer or his business man along in the car with him and, dismissing him with a curt "Well, I'll see if I can finish this to-morrow," would have hastened to her with his best Walter Raleigh manner, and would have produced the cloak, too, if she would but say so. Perhaps she'd have to take him back. Doubtless later on she could manage his prejudices if only he would speak. But how was she to accomplish that?

Still it was lovely being here with Anthony in the park, so green and fresh, so new with the recurring newness of Spring. Anthony touched her hand and said as he had once before, "I'm so content to be with you, Angel. I may call you Angel, mayn't I? You are that to me, you know. Oh if you only knew how happy it makes me to be content, to be satisfied like this. I could get down on my knees and thank God for it like a little boy." He looked like a little boy as he said it. "Happiness is a hard thing to find and harder still to keep."

She asked him idly, "Haven't you always been happy?"

His face underwent a startling change. Not only did the old sadness and strain come back on it, but a great bitterness such as she had never before seen.

"No," he said slowly as though thinking through long years of his life. "I haven't been happy for years, not since I was a little boy. Never once have I been happy nor even at ease until I met you."

But she did not want him to find his happiness in her. That way would only lead to greater unhappiness for him. So she said, to change the subject: "Could you tell me about it?"

But there was nothing to tell, he assured her, his face growing darker, grimmer. "Only my father was killed when I was a little boy, killed by his enemies. I've hated them ever since; I never stopped hating them until I met you." But this was just as dangerous a road as the other plus the possibilities of re-opening old wounds. So she only shivered and said vaguely, "Oh, that was terrible! Too terrible to talk about. I'm sorry, Anthony!" And then as a last desperate topic: "Are you ever going back to Brazil?" For she knew that he had come to the United States from Rio de Janeiro. He had spent Christmas at her house, and had shown her pictures of the great, beautiful city and of his mother, a slender, dark-eyed woman with a perpetual sadness in her eyes.

The conversation languished. She thought: "It must be terrible to be a man and to have these secret hates and horrors back of one." Some Spanish feud, a matter of hot blood and ready knives, a sudden stroke, and then this deadly memory for him.

"No," he said after a long pause. "I'm never going back to Brazil. I couldn't." He turned to her suddenly. "Tell me, Angel, what kind of girl are you, what do you think worthwhile? Could you, for the sake of love, for the sake of being loyal to the purposes and vows of someone you loved, bring yourself to endure privation and hardship and misunderstanding, hardship that would be none the less hard because it really could be avoided?"

She thought of her mother who had loved her father so dearly, and of the wash-days which she had endured for him, the long years of household routine before she and Jimmy had been old enough to help her first with their hands and then with their earnings. She thought of the little, dark, shabby house, of the made-over dresses and turned coats. And then she saw Roger and his wealth and his golden recklessness, his golden keys which could open the doors to beauty and ease and—decency! Oh, it wasn't decent for women to have to scrub and work and slave and bear children and sacrifice their looks and their pretty hands,—she saw her mother's hands as they had always looked on wash day, they had a white, boiled appearance. No, she would not fool herself nor Anthony. She was no sentimentalist. It was not likely that she, a girl who had left her little sister and her home to go out to seek life and happiness would throw it over for poverty,—hardship. If a man loved a woman how could he ask her that?

So she told him gently: "No, Anthony, I couldn't," and watched the blood drain from his face and the old look of unhappiness drift into his eyes.

He answered inadequately. "No, of course you couldn't." And turning over,—he had been sitting on the grass at her feet—he lay face downward on the scented turf. Presently he sat up and giving her a singularly sweet but wistful smile, said: "I almost touched happiness, Angèle. Did you by any chance ever happen to read Browning's 'Two in the Roman Campagna'?"

But she had read very little poetry except what had been required in her High School work, and certainly not Browning.

He began to interpret the fragile, difficult beauty of the poem with its light but sure touch on evanescent, indefinable feeling. He quoted:

> "How is it under our control
> To love or not to love?"

And again:

> "Infinite passion, and the pain
> Of infinite hearts that yearn."

They were silent for a long time. And again she wondered how it would feel to love. He watched the sun drop suddenly below some tree tops and rose to his feet shivering a little as though its disappearance had made him immediately cold.

" 'So the good moment goes.' Come, Angel, we'll have to hasten. It's getting dark and it's a long way to the subway."

The memory of the afternoon stayed by her, shrouding her thoughts, clinging to them like a tenuous, adhering mantle. But she said to herself: "There's no use thinking about that. I'm not going to live that kind of life." And she knew she wanted Roger and what he could give her and the light and gladness which he always radiated. She

wanted none of Anthony's poverty and privation and
secret vows,—he meant, she supposed, some promise to
devote himself to REAL ART,—her visual mind saw it in
capitals. Well, she was sick of tragedy, she belonged to a
tragic race. "God knows it's time for one member of it to
be having a little fun."

"Yes," she thought all through her class, painting
furiously—for she had taken up her work in earnest since
Christmas—"yes, I'll just make up my mind to it. I'll take
Roger back and get married and settle down to a pleasant,
safe, beautiful life." And useful. It should be very useful.
Perhaps she'd win Roger around to helping coloured people. She'd look up all sorts of down-and-outers and give
them a hand. And she'd help Anthony, at least she'd offer
to help him; she didn't believe he would permit her.

Coming out of the building a thought occurred to her:
"Take Roger back, but back to what? To his old status
of admiring, familiar, generous friend? Just that and no
more?" Here was her old problem again. She stopped short
to consider it.

Martha Burden overtook her. "Planning the great mas-
terpiece of the ages, Angèle? Better come along and work
it out by my fireside. I can give you some tea. Are you
coming?"

"Yes," said Angela, still absorbed.

"Well," said Martha after they had reached the house.
"I've never seen any study as deep as that. Come out of it
Angèle, you'll drown. You're not by any chance in love,
are you?"

"No," she replied, "at least I don't know. But tell me,
Martha, suppose—suppose I were in love with one of them,
what do you do about it, how do you get them to propose?"

Martha lay back and laughed. "Such candour have I not
met, no, not in all Flapperdom. Angèle, if I could answer
that I'd be turning women away from my door and handing out my knowledge to the ones I did admit at a hundred
dollars a throw."

"But there must be some way. Oh, of course, I know
lots of them propose, but how do you get a proposal from
the ones you want,—the,—the interesting ones?"

"You really want to know? The only answer I can give
you is Humpty Dumpty's dictum to Alice about verbs and

adjectives: 'It depends on which is the stronger'." She interpreted, for her young guest was clearly mystified. "It depends on (A) whether you are strong enough to make him like you more than you like him; (B) whether if you really do like him more than he does you, you can conceal it. In other words, so far as liking is concerned you must always be ahead of the game, you must always like or appear to like him a little less than he does you. And you must make him want you. But you mustn't give. Oh yes, I know that men are always wanting women to give, but they don't want the women to want to give. They want to take,—or at any rate to compel the giving."

"It sounds very complicated, like some subtle game."

A deep febrile light came into Martha's eyes. "It is a game, and the hardest game in the world for a woman, but the most fascinating; the hardest in which to strike a happy medium. You see, you have to be careful not to withhold too much and yet to give very little. If we don't give enough we lose them. If we give too much we lose ourselves. Oh, Angèle, God doesn't like women."

"But," said Angela thinking of her own mother, "there are some women who give all and men like them the better for it."

"Oh, yes, that's true. Those are the blessed among women. They ought to get down on their knees every day and thank God for permitting them to be their normal selves and not having to play a game." For a moment her still, proud face broke into deeps of pain. "Oh, Angèle, think of loving and never, never being able to show it until you're asked for it; think of living a game every hour of your life!" Her face quivered back to its normal immobility.

Angela walked home through the purple twilight musing no longer on her own case but on this unexpected revelation. "Well," she said, "I certainly shouldn't like to love like that." She thought of Anthony: "A woman could be her true self with him." But she had given him up.

If the thing to do were to play a game she would play one. Indeed she rather enjoyed the prospect. She was playing a game now, a game against public tradition on the one hand and family instinct on the other; the stakes were happiness and excitement, and almost anyone looking at the tricks which she had already taken would prophesy that she would be the winner. She decided to follow all the rules as laid down by Martha Burden and to add any workable ideas of her own. When Roger called again she was still unable to see him, but her voice was a shade less curt over the telephone; she did not cut him off so abruptly. "I must not withhold too much," she reminded herself. He was quick to note the subtle change in intonation. "But you're going to let me come to see you soon, Angèle," he pleaded. "You wouldn't hold out this way against me forever. Say when I may come."

"Oh, one of these days; I must go now, Roger. Good-bye."

After the third call she let him come to spend Friday evening. She heard the blue car rumbling in the street and a few minutes later he came literally staggering into the living-room so laden was he with packages. Flowers, heaps of spring posies had come earlier in the day, lilacs, jonquils, narcissi. Now this evening there were books and candy, handkerchiefs,—"they were so dainty and they looked just like you," he said fearfully, for she had never taken an article of dress from him,—two pictures, a palette and some fine brushes and last a hamper of all sorts of delicacies. "I thought if you didn't mind we'd have supper here; it would be fun with just us two."

How much he pleased her he could not divine; it was the first time he had ever given a hint of any desire for sheer domesticity. Anthony had sought nothing better than to sit and smoke and watch her flitting about in her absurd red or violet apron. Matthew Henson had been speechless with ecstasy when on a winter night she had allowed him to come into the kitchen while she prepared for him a cup of cocoa. But Roger's palate had been so flattered by the concoctions of chefs famous in London, Paris and New York that he had set no store by her simple cooking. Indeed his inevitable comment had been: "Here, what do you want to get yourself all tired out for? Let's go to a restaurant. It's heaps less bother."

But to-night he, too, watched her with humble, delighted eyes. She realized that he was conscious of her every movement; once he tried to embrace her, but she whirled out of his reach without reproach but with decision. He subsided, too thankful to be once more in her presence to take any risks. And when he left he had kissed her hand.

She began going about with him again, but with condescension, with kindness. And with the new vision gained from her talk with Martha she could see his passion mounting. "Make him want you,"—that was the second rule. It was clear that he did, no man could be as persevering as this otherwise. Still he did not speak. They were to meet that afternoon in front of the school to go "anywhere you want, dear, I'm yours to command." It was the first time that he had called for her at the building, and she came out a little early, for she did not want any of the three, Martha, Paulette, nor Anthony, to see whom she was meeting. It would be better to walk to the corner, she thought, they'd be just that much less likely to recognize him. She heard footsteps hurrying behind her, heard her name and turned to see Miss Powell, pleased and excited. She laid her hand on Angela's arm but the latter shook her off. Roger must not see her on familiar terms like this with a coloured girl for she felt that the afternoon portended something and she wanted no side issues. The coloured girl gave her a penetrating glance; then her habitual reserve settled down blotting out the eagerness, leaving her face blurred and heavy. "I beg your pardon, Miss Mory, I'm sure," she murmured and stepped out into the tempestuous traffic of Fourth Avenue. Angela was sorry; she would make it up tomorrow, she thought, but she had not dismissed her a moment too soon for Roger came rushing up, his car resplendent and resplendent himself in a grey suit, soft grey hat and blue tie. Angela looked at him approvingly. "You look just like the men in the advertising pages of the Saturday Evening Post," she said, and the fact that he did not wince under the compliment proved the depth of his devotion, for every one of his outer garments, hat, shoes, and suit, had been made to measure.

They went to Coney Island. "The ocean will be there, but very few people and only a very few amusements," said Roger. They had a delightful time; they were like school children, easily and frankly amused; they entered all the booths that were open, ate pop-corn and hot dogs and other local dainties. And presently they were flying home under the double line of trees on Ocean Parkway and entering the bosky loveliness of Prospect Park. Roger slowed down a little.

"Oh," said Angela. "I love this car."

He bent toward her instantly. "Does it please you? Did you miss it when you made me stay away from you?"

She was afraid she had made a mistake: "Yes, but that's not why I let you come back."

"I know that. But you do like it, don't you, comfort and beauty and dainty surroundings?"

"Yes," she said solemnly, "I love them all."

He was silent then for a long, long time, his face a little set, a worried line on his forehead.

"Well now what's he thinking about?" she asked herself, watching his hands and their clever manipulation of the steering wheel, though his thoughts, she knew, were not on that.

He turned to her with an air of having made up his mind. "Angèle, I want you to promise to spend a day out riding with me pretty soon. I—I have something I want to say to you." He was a worldly young man about town but he was actually mopping his brow. "I've got to go south for a week for my father,—he owns some timber down there with which he used to supply sawmills but since the damned niggers have started running north it's been something of a weight on his hands. He wants me to go down and see whether it's worth his while to hold on to it any longer. It's so rarely that he asks anything of me along a business line that I'd hate to refuse him. But I'll be back the morning of the twenty-sixth. I'll have to spend the afternoon and evening with him out on Long Island but on the twenty-seventh could you go out with me?"

She said as though all this preamble portended nothing: "I couldn't give you the whole day, but I'd go in the afternoon."

"Oh," his face fell a little. "Well, the afternoon then. Only of course we won't be able to go far out. Perhaps you'd like me to arrange a lunch and we'd go to one of the Parks, Central or the Bronx, or Van Cortlandt,——"

"No, not Van Cortlandt," she told him. That park was sacred to Anthony Cross.

"Well, wherever you say. We can settle it even that day. The main thing is that you'll go."

She said to herself. "Aren't men funny! He could have

asked me five times over while he was making all these arrangements." But she was immensely relieved, even happy. She felt very kindly toward him; perhaps she was in love after all, only she was not the demonstrative kind. It was too late for him to come in, but they sat in the car in the dark security of Jayne Street and she let him take her in his arms and kiss her again and again. For the first time she returned his kisses.

Weary but triumphant she mounted the stairs almost stumbling from a sudden, overwhelming fatigue. She had been under a strain! But it was all over now; she had conquered, she had been the stronger. She had secured not only him but an assured future, wealth, protection, influence, even power. She herself was power,—like the women one reads about, like Cleopatra,—Cleopatra's African origin intrigued her, it was a fitting comparison. Smiling, she took the last steep stairs lightly, springily, suddenly reinvigorated.

As she opened the door a little heap of letters struck her foot. Switching on the light she sat in the easy chair and incuriously turned them over. They were bills for the most part, she had had to dress to keep herself dainty and desirable for Roger. At the bottom of the heap was a letter from Virginia. When she became Mrs. Roger Fielding she would never have to worry about a bill again; how she would laugh when she remembered the small amounts for which these called! Never again would she feel the slight quake of dismay which always overtook her when she saw words: "Miss Angèle Mory in account with,——" Outside of the regular monthly statement for gas she had never seen a bill in her father's house. Well, she'd have no difficulty in getting over her squeamish training.

Finally she opened Jinny's letter. Her sister had written: "Angela I'm coming up for an exam on the twenty-eighth. I'll arrive on the twenty-sixth or I could come the day before. You'll meet me, won't you? I know where I'm going to stay,"—she gave an address on 139th Street—"but I don't know how to get there; I don't know your school hours, write and tell me so I can arrive when you're free. There's no reason why I should put you out."

So Virginia was really coming to try her luck in New York. It would be nice to have her so near. "Though I don't suppose we'll be seeing so much of each other," she thought, absently reaching for her schedule. "Less than ever now, for I suppose Roger and I will live in Long Island; yes, that would be much wiser. I'll wear a veil when I go to meet her, for those coloured porters stare at you so and they never forget you."

The twenty-seventh came on Thursday; she had classes in the morning; well, Jinny would be coming in the afternoon anyway, and after twelve she had,—Oh heavens that was *the* day, the day she was to go out with Roger, the day that he would put the great question. And she wrote to Virginia:

"Come the twenty-sixth, Honey, any time after four. I couldn't possibly meet you on the twenty-seventh. But the twenty-sixth is all right. Let me know when your train comes in and I'll be there. And welcome to our city."

CHAPTER VI

The week was one of tumult, almost of agony. After all, matters were not completely settled, you never could tell. She would be glad when the twenty-seventh had come and gone, for then, then she would be rooted, fixed. She and Roger would marry immediately. But now he was so far away, in Georgia; she missed him and evidently he missed her for the first two days brought her long telegrams, almost letters. "I can think of nothing but next Thursday, are you thinking of it too?" The third day brought a letter which said practically the same thing, adding, "Oh, Angèle, I wonder what you will say!"

"But he could ask me and find out," she said to herself and suddenly felt assured and triumphant. Every day thereafter brought her a letter reiterating this strain. "And I know how he hates to write!"

The letter on Wednesday read, "Darling, when you get this I'll actually be in New York; if I can I'll call you up but I'll have to rush like mad so as to be free for Thursday, so perhaps I can't manage."

She made up her mind not to answer the telephone even if it did ring, she would strike one last note of indifference though only she herself would be aware of it.

It was the day on which Jinny was to arrive. It would be fun to see her, talk to her, hear all the news about the queer, staid people whom she had left so far behind. Farther now than ever. Matthew Henson was still in the post-office, she knew. Arthur Sawyer was teaching at Sixteenth and Fitzwater; she could imagine the sick distaste that mantled his face every time he looked at the hideous, discoloured building. Porter had taken his degree in dentistry but he was not practising, on the contrary he was editing a small weekly, getting deeper, more and more hopelessly into debt she was sure . . . It would be fun some day to send him a whopping cheque; after all, he had taken a chance just as she had; she recognized his revolt as akin to her own, only he had not had her luck. She must ask Jinny about all this.

It was too bad that she had to meet her sister,—but she

must. Just as likely as not she'd be car sick and then New York was terrifying for the first time to the stranger,—she had known an instant's sick dread herself that first day when she had stood alone and ignorant in the great rotunda of the station. But she was different from Jinny; nothing about life ever made her really afraid; she might hurt herself, suffer, meet disappointment, but life could not alarm her; she loved to come to grips with it, to force it to a standstill, to yield up its treasures. But Jinny although brave, had secret fears, she was really only a baby. Her little sister! For the first time in months she thought of her with a great surge of sisterly tenderness.

It was time to go. She wore her most unobtrusive clothes, a dark blue suit, a plain white silk shirt, a dark blue, bell-shaped hat—a *cloche*—small and fitting down close over her eyes. She pulled it down even farther and settled her modish veil well over the tip of her nose. It was one thing to walk about the Village with Miss Powell. There were practically no coloured people there. But this was different. Those curious porters should never be able to recognize her. Seymour Porter had worked among them one summer at Broad Street station in Philadelphia. He used to say: "They aren't really curious, you know, but their job makes them sick; so they're always hunting for the romance, for the adventure which for a day at least will take the curse off the monotonous obsequiousness of their lives."

She was sorry for them, but she could not permit them to remedy their existence at her expense.

In her last letter she had explained to Jinny about those two troublesome staircases which lead from the train level of the New York Pennsylvania Railroad station to the street level. "There's no use my trying to tell you which one to take in order to bring you up to the right hand or to the left hand side of the elevator because I never know myself. So all I can say, dear, is when you do get up to the elevator just stick to it and eventually I'll see you or you'll see me as I revolve around it. Don't you move, for it might turn out that we were both going in the same direction."

True to her own instructions, she was stationed between the two staircases, jerking her neck now toward one staircase, now toward the other, stopping short to look at the elevator itself. She thrust up her veil to see better.

A man sprinted by in desperate haste, brushing so closely by her that the corner of his suit-case struck sharply on the thin inner curve of her knee.

"My goodness!" she exclaimed involuntarily.

For all his haste he was a gentleman, for he pulled off his hat, threw her a quick backward glance and began: "I beg your—why darling, darling, you don't mean to say you came to meet me!"

"Meet you! I thought you came in this morning." It was Roger, Roger and the sight of him made her stupid with fear.

He stooped and kissed her, tenderly, possessively. "I did, —oh Angela you *are* a beauty! Only a beauty can wear plain things like that. I did come in this morning but I'm trying to catch Kirby, my father's lawyer, he ought to be coming in from Newark just now and I thought I'd take him down to Long Island with me for the night. I've got a lot of documents for him here in this suitcase—that Georgia business was most complicated—that way I won't have to hunt him up in the morning and I'll have more time to—to arrange for our trip in the afternoon. What are you doing here?"

What was she doing there? Waiting for her sister Jinny who was coloured and who showed it. And Roger hated Negroes. She was lost, ruined, unless she could get rid of him. She told the first lie that came into her mind.

"I'm waiting for Paulette." All this could be fixed up with Paulette later. Miss Lister would think as little of deceiving a man, any man, as she would of squashing a mosquito. They were fair game and she would ask no questions.

His face clouded. "Can't say I'm so wild about your waiting for Paulette. Well we can wait together—is she coming up from Philadelphia? That train's bringing my man too from Newark." He had the male's terribly clarity of understanding for train connections.

"What time does your train go to Long Island? I thought you wanted to get the next one."

"Well, I'd like to but they're only half an hour apart. I can wait. Better the loss of an hour to-day than all of to-morrow morning. We can wait together; see the people are beginning to come up. I wish I could take you home but the minute he shows up I'll have to sprint with him."

"Now God be on my side," she prayed. Sometimes these trains were very long. If Mr. Kirby were in the first car and Jinny toward the end that would make all of ten minutes' difference. If only she hadn't given those explicit directions!

There was Jinny, her head suddenly emerging into view above the stairs. She saw Angela, waved her hand. In another moment she would be flinging her arms about her sister's neck; she would be kissing her and saying, "Oh, Angela, Angela darling!"

And Roger, who was no fool, would notice the name Angela—Angèle; he would know no coloured girl would make a mistake like this.

She closed her eyes in a momentary faintness, opened them again.

"What's the matter?" said Roger sharply, "are you sick?"

Jinny was beside her. Now, now the bolt would fall. She heard the gay, childish voice saying laughingly, assuredly:

"I beg your pardon, but isn't this Mrs. Henrietta Jones?"

Oh, God was good! Here was one chance if only Jinny would understand! In his astonishment Roger had turned from her to face the speaker. Angela, her eyes beseeching her sister's from under her close hat brim, could only stammer the old formula: "Really you have the advantage of me. No, I'm not Mrs. Jones."

Roger said rudely, "Of course she isn't Mrs. Jones. Come, Angèle." Putting his arm through hers he stooped for the suitcase.

But Jinny, after a second's bewildered but incredulous stare, was quicker even than they. Her slight figure, her head high, preceded them; vanished into a telephone booth.

Roger glared after her. "Well of all the damned cheek!"

For the first time in the pursuit of her chosen ends she began to waver. Surely no ambition, no pinnacle of safety was supposed to call for the sacrifice of a sister. She might be selfish,—oh, undoubtedly she had been selfish all these months to leave Jinny completely to herself— but she had never meant to be cruel. She tried to picture the tumult of emotions in her sister's mind, there must have been amazement,—oh she had seen it all on her face, the utter bewilderment, the incredulity and then the settling down on that face of a veil of dignity and pride— like a baby trying to harden its mobile features. She was in her apartment again now, pacing the floor, wondering what to do. Already she had called up the house in 139th Street, it had taken her a half-hour to get the number for she did not know the householder's name and "Information" had been coy,—but Miss Murray had not arrived yet. Were they expecting her? Yes, Miss Murray had written to say that she would be there between six and seven; it was seven-thirty now and she had not appeared. Was there any message? "No, no!" Angela explained she would call again.

But where was Jinny? She couldn't be lost, after all she was grown-up and no fool, she could ask directions. Perhaps she had taken a cab and in the evening traffic had been delayed,—or had met with an accident. This thought sent Angela to the telephone again. There was no Miss Murray as yet. In her wanderings back and forth across the room she caught sight of herself in the mirror. Her face was flushed, her eyes shining with remorse and anxiety. Her vanity reminded her: "If Roger could just see me now." Roger and to-morrow! He would have to speak words of gold to atone for this breach which for his sake she had made in her sister's trust and affection.

At the end of an hour she called again. Yes, Miss Murray had come in. So great was her relief that her knees sagged under her. Yes of course they would ask her to come to the telephone. After a long silence the voice rang again over the wire. "I didn't see her go out but she must have for she's not in her room."

"Oh all right," said Angela, "the main thing was to know that she was there." But she was astonished. Jinny's first night in New York and she was out already! She could not go to see her Thursday because of the engagement with Roger, but she'd make good the next day; she'd be there the first thing, Friday morning. Snatching up a sheet of note-paper she began a long letter full of apologies and excuses. "And I can't come to-morrow, darling, because as I told you I have a very important engagement, an engagement that means very much to me. Oh you'll understand when I tell you about it." She put a special delivery stamp on the letter.

Her relief at learning that Jinny was safe did not ease her guilty conscience. In a calmer mood she tried now to find excuses for herself, extenuating circumstances. As soon as Jinny understood all that was involved she would overlook it. After all, Jinny would want her to be happy. "And anyway," she thought to herself sulkily, "Mamma didn't speak to Papa that day that we were standing on the steps of the Hotel Walton." But she knew that the cases were not analogous; no principle was involved, her mother's silence had not exposed her husband to insult or contumely, whereas Roger's attitude to Virginia had been distinctly offensive. "And moreover," her thoughts continued with merciless clarity, "when a principle *was* at stake your mother never hesitated a moment to let those hospital attendants know of the true status of affairs. In fact she was not aware that she was taking any particular stand. Her husband was her husband and she was glad to acknowledge that relationship."

A sick distaste for her action, for her daily deception, for Roger and his prejudices arose within her. But with it came a dark anger against a country and a society which could create such an issue. And she thought: "If I had spoken to Jinny, had acknowledged her, what good would it have done me or her either? After it was all over she would have been exactly where she was before and I would have lost everything. And I do so want to be happy, to have a good time. At this very hour to-morrow I'll probably be one of the most envied girls in New York. And afterwards I can atone for it all. I'll be good to all sorts of people; I'll really help humanity, lots of coloured folks will be much better off on account of me. And if I had spoken to Jinny I could never have helped them at all." Once she murmured: "I'll help Jinny too, the darling! She shall have everything in the world she wants." But in her heart she knew already that Jinny would want nothing. . . .

PLUM BUN

"PLUM BUN"

CHAPTER IV

Life had somehow come to a standstill; gone was its quality of high adventure and yet with the sense of tameness came no compensating note of assurance, of permanence. Angela pondered much about this; with her usual instinct for clarity, for a complete understanding of her own emotional life, she took to probing her inner consciousness. The fault, she decided, was bound up in her relationship with Roger. At present in a certain sense she might be said to be living for him; at least his was the figure about which her life resolved, revolved. Yet she no longer had the old, heady desire to feel herself completely his, to claim him as completely hers, neither for his wealth nor for the sense of security which he could afford nor for himself. For some reason he had lost his charm for her, much, she suspected, in the same way in which girls in the position which was hers, often lost their charm for their lovers.

And this realization instead of bringing to her a sense of relief, brought a certain real if somewhat fantastic shame. If there was to be no permanence in the relationship, if laying aside the question of marriage, it was to lack the dignity, the graciousness of an affair of long standing, of sympathy, of mutual need, then indeed according to the code of her childhood, according to every code of every phase of her development, she had allowed herself to drift into an inexcusably vulgar predicament. Even when her material safety and security were at stake and she had dreamed vaguely of yielding to Roger's entreaties to ensure that safety and security, there might have been some excuse. Life, she considered, came before creed or code or convention. Or if she had loved and there had been no other way she might have argued for this as the supreme experience of her life. But she was no longer conscious of striving for marriage with Roger; and as for love—she had known a feeling of gratitude, intense interest, even intense possessiveness for him but she did not believe she had ever known love.

But because of this mingling of shame and reproach she found herself consciously striving to keep their relations on the highest plane possible in the circumstances. She wished now not so much that she had never left Jinny and the security of their common home-life, as that the necessity for it had never arisen. Now suddenly she found herself lonely, she had been in New York nearly three years but not even yet had she struck down deep into the lode of genuine friendship. Paulette was kind and generous; she desired, she said, a close woman friend but Paulette was still the adventuress. She was as likely to change her vocation and her place of dwelling as she was to change her lover. Martha Burden, at once more stable and more comprehending in the conduct of a friendship once she had elected for it, was, on the other hand, much more conservative in the expenditure of that friendliness; besides she was by her very nature as reserved as Paulette was expansive, and her native intenseness made it difficult for her to dwell very long on the needs of anyone whose problems did not centre around her own extremely fixed ideas and principles.

As for Anthony Cross,—by some curious, utterly inexplicable revulsion of feeling, Angela could not bring herself to dwell long on the possibilities of a friendship with him. Somehow it seemed to her sacrilegious in her present condition to bring the memory of that far-off day in Van Cortlandt Park back to mind. As soon as his image arose she dismissed it, though there were moments when it was impossible for his vision to come before her without its instantly bringing to mind Rachel Salting's notions of love and self-sacrifice. Well, such dreams were not for her, she told herself impatiently. For her own soul's integrity she must make the most of this state in which she now found herself. Either she must effect through it a marriage whose excuse should be that of safety, assurance and a resulting usefulness; or she must resolve it by patience, steadfastness and affection into a very apotheosis of "free love." Of all possible *affaires du coeur* this must in semblance at any rate, be the ultimate *desideratum,* the finest flower of chivalry and devotion.

· To this end she began devoting herself again to the renewal of that sense of possessiveness in Roger and his affairs which had once been so spontaneous within her. But to this Roger presented unexpected barriers; he grew restive under such manifestations; he who had once fought so bitterly against her indifference resented with equal bitterness any showing of possessive interest. He wanted no claims upon him, he acknowledged none. Gradually his absences, which at first were due to the business interests of his father, occurred for other reasons or for none at all. Angela could not grasp this all at once; it was impossible for her to conceive that kindness should create indifference; in spite of confirmatory stories which she had heard, of books which she had read, she could not make herself believe that devotion might sometimes beget ingratitude, loss of appreciation. For if that were so then a successful relationship between the sexes must depend wholly on the marriage tie without reference to compatibility of taste, training or ideals. This she could scarcely credit. In some way she must be at fault.

No young wife in the first ardour of marriage could have striven more than she to please Roger. She sought by reading and outside questions to inform herself along the lines of Roger's training—he was a mining engineer. His fondness for his father prompted her to numerous inquiries about the interest and pursuits of the older Fielding; she made suggestions for Roger's leisure hours But no matter how disinterested her attitude and tone his response to all this was an increased sullenness, remoteness, wariness. Roger was experienced in the wiles of women; such interest could mean only one thing,—marriage. Well, Angela might just as well learn that he had no thought, had never had any thought, of marrying her or any other woman so far removed from his father's ideas and requirements.

Still Angela, intent on her ideals, could not comprehend. Things were not going well between them; affairs of this kind were often short-lived, that had been one of her first objections to the arrangement, but she had not dreamed that one withdrew when the other had committed no overt offense. She was as charming, as attractive, as pretty as she had ever been and far, far more kind and thoughtful. She had not changed, how could it be possible that he should be different?

A week had gone by and he had not dropped in to see her. Loneliness settled over her like a pall, frightening her seriously because she was realizing that this time she was not missing Roger so much as that a person for whom she had let slip the ideals engendered by her mother's early teaching, a man for whom she had betrayed and estranged her sister, was passing out of her ken. She had rarely called him on the telephone but suddenly she started to do so. For three days the suave voice of his man, Reynolds, told her that Mr. Fielding was "out, m'm."

"But did you give him my message? Did you ask him to call me as soon as he came in?"

"Yes, m'm."

"And did he?"

"That I couldn't tell you, m'm."

She could not carry on such a conversation with a servant.

On the fifth day Roger appeared. She sprang toward him. "Oh Roger, I'm so glad to see you. Did Reynolds tell you I called? Why have you been so long coming?"

"I'd have been still longer if you hadn't stopped 'phoning. Now see here, Angèle, this has got to stop. I can't have women calling me up all hours of the day, making me ridiculous in the eyes of my servants. I don't like it, it's got to stop. Do you understand me?"

Surprised, bewildered, she could only stammer: "But you call me whenever you feel like it."

"Of course I do, that's different. I'm a man." He added a cruel afterword. "Perhaps you notice that I don't call you up as often as I used."

Her pride was in arms. More than once she thought of writing him a brief note telling him that so far as she was concerned their "affair" was ended. But a great stubbornness possessed her; she was curious to see how this sort of thing could terminate; she was eager to learn if all the advice which older women pour into the ears of growing girls could be as true as it was trite. Was it a fact that the conventions were more important than the fundamental impulses of life, than generosity, kindness, unselfishness? For whatever her original motives, her actual relationship with Fielding had called out the most unselfish qualities in her. And she began to see the conventions, the rules that govern life, in a new light; she realized suddenly that for all their granite-like coldness and precision they also represented fundamental facts; a sort of concentrated compendium of the art of living and therefore as much to be observed and respected as warm, vital impulses.

Towards Roger she felt no rancour, only an apathy incapable of being dispersed. The conversation about the telephone left an effect all out of proportion to its actual importance; it represented for her the apparently unbridgeable difference between the sexes; everything was for men, but even the slightest privilege was to be denied to a woman unless the man chose to grant it. At least there were men who felt like that; not all men, she felt sure, could tolerate such an obviously unjust status. Without intent to punish, with no set purpose in her mind, simply because she was no longer interested, she began to neglect Roger. She no longer let other engagements go for him; she made no attempt to be punctual in keeping such engagements as they had already made; in his presence she was often absorbed, absent-minded, lost in thought. She ceased asking him questions about his affairs.

Long before their quarrel they had accepted an invitation from Martha Burden to a small party. Angela was surprised that Roger should remember the occasion, but clearly he did; he was on hand at the correct date and hour and the two of them fared forth. During the brief journey he was courteous, even politely cordial, but the difference between his attitude and that of former days was very apparent. The party was of a more frivolous type than Martha usually sponsored, she was giving it for a young, fun-loving cousin of Ladislas; there was no general conversation, some singing, much dancing, much pairing off in couples. Carlotta Parks was present with Ralph Ashley, the slender, dark man who had appeared with Carlotta when Angela first met her. As soon as Roger appeared Carlotta came rushing toward him.

"I've been waiting for you!" She dragged at his hand and not unwillingly he suffered himself to be led to a small sofa. They chatted a few minutes; then danced; Roger simply must look at Martha's new etchings. The pair was inseparable for the evening. Try as she might Angela could discover no feeling of jealousy but her dignity was hurt. She could not have received less attention from her former lover if they had never met. At first she thought she would make up to Ashley but something malicious in Carlotta's glance deterred her. No, she was sick of men and their babyish, faithless ways; she did not care enough about Roger to play a game for him. So she sat quietly in a deep chair, smoking, dipping into the scattered piles of books which lent the apartment its air of cheerful disorder. Occasionally she chatted; Ladislas Starr perched on the arm of her chair and beguiled her with gay tales of his university days in pre-war Vienna.

But she would never endure such an indignity again. On the way home she was silent. Roger glanced at her curiously, raised his eyebrows when she asked him to come in. She began quietly: "Roger I'll never endure again the treatment—"

But he was ready, even eager for a quarrel. "It looks to me as though you were willing to endure anything. No woman with an ounce of pride would have stood for what you've been standing lately."

She said evenly: "You mean this is the end? We're through?"

"Well, what do you think about it? You certainly didn't expect it to last forever."

His tone was unbelievably insulting. Eyeing him speculatively she replied: "No, of course I didn't expect it to last forever, but I didn't think it would end like this. I don't see yet why it should."

The knowledge of his unpardonable manner lay heavy upon him, drove him to fresh indignity. "I suppose you thought some day I'd kiss your hand and say 'You've been very nice to me; I'll always remember you with affection and gratitude. Good-bye.'"

"Well, why shouldn't you have said that? Certainly I'd expected that much sooner than a scene of this sort. I never dreamed of letting myself in for this kind of thing."

Some ugly devil held him in its grasp. "You knew perfectly well what you were letting yourself in for. Any woman would know it."

She could only stare at him, his words echoing in her

ears: "You knew perfectly well what you were letting yourself in for."

The phrase had the quality of a cosmic echo; perhaps men had been saying it to women since the beginning of time. Doubtless their biblical equivalent were the last words uttered by Abraham to Hagar before she fared forth into the wilderness.

CHAPTER V

Long after Roger had left her she sat staring into the dark shadows of the room. For a long time the end, she knew, had been imminent; she had been curious to see how it would arrive, but the thought had never crossed her mind that it would come with harsh words and with vulgarity. The departure of Roger himself—she shut her hand and opened it—meant nothing; she had never loved, never felt for him one-tenth of the devotion which her mother had known for her father, of the spontaneous affection which Virginia had offered Matthew Henson. Even in these latter weeks when she had consciously striven to show him every possible kindness and attention she had done so for the selfish preservation of her ideals. Now she looked back on those first days of delight when his emotions and her own had met at full tide; when she dreamed that she alone of all people in the world was exempt from ordinary law. How, she wondered futilely, could she ever have suffered herself to be persuaded to tamper with the sacred mysteries of life? If she had held in her hand the golden key,—love! But to throw aside the fundamental laws of civilization for passion, for the hot-headed wilfulness of youth and to have it end like this, drably, vulgarly, almost in a brawl! How could she endure herself? And Roger and his promises of esteem and golden memories!

For a moment she hated him for his fine words and phrases, hated him for tricking her. No matter what she had said, how she had acted, he should have let her go. Better a wound to her passion than later this terrible gash in her proud assurance, this hurt in the core of herself. "God!" she said, raging in her tiny apartment as a tiger in a menagerie rages in its inadequate cage, "God, isn't there any place where man's responsibility to woman begins?"

But she had grown too much into the habit of deliberately ordering her life, of hewing her own path, of

removing the difficulties that beset that path, to let herself
be sickened, utterly prostrated by what had befallen her.
Roger, her companion, had gone; she had been caught up
in an inexcusably needless affair without the pretext of
love. Thank God she had taken nothing from Roger; she
had not sold herself, only bestowed that self foolishly,
unworthily. However upset and harassed her mind might
be it could not dwell too long on this loss of a lover.
There were other problems to consider; for Roger's passing meant the vanishing of the last hope of the successful
marriage which once she had so greatly craved. And
even though she had not actively considered this for some
time, yet as a remote possibility it had afforded a sense of
security. Now that mirage was dispelled; she was brought
with a sudden shock back to reality. No longer was it
enough for her to plan how she could win a pleasant and
happy means of existence, she must be on the *qui vive*
for the maintenance of that very existence itself. New
York had literally swallowed her original three thousand
dollars; part of Virginia's gift was also dissipated. Less
than a thousand dollars stood between her and absolute
penury. She could not envisage turning to Jinny; life
which had seemed so promising, so golden, had failed to
supply her with a single friend to whom she could turn in
an hour of extremity.

Such thoughts as these left her panic-stricken, cold
with fear. The spectre of possible want filled her dreams,
haunted her waking hours, thrust aside the devastating
shame of her affair with Roger to replace it with dread
and apprehension. In her despair she turned more ardently than ever to her painting; already she was capable of
doing outstanding work in portraiture, but she lacked
cachet; she was absolutely unknown.

This condition of her mind affected her appearance;
she began to husband her clothes, sadly conscious that
she could not tell where others would come from. Her
face lost its roundness, the white warmness of her skin
remained but there were violet shadows under her eyes;
her forehead showed faint lines; she was slightly shabby.
Gradually the triumphant vividness so characteristic of
Angèle Mory left her, she was like any one of a thousand
other pitiful, frightened girls thronging New York. Miss

Powell glanced at her and thought: "She looks unhappy, but how can she be when she has a chance at everything in the world just because she's white?"

Anthony marked her fading brightness; he would have liked to question her, comfort her, but where this girl was concerned the rôle of comforter was not for him. Only the instructor, Mr. Paget, guessed at her extremity. He had seen too many students not to recognize the signs of poverty, of disaster in love, of despair at the tardy flowering of dexterity that had been mistaken for talent. Once after class he stopped Angela and asked her if she knew of anyone willing to furnish designs for a well-known journal of fashion.

"Not very stimulating work, but the pay is good and the firm reliable. Their last artist was with them eight years. If you know of anyone,———"

She interrupted: "I know of myself. Do you think they'd take me on?"

"I could recommend you. They applied to me, you see. Doubtless they'd take my suggestions into account."

He was very kind; made all the necessary arrangements. The firm received Angela gladly, offering her a fair salary for work that was a trifle narrow, a bit stultifying. But it opened up possibilities; there were new people to be met; perhaps she would make new friends, form ties which might be lasting.

"Oh," she said hopefully to herself, "life is wonderful! It's giving me a new deal and I'll begin all over again. I'm young and now I'm sophisticated; the world is wide, somewhere there's happiness and peace and a place for me. I'll find it."

But her hope, her sanguineness, were a little forced, her superb self-confidence perceptibly diminished. The radiance which once had so bathed every moment of her existence was fading gently, inexorably into the "light of common day."